Information Visualization

Perception for Design

Information Visualization

Perception for Design

Colin Ware
University of New Hampshire

MORGAN KAUFMANN PUBLISHERS

AN IMPRINT OF ACADEMIC PRESS
A Harcourt Science and Technology Company
SAN FRANCISCO   SAN DIEGO   NEW YORK   BOSTON
LONDON   SYDNEY   TOKYO

Senior Editor: Diane D. Cerra
Director of Production and Manufacturing: Yonie Overton
Production Editor: Heather Collins
Editorial Coordinator: Belinda Breyer
Cover Design: Ross Carron Design
Text Design: Detta Penna, Penna Design and Production
Composition/Color Insert Preparation: Proctor-Willenbacher
Art/Illustrations: Technologies 'N' Typography
Copyeditor: Judith Abrahms
Proofreader: Jennifer McClain
Indexer: Steve Rath
Printer: Courier Corporation

Designations used by companies to distinguish their products are often claimed as trademarks or registered trademarks. In all instances where Morgan Kaufmann Publishers is aware of a claim, the product names appear in initial capital or all capital letters. Readers, however, should contact the appropriate companies for more complete information regarding trademarks and registration.

ACADEMIC PRESS
A Harcourt Science and Technology Company
525 B Street, Suite 1900, San Diego, CA 92101-4495, USA
http://www.academicpress.com

Academic Press
Harcourt Place, 32 Jamestown Road, London, NW1 7BY United Kingdom
http://www.hbuk.co.uk/ap/

Morgan Kaufmann Publishers
340 Pine Street, Sixth Floor, San Francisco, CA 94104-3205, USA
http://www.mkp.com

Library of Congress Cataloging-in-Publication Data
Ware, Colin.
      Information visualization : design for perception / Colin Ware.
            p.   cm.
      Includes bibliographical references and index.
      ISBN 1-55860-511-8
      1. Quality control.   2. Visualization--Data Processing.   3. Engineering inspection.
      I. Title.

TS156.2.W37   1999
671.42'5221   99-051989
                                         CIP

This book is printed on acid-free paper.

Contents

v

Chapter 5   Visual Attention and Information That Pops Out   **151**

Chapter 7   Visual Objects and Data Objects   **241**

**Chapter 8   Space Perception and the
Display of Data in Space   273**

Figure Credits

The following figures are reprinted with permission:

2.11 State et al. (1996) Copyright © 1996 Association for Computing Machinery, Inc.

5.20 Witkin and Kass (1991) Copyright © 1991 Association for Computing Machinery, Inc.

6.21 Turk and Banks (1996) Copyright © 1996 Association for Computing Machinery, Inc.

6.24 Schroeder et al. (1997) Copyright © 1997 Prentice Hall

7.16 Interrante et al. (1997) Copyright © 1997 IEEE

7.17 Norman et al. (1995) Copyright © 1995 Psychonomic Society

7.23 Saito and Takahashi (1990) Copyright © 1990 Association for Computing Machinery, Inc.

8.5 Serra et al. (1997) Copyright 1997 Association for Computing Machinery, Inc.

8.23 Robertson et al. (1993) Copyright © 1991 Association for Computing Machinery, Inc.

8.25 Li (1997) Copyright © 1997 Yanchao Li, University of New Brunswick

9.2 Bellugi and Klima (1976) Copyright © 1976 Annals of the New York Academy of Sciences

9.5 Parker et al. (1998) Copyright © 1998 Academic Press

9.7 Chandler and Sweller (1991) Copyright © 1991 Lawrence Erlbaum

9.8 Kahn (1996b) Copyright © 1996 Association for Computing Machinery, Inc.

9.9 Cypher and Smith (1995) Copyright © 1995 Association for Computing Machinery, Inc.

Preface

In 1973, after I had completed my master's degree in the psychology of vision, I was frustrated with the overly focused academic way of studying perception. Inspired by the legacy of freedom that seemed to be in the air in the late sixties and early seventies, I decided to become an artist and explore perception in a very different way. But after three years with only very small success, I returned, chastened, to the academic fold, though with a broader outlook, a great respect for artists, and a growing interest in the relationship between the way we present information and the way we see. After obtaining a Ph.D. in the psychology of perception at the University of Toronto, I still did not know what to do next. I moved into computer science, via the University of Waterloo and another degree, and have been working on data visualization, in one way or another, ever since. In a way, this book is a direct result of my ongoing attempt to reconcile the scientific study of perception with the need to convey meaningful information. It is about art in the sense that "form should follow function," and it is about science because the science of perception can tell us what kinds of patterns are most readily perceived.

Why should we be interested in visualization? Because the human visual system is a pattern seeker of enormous power and subtlety. The eye and the visual cortex of the brain form a massively parallel processor that provides the highest-bandwidth channel into human cognitive centers. At higher levels of processing, perception and cognition are closely interrelated, which is the reason why the words "understanding" and "seeing" are synonymous. However, the visual system has its own rules. We can easily see patterns presented in certain ways, but if they are presented in other ways, they become invisible. Thus, for example, the word DATA, shown in Figure 1.0, is much more visible in the bottom version shown below than in the one at the top. This is despite the fact that identical parts of the letters are visible in each case and in the lower figure there is more irrelevant "noise" than in the upper figure. The rule that applies here, apparently, is that when the missing pieces are interpreted as foreground objects, continuity between the background letter fragments is easier to infer. The more general point is that when data is presented in certain ways, the patterns can be readily perceived. If we can understand how perception works, our knowledge can be translated into rules for displaying information. Following perception-based rules, we can present our data in such a way that the important and informative patterns stand out. If we disobey these rules, our data will be incomprehensible or misleading.

This is a book about what the science of perception can tell us about visualization. There is a gold mine of information about how we see, to be found in more than a century of work by vision researchers. The purpose of this book is to extract from that large body of research literature those design principles that apply to displaying information effectively.

Visualization can be approached in many ways. It can be studied in the art-school tradition of graphic design. It can be studied within computer graphics as an area concerned with the algorithms needed to display data. It can be studied as part of semiotics, the constructivist approach to symbol systems. These are valid approaches, but a scientific approach based on perception uniquely promises design rules that transcend the vagaries of design fashion, being based on the relatively stable structure of the human visual system.

Figure 1.0   The word DATA is easier to read when the overlapping bars
are visible. Adapted from Nakayama et al. (1989).

The study of perception by psychologists and neuroscientists has advanced enormously over the past three decades, and it is possible to say a
great deal about how we see that is relevant to data visualization. Unfortunately, much of this information is stored in highly specialized journals and
couched in language that is accessible only to the specialist. The research literature concerning human perception is voluminous. Several hundred new
papers are published every month and a surprising number of them have
some application in information display. This information can be extremely
useful in helping us design better displays, both by avoiding mistakes and by
coming up with original solutions. *Information Visualization: Perception for
Design* is intended to make this science and its applications available to the
nonspecialist. It should be of interest to anyone concerned with displaying
data effectively. It is designed with a number of audiences in mind: multimedia designers specializing in visualization, researchers in both industry
and academia, and anyone who has a deep interest in effective information
display. The book presents extensive technical information about various
visual acuities, thresholds, and other basic properties of human vision. It
also contains, where possible, specific guidelines and recommendations.

The book is organized according to bottom-up perceptual principles. The first chapter provides a general conceptual framework and discusses the theoretical context for a vision science–based approach. The next four chapters discuss what can be considered to be the low-level perceptual elements of vision, color, texture, motion, and elements of form. These primitives of vision tell us about the design of attention-grabbing features and the best ways of coding data so that one object will be distinct from another. The later chapters move on to discussing what it takes to perceive patterns in data: first 2D pattern perception, and later 3D space perception. Visualization design, data space navigation, interaction techniques, and visual problem solving are all discussed.

Here is a road map to the book: In general, the pattern for each chapter is first to describe some aspect of human vision and then to apply this information to some problem in visualization. The first chapters provide a foundation of knowledge on which the later chapters are built. Nevertheless, it is perfectly reasonable to randomly access the book to learn about specific topics. When it is needed, missing background information can be obtained by consulting the index.

Chapter 1: Foundation for a Science of Data Visualization   A conceptual framework for visualization design is based on human perception. The nature of claims about sensory representations is articulated, with special attention paid to the work of perception theorist J. J. Gibson. This analysis is used to define the differences between a design-based approach and a science of perception–based approach. A classification of abstract data classes is provided as the basis for mapping data to visual representations.

Chapter 2: The Environment, Optics, Resolution, and the Display   This chapter deals with the basic inputs to perception. It begins with the physics of light and the way light interacts with objects in the environment. Central concepts include the structure of light as it arrives at a viewpoint and the information carried by that light array about surfaces and objects available for interaction. This chapter goes on to discuss the basics of visual optics and issues such as how much detail we can resolve. Human acuity measurements are described and applied to display design.

The applications discussed include: design of 3D environments, how many pixels are needed for visual display systems and how fast they should be updated, requirements for virtual-reality display systems, how much detail can be displayed using graphics and text, and detection of faint targets.

Chapter 3: Lightness, Brightness, Contrast, and Constancy   The visual system does not measure the amount of light in the environment; instead, it measures *changes* in light and color. The way the brain uses this information to discover properties of the surfaces of objects in the environment is presented. This is related to issues in data coding and setting up display systems.

The applications discussed include: integrating the display into a viewing environment, minimal conditions under which targets will be detected, methods for creating gray scales to code data, and errors that occur because of contrast effects.

Chapter 4: Color   This chapter introduces the science of color vision, starting with receptors and trichromacy theory. Color measurement systems and color standards are presented. The standard equations for the CIE standard and the *CIEluv* uniform color space are given. Opponent process theory is introduced and related to the way data should be displayed using luminance and chrominance.

The applications discussed include: color measurement and specification, color selection interfaces, color coding, pseudocolor sequences for mapping, color reproduction, and color for multidimensional discrete data.

Chapter 5: Visual Attention and Information That Pops Out   A "searchlight" model of visual attention is introduced to describe the way eye movements are used to sweep for information. The bulk of the chapter is taken up with a description of the massively parallel processes whereby the visual image is broken into elements of color, form, and motion. Pre-attentive processing theory is applied to critical issues of making one data object distinct from another. Methods for coding data so that it can be perceptually integrated or separated are discussed.

The applications discussed include: display for rapid comprehension, information coding, the use of texture for data coding, the design of symbology, and multidimensional discrete data display.

Chapter 6: Static and Moving Patterns This chapter looks at the process whereby the brain segments the world into regions and finds links, structure, and prototypical objects. These are converted into a set of design guidelines for information display.

The applications discussed include: display of data so that patterns can be perceived, information layout, node-link diagrams, and layered displays.

Chapter 7: Visual Objects and Data Objects Both image-based and 3D structure–based theories of object perception are reviewed. The concept of the object display is introduced as a method for using visual objects to organize information.

The applications discussed include: presenting image data, using 3D structures to organize information, and the object display.

Chapter 8: Space Perception and the Display of Data in Space Increasingly, information display is being done in 3D virtual spaces as opposed to the 2D screen-based layouts. The different kinds of spatial cues and the ways we perceive them are introduced. The latter half of the chapter is taken up with a set of seven spatial tasks and the perceptual issues associated with each.

The applications discussed include: 3D information displays, stereo displays, the choice of 2D versus 3D visualization, 3D graph viewing, and virtual environments.

Chapter 9: Images and Words Visual information and verbal information are processed in different ways and by different parts of the brain. Each has its own strengths, and often both should be combined in a presentation. This chapter addresses when visual and verbal presentation should be used and how the two kinds of information should be linked.

The applications discussed include: integrating images and words, visual programming languages, and effective diagrams.

Chapter 10: Interacting with Visualizations Three major interaction cycles are defined. Within this framework, low-level data manipulation, dynamic control over data views, navigation through data spaces, and problem solving using visual aids are discussed in turn.

The applications discussed include: interacting with data, zooming interfaces, navigation, problem solving with visualization, and creativity.

These are exciting times for visualization design. The computer technology used to produce visualizations has reached a stage at which sophisticated interactive 3D views of data can be produced on ordinary desktop computers. The trend toward more and more visual information is accelerating, and there is an explosion of new visualization techniques being invented to help us cope with our need to analyze huge and complex bodies of information. This creative phase will not last for long. With the dawn of a new technology, there is often only a short burst of creative design before the forces of standardization make what is new into what is conventional. Undoubtedly, many of the visualization techniques that are now emerging will become routine tools in the near future. Even badly designed things can become industry standards. Designing for perception can help us avoid such mistakes. If we can harness the knowledge that has been accumulated about how perception works, we can make visualizations become more transparent windows into the world of information.

I wish to thank the many people who have helped me with this book. The people who most influenced the way I think about perception and visualization are Donald Mitchell, John Kennedy, and William Cowan. I have gained enormously by working with Larry Mayer in developing new tools to map the oceans, as well as with colleagues Kelly Booth, Dave Wells, Tim Dudely, Scott Mackenzie, and Eric Neufeld. It has been my good fortune to work with many talented graduate students and research assistants on visualization-related projects: Daniel Jessome, Richard Guitard, Timothy Lethbridge, Siew Hong Yang, Sean Riley, Serge Limoges, David Fowler, Stephen Osborne, K. Wing Wong, Dale Chapman, Pat Cavanaugh, Ravin Balakrishnan, Mark Paton, Monica Sardesai, Cyril Gobrecht, Suryan Stalin, Justine Hickey, Yanchao Li, Rohan Parkhi, Kathy Lowther, Li Wang, Greg Parker, Daniel Fleet, Jun Yang, Graham Sweet, Roland Arsenault, Natalie Webber, Poorang Inrani, Jordan Lutes, Nhu Le, Irina Padioukova, Glenn Franck, and Lyn Bartram. Many of the ideas presented here have been refined through their efforts.

Peter Pirolli, Doug Gillan, and Nahum Gershon made numerous suggestions that helped me improve the manuscript. As a result, the last two chapters, especially, underwent radical revision. I also wish to thank the editorial staff at Morgan Kaufmann, Diane Cerra, Belinda Breyer, and Heather Collins. Finally, my wife, Dianne Ramey, read every word, made it readable, and kept me going.

Foundation for a Science of Data Visualization

Until recently, the term *visualization* meant *constructing a visual image in the mind* (*Shorter Oxford English Dictionary*). But now it has come to mean something more like *a graphical representation of data or concepts*. Thus, from being an internal construct of the mind, a visualization has become an external artifact supporting decision making. The way we perceive and use external visualizations is the subject of this book.

One of the greatest benefits of data visualization is the sheer quantity of information that can be rapidly interpreted if it is presented well. Figure 1.1 shows a visualization derived from a multibeam echo sounder scanning part of the Passamoquoddy Bay between Maine, in the United States, and New Brunswick, in Canada, where the tides are the highest in the world. Approximately one million measurements were made. Traditionally, this kind of data is presented in the form of a nautical chart with contours and spot soundings. However, when the data is converted to a height field, and displayed using standard computer graphics techniques, many things become visible that were previously invisible on the chart. A pattern of features called *pockmarks* can immediately be seen, and it is easy to see how they form lines. Also visible are various problems with the data. The linear ripples are artifacts, due to the fact that the roll of the ship that made the measurements was not properly taken into account.

The Passamoquoddy Bay image highlights a number of the advantages of visualization:

- Visualization provides an ability to comprehend huge amounts of data. The important information from more than a million measurements is immediately available.

- Visualization allows the perception of emergent properties that were not anticipated. In this visualization, the fact that the pockmarks appear in lines is immediately evident.

- Visualization often enables problems with the data itself to become immediately apparent. It is common for a visualization to reveal things not only about data itself, but about the way it is collected. With an appropriate visualization, errors and artifacts in the data often jump out at you. For this reason, visualizations can be invaluable in quality control.

- Visualization facilitates understanding of both large-scale and small-scale features of the data. It can be especially valuable in allowing the perception of patterns linking local features.

- Visualization facilitates hypothesis formation. For example, the visualization in Figure 1.1 was directly responsible for a research paper concerning the geological significance of the pockmark features (Gray, 1997).

This first chapter has the general goal of defining the scope of a psychology of visualization. Much of it is devoted to outlining the intellectual basis of the endeavor and providing an overview of the kinds of experimental techniques that are appropriate to visualization research. In the latter half of the chapter, a brief overview of human visual processing is introduced to provide a kind of road map to the more detailed analysis of the later chapters. The chapter concludes with a categorization of data itself. It is important to have a reasonably general model of the kinds of data we may wish to visualize so that we can talk in general terms about the ways in which whole classes of data should be represented.

Figure 1.1   Passamoquoddy Bay visualization. Data courtesy of the
Canadian Hydrographic Service.

Visualization Stages

There are four basic stages in the process of data visualization, together with
a number of feedback loops. These are illustrated in Figure 1.2.
    They consist of:

- The collection and storage of data itself

- The preprocessing designed to transform the data into something
  we can understand

- The display hardware and the graphics algorithms that produce an
  image on the screen

- The human perceptual and cognitive system (the perceiver)

    The longest feedback loop involves gathering data itself. A data seeker,
such as a scientist or a stock market analyst, may choose to gather more data
to follow up on an interesting lead. Another loop controls the computational
preprocessing that takes place prior to visualization. The analyst may feel
that if the data is subjected to a certain transformation prior to visualization,
it can be persuaded to give up its meaning. Finally, the visualization process
itself may be highly interactive. For example, in 3D data visualization, the

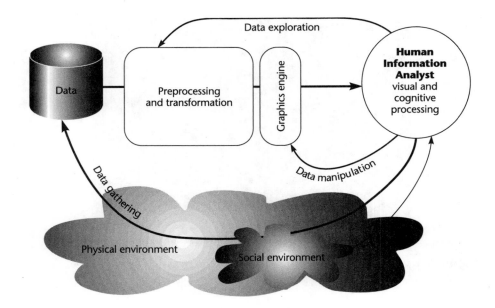

Figure 1.2   A schematic diagram of the visualization process.

scientist may fly to a different vantage point to better understand the emerging structures. Alternatively, a mouse may be used interactively, to select the parameter ranges that are most interesting. Both the physical environment and the social environment are involved in the data-gathering loop: The physical environment is a source of data, while the social environment determines in subtle and complex ways what is collected and how it is interpreted.

In this book, the emphasis is on data, on perception, and on the various tasks to which visualization may be applied. In general, algorithms are discussed only insofar as they are related to perception. The computer is treated, with some reservations, as a universal tool for producing interactive graphics. This means that once we figure out the best way to visualize data for a particular task, we assume that we can construct algorithms to create the appropriate images. The critical question is how best to transform the data into something that people can understand for optimal decision making. However, before plunging into the detailed analysis of human perception and the way it applies in practice, we must establish the conceptual basis for the endeavor. The purpose of this discussion is to stake out a theoretical framework wherein claims about visualizations being "visually efficient" or "natural" can be pinned down in the form of testable predictions.

Experimental Semiotics Based on Perception

This book claims to be about the science of visualization, as opposed to the craft or art of visualization. However, some scholars argue that visualization is best understood as a kind of learned language and not as a science at all. In essence, the language argument is as follows: Visualization is about diagrams and how they can convey meaning. Diagrams are generally held to be made up of symbols, and symbols are based on social interaction. The meaning of a symbol is normally understood to be created by convention, established in the course of person-to-person communication. Diagrams are arbitrary and are effective in much the same way as the written words on this page are effective—we must learn the conventions of the language, and the better we learn them, the clearer that language will be. Thus, one diagram may ultimately be as good as another; it is just a matter of learning the code, and the laws of perception are largely irrelevant. This view has strong philosophical proponents. Although it is not the position adopted here, the debate can help us define where vision research can assist us in designing better visualizations, and where we would be wise to consult a graphic designer trained in an art college.

Semiotics of Graphics

The study of symbols and how they convey meaning is called *semiotics*. This discipline was originated in the United States by C. S. Peirce and later developed in Europe by the French philosopher and linguist Ferdinand de Saussure (1959). Semiotics has mostly been dominated by philosophers and by those who construct arguments based on example rather than on formal experiment. In his great masterwork, *The Semiology of Graphics,* Jacques Bertin (1983) attempted to classify all graphic marks in terms of how they could express data. The work is for the most part based on his own judgment, though it is a highly trained and sensitive judgment. There are few, if any, references to theories of perception or scientific studies.

It is often claimed that visual languages are easy to learn and use, although in certain cases these languages are visual only to the extent that a written document is visual. It can be just as hard to learn to read some diagrams as it is to learn to read written language. Figure 1.3 shows three examples of languages that have some claim to being visual. The first is based on a cave painting. We can readily interpret human figures and infer that the

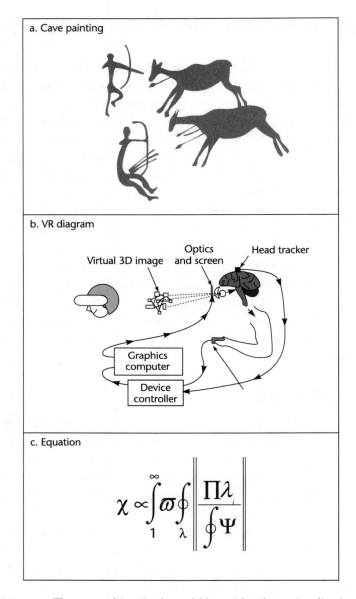

a. Cave painting

b. VR diagram

Virtual 3D image   Optics and screen   Head tracker

Graphics computer

Device controller

c. Equation

$$\chi \propto \int_{1}^{\infty} \varpi \oint_{\lambda} \left\| \frac{\Pi \lambda_i}{\oint \Psi} \right\|$$

Figure 1.3   Three graphics. Each could be said to be a visualization.

people are hunting deer with bows and arrows. The second is a schematic diagram showing the interaction between a person and a computer in a virtual environment system; the brain in the diagram is a simplified picture, but it is a part of the anatomy that few have directly perceived. The arrows show data flows and are arbitrary conventions, as are the printed words. The third is the expression of a mathematical equation that is utterly obscure to all but the initiated. These examples clearly show that some visual languages are easier to "read" than others. But why? Perhaps it is simply that we have more experience with the kind of pictorial image shown in the cave painting and less with the mathematical notation. Perhaps the concepts expressed in the cave painting are more familiar than those in the equation.

The most profound threat to the idea that there can be a science of visualization originates with Saussure. He defined a principle of *arbitrariness* as applying to the relationship between the symbol and the thing that is signified. Saussure was also a founding member of a group of structuralist philosophers and anthropologists who, although they disagreed on many fundamental issues, were unified in their general insistence that truth is relative to its social context. Meaning in one culture may be nonsense in another. A trash can as a visual symbol for deletion is meaningful only to those who know how trash cans are used. Thinkers such as Levi-Strauss, Barthes, and Lacan have condemned the cultural imperialism and intellectual arrogance implicit in applying our intellects to characterizing other cultures as "primitive," and as a result, they have developed the theory that all meaning is relative to the culture. Indeed, meaning is created by society. They claim that we can interpret another culture only in the context of our own culture and using the tools of our own language. Languages are conventional means of communication in which the meanings of symbols are established through custom. The point is that no one representation is "better" than another. All representations have value. All are meaningful to those who understand them and agree to their meanings. Since it seems entirely reasonable to consider visualizations as communications, this argument strikes at the root of the idea that there can be a natural science of visualization.

Pictures as Sensory Languages

A good place to begin reviewing the evidence is the perception of pictures. There has been a debate over the last century between those who claim that pictures are every bit as arbitrary as words and those who believe that there may be a measure of *similarity* between pictures and the things that they represent. This debate is crucial to the theory presented here, because if even "realistic" pictures do not embody a sensory language, it will be impossible to make claims that certain diagrams and other visualizations are better designed perceptually. The nominalist philosopher Nelson Goodman has delivered some of the more forceful attacks on the notion of similarity in pictures (1968):

> Realistic representation, in brief, depends not upon imitation or illusion or information but upon inculcation. Almost any picture may represent almost anything; that is, given picture and object there is usually a system of representation, a plan of correlation, under which the picture represents the object. (p. 38)

For Goodman, realistic representation is a matter of convention; it "depends on how stereotyped the model of representation is, how commonplace the labels and their uses have become" (p. 36). Biesheuvel (1947) expressed the same opinion: "The picture, particularly one printed on paper, is a highly conventional symbol, which the child reared in Western culture has learned to interpret." These statements, taken at face value, invalidate any meaningful basis for saying that a certain visualization is fundamentally better or more natural than another. This would mean that all languages are equally valid, all are learned. If we accept this position, the best approach to designing visual languages would be to establish graphical conventions early and stick to them. It would not matter what the conventions were, only that we adhered to them in order to reduce the labor of learning new conventions.

In support of the nominalist argument, a number of anthropologists have reported expressions of puzzlement from people who encounter pictures for the first time. "A Bush Negro woman turned a photograph this way and that, in attempting to make sense out of the shadings of gray on the piece of paper she held" (Herkovits, 1948).

The evidence related to whether or not we must learn to see pictures has been carefully reviewed and analyzed by Kennedy (1974). He rejects the strong position that pictures and other visual representations are entirely arbitrary. In the case of the reported puzzlement of people who are seeing pictures for the first time, Kennedy argues that these people are amazed by the technology rather than unable to interpret the picture. After all, a photograph is a remarkable artifact. What curious person would not turn it over to see if, perhaps, the reverse side contains some additional interesting information? Here are two of the many studies that contradict the nominalist position and suggest that people can interpret pictures without training. Deregowski (1968) reported studies of adults and children, in a remote area of Zambia, who had very little graphic art. Despite this, these people could easily match photographs of toy animals with the actual toys. In an extraordinary but very different kind of experiment, Hochberg and Brooks (1962) raised their daughter nearly to the age of two in a house with no pictures. She was never read to from a picture book and there were no pictures on the walls in the house. Although her parents could not completely block the child's exposure to pictures on trips outside the house, they were careful never to indicate a picture and tell the child that it was a representation of something. Thus, she had no social input telling her that pictures had any kind of meaning. When the child was finally tested, she had a reasonably large vocabulary, and she was asked to identify objects in line drawings and in black-and-white photographs. Despite her lack of instruction in the interpretation of pictures, she was almost always correct in her answers.

However, the issue of how pictures, and especially line drawings, are able to unambiguously represent things is still not fully understood. Clearly, a portrait is a pattern of marks on a page; in a physical sense, it is utterly unlike the flesh-and-blood person it depicts. The most probable explanation is that at some stage in visual processing, the pictorial outline of an object and the object itself excite similar neural processes (Pearson et al., 1990). This view is made plausible by the ample evidence that one of the most important products of early visual processing is the extraction of linear features in the visual array. These may be either the visual boundaries of objects or the lines in a line drawing. The nature of these mechanisms is discussed further in Chapter 6.

Although we may be able to understand certain pictures without learning, it would be a mistake to underestimate the role of convention in representation. Even with the most realistic picture or sculpture, it is very rare for the artifact to be mistaken for the thing that is represented. Trompe l'oeil art is designed to "fool the eye" into the illusion that a painting is real. Artists are paid to paint pictures of niches containing statues that look real, and sometimes, for an instant, the viewer will be fooled. On a more mundane level, a plastic laminate on furniture may contain a photograph of wood grain that is very difficult to tell from the real thing. But in general, a picture is intended to represent an object or a scene; it is not intended to be mistaken for it. Many pictures are highly stylized. They violate the laws of perspective and develop particular methods of representation that no one would call realistic.

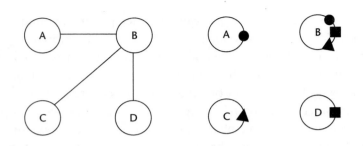

Figure 1.4   Two different graphical methods for showing relationships between entities.

When we turn to diagrams and nonpictorial visualizations, it is clear that convention must play a greater role. Figure 1.3(b) is not remotely "like" any scene in the real world under any system of measurement. Nevertheless, we can argue that many elements in it are constructed in ways that, for perceptual reasons, make the diagram easy to interpret. The lines that connect the various components, for example, are a notation that is easy to read, because the visual cortex of the brain contains mechanisms specifically designed to seek out continuous contours. Other possible graphical notations for showing connectivity would be far less effective. Figure 1.4 shows two different conventions for showing relationships between entities. The connecting lines on the left are much more effective than the symbols on the right. Thus, not all diagrammatic notations are equal.

Sensory versus Arbitrary Symbols

In this book, the word *sensory* is used to refer to symbols and aspects of visualizations that derive their expressive power from their ability to use the perceptual processing power of the brain without learning. The word *arbitrary* is used to define aspects of representation that must be learned, having no perceptual basis. For example, the written word *dog* bears no perceptual relationship to any actual animal. Probably very few graphical languages consist of entirely arbitrary conventions, and probably none are entirely sensory. However, the sensory-versus-arbitrary distinction is important. Sensory representations are effective (or misleading) because they are well matched to the early stages of neural processing. They tend to be stable across individuals and cultures and time. A cave drawing of a hunt still conveys much of its meaning across several millennia. Conversely, arbitrary conventions derive their power from culture and are therefore dependent on the particular cultural milieu of an individual.

The theory of sensory languages is based on the idea that the human visual system has evolved as an instrument to perceive the physical world. It rejects the idea that the visual system is a truly universal machine. It used to be widely held that the brain at birth was an undifferentiated neural net, capable of configuring itself to perceive in any world, no matter how strange. According to this theory, if a newborn human infant were to be born into a world with entirely different rules for the propagation of light, that infant would nevertheless learn to see. Partly, this view came from the fact that all cortical brain tissue looks more or less the same, a uniform pinkish gray, so it was thought to be functionally undifferentiated. This "tabula rasa" view has been overthrown as neurologists have come to understand that the brain has a great many specialized regions. Figure 1.5 shows the major neural pathways between different parts of the brain involved in visual processing (Distler et al., 1993). Although much of the functionality remains unclear, this diagram represents an amazing achievement and summarizes the work of dozens of researchers. These structures are present both in higher primates and in humans. The brain is clearly not an undifferentiated mass; it is more like a collection of highly specialized parallel-processing machines with high-bandwidth interconnections. The entire system is designed to extract information from the world in which we live, not from some other environment with entirely different physical properties.

Certain basic elements are necessary for the visual system to develop normally. For example, cats reared in a world consisting only of vertical stripes develop distorted visual cortices, with an unusual preponderance of vertical-edge detectors. Nevertheless, the basic elements for the development of normal vision are present in all but the most abnormal circumstances. The interaction of the growing nervous system with everyday reality leads to a more or less standard visual system. This should not surprise us; the everyday world has ubiquitous properties that are common to all environments. All earthly environments consist of objects with well-defined surfaces, surface textures, surface colors, and a variety of shapes. Objects exhibit temporal persistence: They do not randomly appear and vanish, except when there are specific causes. At a more fundamental level, light travels in straight lines and reflects off surfaces in certain ways. The law of gravity continues to operate. Given these ubiquitous properties of the everyday world, the evidence suggests that we all develop essentially the same visual systems, irrespective of cultural milieu. Monkeys and even cats have visual structures very similar to those of humans. For example, although Figure 1.5 is based on the visual pathways of the Macaque monkey, a number of lines of evidence show that the same structures exist in humans. First, the same areas can be identified anatomically in humans and animals. Second, specific patterns of blindness occur that point to the same areas having the same functions in humans and animals. For example, if the brain is injured in area V4, patients suffer from achromatopsia (Zeki, 1992; Milner and Goodale, 1995). These patients perceive only shades of gray. They also cannot recall colors from times before the lesion was formed. Color processing occurs in the same region of the monkey cortex. Third, new research imaging technologies such as positron emission tomography (PET) and fast magnetic resonance imaging (MRI) show that in response to colored or moving patterns, the same areas are active in people as in the Macaque monkey (Zeki, 1992; Beardsley, 1997). The key implication of this is that because we all have the same visual system, it is likely that we all see in the same way, at least as a first approximation. Hence the same visual designs will be effective for all of us.

Sensory aspects of visualizations derive their expressive power from being well designed to stimulate the visual sensory system. In contrast, arbitrary, conventional aspects of visualizations derive their power from how well they are learned. Sensory and arbitrary representations differ radically in the ways they should be studied. In the former case, we can apply the full rigor of the experimental techniques developed by sensory neuroscience, while in the latter case visualizations and visual symbols can best be studied with the very different interpretive methodology derived from the structuralist social sciences. With sensory representations, we can also make claims that transcend cultural and racial boundaries. Claims based on a generalized perceptual processing system will apply to all humans, with obvious exceptions such as color blindness.

This distinction between the sensory and social aspects of the symbols used in visualization also has practical consequences in terms of research methodology. It is not worth expending a huge effort carrying out intricate and highly focused experiments to study something that is only this year's fashion. However, if we can develop generalizations that apply to large classes of visual representations, and for a long time, the effort is worthwhile.

If we accept the distinction between sensory and arbitrary codes, we nevertheless must recognize that most visualizations are hybrids. In the

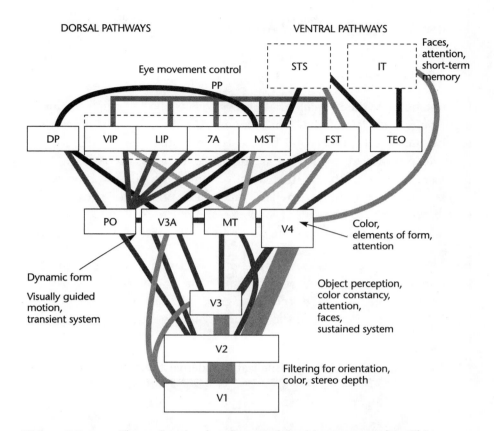

DORSAL PATHWAYS

VENTRAL PATHWAYS

Faces, attention, short-term memory

Eye movement control
PP

STS

IT

DP | VIP | LIP | 7A | MST | FST | TEO

PO | V3A | MT | V4

Color, elements of form, attention

Dynamic form

Visually guided motion, transient system

Object perception, color constancy, attention, faces, sustained system

V3

V2

Filtering for orientation, color, stereo depth

V1

Figure 1.5 The major visual pathways of the Macaque monkey. This diagram is included both to illustrate the structural complexity of the visual system and because a number of these areas are referenced in different sections of this book. Adapted from Distler et al. (1993); notes added. V1–V4, visual areas 1–4; PO, parieto-occipital area; MT, middle temporal area (also called V5); DP, dorsal prestiate area; PP, posterior parietal complex; STS, superiotemporal sulcus complex; IT, inferotemporal cortex.

obvious case, they may contain both pictures and words. But in many cases, the sensory and arbitrary aspects of a representation are much more difficult to tease apart. There is an intricate interweaving of learned conventions and hard-wired processing. The distinction is not as clean as we would like, but there are ways of distinguishing the different kinds of codes.

Properties of Sensory and Arbitrary Representation

The following paragraphs summarize some of the important properties of sensory representations.

Understanding without training: A sensory code is one for which the meaning is perceived without additional training. Usually, all that is necessary is for the audience to understand that *some* communication is intended. For example, it is immediately clear that the image in Figure 1.6 has an unusual spiral structure. Even though this visually represents a physical process that cannot actually be seen, the detailed shape can be understood because it has been expressed using an artificial shading technique to make it look like a 3D solid object. Our visual systems are built to perceive the shapes of 3D surfaces.

Resistance to instructional bias: Many sensory phenomena, such as the illusions shown in Figure 1.7, persist despite the knowledge that they are illusory. When such illusions occur in diagrams, they are likely to be misleading. But what is important to the present argument is that some aspects of

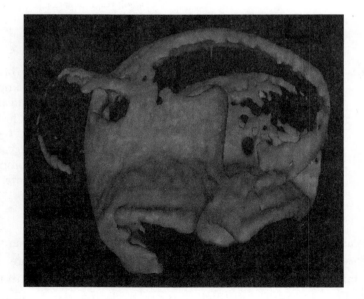

Figure 1.6   The expanding wavefront of a chemical reaction is visualized (Cross et al., 1997). Even though this process is alien to most of us, the shape of the structure can be readily perceived.

perception can be taken as bottom-line facts that we ignore at our peril. In general, perceptual phenomena that persist and are highly resistant to change are likely to be hard-wired into the brain.

Sensory immediacy: The processing of certain kinds of sensory information is hard-wired and fast. We can code information in certain ways that are processed in parallel. This point is illustrated in Figure 1.8, which shows four

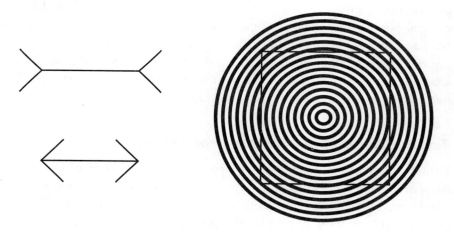

Figure 1.7   In the Muller-Lyer illusion, on the left, the horizontal line in the upper figure appears longer than the same line in the lower figure. On the right, the rectangle is distorted into a "pincushion" shape.

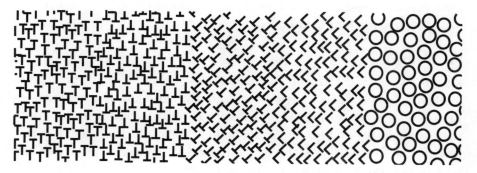

Figure 1.8   Five regions of texture. Some are easier to visually distinguish than others. Adapted from Beck (1966).

different textured regions. The two regions on the left are almost impossible to separate. The upright Ts and inverted Ts appear to be a single patch. The region of oblique Ts is easy to differentiate from the neighboring region of inverted Ts at the middle boundary. The circles are the easiest to distinguish (Beck, 1966). The way in which the visual system divides the visual world into regions is called segmentation. The evidence suggests that this is a function of early rapid-processing systems. (Chapter 5 presents a theory of texture discrimination.)

Cross-cultural validity: A sensory code will, in general, be understood across cultural boundaries. These may be national boundaries, or the boundaries between different user groups. Instances in which a sensory code is misunderstood occur when some group has dictated that a sensory code be used arbitrarily in contradiction to the natural interpretation. In this case, the natural response to a particular pattern will, in fact, be wrong.

Testing Claims about Sensory Representations

Entirely different methodologies are appropriate to the study of representations of the sensory and arbitrary types. In general, the study of sensory representations can employ the methods of vision researchers and biologists. The study of arbitrary conventional representations is best done using the techniques of the social sciences, such as sociology and anthropology; philosophers and cultural critics have much to contribute.

The following is a brief summary of the research methodologies that apply to the study of sensory representations. All are based on the concept of the controlled experiment. For more detailed information on techniques used in vision research and human-factors engineering, see Sekuler and Blake (1990) and Wickens (1992).

Psychophysics

Psychophysics is the set of techniques that are based on applying the methods of physics to measurements of human sensation. These techniques have been extremely successful in defining the basic set of limits of the visual system. For example, how rapidly must a light flicker before it is perceived as steady, or what is the smallest relative brightness change that can be detected? Psychophysical techniques are ideal for discovering the important sensory dimensions of color, visual texture, sound, and so on, and more than a century of work already exists. Psychophysicists insist on a precise physical definition of the stimulus pattern. Light levels, temporal characteristics, and spatial characteristics must all be measured and controlled.

Psychophysical techniques are normally used for studies intended to reveal early sensory processes, and it is usually assumed (sometimes wrongly) that instructional biases are not significant in these experiments. Extensive studies are often carried out using only one or two observers, frequently the principal investigator and a lab assistant or student. These results are then generalized to the entire human race, with a presumption that can infuriate social scientists. Nevertheless, for the most part, this has not been a problem. Results obtained in the nineteenth century have withstood the test of time and dozens of replications. Indeed, because some of the experiments require hundreds of hours of careful observation, experiments with large subject populations are usually out of the question.

If a phenomenon is easily altered because of instructional bias, we must question whether it represents the operation of low-level sensory mechanisms. This can be used as a method for teasing out what is sensory and what is arbitrary. If a psychophysical measurement is highly sensitive to changes in instructions, it is likely to be measuring something that has higher-level cognitive or cultural involvement.

Cognitive Psychology

In cognitive psychology, the brain is treated as a set of interlinked processing modules. A classical example of a cognitive model is the separation of short-term and long-term memory. Short-term memory, also called working memory, is the temporary buffer where we hold concepts, recent percepts, and plans for action. Long-term memory is a more or less permanent store of information that we have accumulated over a lifetime. Methods in cognitive psychology may involve measuring reaction time or measuring errors. Typically, interference patterns are used as evidence that different channels of information processing converge at some point. For example, if the task of mentally counting down in sevens from 100 were to interfere with short-term memory for the locations of objects in space, these skills would be taken to share some common cognitive processing. The fact that there is little or no interference suggests that visual short-term memory and verbal short-term memory are separate (Postma and De Haan, 1996). Recently, some cognitive theories have gained a tremendous boost because of advances in brain imaging. MRI techniques have been developed that allow researchers to actually see which parts of the brain are active when subjects perform certain tasks. In this way, functional units that had only been inferred have actually been pinpointed (Zecki, 1992).

Structural Analysis

In the structuralist tradition, researchers conduct studies that are more like interviews than formal experiments. Often the subjects are required to carry out certain simple tasks and report at the same time on their understanding and their perceptions. Using these techniques, researchers such as Piaget have been able to open up large areas of knowledge very rapidly and to establish the basic framework of our scientific understanding. However, in some cases, the insights obtained have not been confirmed by subsequent, more careful experiments. In structuralism, emphasis is given to hypothesis formation, which at times may seem more like the description and classification of behavior than a true explanation. A structuralist analysis is often especially appropriate to the study of computer interfaces, because it is fast-moving and can take a variety of factors into account. We can quantify judgments to some extent through the use of rating scales. By asking observers to assign numbers to such things as subjective effectiveness, clarity, and so on, we can obtain useful numerical data that compares one representation to another.

Cross-Cultural Studies

If sensory codes are indeed interpreted easily by all humans, this proposition should be testable by means of cross-cultural studies. In a famous study by Berlin and Kay (1969), they compared color naming in more than 100 languages. In this way, they established the universality of certain color terms, equivalent to our red, green, yellow, and blue. This study is supported by neurophysiological and psychophysical evidence that suggests these basic colors are hard-wired into the human brain. Such studies are rare, for obvious reasons, and with the globalization of world culture, meaningful studies of this type are rapidly becoming impossible. Television is bringing about an explosive growth in universal symbols.

Child Studies

By using the techniques of behaviorism, it is possible to discover things about a child's sensory processing even before the child is capable of speech. Presumably, very young children have only minimal exposure to the graphic conventions used in visualization. Thus, the way they respond to simple patterns can reveal basic processing mechanisms. This, of course, is the basis for the Hochberg and Brooks study discussed earlier.

It is also possible to gain useful data from somewhat older children, such as five-year-olds. They presumably have all the basics of sensory processing in place, but still have a long way to go in learning the graphic conventions of our culture, particularly in those obscure areas that deal with data visualization.

Arbitrary Conventional Representations

Some basic properties of arbitrary codes can be stated in general terms.

Hard to learn: It takes a child hundreds of hours to learn to read and write, even if the child has already acquired spoken language. The graphical codes of the alphabet and their rules of combination must be laboriously learned. The Chinese character set is reputed to be even harder to work with than the Roman.

Easy to forget: Arbitrary conventional information that is not overlearned can easily be forgotten. It is also the case that arbitrary codes can interfere with each other. In contrast, the sensory codes cannot be forgotten; they are hard-wired; forgetting them would be like learning not to see. Still, some arbitrary codes, such as written numbers, are overlearned to the extent that they will never be forgotten. Thus, we cannot always choose to use the most easily perceived display solution.

Embedded in culture and applications: An Asian student in my laboratory was working on an application to visualize changes in computer software. She chose to represent deleted entities with the color green and new entities with red. I suggested to her that red is normally used for a warning, while green symbolizes renewal, and perhaps the reverse coding would be more appropriate. She protested, explaining that green symbolizes death in China, while red symbolizes luck and good fortune. The use of color codes to indicate meaning is highly culture-specific.

Many graphical symbols are transient and tied to a local culture or application. Think of the graffiti of street culture, or the hundreds of new graphical icons that are being created on the Internet. These tend to stand alone, conveying meaning; there is little or no syntax to bind the symbols into a

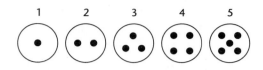

Figure 1.9   Two methods for representing the first five digits. The code given below is probably easier to learn. However, it is not easily extended.

formal structure. On the other hand, in some cases, arbitrary representations can be almost universal. The Arabic numerals shown in Figure 1.9 are widely used throughout the world, and even if a more perceptually valid code could be constructed, the effort would be wasted. The designer of a new symbology for Air Force or Navy charts must live within the confines of existing symbols because of the huge amount of effort invested in the standards. We have many standardized visualization techniques that work well and are solidly embedded in work practices, and attempts to change them would be foolish. In many applications, good design is standardized design.

Culturally embedded aspects of visualizations persist because they have become embedded in ways in which we think about problems. For many geologists, the topographic contour map is the ideal way to understand relevant features of the earth's surface. They often resist shaded computer graphics representations, even though these appear to be much more intuitively understandable to most people. Contour maps are embedded in cartographic culture and training.

Formally powerful: Arbitrary graphical notations can be constructed that embody formally defined, powerful languages. Mathematicians have created hundreds of graphical languages to express and communicate their concepts. The expressive power of mathematics to convey abstract concepts in a way that is formal and rigorous is unparalleled. However, the languages of mathematics are extremely hard to learn (at least for most people). Clearly, the fact that something is expressed in a visual code does not mean that it is easy to understand.

Capable of rapid change: One way of looking at the sensory/arbitrary distinction is in terms of the time the two modes have taken to develop. Sensory codes are the products of the millions of years it has taken for our visual systems to evolve. Although the time frames for the evolution of arbitrary conventional representations are much shorter, they can still have lasted for thousands of years (e.g., the number system). But many more have had only a few decades of development. High-performance interactive computer graphics have greatly enhanced our capability to create new codes. We can now control motion and color with great flexibility and precision. For this reason, we are currently witnessing an explosive growth in the invention of new graphical codes.

The Study of Arbitrary Conventional Symbols

The appropriate methodology for studying arbitrary symbols is very different from that used to study sensory symbols. The tightly focused, narrow questions addressed by psychophysics are wholly inappropriate to investigating visualization in a cultural context. A more appropriate methodology for the researcher of arbitrary symbols may derive from the work of anthropologists such as Clifford Geertz (1973), who advocated "thick description." This approach is based on careful observation, immersion in culture, and an effort to keep "the analysis of social forms closely tied . . . to concrete social events and occasions." Also borrowing from the social sciences, Carroll and coworkers have developed an approach to understanding complex user interfaces that they call *artifact analysis* (Carroll, 1989). In this approach, user interfaces (and presumably visualization techniques) are best viewed as artifacts and studied much as an anthropologist studies cultural artifacts of a religious or practical nature. Formal experiments are out of the question in such circumstances, and if they were actually carried out, they would undoubtedly change the cultural symbols being studied.

Unfortunately for researchers, sensory and social aspects of symbols are closely intertwined in many representations. Although sensory and arbitrary representations have been presented here as distinct categories, the boundary between them is very fuzzy. There is no doubt that culture influences cognition; it is also true that the more we know, the more we may perceive. Pure instances of sensory or arbitrary coding may not exist, but this does not mean that the analysis is invalid. It simply means that for any given example we must be careful to determine which aspects of the visual coding belong in each category.

In general, the science of visualization is still in its infancy. There is much about visualization and visual communication that is more craft than science. For the visualization designer, training in art and design is at least as useful as training in perceptual psychology. For those who wish to do good design, the study of design by example is generally most appropriate. But the science of visualization can inform the process by providing a scientific basis for design rules, and it can suggest new design ideas and methods for displaying data that have not been thought of before. Ultimately, our goal should be to create a new set of conventions for information visualization, designed to be optimal based on sound perceptual principles.

Gibson's Affordance Theory

The great perception theorist J. J. Gibson brought about radical changes in the ways we think about perception with his theories of *ecologocial optics, affordances,* and *direct perception.* Aspects of each of these theoretical concepts are discussed throughout this book. We begin with affordance theory (Gibson, 1979).

Gibson assumed that we perceive in order to operate on the environment. Perception is designed for action. Gibson called the perceivable possibilities for action *affordances;* he claimed that we perceive these properties of the environment in a direct and immediate way. This theory is clearly attractive from the perspective of visualization, because the goal of most visualization is decision making. Thinking about perception in terms of action is likely to be much more useful than thinking about how two adjacent spots of light influence each other's appearance (which is the typical approach of classical psychophysicists).

Much of Gibson's work was in direct opposition to the approach of theorists who reasoned that we must deal with perception from the bottom up, as with geometry. The pre-Gibsonian theorists tended to have an atomistic view of the world. They thought we should first understand how single points of light were perceived, and then we could gradually work on understanding how pairs of lights interacted and gradually build up to understanding the vibrant, dynamic visual world that we live in.

Gibson took a radically different approach. He claimed that we do not perceive points of light; rather, we perceive possibilities for action. We perceive surfaces for walking, handles for pulling, space for navigating, tools for manipulating, and so on. In general, our whole evolution has been geared toward perceiving useful possibilities for action. In an experiment that supports this view, Warren (1984) showed that subjects were capable of accurate judgments of the "climbability" of staircases. These judgments depended on their own leg lengths. Gibson's affordance theory is tied to a theory of direct perception. He claimed that we perceive affordances of the environment *directly,* not indirectly by piecing together evidence from our senses.

Translating the affordance concept into the interface domain, we might construct the following principle: To create a good interface, we must create it with the appropriate affordances to make the user's task easy. Thus, if we have a task of moving an object in 3D space, it should have clear handles, for us to rotate and lift the object. Figure 1.10 shows a design for a 3D object-manipulation interface from Houde (1992). When an object is selected, "handles" appear that allow the object to be lifted or rotated. The function of these handles is made more explicit by illustrations of gripping hands that show the affordances.

However, Gibson's theory presents problems if it is taken literally. According to Gibson, affordances are *physical* properties of the environment that we *directly* perceive. Many theorists, unlike Gibson, think of perception as a very active process: The brain deduces certain things about the environment based on the available sensory evidence. Gibson rejected this view in favor of the

Figure 1.10   Small drawings of hands pop up to show the user what interactions are possible in the prototype interface. Reproduced, with permission, from Houde (1992).

idea that our visual system is tuned to perceiving the visual world and that we perceive it accurately except under extraordinary circumstances. He preferred to concentrate on the visual system as a whole and not to break perceptual processing down into components and operations. He used the term *resonating* to describe the way the visual system responds to properties of the environment. This view has been remarkably influential and has radically changed the way vision researchers think about perception. Nevertheless, few would accept it today in its pure form.

There are three problems with Gibson's direct perception in developing a theory of visualization. The first problem is that even if perception of the environment is direct, it is clear that visualization of data through computer graphics is very indirect. There are typically many layers of processing between the data and its representation. In some cases, the source of the data may be microscopic or otherwise invisible. The source of the data may be quite abstract, such as company statistics in a stock market database. Direct perception is not a meaningful concept in these cases.

Second, there are no clear *physical* affordances in *any* graphical user interface. To say that a screen button "affords" pressing in the same way as a flat surface affords walking is to stretch the theory beyond reasonable limits. In the first place, it is not even clear that a real-world button affords pressing. In another culture, these little bumps might be perceived as rather dull architectural decorations. Clearly, the use of buttons is arbitrary; we must learn that buttons, when pressed, do interesting things in the real world. Things are even more indirect in the computer world; we must learn that a *picture* of a button can be "pressed" using a mouse, a cursor, or yet another button. This is hardly a direct interaction with the physical world.

Third, Gibson's rejection of visual mechanisms is a problem. To take but one example, much that we know about color is based on years of experimentation, analysis, and modeling of the perceptual mechanisms. Color television and many other display technologies are based on an understanding of these mechanisms. To reject the importance of understanding visual mechanisms would be to reject a tremendous proportion of vision research as irrelevant. This entire book is based on the premise that an understanding of perceptual mechanisms is basic to a science of visualization.

Despite these reservations, Gibson's theories color much of this book. The concept of affordances can be extremely useful from a design perspective if it is loosely construed. The idea suggests that we build interfaces that beg to be operated in appropriate and useful ways. We should make virtual handles for turning, virtual buttons for pressing. If components are designed to work together, this should be made perceptually evident, perhaps by creating shaped sockets that afford the attachment of one object to another. This is the kind of design approach advocated by Norman in his famous book, *The Psychology of Everyday Things* (1988). Nevertheless, screen widgets present affordances only in an indirect sense. They borrow their power from our ability to represent pictorially, or otherwise, the affordances of the everyday world. Therefore, we can be inspired by affordance theory to produce good designs, but we cannot expect much help from that theory in building a science of visualization.

A Model of Perceptual Processing

In this section, we introduce an overview of the information processing model of human visual perception. What is provided here is a simplification that should not be taken too literally. As Figure 1.5 shows, there are many subsystems in vision and we should always be wary of overgeneralization. Still, an overall conceptual framework is often useful in providing a starting point for more detailed analysis. Figure 1.11 gives a much broader overview of a two-stage model of perception. In the first stage, information is processed in parallel to extract basic features of the environment. In the second stage, visual attention plays a much more active role and items in the environment tend to be examined in sequence.

Stage 1: Parallel Processing to Extract Low-Level Properties of the Visual Scene

Visual information is first processed by large arrays of neurons in the eye and in the primary visual cortex at the back of the brain. Individual neurons are selectively tuned to certain kinds of information, such as the orientation of edges or the color of a patch of light. In each subarea, large arrays of neurons work in parallel, extracting particular features of the environment. At the early stages, this parallel processing proceeds whether we like it or not, and it is largely independent of what we choose to attend to (although not where we look). It is also rapid. If we want people to understand information fast,

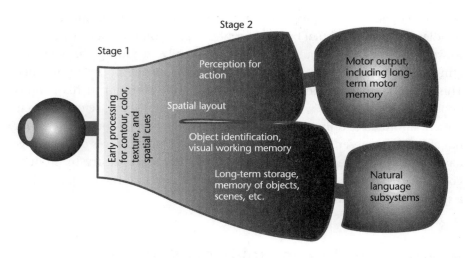

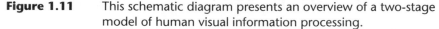

Figure 1.11   This schematic diagram presents an overview of a two-stage model of human visual information processing.

we should present it in such a way that it can easily be detected by these large, fast computational systems in the brain.

Important characteristics of Stage 1 processing include:

- Rapid parallel processing

- Extraction of features, orientation, color, texture, and movement patterns

- Transitory nature of information, which is briefly held in an iconic store

- Bottom-up, data-driven model of processing

Stage 2: Sequential Goal-Directed Processing

At the second stage, there is a bifurcation into a subsystem specialized for object recognition and a subsystem specialized for interacting with the environment. In the case of object recognition, factors such as visual attention and memory become important. Clearly, for people to identify an object, they must somehow match its visual characteristics with properties of the object stored in memory. In general, the tasks that the observer is performing will also influence what is perceived. One of the primary mechanisms relating what is perceived to the task is visual attention. We know that some aspects of this second-stage processing occur sequentially; one visual object at a time is processed.

There is increasing evidence that tasks involving eye-hand coordination and locomotion may be processed in pathways distinct from those involved in object recognition. In this case, there are tight connections with the motor control centers of the brain. This is the two-visual-system hypothesis: one system for locomotion and action, another for symbolic object manipulation. A detailed and convincing account of it can be found in Milner and Goodale (1995).

Important characteristics of Stage 2 processing include:

- Slow serial processing

- Involvement of both working memory and long-term memory

- More emphasis on arbitrary aspects of symbols

- Top-down processing

- Different pathways for object recognition and visually guided motion

A number of theorists have suggested that there is a kind of intermediate representation of the world at the boundary between Stage 1 and Stage 2 processing. Marr (1982) called this the 2½D sketch. Triesman (1980) called it a feature map. But much is still unknown about how visual objects are constructed from features and memories and the locus of visual attention.

Beyond the visual processing stages shown in Figure 1.11 are interfaces to other subsystems. The visual object identification process interfaces with the verbal linguistic subsystems of the brain so that words can be connected to images. The perception-for-action subsystem interfaces with the motor systems that control muscle movements.

The two-stage model is the basis for the structure of this book: The first chapters deal mainly with Stage 1 issues and the later chapters deal with Stage 2 issues. The final two chapters also deal with the interfaces between perceptual and other cognitive processes, such as those involved in language and decision making.

Types of Data

If the goal of visualization research is to transform data into a perceptually efficient visual format, and if we are to make statements with some generality, we must be able to say something about the types of data that can exist for us to visualize. It is useful, but less than satisfying, to be able to say that color coding is good for stock market trends but texture coding is good for geological maps. It is far more useful to be able to define broader categories of information, such as continuous-height maps (scalar fields), continuous-flow fields (vector maps), and category data, and then to make general statements such as "Color coding is good for category information" and "Motion coding is good for highlighting selected data." If we can give perceptual reasons for these generalities, we have a true science of visualization.

Unfortunately, the classification of data is a *big* issue. The classification of data is closely related to the classification of knowledge, and it is with great caution that we approach the subject. What follows is an informal classification of data classes using a number of concepts that we will find helpful in later chapters. We make no claims that this classification is especially profound or all-encompassing.

Bertin (1977) has suggested that there are two fundamental forms of data: data values and data structures. A more modern way of expressing this idea is to divide data into entities and relationships (often called relations). Entities are the objects we wish to visualize; relations define the structures and patterns that relate entities to one another. Sometimes the relationships are provided explicitly; sometimes discovering relationships is the very purpose of visualization. We can also talk about the attributes of an entity or a relationship. Thus, for example, an apple can have color as one of its attributes. The concepts of entity, relationship, and attribute have a long history in database design, and have been adopted more recently in systems modeling. However, we shall extend these concepts beyond the kinds of data that are traditionally stored in a relational database. In visualization, it is necessary to deal with entities that are more complex.

Entities

Entities are generally the objects of interest. People can be entities; hurricanes can be entities. Both fish and fishponds can be entities. A group of things can be considered a single entity if it is convenient—for example, a school of fish.

Relationships

Relationships form the structures that relate entities. There can be many kinds of relationships. A wheel has a "part-of" relationship to a car. One employee of a firm may have a supervisory relationship to another. Relationships can be structural and physical, as in defining the way a house is made of its many component parts, or they can be conceptual, as in defining the relationship between a store and its customers. Relationships can be causal, as when one event causes another, and they can be purely temporal, defining an interval between two events.

Attributes of Entities or Relationships

Both entities and relationships can have attributes. In general, something should be called an attribute (as opposed to an entity itself) when it is a property of some entity and cannot be thought of independently. Thus, the color of an apple is an attribute of the apple. The temperature of water is an attribute of the water. Duration is an attribute of a journey. However, defining what should be an entity and what should be an attribute is not always straightforward. For example, the salary of an employee could be thought of as an attribute of the employee, but we can also think of an amount of money as an entity unto itself, in which case we would have to define a relationship between the employee entity and the sum-of-money entity.

Attribute Quality

It is often useful to describe data visualization methods in light of the quality of attributes they are capable of conveying. A useful way of considering the quality of data is the taxonomy of number scales defined by the statistician S. S. Stevens (1946). According to Stevens, there are four levels of measurement: nominal, ordinal, interval, and ratio scales.

1. **Nominal:** This is the labeling function. Fruit can be classified into apples, oranges, bananas, and so on. There is no sense in which the fruit can be placed in an ordered sequence. Sometimes numbers are used in this way. Thus, the number on the front of a bus generally has a purely nominal value. It identifies the route on which the bus travels.

2. **Ordinal:** The ordinal category encompasses numbers used for ordering things in a sequence. It is possible to say that a certain item

comes before or after another item. The position of an item in a queue or list is an ordinal quality. When we ask people to rank some group of things (films, political candidates, computers) in order of preference, we are requiring them to create an ordinal scale.

3. **Interval:** When we have an interval scale of measurement, it becomes possible to derive the gap between data values. The time of departure and the time of arrival of an aircraft are defined on an interval scale.

4. **Ratio:** With a ratio scale, we have the full expressive power of a real number. We can make statements such as "Object A is twice as large as Object B." The mass of an object is defined on a ratio scale. Money is defined on a ratio scale. The use of a ratio scale implies a zero value used as a reference.

In practice, only three of Stevens's levels of measurement are widely used, and these in somewhat different form. The typical basic data classes most often considered in visualization have been greatly influenced by the demands of computer programming. They are the following.

Category data: This is like Stevens's nominal class.

Integer data: This is like his ordinal class in that it is discrete and ordered.

Real-number data: This combines the properties of interval and ratio scales.

These classes of data can be very useful in discussing the expressive power of visualization techniques. For example, here are two generalizations: (1) Using graphic size (as in a bar chart) to display category information is likely to be misleading, because we tend to interpret size as representing quantity. (2) If we map measurements to color, we can perceive nominal or, at best, ordinal values, with a few discrete steps. Perceiving metric intervals using color is not very effective. As we will see, many visualization techniques are capable of conveying only nominal or ordinal data qualities. These points will be brought out in more detail in later chapters.

Attribute Dimensions: 1D, 2D, 3D, ...

An attribute of an entity can have multiple dimensions. We can have a single *scalar* quantity, such as the weight of a person. We can have a *vector* quantity, such as the direction in which that person is traveling. *Tensors* are higher-order quantities that describe both direction and shear forces, such as occur in materials that are being stressed.

We can have a *field* of scalars, vectors, or tensors. The gravitational field of the earth is a three-dimensional attribute of the earth. In fact, it is a three-dimensional vector field attribute. If we are interested only in the strength of gravity at the earth's surface, it is a two-dimensional scalar attribute. Often the term *map* is used to describe this kind of field. Thus, we talk about a gravity map or a temperature map.

Operations Considered as Data

An entity relationship model can be used to describe most kinds of data. However, it does not capture the operations that may be performed on entities and relationships. We tend to think of operations as somehow different from the data itself, neither entities nor relationships nor attributes. The following are but a few common operations:

- Mathematical operations on numbers—multiplication, division, and so on

- Merging two lists to create a longer list

- Inverting a value to create its opposite

- Bringing an entity or relationship into existence (a new concept is formed)

- Deleting an entity or relationship (a marriage breaks up)

- Transforming an entity in some way (the chrysalis turns into a butterfly)

- Forming a new object out of other objects (a pie is baked from apples and pastry)

- Splitting a single entity into its component parts (a machine is disassembled)

In some cases, these operations can themselves form a kind of data that we may wish to capture. Chemistry contains a huge catalog of the compounds that result when certain operations are applied to combinations of other compounds. These operations may form part of the data that is stored. Certain operations are easy to visualize; for example, the merging of two entities can easily be represented by showing two visual objects that combine (visually merge) into a single entity. Other operations are not at all easy to represent in any visualization. For example, the detailed logical structure of a computer program may be better represented using a written code that has its basis in natural language than using any kind of diagram. What should and should not be visualized is a major topic in Chapter 9.

Operations and procedures often present a particularly difficult challenge for visualization. It is difficult to express operations effectively in a static diagram, and this is especially a problem in the creation of visual languages. On the other hand, the use of animation opens up the possibility of expressing at least certain operations in an immediately accessible visual manner. We shall deal with the issue of animation and visual languages in Chapter 9.

Metadata

When we are striving to understand data, certain products are sure to emerge as we proceed. We may discover correlations between variables or clusters of data values. We may postulate certain underlying mechanisms that are not immediately visible. The result is that theoretical entities come into being. Atoms, photons, black holes, and all the basic constructs of physics are like this. As more evidence accumulates, the theoretical entities seem more and more real, but they are nonetheless only observable in the most indirect ways. These theoretical constructs that emerge from data analysis have sometimes been called *metadata* (Tweedie, 1997). They are generally called *derived data* in the database modeling community. Metadata can be of any kind. It can consist of new entities, such as identified classes of objects, or new relationships, such as postulated interactions between different entities, or new rules. We may impose complex structural relationships on the data, such as tree structures or directed acyclic graphs, or we may find that they already exist in the data.

The problem with the view that metadata and primary data are somehow essentially different is that all data is interpreted to some extent—there is no such thing as raw data. Every data-gathering instrument embodies some particular interpretation in the way it is built. Also, from the practical viewpoint of the visualization designer, the problems of representation are the same for metadata as for primary data. In both cases, there are entities, relationships, and their attributes to be represented, although some are more abstract than others.

Conclusion

Visualization applies vision research to practical problems of data analysis in much the same way as engineering applies physics to practical problems of building manufacturing plants. Just as engineering has influenced physicists to become more concerned with areas such as semiconductor technology, so we may hope that the development of an applied discipline of data visualization can encourage vision researchers to intensify their efforts in addressing such problems as 3D space and task-oriented perception. Now there is considerable practical benefit in understanding these things.

We have introduced a key distinction between the ideas of sensory and arbitrary conventional symbols. This is a difficult and sometimes artificial distinction. Readers can doubtless come up with counterexamples and reasons why it is impossible to separate the two. Nonetheless, the distinction is essential. With no basic model of visual processing on which we can support the idea of a good data representation, ultimately the problem of visualization comes down to establishing a consistent notation. If the best representation is simply the one we know best, because it is embedded in our culture, then standardization is everything—there is no good representation, only widely shared conventions. In opposition to the view that everything is arbitrary, this book takes the view that all humans do have more or less the same visual system. This visual system has evolved over tens of millions of years to enable creatures to perceive and act within the natural environment. Although very flexible, the visual system is tuned to receiving data presented in certain ways, but not in others. If we can understand how the mechanism works, we can produce better displays.

The Environment, Optics, Resolution, and the Display

We can think of the world itself as an information display. Objects may be used as tools or as construction materials, or they may be obstacles to be avoided. Every intricate surface reveals the properties of the material from which it is made. Creatures signal their intentions inadvertently or deliberately through movement. There are almost infinite levels of detail in nature and we must be responsive to both small and large things, but in different ways: Large things, such as boulders, are obstacles; smaller things, such as rocks, can be used as tools; still smaller things, such as grains of sand, are useful by the handful. If our extraordinary skill in perceiving the information inherent in the environment can be applied to data visualization, we will have gained a truly powerful tool.

The visual display of a computer is only a single rectangular planar surface, divided into a regular grid of small colored dots. It is astonishing how successful it is as an information display, given how little it resembles the world we live in. This chapter concerns the lessons we can learn about information display by appreciating the environment in broad terms and how the same kind of information can be picked up from a flat screen. It begins with a discussion of the most general properties of the visual environment, then considers the lens-and-receptor system of the eye as the principal instrument of vision. The basic abilities of the eye are related to the problem of creating an optimal display device.

This low-level analysis bears on a number of display problems. If we want to make virtual objects seem real, how should we simulate the interaction of light with their surfaces? What is the optimal display device and how do current display devices measure up? How much detail can we see? How faint a target can we see? How good is the lens system of the human eye? This is a kind of foundation chapter; it introduces much of the basic vocabulary of vision research.

The Environment

A strategy for designing a visualization is to transform the data so that it appears like a common environment—a kind of data landscape. We should then be able to transfer skills obtained in interpreting the real environment to understanding our data. This is not to say that we should represent data by means of synthetic trees, flowers, and undulating lawns—that would be quaint and ludicrous. It seems less ludicrous to create synthetic offices, with desks, filing cabinets, phones, books, and Rolodexes, and this is already being done in a number of computer interfaces.

Understanding the general properties of the environment is important for a more basic reason. When you are trying to understand perception, it is always a good strategy to try to understand what perception is *for*. The theory of evolution tells us that the visual system must have survival value, and adopting this perspective allows us to understand visual mechanisms in the broader context of useful skills, such as navigation, food seeking (which is like information seeking), and tool use (which depends on object-shape perception).

What follows is a short tour of the visual environment, beginning with light.

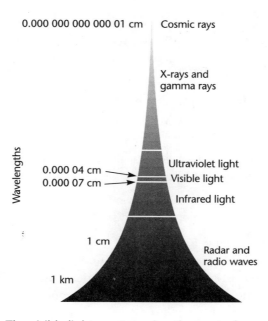

Figure 2.1   The visible light spectrum is a tiny part of a much larger spectrum of electromagnetic radiation.

Visible Light

Perception is about understanding patterns of light. Visible light constitutes a very small part of the electromagnetic spectrum, as is shown in Figure 2.1. Some animals, such as snakes, can see in the infrared, while certain insects can see in the ultraviolet. Humans can perceive light only in the range of 400 to 700 nanometers. (In vision research, wavelength is generally expressed in units of 10^{-9} meters, called nanometers). At wavelengths shorter than 400 nm are ultraviolet light and X-rays. At wavelengths longer than 700 nm are infrared light, microwaves, and radio waves.

Ecological Optics

The most useful broad framework for describing the visual environment is given by ecological optics, a discipline developed by J. J. Gibson. Gibson radically changed the way we think about perception of the visual world. Instead of concentrating on the image on the retina, as did other vision researchers, Gibson emphasized perception of *surfaces in the environment.* The following quotations strikingly illustrate how he broke with a traditional approach to space perception that was grounded in the classical geometry of points, lines, and planes:

> A surface is substantial; a plane is not. A surface is textured; a plane is not. A surface is never perfectly transparent; a plane is. A surface can be seen; a plane can only be visualized.

> A fiber is an elongated object of small diameter, such as a wire or thread. A fiber should not be confused with a geometrical line.

> In surface geometry the junction of two flat surfaces is either an edge or a corner; in abstract geometry the intersection of two planes is a line.

From these statements (Gibson, 1979, p. 35), it is clear that for Gibson, perception of surfaces is one of the keys to understanding perception. Much of human visual processing becomes more understandable if we assume that a key function of the visual system is to extract properties of surfaces. As our primary contact with objects, surfaces are essential to understanding the potential for interaction and manipulation in the environment.

A second key concept in Gibson's ecological optics is the ambient optical array (Gibson, 1986). To understand the ambient optic array, consider what happens to light entering the environment from some source such as the sun. It is absorbed, reflected, refracted, and diffracted as it interacts with various objects such as stones, grass, trees, and water. The environment, considered in this way, is a hugely complex matrix with photons traveling in all directions, consisting of different mixtures of wavelengths and polarized in various ways. This complexity is quite impossible to simulate. However, from any particular stationary point in the environment, critical information is contained in the structure of the light arriving at that point. This vast simplification is what Gibson called the ambient optical array. This array encompasses all the rays arriving at a particular point as they are structured in both space and time. Figure 2.2 is intended to capture the flavor of the concept.

Much of the effort of computer graphics can be characterized as an attempt to model the ambient optical array. Because the interactions of light with surfaces are vastly complex, it is not possible to directly model entire environments. But the ambient array provides the basis for simplifications such as those used in ray tracing, so that approximations can be computed (Foley et al., 1990). If we can capture the structure of a bundle of rays passing through a glass rectangle on their way to the stationary point, we have something that we may be able to reproduce on a screen (see Figure 2.2).

Figure 2.2   *Ambient optical array* is a term that describes the array of light
that arrives from all directions at some designated point in the
environment. Simulating the appearance of the bundle of rays
that would pass through a glass rectangle is one of the goals
of computer graphics.

Optical Flow

The ambient optical array is dynamic, changing over time both as the viewpoint moves and as objects move. As we advance into a static environment,
a characteristic flow field develops. Figure 2.3 illustrates the visual field
expanding outward as a result of forward motion. There is evidence that the
visual system includes processes to interpret such flow patterns and that
they are important in understanding how animals (including humans) navigate through space, avoid obstacles, and generally perceive the layout of
objects in the world. The flow pattern in Figure 2.3 is only a very simple
case; if we follow something with our eyes while we move forward, the
pattern becomes more complex. The perceptual mechanisms to interpret
flow patterns must therefore be sophisticated. The key point here is that
visual images of the world are dynamic, so that the perception of motion
patterns may be as important as the perception of the static world, albeit less
well understood. Chapter 8 deals with motion perception in the context of
space perception and 3D information display. This man has no pens

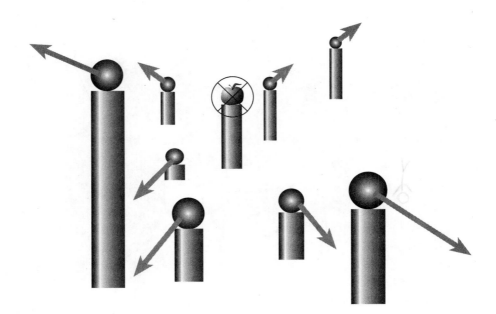

Figure 2.3   An expanding flow pattern of visual information is created as an observer moves forward through the environment.

Textured Surfaces and Texture Gradients

Gibson pointed out that surface texture is one of the fundamental visual properties of an object. In visual terms, a surface is merely an unformed patch of light unless it is textured. Texture is critical to perception in a number of ways. The texture of an object helps us see where an object is and what shape it has. On a larger scale, the texture of the ground plane on which we walk, run, and crawl is important in judging distances and other aspects of space. Figure 2.4 shows that the texture of the ground plane produces a characteristic texture gradient that is important in space perception. Of course, surfaces themselves are infinitely varied. The surface of a wooden table is very different from the surface of an ocelot. Generally speaking, most surfaces have clearly defined boundaries; diffuse, cloud-like objects are exceptional. Perhaps because of this, we have great difficulty in visualizing diffuse data fields such as uncertainty distributions.

At present, most computerized visualizations present objects as smooth and untextured. This may be partly because texturing is not yet easy to do in many visualization packages. Perhaps visualization designers have avoided texturing surfaces by applying the general esthetic principle that we should avoid irrelevant decoration in displays—"chart junk," to use Tufte's

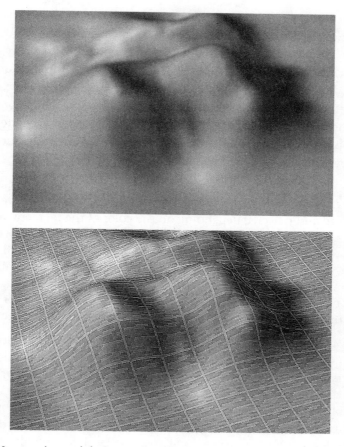

Figure 2.4   An undulating surface with and without surface texture.

memorable phrase (Tufte, 1983). But texturing surfaces is not chart junk, especially in 3D visualizations. Even if we texture all objects in exactly the same way, this can help us perceive the orientation, shape, and spatial layout of a surface. Textures need not be garish or obtrusive, but when we want something to appear to be a 3D surface, it should have at least a subtle texture. As we shall see in Chapter 5, texture can also be used to code information.

The Paint Model of Surfaces

Surfaces in nature are endlessly varied and complex. Microtextures give irregular patterns of reflection, so the amount and color of reflected light can vary with both the illumination angle and the viewing angle. However, there is a simple model that approximates many common materials. This model can be understood by considering a glossy paint. The paint has pigment particles embedded in a more or less clear medium, as shown in Figure 2.5. Some of the light is reflected from the surface of the glossy medium and is unchanged in color. Most of the light penetrates the medium and is selectively absorbed by the pigment particles, altering its color. According to this model, there are three important direct interactions of light with surfaces, as described below. An additional (fourth) property is related to the fact that parts of objects cast shadows, revealing more information about their shapes. (See Figures 2.5 and 2.6.)

- *Lambertian shading.* Some light penetrates the material's surface and interacts with the pigment in the medium. This light is selectively absorbed and reflected depending on the color of the pigment, and some of it is scattered back through the surface out into the environment. This scattered light tends to be distributed roughly equally in all directions. The equal scattering of light in all directions is called the lambertian model. Figure 2.6(a) shows a surface with only lambertian shading. Lambertian shading is the simplest method for representing surface shape from shading. It can also be highly effective.

- *Specular shading.* The light that is reflected directly from a surface is called specular light. This is what we see as the highlights on glossy objects. Specular reflection obeys the optical principle of mirror reflection: The angle of reflection equals the angle of incidence. It is possible to simulate high-gloss, semigloss, or eggshell finishes by causing the specular light to spread out somewhat, simulating different degrees of roughness at a microscopic level. Specular light reflected from a surface retains the color of the illuminant; it is not affected by the color of the underlying pigment. Hence, we see white highlights gleaming from the surface of a red automobile. Both the viewing direction and the positions of the light sources affect the locations where hightlights appear. Figure 2.6(b) shows a surface with both lambertian and specular shading.

- *Ambient shading.* Ambient light is the light that illuminates a surface from everywhere in the environment, except for the actual sources. In reality, ambient light is as complex as the scene itself. However, in computer graphics, ambient light is often grossly simplified by treating it as a constant, which is like assuming that an object is situated in a uniformly gray room. The radiosity technique (Cohen and Greenberg, 1985) properly models the complexity of ambient light, but is rarely used for visualization. One of the consequences of modeling ambient light as a constant is that no shape-from-shading

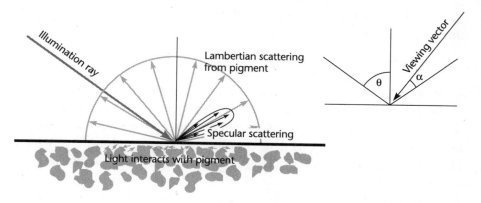

Figure 2.5   This simplified model of light interacting with surfaces is used in most computer graphics. Specular reflection is light that is reflected directly from the surface without penetrating to the underlying pigment.

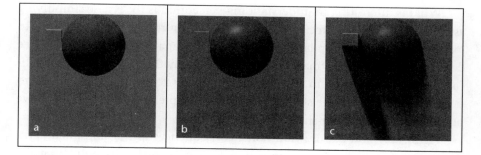

Figure 2.6   (a) Lambertian shading only. (b) Lambertian shading with specular and ambient shading. (c) Lambertian shading with specular, ambient, and cast shadows. See also color plates.

information is available in areas of cast shadow. In Figures 2.6(b) and 2.6(c), ambient light is simulated by the assumption that a constant amount of light is reflected from all points on the surface.

- *Cast shadows.* An object can cast shadows either on itself or on other objects. As shown in Figure 2.6(c), cast shadows can greatly influence the perceived height of an object.

The mathematical expression for the amount reflected, R, according to this simplified model, is as follows:

$$R = a + b\cos\theta + c\cos^k(\alpha)$$

where θ is the angle between the incident ray and the surface normal and α is the angle between the reflected ray and the view vector. a, b, and c represent the relative amounts of ambient, lambertian, and specular light, respectively. The exponent k is used to control the degree of glossiness. A high value of k, such as 50, models a very shiny surface, while a lower value, such as 6, results in a semigloss appearance.

Note that this is a simplified treatment, providing only the crudest approximation to the way light interacts with surfaces, but nevertheless it is so effective in creating real-looking scenes that it is widely used in computer graphics with only a small modification to simulate color. It assumes light sources at infinity and deals only with the amount of reflected light and not with its color. This surface/light interaction model and others are covered extensively by computer graphics texts concerned with realistic image synthesis. The reader is referred to Foley et al. (1990) for more information.

What is interesting in understanding perception is that these simplifying assumptions may, in effect, be embedded in our visual systems. The brain may assume a model similar to this when we estimate the shape of a surface defined by shading information. Indeed, it is likely that using more sophisticated modeling of light in the environment may actually be detrimental to our understanding of the shapes of surfaces. Chapter 7 discusses the way we perceive this shape-from-shading information.

Figures 2.7 and 2.8 illustrate some consequences of the simplified lighting model. Figure 2.7 shows some glossy leaves to make the point that the simplified model is representative of at least some nonsynthetic objects. In this picture, the specular highlights from the shiny surface are white because the illuminant is white. The nonspecular light from the leaf pigmentation is green. As a tool in data visualization, specular reflection is useful in visualization of fine surface features, such as scratches on glass. These can be brought out by deliberately arranging the lighting so that a specular highlight falls across the surface. Specular highlights can be similarly useful in revealing subtle differences in surface microroughness. The nonspecular reflection is more effective in giving an overall impression of the shape of the surface.

To summarize this brief introduction to the visual environment, we have seen that much of what is useful to organisms is related to objects, to their

Figure 2.7   Glossy leaves. Note that the highlights are the color of the illuminant. See also color plates.

Figure 2.8   Specular light reveals fine details of surface structure. However, it depends on the viewpoint.

layout in space, and to the properties of their surfaces. As Gibson so effectively argued, in understanding how surfaces are perceived, we must understand how light becomes structured when it arrives at the eye. We have covered two important kinds of structuring thus far. One is the structure that is present in the ambient array of light that arrives at a viewpoint. This structure has both static pattern components and dynamic pattern flows as we move through the world. The second is the more detailed structuring of light that results from the interaction of light with surfaces.

The Eye

We now move from taking a broad view of the visual environment to considering the eye as the instrument of sight. The human eye, like a camera, contains the equivalents of a lens, an aperture (the pupil), and a film (the retina). Figure 2.9 illustrates these parts. The lens focuses a small, inverted picture of the world onto the retina. The iris performs the function of a variable aperture, helping the eye to adjust to different lighting conditions. For some people, the fact that the image is upside down is a problem. But we do not perceive what is on the retina; instead, our brains compute a percept based on sensory information. Inversion of the images is the least of the computational problems.

We should not take the eye/camera analogy too far. If seeing were like photography, you would only have to copy the image on the back of the eye to produce a perfect likeness of a friend; anyone could be a great portrait painter. Yet artists spend years studying perspective geometry and anatomy, and constantly practicing their skills. Early cave artists represented human figures with spindly lines for arms and legs. Children still do this. It took thousands of years, culminating in the golden age of Greek art, for artists to develop the skills to draw natural figures, properly shaded and foreshortened. Following this, the skill was largely lost again until the Renaissance, in the fifteenth century. Yet in the image on the back of the eye, everything is in perfect proportion and in perspective. Clearly, we do not "see" what is on the retina. The locus of conscious perception is farther up the chain of processing, and at this later stage most of the simple properties of the retinal image have been lost. The world that we perceive is not at all what is imaged on the retina.

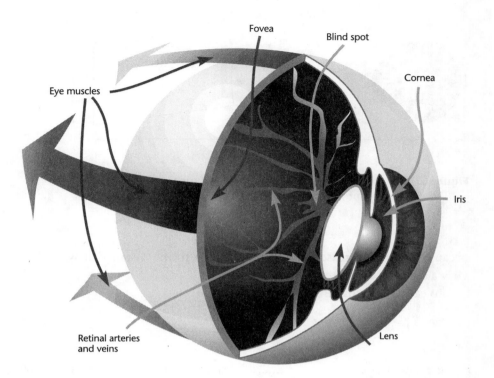

Figure 2.9   The human eye. Important features include the fovea, where vision is sharpest; the iris, which determines the amount of light that enters the eye; and the large eye muscles that enable eye movements. The blind spot is caused by the absence of receptors where the retinal arteries enter the eyeball and in the two principal optical elements, the lens and the cornea.

The Visual Angle Defined

The visual angle is a key concept in defining the properties of the eye and early vision. As Figure 2.10 illustrates, a visual angle is the angle subtended by an object at the eye of an observer. Visual angles are generally defined in degrees, minutes, and seconds of arc. (A minute is $\frac{1}{60}$ degree and a second is $\frac{1}{60}$ minute). As a general rule, a thumbnail held at arm's length subtends about 1 degree of visual angle. Another useful fact is that a 1-cm object viewed at 57 cm has a visual angle of approximately 1 degree. This is useful,

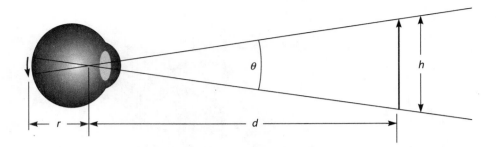

Figure 2.10   The visual angle of an object is measured from the optical center of the eye.

because 57 cm is a reasonable approximation to the distance at which we view a computer monitor.

To calculate visual angle, use this equation:

$$\tan\left(\frac{\theta}{2}\right) = \frac{h}{2} \tag{2.1}$$

or

$$\theta = 2\arctan\left(\frac{h}{2d}\right) \tag{2.2}$$

The Lens

The human eye contains a compound lens. This lens has two key elements, the curved front surface of the cornea and the crystalline lens. The nodal point is the optical center of the compound; it is positioned approximately 17 mm from the retina. The distance from the eye is usually measured from the cornea, but in terms of optics it is better to estimate the distance to the first nodal point. (See Figure 2.10.)

The following equation describes the imaging properties of a simple lens.

$$\frac{1}{f} = \frac{1}{d} + \frac{1}{r} \tag{2.3}$$

where f is the focal length of the lens, d is the distance to the object that is imaged, and r is the distance to the image that is formed.

If the units are meters, the *power* of a lens is given by the reciprocal of the focal length ($1/f$) in units of *diopters*. Thus, a 1-diopter lens has a focal length of 1 m.

As a first approximation, the power of a compound lens can be computed by adding the powers of the components. We obtain the focal length of a two-part compound lens by using the following equation:

$$\frac{1}{f_3} = \frac{1}{f_1} + \frac{1}{f_2} \tag{2.4}$$

f_3 is the result of combining lenses f_1 and f_2.

The human lens system has a focal length of about 17 mm, corresponding to a power of 59 diopters. Most of this power, about 40 diopters, comes from the front surface of the cornea; the remainder comes from the variable-focus lens. When the cillary muscle that surrounds the lens contracts, the lens assumes a more convex, more powerful shape and nearby objects come into focus.

Young children have very flexible lenses, capable of adjusting over a range of 12 diopters or more, which means that they can focus on an object as close as 8 cm. However, the eye becomes less flexible with age, at roughly the rate of 2 diopters per decade, so that at the age of 60, the lens is almost completely rigid (Sun et al., 1988). Hence the need for reading glasses at about the age of 48 when only a few diopters of accommodation are left.

The *depth of focus* of a lens is the distance over which objects are in focus without changes in focus. The depth of focus of the human eye varies with the size of the pupil (Smith and Atchison, 1997), but assuming a 3-mm pupil and a human eye focused at infinity, objects between about 3 m and infinity are in focus. Depth of focus can usefully be described in terms of the power change that takes place without the image's becoming significantly blurred. This is about ⅓ diopter, assuming a 3-mm pupil.

Assuming the ⅓-diopter depth-of-focus value, and an eye focused at distance d, objects in the range

$$\left[\frac{3d}{d+3}, \frac{-3d}{d-3} \right]$$

will be in focus.

To illustrate, for an observer focusing at 50 cm, roughly the normal monitor-viewing distance, an object can be about 7 cm in front of the screen or 10 cm behind the screen before it appears to be out of focus. In helmet-mounted displays, it is common to set the screen at a focal distance of 2 m. This means that in the range 1.2 m to 6.0 m, it is not necessary to worry about simulating depth-of-focus effects, something that is difficult and computationally expensive to do. However, the large pixels in typical

Table 2.1   Depth of focus at various viewing distances.

Viewing Distance	Near	Far
50 cm	43 cm	60 cm
1 m	75 cm	1.5 m
2 m	1.2 m	6.0 m
3 m	1.5 m	Infinity

virtual-reality displays prevent us from modeling image blur to anywhere near this resolution.

Table 2.1 gives the range that is in focus for a number of viewing distances, given a 3-mm pupil. For more detailed modeling of depth of focus as it varies with pupil diameter, consult Smith and Atchison (1997).

Focus and Augmented-Reality Systems

Augmented-reality systems involve superimposing visual imagery on the real world so that people can see a computer-graphics-enhanced view of the world. For this blending of real and virtual imagery to be achieved, the viewpoint of the observer must be accurately known and the objects' positions and shapes in the local environment must also be stored in the controlling computer. With this information, it is a straightforward application of standard computer graphics techniques to draw 3D images that are superimposed on the real-world images. However, the technical difficulties in getting precise registration information and in designing optical systems that are light and portable should not be underestimated.

Figure 2.11 illustrates an experimental augmented-reality system in which a radiologist can see within a woman's breast to guide a biopsy needle in taking a tissue sample (from State et al., 1996). Given how difficult it is for the surgeon to accomplish this task with a gland that is easily deformed, such a development would have very large benefits. Other applications for augmented displays include automobile servicing machines in which the mechanic sees instructions and structural diagrams superimposed on the actual machinery; tactical military displays in which the pilot or tank driver sees indicators of friendly or hostile targets superimposed on a view of the landscape; and medical technology in which the surgeon sees an internal object, such as a brain tumor, highlighted within the brain during surgical planning or actual surgery. In each case, visual data is superimposed on real

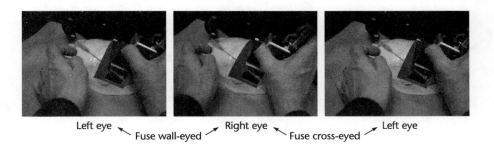

Left eye   Fuse wall-eyed   Right eye   Fuse cross-eyed   Left eye

Figure 2.11   Augmented system for assisting in breast biopsies. This is a simulation of a system that is under development. The inside of the breast has been imaged using ultrasound, allowing the surgeon to guide the biopsy needle to the suspicious-looking tissue. Reprinted with permission (State et al., 1996).

objects to supplement the information available to the user and enable better or more rapid decision making. This data may take the form of written text labels or sophisticated symbology.

In many augmented-reality systems, computer graphics imagery is superimposed on the environment using a device called a beam-splitter. The splitter is actually used not to split, but to *combine* the images coming from the real world with those presented on a small computer monitor. The result is a like a double-exposed photograph. A typical beam-splitter allows approximately half the light to pass through and half the light to be reflected. Figure 2.12 illustrates the essential optical components of this type of augmented-reality display.

Because the optics are typically fixed in augmented-reality systems, there is only one depth at which both the computer-generated imagery and the real-world imagery are in focus. This can be both good and bad. If both real-world and virtual-world scenes are simultaneously in focus, it will be easier to perceive them together. If this is desirable, care should be taken to set the focal plane of the virtual imagery at the typical depth of the real imagery. However, it is sometimes desirable that the computer imagery remain perceptually distinct from the real-world image. For example, a transparent layer of text from an instruction manual might be presented on a see-through display (Feiner et al., 1993). If the focal distances are different, the user can choose to focus either on the text or on the imagery, and in this way selectively attend to one or the other.

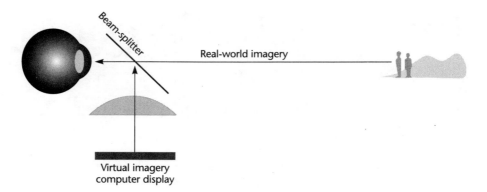

Figure 2.12   In augmented-reality displays, computer graphics imagery is superimposed on the real-world environment using a beam-splitter. The effect is like a transparent overlay on the environment. The focal distance of the computer imagery depends on the power of the lenses used.

There is evidence that focus can cause problems with distance estimation in aircraft heads-up displays (HUDs). In these displays, the virtual image is set at optical infinity, because only distant objects are normally seen through a cockpit screen. Despite this, experiments have shown that observers tend to focus at a distance closer than infinity with HUDs, and this can cause overestimation of distances to objects in the environment (Roscoe, 1991). This may be a serious problem; according to Roscoe, it has been at least partially responsible for large numbers (one per month) of generally fatal "controlled flight into the terrain" accidents.

Roscoe's theory of what occurs is that the average apparent size of objects is almost perfectly correlated with the distance at which the eyes are focused (Iavecchia et al., 1988). But with HUDs, the eyes are focused closer (for reasons that are not fully understood), leading to an underestimation of size and an overestimation of distance. Roscoe suggests that this can also partially account for the fact that when virtual imaging is used, either in simulators or in real aircraft with HUDs, pilots make fast approaches and land hard.

Focus in Virtual-Reality Displays

In virtual-reality (VR) displays, unlike the augmented-reality displays discussed above, the system designer need only be concerned with computer-generated imagery. However, it is still highly desirable that correct depth-of-focus information be presented to the user. Objects that the user fixates should be in sharp focus, while objects both farther away and nearer should be blurred to the appropriate extents. Focus is important in helping us to differentiate objects that we wish to attend to from other objects in the environment. Unfortunately, simulating depth of focus using a flat-screen display is a major technical problem. It has two parts: simulating optical blur and simulating the optical distance of the virtual object. There is also the problem of knowing what the user is looking at so that the object of attention can be made sharp while other objects are displayed as though out of focus. Figure 2.13 illustrates one way that correct depth-of-focus information could be presented on a flat-screen VR display. An eye tracker is used to determine where in the scene the eye is fixated. If binocular eye trackers were used in a stereoscopic display, this information would be even more accurate, because eye convergence information can be used to estimate the distance to the fixated

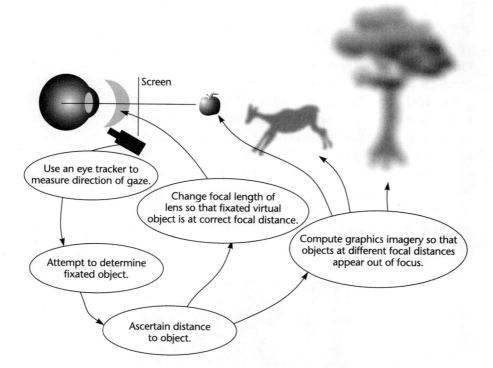

Figure 2.13   A possible solution to the problem of how correct depth-of-focus information might be displayed in a virtual-reality (VR) display. The apple is the fixated object and is drawn in sharp focus. The other objects are drawn out of focus, depending on their relative depths.

object. Once the object of attention is identified, an image is computed in such a way that the fixated object is in sharp focus and other objects are appropriately out of focus. A sophisticated system might measure pupil diameter and take this information into account. At the same time, other system components change the focal lengths of the lenses in the display system so that the attended virtual object is placed at the correct focal distance. All virtual objects are actually displayed on the screen in the conventional way, but with simulated depth of focus. Neveau and Stark (1998) describe the optical and control requirements of such a system.

Chromatic Aberration

The human eye is not corrected for chromatic aberration. This means that different wavelengths of light are focused at different distances within the eye. Short-wavelength blue light is refracted more than long-wavelength red light. A typical monitor has a blue phosphor peak wavelength at about 480 nm and a red peak at about 640 nm, and a lens with a power of 1.5 diopters is needed to make blue and red focus at the same depth. This is the kind of blur that causes people to reach for their reading glasses. Thus, if we focus on a patch of light produced by the red phosphor, an adjacent blue patch will be significantly out of focus. Because of chromatic aberration, it is inadvisable to make fine patterns that use the undiluted blue phosphor. Pure blue text on a black background can be almost unreadable if there is white or red text nearby to attract the focusing mechanism. The addition of even a small amount of red and green will alleviate the problem, because they will provide luminance edges to perceptually define the color boundary.

The chromatic aberration of the eye can give rise to strong illusory depth effects (Jackson et al., 1994). This is illustrated in Figure 2.14, where both blue

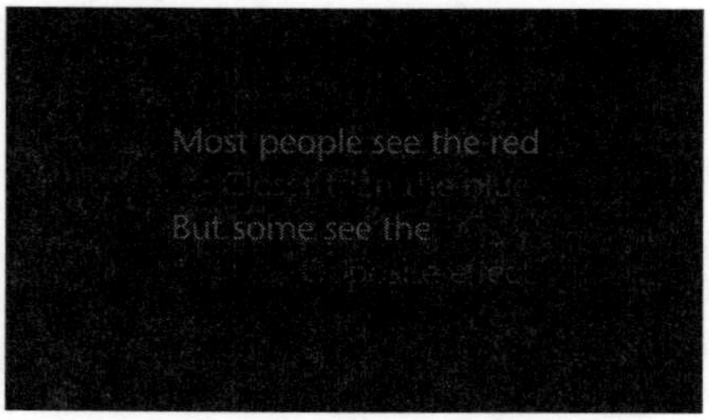

Figure 2.14   Chromostereopsis. For most people, the red advances and the blue recedes. See also color plates.

text and red text are superimposed on a black background. For about 60% of observers, the red appears closer. But 30% see the reverse, and the remaining 10% see the colors lying in the same plane. It is common to take advantage of this in slide presentations by making the background a deep blue, which makes white or red lettering appear to stand out.

Receptors

The lens focuses an image on a mosaic of photoreceptor cells that line the back of the eye in a layer called the retina. There are two types of such cells: rods, which are extremely sensitive at low light levels, and cones, which are sensitive under normal working light levels. There are about 100 million rods and only 6 million cones. Rods contribute far less to normal daytime vision than do cones. The input from rods is pooled over large areas, with thousands of rods contributing to the signal that passes up through a single fiber in the optic nerve. Rods are so sensitive that they are overloaded in daylight and effectively shut down; therefore, most vision researchers ignore their very slight contribution to normal daylight vision.

The fovea is a small area in the center of the retina that is densely packed only with cones, and it is here that vision is sharpest. Cones at the fovea are packed about 20 sec of arc apart (180 per degree). There are more than 100,000 cones packed into a small area subtending a visual angle of 1.5 to 2 degrees. Although it is usual to speak of the fovea as a 2-degree field, the greatest resolution of detail is obtained only in the central ½ degree of this region. Figure 2.15 is an image of the receptor mosaic in the fovea. As you can see, the receptors are arranged in an irregular but roughly hexagonal pattern.

Simple Acuities

Visual acuities are measurements of our ability to see detail. Acuities are important in display technologies because they give us an idea of the ultimate limits on the information densities that we can perceive. Some of the basic acuities are summarized in Figure 2.16.

Most of the acuity measurements in Figure 2.16 suggest that we can resolve things, such as the presence of two distinct lines, down to about 1 minute. This is in rough agreement with the spacing of receptors in the center of the fovea. For us to see that two lines are distinct, the blank space between them should lie on a receptor; therefore, we should only be able to perceive lines separated by roughly twice the receptor spacing. However, there are a number of superacuities, of which vernier acuity and stereo

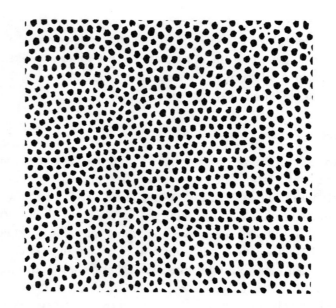

Figure 2.15   The receptor mosaic in the fovea. From Frisby, J. P. (1979), p. 34.

acuity are examples. A superacuity is the ability to perceive visual properties of the world to a greater precision than could be achieved based on a simple receptor model. Superacuities can be achieved only because postreceptor mechanisms are capable of integrating the input from many receptors to obtain better than single-receptor resolution. A good example of this is vernier acuity, the ability to judge the collinearity of two fine line segments. This can be done with amazing accuracy to better than 10 seconds of arc. To give an idea of just how accurate this is, a normal computer monitor has about 40 pixels (picture elements) per centimeter. We can perform vernier acuity tasks that are accurate to about $\frac{1}{10}$ of a pixel.

Neural postprocessing can efficiently combine input from two eyes. Campbell and Green (1965) found that binocular viewing improves acuity by 7% as compared with monocular viewing. They also found a $\sqrt{2}$ improvement in contrast sensitivity. This latter finding is remarkable because it supports the theory that the brain is able to perfectly pool information from the two eyes, despite the fact that three or four synaptic connections lie between the receptors and the first point at which the information from the two eyes can be combined.

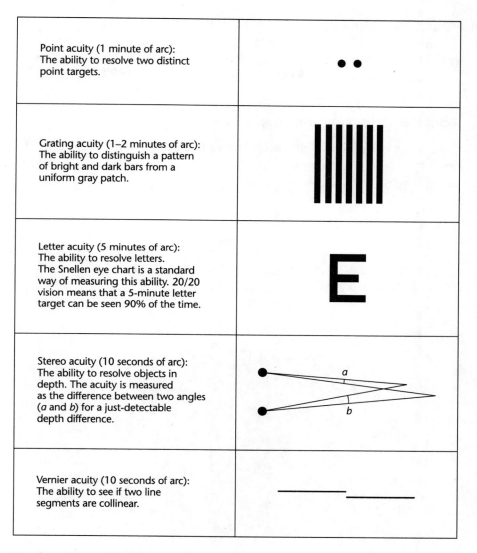

Point acuity (1 minute of arc): The ability to resolve two distinct point targets.	
Grating acuity (1–2 minutes of arc): The ability to distinguish a pattern of bright and dark bars from a uniform gray patch.	
Letter acuity (5 minutes of arc): The ability to resolve letters. The Snellen eye chart is a standard way of measuring this ability. 20/20 vision means that a 5-minute letter target can be seen 90% of the time.	
Stereo acuity (10 seconds of arc): The ability to resolve objects in depth. The acuity is measured as the difference between two angles (*a* and *b*) for a just-detectable depth difference.	
Vernier acuity (10 seconds of arc): The ability to see if two line segments are collinear.	

Figure 2.16 The basic acuities.

Interestingly, Campbell and Green's findings suggest that we should be able to use the ability of the eye to integrate information over space and time to allow perception of higher-resolution information than is actually available on our display device. One technique for achieving higher-than-device resolution is antialiasing, which is discussed later in this chapter. There is also an intriguing possibility that the temporal-integration capability of the human eye could be used to advantage. It may be possible to distribute the information in a high-resolution image over a sequence of frames on a lower-resolution display in such a way that the brain integrates the information.

Acuity Distribution and the Visual Field

The human eye accepts light through a wide field of view, as shown in Figure 2.17. There is a roughly triangular region of binocular overlap within which both eyes receive input.

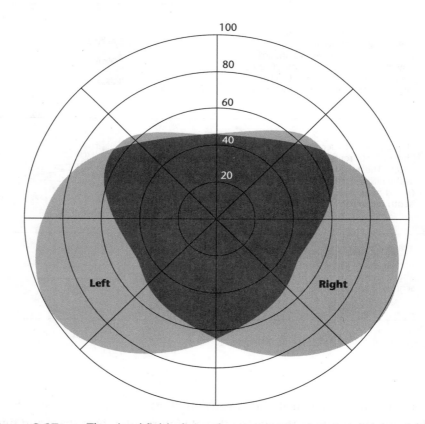

Figure 2.17 The visual field of view for a person gazing straight ahead. The irregular boundaries of the left and right fields are caused by facial features such as the nose. The darker-gray area shows the region of binocular overlap.

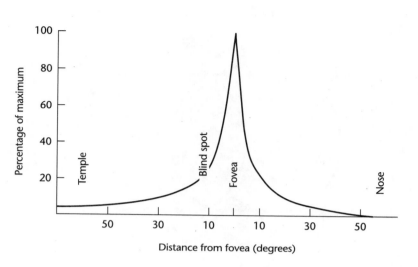

Figure 2.18 The acuity of the eye falls off rapidly with distance from the fovea.

Visual acuity is very nonuniformly distributed over this field. As shown in Figure 2.18, acuity outside of the fovea drops rapidly, so that we can only resolve about ⅕ the detail at 10 degrees from the fovea. Normal acuity is a linear measure; if we consider detail perceived per unit area, the amount that can be seen falls to ¹⁄₂₅.

Figure 2.17 suggests that the ultimate immersive virtual-reality display should have a very wide field of view. However, achieving high resolution over such a large field is not currently possible, and in any case is wasteful of resources, because we can see fine detail only at the fovea. One solution to the problem is to display more detail at the fovea than at the periphery of vision. This requires technology to track eye movements and project a high-resolution patch onto the region around the fovea.

The CAE FOHMD is one of the widest-field displays made (Shenker, 1987). Designed for helicopter simulators, it has a 127-×-66-degree low-resolution field of view, with a high-resolution 24-×-19-degree insert that is coupled to the user's eye position via an eye-tracking system. It has 5 arc minutes in the background and 1.5 arc minutes in the insert (see Figure 2.19). However, even this advanced system provides computer graphics imagery to less than half the total visual field. The region of binocular overlap is even more impoverished, less than 15% of that available under real-world viewing conditions.

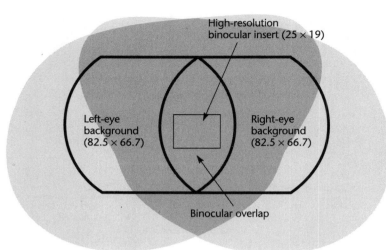

Figure 2.19   The CAE FOHMD has a low-resolution background display for each eye and a high-resolution inset slaved to the user's line of gaze. The gray region illustrates the human visual field of view for comparison. The high-resolution inset is approximately the size of a computer monitor at a normal viewing distance.

Spatial Contrast Sensitivity Function

The rather simple pattern shown in Figure 2.20 has become one of the most useful tools in measuring basic properties of the human visual system. This pattern is called a sine wave grating, because its brightness varies sinusoidally in one direction only. However, there are actually five ways in which this pattern can be varied:

1. Spatial frequency (the number of bars of the grating per degree of visual angle)

2. Orientation

3. Contrast (the amplitude of the sine wave)

4. Phase angle (the lateral displacement of the pattern)

5. Area covered by the grating pattern

Figure 2.20   A sine wave grating.

The grating luminance is defined by the following equation:

$$L = 0.5 + \frac{a}{2}\sin\left(\frac{2\pi x}{\omega} + \frac{\phi}{\omega}\right)$$

(2.5)

where a is the contrast (amplitude), ω is the wavelength, ϕ is the phase angle, and x is the position on the screen. L denotes the resulting output light level in the range [0, 1], assuming that the monitor is linear (see the discussion of gamma correction in Chapter 3).

One of the ways of using a sine wave grating is to measure the sensitivity of the eye/brain system to the lowest contrast that can be detected and to see how this varies with spatial frequency.

Contrast is defined by

$$C = \frac{L_{max} - L_{min}}{L_{max} + L_{min}}$$

(2.6)

where L_{max} is the peak luminance and L_{min} is the minimum luminance.

The result is called a spatial modulation sensitivity function.

Figure 2.21 is a pattern designed to allow you to directly see the high-frequency fall-off in the sensitivity of your own visual system. It is a sinusoidally modulated pattern of stripes that varies from left to right in terms of spatial frequency and from top to bottom in terms of contrast. If you view this from 2 m, you can see how your sensitivity to high-frequency patterns is reduced.

The human spatial contrast sensitivity function varies dramatically with spatial frequency, falling off at both high and low values. We are most sensitive to patterns of bright and dark bars occurring at about 2 or 3 cycles per degree. Figure 2.22 shows typical functions for three different age groups.

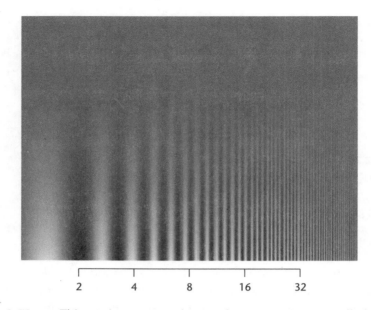

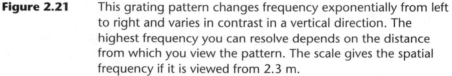

| 2 | 4 | 8 | 16 | 32 |

Figure 2.21   This grating pattern changes frequency exponentially from left to right and varies in contrast in a vertical direction. The highest frequency you can resolve depends on the distance from which you view the pattern. The scale gives the spatial frequency if it is viewed from 2.3 m.

Sensitivity falls off to zero for fine gratings of about 60 cycles per degree for younger people. As we age, we become less and less sensitive to higher spatial frequencies (Owlsley et al., 1983). It is not just that the finest detail we can resolve declines with age. We actually become less sensitive to any pattern components above 1 cycle per degree.

What is perhaps surprising about Figure 2.23 is that there is also a fall-off at low spatial frequencies. We are insensitive to gradual changes and very rapid changes in light patterns. One of the practical implications of the low-frequency fall-off in sensitivity is that many monitors are very nonuniform, yet this goes unremarked. A typical monitor or television display may vary by as much as 30% or more over its face (it is usually brightest in the center), even if it is displaying a supposedly uniform field, but because we are insensitive to this very gradual (low-frequency) variation, we fail to notice the poor quality.

Most tests of visual acuity, such as letter or point acuity, are really tests of high-frequency resolution, but this may not always be the most useful thing

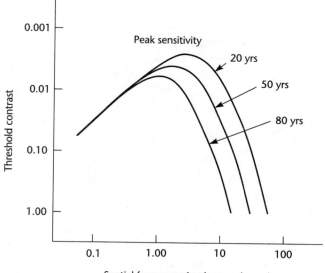

Figure 2.22   Contrast sensitivity varies with spatial frequency. The function is illustrated for three age groups. As we age, our sensitivity to higher spatial frequencies is reduced. Redrawn from Owlsley et al. (1983).

to measure. In tests of pilots' performance, it has been shown that low-frequency contrast sensitivity is actually more important than simple acuity in measuring their performance in flight simulators (Ginsburg et al., 1982).

Visual images on the retina vary in time as well as in space. We can measure the temporal sensitivity of the visual system in much the same way as we measure the spatial sensitivity. This involves taking a pattern such as that shown in Figure 2.20 and causing it to oscillate in contrast from high to low and back again over time. This oscillation in contrast is normally done using a sinusoidal function. Over time, the dark bars become bright bars and then darken again. When this technique is used, both the spatial and the temporal sensitivity of human vision can be mapped out. Once this is done, it becomes evident that spatial-frequency sensitivity and temporal-frequency sensitivity are interdependent. Figure 2.23 shows the contrast threshold of a flickering grating as a function of its temporal frequency and its spatial frequency (Kelly, 1979). This shows that optimal sensitivity is obtained for a grating flickering at between 2 and 10 cycles per second (Hz). It is interesting

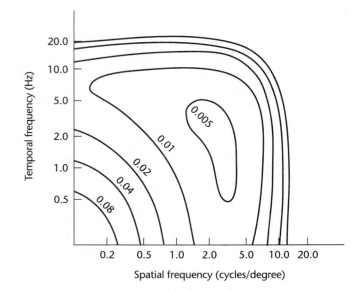

Figure 2.23   Contour map of the human spatiotemporal threshold surface (adapted from Kelly, 1979). Each contour represents the contrast at which a particular combination of spatial and temporal frequencies can be detected.

to note that the low-frequency fall-off in sensitivity is much less when a pattern is flickering at between 5 and 10 Hz. If we were interested only in being able to detect the presence of patterns in data, making those patterns flicker at 7 or 8 Hz would be the best way to present them. There are many other reasons, however, why this is not a good idea; in particular, it would undoubtedly be extremely irritating. The limit of human sensitivity to flicker is about 50 Hz.

When the spatial- and temporal-frequency analysis of the visual system is extended to color, we see that chromatic spatial sensitivity is much lower, especially for rapidly changing patterns. In Chapter 4, the spatial and temporal characteristics of color vision are compared to those of the black-and-white vision we have been discussing up to this point.

Visual Stress

On December 17, 1997, a Japanese television network canceled broadcasts of an action-packed cartoon because its brightly flashing scenes caused convulsions, and even vomiting of blood, in more than 700 children. The primary cause was determined to be the repetitive flashing lights produced by the computer-generated graphics. The harmful effects were exacerbated by the tendency of children to sit very close to the screen. Vivid, repetitive, large-field flashes are known to be extremely stressful to some people.

The disorder known as pattern-induced epilepsy has been reported and investigated for decades. Some of the earliest reported cases were caused by the flicker from helicopter rotor blades, and this resulted in prescreening of pilots for the disorder. In an extensive study of the phenomenon, Wilkins (1995) concludes that a particular combination of spatial and temporal frequencies is especially potent: Striped patterns of about 3 cycles per degree and flicker rates of about 20 Hz are most likely to induce seizures in susceptible individuals. Figure 2.24 illustrates a static pattern likely to cause visual stress. The ill effects also increase with the overall size of the pattern. But visual stress may not be confined to individuals with a particular disorder.

> **Warning! This pattern can cause seizures in some individuals.
> If it causes you to feel ill effects, avoid looking at it.**

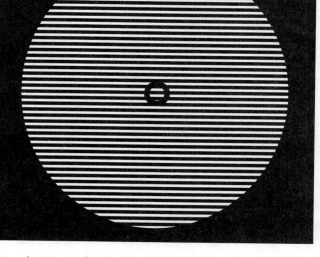

Figure 2.24　　A pattern that is designed to be visually stressful. If it is viewed from 40 cm, the spacing of the stripes is about 3 cycles per degree.

Wilkins argues that striped patterns can cause visual stress in most people. He gives normal text as an example of a pattern that may cause problems because it is laid out in horizontal stripes, and shows that certain fonts may be worse than others.

The Optimal Display

Acuity information is useful in determining what is needed to produce an adequate or optimal visual display. A modern high-resolution monitor has about 40 pixels per cm. This translates to 40 cycles per degree at normal viewing distances. Given that the human eye has receptors packed into the fovea at roughly 180 per degree of visual angle, we can claim that in linear resolution, we are about a factor of four from having monitors that match the resolving power of the human retina in each direction. A 4000-×-4000-resolution monitor should be adequate for any conceivable visual task, leaving aside, for the moment, the problem of superacuities. Such a monitor would require 16 million pixels. The highest-resolution monitors that are currently widely available have 1920 × 1280 pixels, more than two million.

We come to a similar conclusion about the ultimate display from the spatial modulation transfer function. Humans can resolve a grating of approximately 50 cycles per degree. If we take into account the sampling theory that states that we must sample at more than twice the highest frequency we wish to detect, this suggests that we need more than 100 pixels per degree. Perhaps 150 pixels per degree would be reasonable.

If 150 pixels per degree is sufficient, we must ask why manufacturers produce laser printers capable of 1200 dots per inch (460 dots per centimeter). There are three reasons: aliasing, gray levels, and superacuities. The first two of these are essentially technical, not perceptual, but they are worth discussing because they have significant implications in perception. The problems are significant for most display devices, not just for printers.

Aliasing

A fundamental theorem of signal transmission tells us that a signal can be reconstructed from its samples only if the samples are obtained at a frequency at least twice the highest frequency contained in the source (Gonzalez and Winz, 1987). Aliasing effects occur when a regular pattern is sampled by another regular pattern at a different frequency. Figure 2.25 illustrates what happens when a pattern of black and white stripes is sampled by an array of pixels whose spacing is slightly greater than the wavelength. We assume that the pattern of input stripes is sampled at the center of each pixel. The resulting pattern has a much wider spacing. Aliasing can cause all kinds of unwanted effects. Patterns that should be invisible because they are beyond the resolving power of the human eye can become all too visible. Patterns that are unrelated to the original data can occur in moiré fringes. Aliasing effects are especially bad when some regular pattern is sampled by another regular pattern. This is surely the reason that the retinal mosaic of receptor cells is not regular except in small patches (Figure 2.15).

Another aliasing effect is illustrated in Figure 2.26. The line shown in the top part of the figure becomes a staircase pattern when it is drawn using large pixels. The problem is that each pixel samples the line at a single point. Either the point is on the line, in which case the pixel is colored black, or it is not, in which case the pixel is colored white. A set of techniques known as antialiasing can help with this. Antialiasing consists of computing the *average* of the light pattern that is represented by each pixel. The result is shown in the lower part of Figure 2.26. Proper antialiasing can be a more cost-effective solution than simply increasing the number of pixels in the display. With it, a low-resolution display can be made as effective as a much higher-resolution display. However, this does require extra computation. In addition to antialiasing, a full-color image requires properly averaging the three color components, not just the brightness levels.

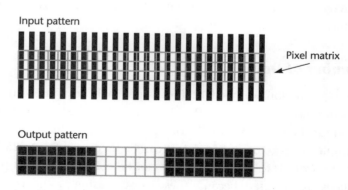

Figure 2.25   A striped pattern is sampled by pixels. The result is shown in the lower diagram.

Figure 2.26   Aliasing artifacts, with antialiasing as a solution.

Figure 2.27   An aliased line that is not quite horizontal.

In data visualization, aliasing effects can sometimes actually be useful. For example, it is much easier to judge whether a line is perfectly horizontal on the screen with aliasing than without (Figure 2.27). Because of our ability to see very small line displacements (vernier acuity), aliasing makes small misalignments completely obvious. It is also possible that the spatial-frequency amplification illustrated in Figure 2.25 can be used as a deliberate technique to magnify certain kinds of regular patterns, to make invisibly fine variations visible.

Number of Dots

The main reason we need 1200 dots per inch on a laser printer is that the dots of a laser printer are either black or white and to represent gray, many dots must be used. Essentially, one pixel is made up of many dots. Thus, for example, a 16-×-16 matrix of dots can be used to generate 257 levels of gray because from 0 to 256 of the dots can be colored black. In practice, square patches are not used, because these cause aliasing problems. To correct aliasing effects, randomness is used in distributing the dots and errors are propagated from one patch to neighboring patches. Most graphics textbooks provide an introduction to these techniques (e.g. Foley et al., 1990). The fact that grays are made from patterns of black and white dots means that the resolution of a laser printer actually is 1200 dots per inch only for black-and-white patterns. For gray patterns, the resolution is at least ten times lower than this.

Superacuities and Displays

Superacuities provide a reason why we might wish to have very high-resolution monitors. As discussed earlier, superacuities occur because the human visual system can integrate information from a number of receptors to give better-than-receptor resolution. For example, in vernier acuity, better than 10-arc-second resolution is achievable.

However, in my laboratory, we have obtained experimental evidence that antialiasing can result in superacuity performance on vernier acuity tasks. This involves making judgments to see differences that are actually smaller than individual pixels. Figure 2.28 shows previously unpublished

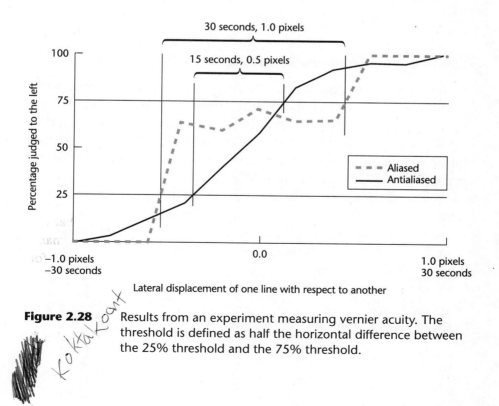

Figure 2.28 Results from an experiment measuring vernier acuity. The threshold is defined as half the horizontal difference between the 25% threshold and the 75% threshold.

data from an experiment that my research assistant, Tim Millar, and I carried out to determine whether vernier acuity performance can be achieved to higher-than-pixel resolution if the lines are antialiased.

In the standard vernier acuity task, subjects judge whether one vertical line is to the left of another (as in Figure 2.26, only with the lines arranged vertically). The lines are placed end to end with a small lateral displacement between them. The purpose of the experiment is to determine how small a displacement can be perceived more than 50% of the time (Berry, 1948). In our study, one line was displaced horizontally by an amount that varied randomly in a range between 1 pixel and –1 pixel. At the viewing distance we chose, this corresponded to ± 30 seconds of arc. The question asked was "Is the lower line to the right of the upper line?" The percentage correct was computed based on the answers given over a large number of trials. By convention, vernier acuity is defined as half the difference between 25% correct performance and 75% correct performance. In Figure 2.28, two of our results are shown for aliased and antialiased lines. The actual threshold is half of each range on the x-axis. Thus, Figure 2.28 shows a 15-sec vernier acuity threshold (30 sec × 0.5) for aliased lines and a 7.5-sec threshold (15 sec × 0.5) for antialiased lines. This data shows that given proper antialiasing, superacuity performance to better-than-pixel resolution can be achieved.

Temporal Requirements of the Perfect Display

Just as we can evaluate the spatial requirements for a perfect monitor, so we can evaluate the temporal requirements. 50-Hz flicker is about the limit of resolution that most of us can perceive. Hence the 50-Hz-to-75-Hz refresh rate of the typical monitor would seem to be adequate. However, temporal aliasing artifacts are common in computer graphics and movies. The "reversing wagon wheel" effect is the one most often noticed (the wheel of a wagon in a Western movie appears to rotate in the wrong direction). Temporal aliasing effects are especially pronounced when the image update rate is low. It is common in animated data visualization systems to have graphic images that are updated only about 10 times per second even though the screen is refreshed at 60 Hz or better. An obvious result is the breaking up of a moving object into a series of discrete objects. If data contains a repetitive temporal pattern, aliasing and sampling effects can occur that are the exact analogs of the spatial-frequency effects.

To correct these problems, temporal antialiasing can be employed. Part of an image that is moving may pass through several pixels over the course of a single animation frame. The correct antialiasing solution is to color each pixel according to the percentage contributions of all the different objects as they pass through it for the duration of the animation frame. Thus, if the refresh rate is 60 Hz, a program must calculate the *average* color for each pixel that is affected by the moving pattern for each $\frac{1}{60}$-second interval. This technique is often called motion blur. It can be computationally expensive in practice and is rarely done except in the case of high-quality animations created for the movie industry. As computers become faster, we can expect antialiasing to be more widely used in data visualization, since there is no doubt that aliasing effects can be visually disturbing and occasionally misleading.

Conclusion

In comparison with the richness of the visual world, the cathode ray tube (CRT) screen is simple indeed. It is remarkable that we can achieve so much with such a limited device. In the world, we perceive subtly textured, visually rich surfaces, differentiated by shading, depth-of-focus effects, and texture gradients. The CRT screen merely produces a two-dimensional array of colors. Gibson's concept of the ambient optical array, introduced at the beginning of this chapter, provides a context for understanding the success of this device. Given a particular direction, and a viewing angle of 20 degrees or so, the CRT is capable of reproducing many (but not all) of those aspects of the ambient array that are most important to perception. As we shall see in Chapter 4, this is especially true in the realm of color, where a mere three colors are used to effectively reproduce much of the gamut to which humans are sensitive. Spatial information, in the form of texture gradients and other spatial cues, is also reproducible to some extent on a CRT. However, there are problems in the reproduction of fine texture. The actual pixel pattern, or phosphor-dot pattern, of a CRT may provide a texture that visually competes with the texture designed for display.

A typical monitor only stimulates perhaps 5% to 10% of the visual field at normal viewing distances, as shown in Figure 2.19. However, this is not as serious a shortcoming as it might seem, because the central field of view is heavily overweighted in human visual processing. In fact, looking at the center of a typical monitor screen from a normal viewing distance stimulates considerably more than 50% of the visual processing mechanisms in the brain (Wilkins, 1995). A monitor is also deficient in that it has limited dynamic range compared to the huge range of light levels that can occur in the environment. But this is not so bad, because the eye neglects the absolute light level and adapts to the prevailing conditions. At any given time, the range over which the eye functions is no more than two orders of magnitude, and the dynamic range of a CRT is not much worse than this.

Nevertheless, the CRT has some serious deficiencies as a device for presenting visual data. One of these is its lack of ability to provide focal depth-of-focus information. In the real world, the eye must refocus on objects at different distances. Since this is not the case for computer graphics presented on the screen, it can confuse our spatial processing systems. This problem will be discussed further in Chapter 8 under the heading "The Vergence-Focus Problem."

A second major problem with the CRT is perhaps more profound. Although we may be able to fool the eye into thinking that the abstractions displayed on a CRT are in some ways like objects in the real world, the illusion becomes painfully evident when it comes to interacting with these objects. To use Gibson's terminology, we may be able to fool the eye into believing that a certain set of affordances exists, but when users wish to take advantage of these affordances and reach out and touch the artificial objects, the artifice is revealed. There are no haptic affordances on a CRT screen. All interaction is necessarily indirect and more or less artificial.

Lightness, Brightness, Contrast, and Constancy

How bright is that patch of light? What is white? What is black? What is a middle gray? These are simple-sounding questions, but the answers are complex and lead us to consider many of the fundamental mechanisms of perception. The fact that we have light-sensing receptors in our eyes might seem like a good starting point. But in fact, the receptor signals tell us very little. The nerves that transmit information from the eyes to the brain transmit nothing about the amount of light falling on the retina. Instead, they signal the *relative* amount of light: how a particular patch differs from a neighboring patch, or how a particular patch of light has changed in the past instant. Neurons in the early stages of the visual system do not behave like light meters; they behave like change meters.

The signaling of differences is not special to lightness and brightness. This is a general property of many early sensory systems, and we will come across it again and again throughout this book. The implications of this are fundamental to the way we perceive information. The fact that differences, and not absolute values, are transmitted to the brain accounts for contrast illusions that can cause substantial errors in the way data is "read" from a visualization. The signaling of differences also means that the perception of lightness is nonlinear, and this has implications for the gray-scale coding of information.

To belabor the occasional inaccuracies of perception does not do justice to millions of years of evolution. The fact that the early stages of vision are nonlinear does not mean that all perception is inaccurate. On the contrary, most of the time we can make quite sophisticated judgments about the lightness of surfaces in our environments. This chapter shows how simple early visual mechanisms can help our brains do sophisticated things, such as see objects correctly no matter what the illumination level. Difference signaling is a mechanism designed to support accurate judgments about the reflectance of surfaces, not about amounts of light. It is much more important for organisms to know about the surface properties of objects in the environment than to act as light-measuring instruments. Part of the problem of data display systems is that computer graphics images are not like the real world; they usually consist of rather simple luminous light patches. Much of the detailed texture and shadow information that helps us understand the world is missing, and some of the errors and distortions that occur in information displays may occur because of this impoverished visual environment. Without enough high-level information to make accurate judgments, the brain falls back on low-level mechanisms and this leads to errors.

This chapter has the additional function of being the first part of a presentation of color vision. Luminance perception can be regarded as one of three color dimensions. Discussing this dimension in isolation gives us an opportunity to examine many of the basic concepts of color with a simpler model. (This is expanded, in Chapter 4, into a full three-color-channel model.) We start by introducing neurons and the concept of the visual receptive field and a number of display distortion effects that can be explained by these simple mechanisms. The bulk of this chapter is taken up with a discussion of the concepts of luminance, lightness, and brightness and the implications of these for data display.

The practical lessons of this chapter are related to the way data values can be mapped to gray values using gray-scale coding. The kinds of perceptual "errors" that can occur owing to simultaneous contrast are discussed at length. More fundamentally, the reasons why the visual system makes these errors provide a very general lesson. The nervous system works by computing difference signals at almost every level. Brightness contrast effects are just one instance of this process. The lesson is that visualization is not good for representing precise absolute numerical values, but rather for displaying patterns of differences or changes over time, to which the eye and brain are extremely sensitive.

Neurons, Receptive Fields, and Brightness Illusions

Neurons are the basic circuits of information processing in the brain. In some respects they are like transistors, only much more complex. Like the digital circuits of a computer, neurons respond with discrete pulses of electricity. However, unlike transistors, neurons are connected to hundreds and sometimes thousands of other neurons. Much of our knowledge about the behavior of neurons comes from single-cell recording techniques whereby a tiny microelectrode is actually inserted into a cell and the cell's electrical activity is monitored. Most neurons are constantly active, emitting pulses of electricity through connections with other cells. Depending on the input, the rate of firing can be increased or decreased as the neuron is excited or inhibited. Neuroscientists often set up amplifiers and loudspeakers in their laboratories so that they can hear the activity of cells that are being probed. The result is like the clicking of a Geiger counter, becoming rapid when the cell is excited and slowing when it is inhibited.

There is considerable neural processing of information in the eye itself. Several layers of cells in the eye culminate in retinal ganglion cells. These ganglion cells send information through the optic nerve via a way station called the lateral geniculate nucleus, on to the primary visual processing areas at the back of the brain, as shown in Figure 3.1.

The *receptive field* of a cell is the visual area over which a cell responds to light. This means that patterns of light falling on the retina influence the way the neuron responds, even though it may be many synapses removed from receptors. Retinal ganglion cells are organized with circular receptive fields and they can be either on-center or off-center. The activity of an on-center cell is illustrated in Figure 3.2. When this cell is stimulated in the center of its

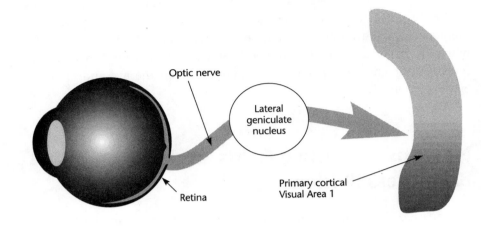

Optic nerve

Lateral geniculate nucleus

Retina

Primary cortical Visual Area 1

Figure 3.1   Signals from the retina are transmitted along the optic nerve to the lateral geniculate nucleus. From there, they are distributed to a number of areas, but go mostly to Visual Area 1 of the cortex, located at the back of the head.

receptive field, it emits pulses at a greater rate. When the cell is stimulated outside of the center of its field, it emits pulses at a lower-than-normal rate and is said to be inhibited. Figure 3.2 also shows the output of an array of such neurons being stimulated by a bright edge. The output of this system is an enhanced response on the bright side of the edge and a depressed response on the dark side of the edge, with an intermediate response to the uniform areas on either side. The cell fires more on the bright side because there is less light in the inhibitory region and hence it is less inhibited.

A widely used mathematical description of the concentric receptive field is the Difference of Gaussians model (often called the DOG function):

$$f(x) = \alpha_1 e^{-\left(\frac{x}{w_1}\right)^2} - \alpha_2 e^{-\left(\frac{x}{w_2}\right)^2}$$

In this model, the firing rate of the cell is the difference between two Gaussians. One of the Gaussians represents the center and the other represents the surround, as illustrated in Figure 3.3. The variable x represents the distance from the center of the field, w_1 defines the width of the center, and w_2 defines the width of the surround. The amount of excitation or inhibition is given by the amplitude parameters α_1 and α_2.

We can easily calculate the effect of the DOG-type receptor on various patterns. In doing this, we can either think of the pattern passing over the receptive field of the cell, or think of the output of a whole array of DOG cells arranged in a line across the pattern. When we do this, we discover that the DOG receptive field can be used to explain a variety of brightness contrast effects.

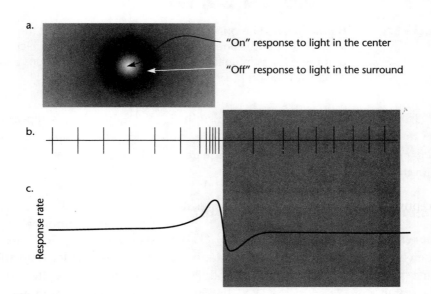

a.

"On" response to light in the center

"Off" response to light in the surround

b.

c.

Response rate

Figure 3.2   (a) The receptive field structure of an on-center simple lateral geniculate cell. (b) As the cell passes over from a light region to a dark region, the rate of neural firing increases just to the bright side of the edge and decreases on the dark side. (c) A smoothed plot of the cell activity level.

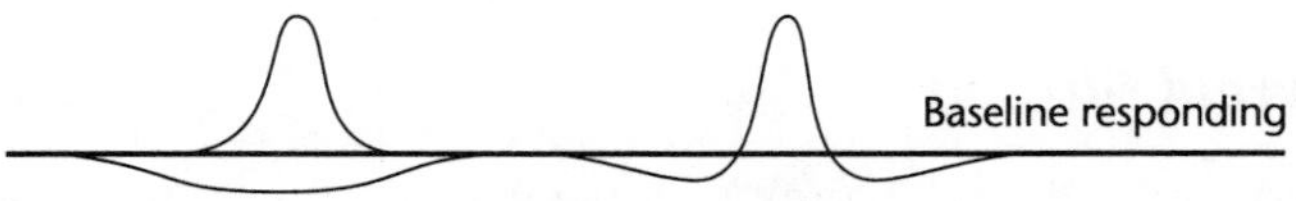

Baseline responding

Figure 3.3   Difference of Gaussians (DOG) model of a receptive field.

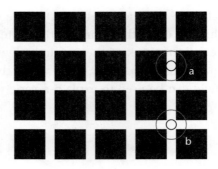

Figure 3.4   Hermann Grid Illusion. The black spots that are seen at the intersections of the lines are thought to result from the fact that there is less inhibition when a receptive field is at position a than at position b.

In the Hermann Grid illusion, shown in Figure 3.4, black spots appear at the intersections of the bright lines. The explanation is that there is *more inhibition* at the points between two squares, and hence they seem brighter than the points at the intersections.

Simultaneous Brightness Contrast

The term *simultaneous brightness contrast* is used to explain the general effect whereby a gray patch placed on a dark background looks lighter than the same gray patch on a light background. Figure 3.5 illustrates this effect and the way it is predicted by the DOG model of concentric opponent receptive fields.

Mach Bands

Figure 3.6 shows a Mach band effect. At the point where a uniform area meets a luminance ramp, a bright band is seen. In general, Mach bands appear where there is an abrupt change in the first derivative of a brightness profile. The lower plot on the right shows how this is simulated by the DOG model.

The Chevreul Illusion

When a sequence of gray bands is generated as shown in Figure 3.7, the bands appear darker at one edge than at the other. The diagram to the right in Figure 3.7 shows that this visual illusion can be simulated by the application of a DOG model of the neural receptive field.

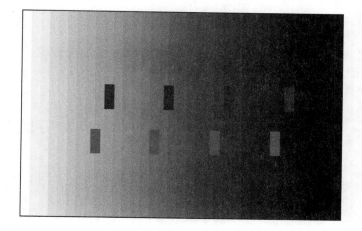

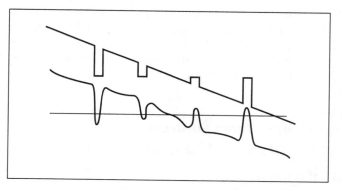

Figure 3.5   An Illustration of simultaneous brightness contrast. The upper row of rectangles are an identical gray. The lower rectangles are a lighter gray, but are also all identical. The graph below illustrates the effect of a DOG filter applied to this pattern.

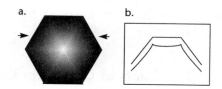

Figure 3.6   Illustration of Mach banding. (a) Bright Mach bands are evident at the boundaries between the internal triangles. (b) At the top, the actual brightness profile is shown between the two arrows. The curve below shows how the application of a DOG filter models the bright bands that are seen.

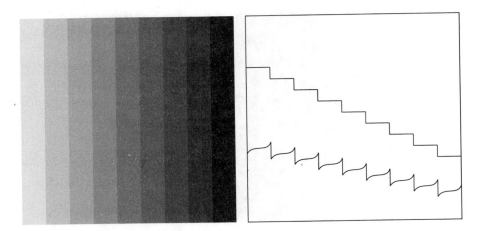

Figure 3.7   The Chevreul illusion. The measured lightness pattern is shown by the staircase pattern on the right. What is perceived can be closely approximated by a DOG model. The lower plot on the right shows the application of a DOG filter to the staircase pattern shown above.

Simultaneous Contrast and Errors in Reading Maps

The most obvious relevance of contrast effects to visualization is that they can result in errors of judgment during the reading of quantitative (value) information that is encoded using a gray scale (Cleveland and McGill, 1983). For example, Figure 3.8 shows a gravity map of part of the North Atlantic where the local strength of the gravitational field is encoded in shades of gray. In an experiment to measure the effects of contrast on data encoded in this way, we found substantial errors that averaged 20% of the entire scale in the worst case (Ware, 1988).

Contrast Effects and Artifacts in Computer Graphics

One of the consequences of Mach bands, and of contrast effects in general, is that they tend to show up the deficiencies in the common shading algorithms used in computer graphics. These effects can also lead to the perception of illusory patterns that result from two artifacts. The first is the way that

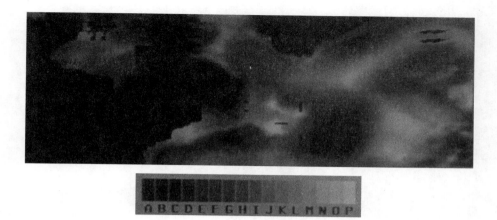

Figure 3.8   A gravity map of the North Atlantic (Ware, 1988). Large errors can occur when values are read using the key.

smooth surfaces are often displayed using polygons, both for simplicity and to speed the computer graphics rendering process. The second is the way the visual system enhances the boundaries at the edges of polygons. Figure 3.9 illustrates the effects of the DOG model on three surface-shading methods. In this example, a cylinder has been broken into a series of rectangular facets.

1. **Uniform shading:** The light reflected from each rectangular facet is computed by taking into account the incident illumination and the orientation of the surface with respect to the light. Then the entire facet is uniformly filled with the resulting color. Scanning across an object modeled in this way reveals stepwise changes in color. The steps are exaggerated by the Chevreul illusion.

2. **Gouraud shading:** A shading value is calculated not for the facets, but for the edges between the facets. This is done by averaging the surface normals at the boundaries where facets meet. As each facet is painted during the rendering process, the color is linearly interpolated between the facet boundaries. Scanning across the object, we see linear changes in color across polygons, with abrupt transitions in gradient where the facets meet. Mach banding occurs at these facet boundaries, enhancing the discontinuities.

3. **Phong shading:** As with Gouraud shading, surface normals are calculated at the facet boundaries. However, in this case, the surface normal is interpolated between the edges. The result is smooth changes in lightness with no appreciable Mach banding.

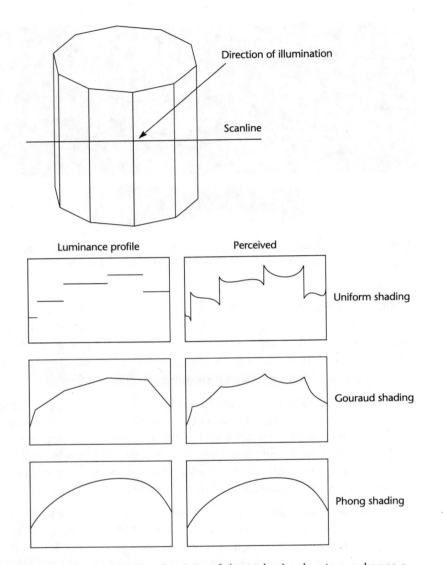

Figure 3.9   The contrast mechanisms of the early visual system enhance a number of artifacts that occur in computer graphics shading algorithms. The illustration at the top illustrates a single line of pixels through a rendering of a cylinder that is approximated by a set of rectangular panels. The plots in the left-hand column illustrate the actual light-level distributions that result from three common techniques used in computer graphics. The plots in the right-hand column show how the lack of smoothness in the result is increased by the application of the DOG model.

Edge Enhancement

Lateral inhibition can be considered a first stage of an edge detection process that signals the positions and contrasts of edges in the environment. One of the consequences is that pseudo-edges can be created; two areas that physically have the same lightness can be made to look different by having an edge between them that shades off gradually to the two sides (Figure 3.10). The brain does perceptual interpolation so that the entire central region appears lighter than surrounding regions. This is called the Cornsweet effect, after the researcher who first described it (Cornsweet, 1970).

The enhancement of edges is also an important part of the techniques of some artists. It is a way to make objects more clearly distinct, given the limited dynamic range of paint. The example given in Figure 3.11 is from Seurat's painting of bathers. This technique can be used to adjust the background of a sophisticated data visualization to enhance key parts of the image.

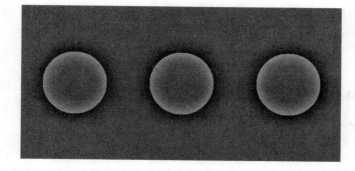

Figure 3.10   The Cornsweet effect. The areas in the centers of the circles tend to look lighter than the surrounding area, even though they are actually the same shade. This provides evidence that the brain constructs surface color based largely on edge contrast information.

Figure 3.11   Seurat deliberately enhanced edge contrast to make his figures stand out.

Luminance, Brightness, Lightness, and Gamma

Contrast effects can be viewed as annoying problems in the presentation of data, but a deeper analysis shows that they can also be used to reveal the mechanisms underlying normal perception. The way the contrast mechanism works to enable us to accurately perceive our environment, under all but unusual circumstances, is the main subject in the discussion that follows. We will argue that contrast effects are severe in computer displays as a consequence of the impoverished nature of those displays, not of any inadequacy of the visual system.

It should now be evident that the perceived brightness of a particular patch of light has almost nothing to do with the amount of light coming from that patch as we might measure it with a photometer. Thus, what might seem like a simple question—"How bright is that patch of light?"—is not at all straightforward. We start with an ecological perspective, then consider perceptual mechanisms, and finally discuss applications in visualization.

In order to survive, we need to be able to manipulate objects in the environment and determine their properties. Generally, information about the quantity of illumination is of very little use to us. Illumination is a prerequisite for sight, but otherwise we do not need to know whether the light we are seeing by is dim because it is late on a cloudy day, or brilliant because of the noonday sun. What we do need to know about are objects—food, tools, plants, animals, other people, and so on—and we can find out a lot about objects from their surface properties. In particular, we can obtain knowledge of the spectral reflectance characteristics of objects—what we call their color and lightness. The human vision system evolved to extract information about surface properties of objects, often at the expense of losing information about the quality and quantity of light entering the eye. This phenomenon, the fact that we experience colored surfaces and not colored light, is called *color constancy.* When we are talking about the apparent overall reflectance of a surface, it is called *lightness constancy.* Three terms are commonly used to describe the general concept of quantity of light: *luminance, brightness,* and *lightness.* The following brief definitions are followed by more extensive descriptions.

Luminance is the easiest to define; it refers to the measured amount of light coming from some region of space. It is measured in units such as candelas per square meter. Of the three terms, only *luminance* refers to something that can be physically measured. The other two terms refer to psychological variables.

Brightness generally refers to the perceived amount of light coming from a source. In the following discussion, it is used to refer only to things that are perceived as self-luminous. Sometimes people talk about bright colors, but *vivid* and *saturated* are better terms.

Lightness generally refers to the perceived reflectance of a surface. A white surface is light. A black surface is dark. The shade of paint is another concept of lightness.

Luminance

Luminance is not a perceptual quantity at all. It is a physical measure that is used to define an amount of light in the visible region of the electromagnetic spectrum. Unlike lightness and brightness, luminance can be read out directly from a scientific measuring instrument. Luminance is a measurement of light energy weighted by the spectral sensitivity function of the human visual system. We are about 100 times less sensitive to light at 450 nanometers than we are to light at 510 nanometers, and it is clearly important to take this difference into account when we are measuring light levels with human observers in mind. The human spectral sensitivity function is illustrated in Figure 3.12 and given at 10-nm intervals in Table 3.1. This function is called the $V(\lambda)$ function. It is an international standard maintained by the Commission Internationale de L'Éclairage (CIE). The $V(\lambda)$ function represents the spectral sensitivity curve of an ideal standard human observer. To find the luminance of a light, we integrate the light distribution $E(\lambda)$ with the CIE estimate of the human sensitivity function $V(\lambda)$. λ represents wavelength.

$$L = \int_{400}^{700} V_\lambda E_\lambda \delta\lambda \qquad\qquad (3.1)$$

When multiplied by the appropriate constant, output is luminance L in units of candelas per square meter. Note that a great many technical issues must be considered when we are measuring light, such as the configuration of the measuring instrument and the sample. Wyszecki and Stiles (1982) is an excellent reference.

It is directly relevant to data display that the blue phosphor of a monitor has a peak at about 450 nm. Table 3.1 shows that at this wavelength, human sensitivity is only 4 percent of the maximum in the green range. In Chapter 2, we noted that the chromatic aberration of the human eye means that a monitor's blue light is typically out of focus. The fact that we are also insensitive to it is another reason why representing text and other detailed information using the pure blue of a monitor is not a good idea.

The $V(\lambda)$ function is extremely useful because it provides a close match to the combined sensitivities of the individual cone receptor sensitivity functions. It is reasonable to think of the $V(\lambda)$ function as measuring the luminance efficiency of the first stage of processing in an extended process that ultimately allows us to perceive useful information such as surface lightness

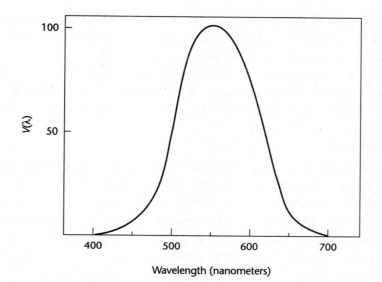

Figure 3.12 The CIE *V(λ)* function representing the relative sensitivity of the human eye to light of different wavelengths.

Table 3.1 Values show the sensitivity of the eye to light of different wavelengths relative to the maximum sensitivity at 555 nanometers.

Wavelength (nanometers)	Relative Sensitivity	Wavelength (nanometers)	Relative Sensitivity	Wavelength (nanometers)	Relative Sensitivity
400	.0004	510	.5030	620	.3810
410	.0012	520	.7100	630	.2650
420	.0040	530	.8620	640	.1750
430	.0116	540	.9540	650	.1070
440	.0230	550	.9950	660	.0610
450	.0380	560	.9950	670	.0320
460	.0600	570	.9520	680	.0170
470	.0910	580	.8700	690	.0082
480	.1390	590	.7570	700	.0041
490	.4652	600	.6310	710	.0010
500	.3230	610	.5030	720	.0005

and the shapes of surfaces. Technically, it defines the way the sensitivity of the so-called *luminance channel* varies with wavelength. The luminance channel is an important theoretical concept in vision research; it is held to be the basis for most pattern perception, depth perception, and motion perception. In Chapter 4, the properties of the luminance channel are discussed in more detail in comparison to the color-processing *chrominance* channels.

Text Contrast

For ease of reading, it is essential that text have a reasonable luminance difference from its background. The International Standards Organization (ISO 9241, part 3) recommends a minimum 3:1 luminance ratio of text and background; 10:1 is preferred. This recommendation can be generalized to the display of any kind of information where fine-detail resolution is desirable. In fact, as the spatial modulation sensitivity function shows (Figure 2.22, Chapter 2), the finer the detail, the greater the contrast required.

Brightness

The term *brightness* is usually used to refer to the perceived amount of light coming from self-luminous sources. Thus, it is relevant to the perception of the brightness of indicator lights in an otherwise darkened display—for example, nighttime instrument displays in the cockpits of aircraft and on the darkened bridges of ships.

Perceived brightness is a very nonlinear function of the amount of light emitted by a lamp. Stevens (1961) popularized a technique known as magnitude estimation to provide a way of measuring the perceptual impact of simple sensations. In magnitude estimation, subjects are given a stimulus such as a patch of light viewed in isolation. They are told to assign this stimulus a standard value (e.g., 10) to denote its brightness. Subsequently, they are shown other patches of light, also in isolation, and asked to assign them values relative to the standard that they have set. If a patch seems twice as bright as the reference sample, it is assigned the number 20; if it seems half as bright, it is assigned the number 5, and so on. Applying this technique, Stevens discovered that a wide range of sensations could be described by a simple power law:

$$S = aI^n \qquad (3.2)$$

This law states that perceived sensation S is proportional to the stimulus intensity, I, raised to a power n. The power law has been found to apply to many types of sensations, including loudness, smell, taste, heaviness, force, and touch. Stevens found that his power law also applied to the perceived brightness of lights viewed in the dark.

$$\text{Brightness} = \text{Luminance}^n \tag{3.3}$$

However, the value of n depends on the size of the patch of light. For circular patches of light subtending 5 degrees of visual angle, n is 0.333, whereas for point sources of light, n is close to 0.5.

These findings are really only applicable to lights viewed in relative isolation in the dark. Thus, although they have some practical relevance to the design of control panels to be viewed in dark rooms, many other factors must be taken into account in more complex displays. Before we go on to consider these perceptual issues, it is useful to know something about the way computer monitors are designed.

Monitor Gamma

Most visualizations are produced on monitor screens. Anyone who is serious about producing such a thing as a uniform gray scale, or color reproductions in general, must come to grips with the properties of computer monitors. The relationship of physical luminance to voltage on a monitor is approximated by a gamma function:

$$L = V^\gamma \tag{3.4}$$

V is the voltage driving one of the electron guns in the monitor, L is the luminance, and γ is an empirical constant that varies widely from monitor to monitor (values can range from 1.4 to 3.0). The reader is referred to Cowan (1983) for a thorough treatise on monitor calibration. Monitor nonlinearity is not accidental; it was created by early television engineers to make the most of the available signal bandwidth. They made television screens nonlinear precisely because the human visual system is nonlinear in the opposite direction, as described above. For example, a gamma value of 3 will exactly cancel a brightness power function exponent of 0.333, resulting in a display that produces a linear relationship between voltage and perceived brightness. Most monitors have a gamma value much less than 3.0, for reasons that will be explained later.

Adaptation, Contrast, and Lightness Constancy

It cannot be emphasized enough that luminance is completely unrelated to perceived lightness or brightness. If we lay out a piece of black paper in full sunlight on a bright day and we point a photometer at it, we may easily measure a value of 1000 candelas per square meter (a typical "black" surface reflects about 10% of the available light). If we now take our photometer into a typical office and point it at a white piece of paper, we will probably measure a value of about 50 candelas per square meter. Thus, a black object on a bright day in a beach environment may reflect 20 times more light than white paper in an office. Even in the same environment, white paper lying under the boardwalk may reflect less light than black paper lying in the sun.

Figure 3.13 illustrates the range of light levels we encounter, from bright sunlight to starlight. A normal interior will have an artificial illumination level of approximately 50 lux. (Lux is a measure of incident illumination that incorporates the $V(\lambda)$ function.) On a bright day in summer, the light level can easily be 50,000 lux. Except for the brief period of adaptation that occurs when we come indoors on a bright day, we are generally almost

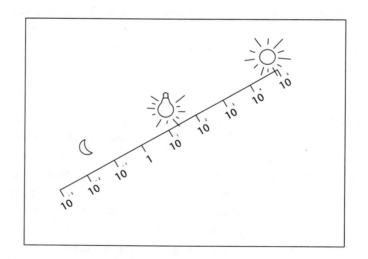

Figure 3.13   The eye/brain system is capable of functioning over a huge range of light levels. The amount of light available on a bright day at the beach is 10,000 times greater than the light available in a dimly lit room.

totally oblivious to this huge variation. A change in overall light level of a factor of 2 is barely noticed. Remarkably, our visual systems can achieve lightness constancy over virtually this entire range; in bright sunlight or dim moonlight, we can easily tell whether a surface is black, white, or gray.

The first-stage mechanism of lightness constancy is adaptation. The second stage of level invariance is lateral inhibition. Both mechanisms help the visual system to factor out the effects of the amount and color of the illumination.

The role of adaptation in lightness constancy is straightforward. The changing sensitivity of the receptors and neurons in the eye helps factor out the overall level of illumination. One mechanism is the bleaching of photo-pigment in the receptors themselves. At high light levels, more photopigment is bleached and the receptors become less sensitive. At low light levels, photo-pigment is regenerated and the eyes regain their sensitivity. This regeneration can take some time, and this is why we are briefly blinded when coming into a darkened room out of bright sunlight. It can take up to half an hour to develop maximum sensitivity to very dim light, such as moonlight. In addi-tion to the change in receptor sensitivity, the iris of the eye opens and closes and this also modulates the amount of light entering the pupil, but this is much less significant than the change in receptor sensitivity. In general, adap-tation allows the visual system to adjust overall sensitivity to the ambient light level.

Contrast and Constancy

Contrast mechanisms, such as the concentric opponent receptive field, help us achieve constancy by signaling differences in light levels, especially at the edges of objects. Consider the simple desktop environment illustrated in Figure 3.14. A desk lamp, just to the right of the picture, has created very non-uniform illumination over a wooden desk that has two pieces of paper lying on it. The piece nearer to the lamp is a medium gray. Because it is receiving more light, it reflects about the same amount of light as the white paper, which is farther from the light. In the original scene, it is easy for people to tell which piece of paper is gray and which is white, and simultaneous con-trast can help to explain this. Because the white paper is lighter *relative to its background* than the gray paper is, relative to *its* background, the same mecha-nism that caused contrast in Figure 3.5 is responsible for enabling an accurate

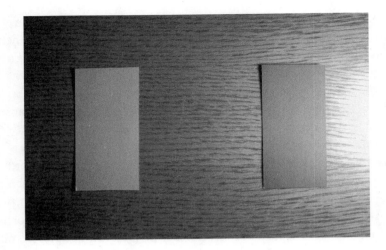

Figure 3.14   These two pieces of paper are illuminated by a desk lamp just to the right of the picture. See also color plates.

judgment to be made here. An illumination profile across the desk and the pieces of paper will be similar to that illustrated in Figure 3.5, except that in this case, contrast does not result in an illusion; instead, it helps us to achieve lightness constancy.

Contrast on Paper and on Screen

There is a subtlety here that is worth exploring. It is often the case that paper reproductions of contrast and constancy effects are less convincing than these effects are in the laboratory. Looking at Figure 3.14, the reader may well be excused for being less than convinced. The two pieces of paper may not look very different. But try the experiment with your own desk lamp and paper. Two holes punched in a piece of opaque cardboard can be used as a mask, enabling you to compare the brightness of the gray and white pieces of paper. Under these real-world viewing conditions, it is usually impossible to perceive the true relative *brightness*; instead, the surface *lightness* is perceived. But take a photograph of the scene, like Figure 3.14, and the effect is less strong. Why is this? The answer lies in the dual nature of pictures. The photograph itself has a surface, and to some extent we perceive the actual gray levels of the photographic pigment, as opposed to the gray levels of what is depicted. The mechanism of lightness constancy makes it difficult to illustrate contrast effects in a book. The poorer the reproduction, the more we see the actual color printed on the paper as opposed to what is depicted. This duality will crop up again in Chapter 8, when we discuss the depiction of 3D scenes.

Contrast illusions are generally much worse in CRT displays. On a CRT screen there is no texture, except for the uniform pattern of pixels and phosphor dots. Moreover, the screen is self-luminous, which may also confound our lightness constancy mechanisms. Scientists studying simultaneous contrast in the laboratory generally use perfectly uniform textureless fields and obtain extreme contrast effects—after all, under these circumstances, the only information is the differences between patches of light. CRT images lie somewhere between real-world surfaces and the artificial featureless patches of light used in the laboratory. The way lightness is judged will depend on exactly how images are designed and presented. On the one hand, a CRT can be set up in a dark room and made to display featureless gray patches of light; in this case, simple contrast effects will dominate. However, if the CRT is used to simulate a very realistic 3D model of the environment, surface lightness constancies can be obtained depending on the degree of realism, the quality of the display, and the overall setup.

Perception of Surface Lightness

Although both adaptation and contrast can be seen as mechanisms that act in the service of lightness constancy, they are clearly not sufficient. Ultimately, the solution to this perceptual problem can involve every level of perception. Three additional factors seem especially important. The first is that the brain must somehow take the direction of illumination and surface orientation into account in lightness judgments. If a flat white surface is turned away from the light, it will reflect less light than one turned toward the light. Figure 3.15 illustrates two surfaces being viewed, one turned away from the light and one turned toward it. Under these circumstances, people can still make reasonably accurate lightness judgments, showing that our brains can take into account both the direction of illumination and the spatial layout (Gilchrist, 1980).

The second important factor is that the brain seems to use the lightest object in the scene as a kind of *reference white* to determine the gray values of all other objects (Cataliotti and Gilchrist, 1995). This is discussed in the following section in the context of lightness-scaling formulas.

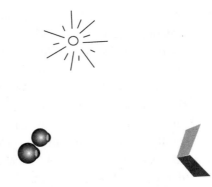

Figure 3.15   When making surface lightness judgments, the brain can take into account the fact that a surface turned away from the light receives less light than a surface turned toward the light.

The third factor is that the ratio of specular and nonspecular reflection can be important under certain circumstances. Figure 3.16(a) is a picture of a world where everything is black, while Figure 3.16(b) shows a world in which everything is white. If we consider these images as slides projected in a darkened room, it is obvious that every point on the black image is brighter than the surroundings. How can we perceive something to be black when it is a bright image? In this case, the most important factor differentiating black from white is the ratio between the specular and the nonspecular reflected light. In the all-black world, the ratio between specular and nonspecular is much larger than in the all-white world.

Lightness Differences and the Gray Scale

Suppose that we wish to display map information using a gray scale. We might, for example, wish to illustrate the variability in population density within a geographical region, or a gravity map as shown in Figure 3.8. For this kind of application, we ideally would like a gray scale such that equal differences in data values are displayed as perceptually equally spaced gray steps (an interval scale). Although the gray scale is probably not the best way of coding this kind of information because of contrast effects (better methods are discussed in Chapter 4 and in Chapter 7), the problem does merit some attention because it allows us to discuss some fundamental and quite general issues related to perceptual scales.

a.

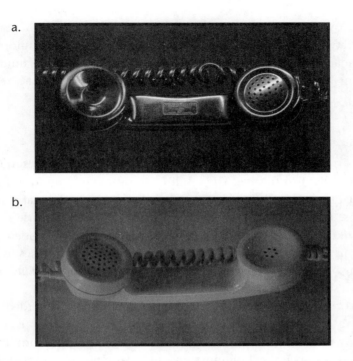

b.

Figure 3.16   These two photographs show scenes in which (a) everything is black and (b) everything is white. See also color plates.

Leaving aside contrast effects, the perception of brightness differences depends on whether those differences are small or large. At one extreme, we can consider the smallest difference that can be distinguished between two gray values. In this case, one of the fundamental laws of psychophysics applies. This is called Weber's law, after the nineteenth-century physicist Max Weber (Wyszecki, 1982). Weber's law states that if we have a background with luminance L, and superimposed on it is a patch that is a little bit brighter $(L + \delta L)$, the value of δ that makes this small increment just visible is independent of the overall luminance. Thus, $\delta L/L$ is constant at threshold. Typically, under optimal viewing conditions, we can detect the brighter patch if δ is greater than about 0.005. In other words, we can just detect about an 0.5-percent change in brightness.

Weber's law applies only to small differences. When large differences between gray samples are judged, many other factors become significant, such as those listed in the previous section. A typical experimental procedure used to study large differences involves asking subjects to select a gray value midway between two other values. The CIE has produced a uniform gray-scale standard based on a synthesis of the results from large numbers of experiments of this kind. This formula includes the concept of a reference white, although many other factors are still neglected.

$$L* = 116(Y/Y_n)^{\frac{1}{3}} - 16 \qquad Y/Y_n > 0.01 \tag{3.5}$$

Y_n is a reference white in the environment, normally the surface that reflects most light to the eye. The result $L*$ is a value in a uniform lightness scale. Equal measured differences on this scale approximate equal perceptual differences. It is reasonable to assume that $Y/Y_n > 0.01$ because even the blackest inks and fabrics still reflect more than 1 percent of incident illumination. This standard is used by the paint and lighting industries to specify such things as color tolerances. Equation 3.5 is part of the *CIEluv* uniform color space standard, which is described more fully in Chapter 4.

Uniform lightness and color scales should always be regarded as providing only rough approximations. Because the visual field is radically changed by many factors that are not taken into account by formulas such as Equation 3.5—perceived illumination, specular reflection from glossy surfaces, and local contrast effects—the goal of obtaining a perfect gray scale is not realizable.

Contrast Crispening

Another perceptual factor that distorts gray values is called contrast *crispening* (see Wyszecki, 1982). Generally, differences are perceived as larger when samples are similar to the background color. Figure 3.17 shows a set of identical gray scales on a range of different gray backgrounds. Notice how the scales appear to divide perceptually at the value of the background. More subtle gray values can be distinguished at the point of crossover. The crispening is not taken into account by uniform gray-scale formulas.

Monitor Illumination and Monitor Surrounds

In some visualization applications, the accurate perception of surface lightness and color is critical. One example is the use of a computer monitor to display wallpaper or fabric samples for customer selection. It is also important for graphic designers that colors be accurately perceived. In these cases, not only is it necessary to calibrate the monitor so that it actually displays

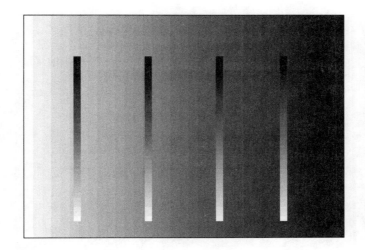

Figure 3.17　　Perceived differences between gray-scale values are enhanced where the values are close to the light part of the background. The effect is known as crispening.

the specified color range, but other factors affecting the state of adaptation of the user's eyes must also be taken into account. The color and the brightness of the *surround* of the monitor can be very important in determining how screen objects appear. The adaptation effect produced by room lighting can be equally important.

How should the lighting surrounding a monitor be set up? A monitor used for visual displays engages only the central part of the visual field, so the overall state of adaptation of the eye is maintained at least as much by the ambient room illumination. There are good reasons for maintaining a reasonably high level of illumination in a viewing room, such as the ability to take notes and see other people. However, a side effect of a high level of room illumination is that some light falls on the monitor screen and is scattered back to the eye, degrading the image. In fact, under normal office conditions, between 15% and 40% of the illumination coming to the eye from the monitor screen will come indirectly from the room light, not from the luminous phosphors. Figure 3.18 shows a monitor display with a shadow lying across its face. Although this is a rather extreme example, the effects are clear. Overall contrast is much reduced where the room light falls on the display.

We can model the effects of illumination on a monitor by adding a constant to Equation 3.4.

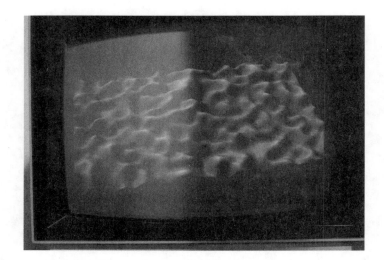

Figure 3.18   A monitor with a shadow falling across its face. Under normal viewing conditions, a significant proportion of the light coming from the screen is reflected ambient room illumination. See also color plates.

$$L = V^{\gamma} + A \tag{3.6}$$

where A is the ambient room illumination reflected from the screen, V is the voltage to the monitor, and L is the luminance output for a given gamma.

If we wish to create a monitor for which equal voltage steps result in equal perceptual steps under conditions where ambient light is reflected, a lower gamma value is needed. Figure 3.19 shows the effects of different gamma values, assuming that 15% of the light coming from the screen is reflected ambient light. The CIE luminance correction equation (3.5) has been used to model lightness scaling. As you can see, under these assumptions, a monitor is a perceptually more linear device with a gamma of only 1.5 than with a gamma of 2.5 (though under dark viewing conditions, a higher gamma is needed).

If you cover part of your monitor screen with a sheet of white paper, under normal working conditions (when there are lights on in the room), you will probably find that the white of the paper is very different from the white of the monitor screen. The paper may look relatively blue, or yellow, and it may appear darker or lighter. There are often large discrepancies between monitor colors and colors of objects in the surrounding environment.

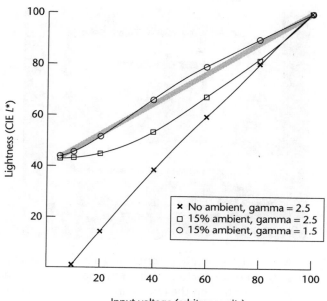

Figure 3.19   The three curves show how monitor gun voltage is transformed into lightness, according to the CIE model, with different ambient light conditions and gamma values.

For the creation of an environment where computer-generated colors are comparable to colors in a room, the room should have a standard light level and illuminant color. The monitor should be carefully calibrated and balanced so that the monitor's white matches that of a sheet of white paper held up beside the screen. In addition, only a minimal amount of light should be allowed to fall on the monitor screen.

Figure 3.20 shows a computer display set up so that the lighting in the virtual environment shown on the monitor is matched with the lighting in the real environment surrounding the monitor. This is achieved by illuminating the region surrounding the monitor with a projector that contains a special mask. This mask was custom-designed so that light was cast on the monitor casing and the desktop surrounding the computer, but no light at all fell on the part of the screen containing the picture. In addition, the direction and color of the light in the virtual environment were adjusted to exactly match the light from the projector. Simulated cast shadows were also created to match the cast shadows from the projector. Using this setup, it is

Figure 3.20   A projector was set up containing a mask especially designed so that no light actually fell on the portion of the monitor screen containing the image. In this way, the illumination in the virtual environment displayed on the monitor was made to closely match the illumination falling on the monitor and surrounding region. See also color plates.

possible to create a virtual environment whose simulated colors and other material properties can be directly compared to the colors and material properties of objects in the room. (This previously unpublished work was done by Justin Hickey and the author.)

Conclusion

As a general observation, the use of gray-scale colors is not a particularly good method for coding data, and not just because contrast effects reduce accuracy. Because the luminance channel of the visual system is fundamental to so much of perception, it is generally a waste of perceptual resources to use gray-scale encoding. Nevertheless, it is important to understand the problems of brightness and lightness perception because they point to issues that are fundamental to all perceptual systems. One of these basic problems is how perception functions effectively in visual environments where the light level can vary by six orders of magnitude. The solution, arrived at over the course of evolution, is a system that essentially neglects the level of illumination. This may seem like an exaggeration—after all, we can certainly tell the difference between bright sunlight and dim room illumination—but we are barely aware of a change of light level on the order of a factor of 2. For example, in a room lit with a two-bulb fixture, if one bulb burns out, this is often not noticed, as long as the bulbs are hidden within a diffusing surround.

A fundamental point made in this chapter is the relativistic nature of early visual processing. As a general rule, nerve cells situated early in the visual pathway do not respond to absolute signals. Rather, they respond to differences in both space and time. At later stages in the visual system, more stable percepts such as the perception of surface lightness can emerge, but this is only because of sophisticated image analysis that takes into account such factors as the position of the light, cast shadows, and the orientation of the object. The relativistic nature of lightness perception can be regarded mainly as a source of errors. However, the same mechanism is the reason that we can perceive subtle changes in data values, and can pick out patterns despite changes in the background light level.

Luminance contrast is an especially important consideration for choosing backgrounds and surrounds for a visualization. The way a background is chosen depends on what is important. If the outline shapes of objects are critical, the background should be chosen for maximum luminance contrast with foreground objects. If it is important to see subtle gradations in gray level, the crispening effect suggests that choosing a background in the midrange of gray levels will help us to see more of the important details.

When people care about image quality on a computer display, they typically reduce the room illumination as much as possible. The main reason for doing this is to reduce the amount of ambient room light that falls on the viewing screen, degrading the image. But this can have unfortunate side effects. Low room illumination causes a kind of visual shock in looking at the screen and away from it. In addition, it is impossible for observers to take notes. When people spend lots of time in a dimly lit work environment, it can also cause depression and reduced job satisfaction (Rosenthal, 1993). For these reasons, the optimal visualization viewing environment is one that is carefully engineered so that there is a high level of ambient light in the room, but the lights are arranged so that minimal illumination falls on the viewing screen.

Luminance is but one dimension of color space. In Chapter 4, this one-dimensional model is expanded to a three-dimensional color perception model. The luminance channel, however, is special. We could not get by without luminance perception, but we can certainly get by without color perception. This is demonstrated by the historic success of black-and-white movies and television. Later chapters describe how information encoded in the luminance "channel" is fundamental to perception of fine detail, discrimination of the shapes of objects through shading, in stereoscopic depth perception, motion perception, and many aspects of pattern perception.

Color

In the summer of 1997, I designed an experiment to measure human ability to trace paths between connected parts in a 3D diagram. Then, as is my normal practice, I ran a pilot study in order to see whether the experiment was well constructed. By ill luck, the first person tested was a research assistant who worked in my lab. He had far more difficulty with the task than anticipated—so much so that I put the experiment back on the drawing board to reconsider, without trying any more pilot subjects. Some months later, my assistant told me he had just had an eye test and the optometrist had determined that he was color-blind. This explained the problems with the experiment. Although it was not about color perception, I had marked the targets red in my experiment and he therefore had had great difficulty in finding them, which rendered the rest of the task meaningless.

The remarkable aspect of this story is that my assistant had gone through 21 years of his life without knowing that he was blind to many color differences. This is not uncommon and it strongly suggests that color vision cannot be all that important to everyday life. In fact, color vision is irrelevant to much of normal vision. It does not help us determine the layout of objects in space, how they are moving, or what their shapes are. It is not much of an overstatement to say that color vision is largely superfluous in modern life. Nevertheless, color is extremely useful in data visualization.

Color vision does have a critical function, which is hardly surprising since this sophisticated ability must surely provide some evolutionary advantage. Color helps us break camouflage. Some things differ visually from their surroundings only by their color. An especially important example is illustrated in Figure 4.1. If we have color vision, we can easily see the berries hidden in the leaves. If we do not, this becomes much harder. Color also tells us much that is useful about the material properties of objects. This is crucial in judging the condition of our food. Is this fruit ripe or not? It this meat fresh or putrid? What kind of mushroom is this? It is also useful if we are making tools. What kind of stone is this? Clearly, these can be life-or-death decisions. In modern hunter-gatherer societies, men are the hunters and women are the gatherers. This may have been true for long periods of human evolution and this could explain why it is mostly men who are color-blind. As gatherers, they would have been more than likely to bring home poison berries—a selective disadvantage. In the modern age of supermarkets, these skills are much less valuable; this is perhaps why color deficiencies so often go unnoticed.

The role that color plays ecologically suggests ways that it can be used in information display. It is useful to think of color as an attribute of an object rather than as its primary characteristic. It is excellent for labeling

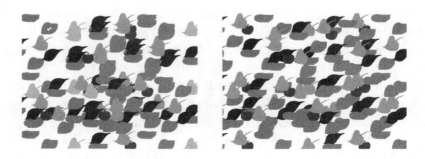

Figure 4.1   Finding the cherries among the leaves is much easier if we have color vision. See also color plates.

and categorization, but poor for displaying shape, detail, or space. These points are elaborated in this chapter. We begin with an introduction to the basic theory of color vision to provide a foundation for the applications. The latter half of the chapter consists of a set of five visualization problems requiring the effective use of color; these have to do with color selection interfaces, color labeling, pseudocolor sequences for mapping, color reproduction, and color for multidimensional discrete data. Each represents a different use of color, with its own special set of requirements. Some readers may wish to skip directly to the applications and to sample the more technical introduction only as needed.

Trichromacy Theory

The most important fact about color vision is that we have three distinct color receptors, called cones, in our retinas that are active at normal light levels—hence *trichromacy.* We also have rods, sensitive at low light levels, but they are so overstimulated in all but the dimmest light that their influence can be ignored. Thus, in order to understand color vision, we need only consider the cones. The fact that there are only three receptors is the reason for the basic three-dimensionality of human color vision. In this chapter, a number of color spaces, designed for different purposes, are discussed. Complex transformations are sometimes required to convert from one to another, but they are all three-dimensional, and this three-dimensionality derives ultimately from the three cone types. This is the reason that there are three differently colored phosphors in a television tube—red, green, and blue—and this is the reason that we learn in school that there are three primary paint colors—red, yellow, and blue. It is also the reason that the printer has a minimum of three colored inks for color printing—cyan, magenta, and yellow. Engineers should be grateful that humans have only three color receptors. Some birds, such as chickens, have as many as twelve different kinds of color-sensitive cells. A television set for chickens would have to have twelve electron beams and twelve differently colored phosphors!

Figure 4.2 shows the cone sensitivity functions. The plots show how light of different wavelengths is absorbed by the different receptors. It is evident that two of the functions, which peak at 540 nanometers and 580 nanometers, overlap considerably, while the third is much more distinct, with peak sensitivity at 450 nanometers.

Because only three different receptor types are involved in color vision, it is possible to match a particular patch of colored light with a mixture of just three primaries. It does not matter that the target patch may have a completely different spectral composition. The only thing that matters is that the matching primaries are balanced to produce the same response from the receptors as the patch of light to be matched. Figure 4.3(a) illustrates the three-dimensional space formed by the responses of the three cones.

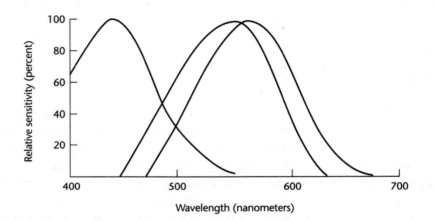

Figure 4.2   Cone sensitivity functions.

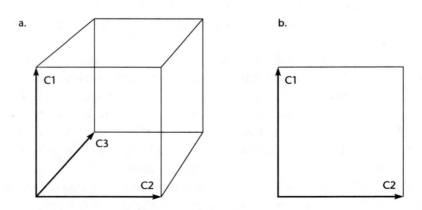

Figure 4.3   (a) Cone response space, defined by the response of each of the three cone types. (b) The space becomes two-dimensional in the case of the common color deficiencies.

Color Blindness

About 10% of the male population and about 1% of the female population suffer from some form of color vision deficiency. The most common deficiencies are explained by lack of either the long-wavelength-sensitive cones (protanopia) or the medium-wavelength-sensitive cones (deuteranopia). Both protanopia and deuteranopia result in an inability to distinguish red and green, meaning that the cherries in Figure 4.1 will be difficult for people with these deficiencies to see. One way of describing color vision deficiency is by pointing out that the three-dimensional color space of normal color vision collapses to a two-dimensional space, as shown in Figure 4.3(b). An unfortunate result is that if color is widely used for information coding, we immediately create a new class of people with a disability. Color blindness already disqualifies applicants for jobs such as those of telephone linespeople, because of the myriad colored wires, and pilots, because of the need to distinguish color-coded lights.

Color Measurement

The fact that we can match any color with a mixture of no more than three lights (usually called primaries) is the basis of *colorimetry*. An understanding of colorimetry is essential for anyone who wishes to precisely specify colors for reproduction.

We can describe a color by the following equation:

$$C \equiv rR + gG + bB \tag{4.1}$$

where C is the color to be matched, R, G, and B are the primary sources to be used to create a match, and r, g, and b represent the amounts of each primary light. The $\equiv$ symbol is used to denote a perceptual match—the sample and the mixture of the red, green, and blue primaries look identical. Figure 4.4 illustrates the concept. Three projectors are set up with overlapping beams. In the figure, the beams only partially overlap so that the mixing effect can be illustrated, but in a color-matching experiment they would overlap completely. To match the lilac-colored sample, the projectors are adjusted so that a large amount of light comes from the red and blue projectors and only a small amount of light comes from the green projector.

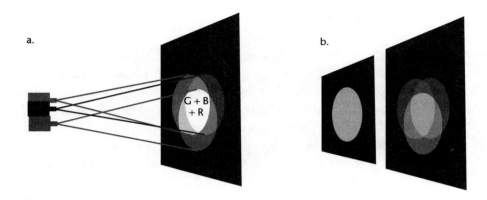

Figure 4.4   A color-matching setup. (a) When the light from three projectors is combined, the results are as shown. Yellow light is a mixture of red and green. Purple light is a mixture of red and blue. Cyan light is a mixture of blue and green. White light is a mixture or red, green, and blue. (b) Any other color can be matched by adjusting the proportions of red, green, and blue light. See also color plates.

The *RGB* primaries form the coordinates of a color space, as is illustrated in Figure 4.5. If the red, green, and blue primaries are formed by the phosphor colors of a color monitor, this space defines the *gamut* of the monitor. In general, a gamut is the set of all colors that can be produced by a device or sensed by a receptor system.

It seems obvious that restrictions must be placed on the above formulation. For example, what if we were to choose different primary lights, for example, yellow, blue, and purple? There is no rule that says they have to be red, green, and blue. How could we possibly reproduce a patch of red light out of combinations of these lights? In fact, we can only reproduce colors that lie within the *gamut* of the three primaries. Yellow, blue, and purple would simply have a smaller gamut, meaning that if we used them, a smaller range of colors could be reproduced.

The relationship defined in Equation 4.1 is a linear relationship. This has the consequence that if we double the amount of light on the left, we can double the amount of light on each of our primaries and the match will still hold. To make the math simpler, it is also useful to allow the concept of negative light. Thus, we may allow expressions such as

$$C \equiv -rR + gG + bB \tag{4.2}$$

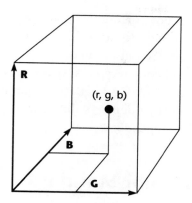

Figure 4.5 The three-dimensional space formed by three primary lights. Any color can be created by varying the amount of light produced by each of the primaries.

While this concept may seem nonsensical, because negative light does not exist in nature, it is, in fact, practically useful in the following situation. Suppose we have a colored light that cannot be matched because it is outside the gamut of our three primary sources. We can still achieve a match by adding part of one of the primaries to our sample. If the test samples and the *RGB* primaries are all projected as shown in Figure 4.4, this can be achieved by swiveling one of the projectors around and adding its light to the light of the sample.

If the red projector were redirected in this way, we would have

$$C + rR \equiv gG + bB \tag{4.3}$$

which can be rewritten

$$C \equiv -rR + gG + bB \tag{4.4}$$

Once we allow the concept of negative values for the primaries, it becomes possible to state that *any* colored light can be matched by a weighted sum of *any* three distinct primaries.

Change of Primaries

Primaries are arbitrary from the point of view of color mixture—there is no special red, green, or blue light that must be used. Fundamental to colorimetry is the ability to change from one set of primaries to another. This gives us freedom to choose any set of primaries we want. We can choose as primaries the three phosphors of a monitor, three differently colored lasers, or some hypothetical set of lamps. We can even choose to base our primaries on the sensitivities of the human cone receptors. Given a standard way of specifying colors (using a standard set of primaries), we can use a transformation to create that same color on any number of different output devices. This transformation is described in Appendix A.

CIE System of Color Standards

We now have the foundations of a color measurement and specification system. First we standardize three primary lights (*RGB*), so that an identical set of lights is available to anyone, anywhere in the world. Now to give a precise color specification to someone with the standard primaries, we simply need to make a match and then send that person the amounts of each of the three primaries needed for the match. The recipient can then adjust the standard lamps to reproduce the color. Of course, although this approach is theoretically sound, it is not very practical to create standard primary lamps. They would be very difficult to maintain and calibrate. But we can apply the principle by creating a set of abstract primary lamps defined on the basis of the human receptor characteristics. This assumes that everyone has the same receptor functions. In fact, although humans do not display exactly the same sensitivities to different colors, with the exception of the color deficiencies, they come close. One of the basic concepts in any color standard is that of the standard observer. This is a hypothetical person whose color sensitivity functions are held to be typical of all humans. Most serious color specification is done using the Commission Internationale de L'Éclairage (CIE) system of color standards. These are based on standard observer measurements that were made prior to 1931.

The CIE system uses a set of abstract primaries called tristimulus values; these are labeled *XYZ*. These primaries are chosen for their mathematical properties, not because they match any set of actual lights. One important feature of the system is that the *Y* tristimulus value is the same as luminance. More details of the way the system is derived are given in Appendix B.

Figure 4.6 illustrates the color volume created by the *XYZ* tristimulus primaries of the CIE system. The colors that can actually be perceived are represented as a gray volume entirely contained within the positive space defined by the axes. The colors that can be created by a set of three colored

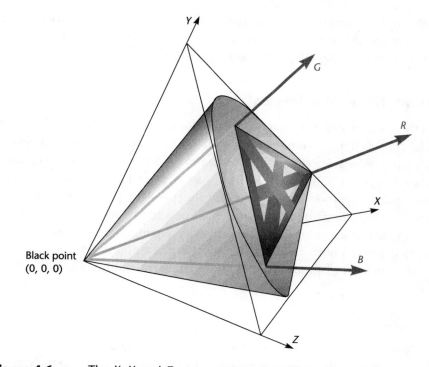

Figure 4.6   The *X*, *Y*, and *Z* axes represent the CIE standard virtual primaries. Within the positive space defined by the axes, the gamut of perceivable colors is represented as a gray solid. The colors that can be created by means of the red, green, and blue monitor primaries are also shown. See also color plates.

lights, such as the red, green, and blue monitor phosphors, are defined by the volume within the *RGB* axes as shown.

The CIE tristimulus system based on the standard observer is by far the most widely used standard for measuring colored light. For this reason, it should always be used when precise color specification is required. Because a monitor is a light-emitting device with three primaries, it is relatively straightforward to calibrate a monitor in terms of the CIE coordinates. If a color generated on one monitor is to be reproduced on another, for example, a liquid crystal display, the best procedure will be first to convert the colors into the CIE tristimulus values and then to convert them into the primary space of the second monitor.

The specification of surface colors is far more difficult than the specification of lights, because an illuminant must be taken into account and because, unlike lights, pigment colors are not additive. A treatment of surface color measurement is beyond the scope of this book, although we will later deal with perceptual issues related to color reproduction.

Chromaticity Coordinates

The three-dimensional abstract space represented by the *XYZ* coordinates is useful for specifying colors, but it is difficult to understand. As discussed in Chapter 3, there are good reasons for treating lightness, or luminance, information as special. In everyday speech, we often refer to the color of something and its lightness as different and independent properties. Thus, it is useful to have a measure that defines the hue and vividness of a color while ignoring the amount of light. Chromaticity coordinates have exactly this property through normalizing with respect to the amount of light.

To transform tristimulus values to chromaticity coordinates, use

$$x = X/(X+Y+Z)$$
$$y = Y/(X+Y+Z) \qquad\qquad (4.5)$$
$$z = Z/(X+Y+Z)$$

Because $x + y + z = 1$, it is sufficient to use x, y values. It is common to specify a color by its luminance and its x, y chromaticity coordinates (x, y, Y). The inverse transformation from x, y, Y to tristimulus values is

$$X = Yx/y$$
$$Y = Y \qquad\qquad (4.6)$$
$$Z = (1 - x - y)Y/y$$

Figure 4.7 shows a CIE chromaticity diagram and graphically illustrates some of the colorimetric concepts associated with it. Here are some of the useful and interesting features of the chromaticity diagram:

1. If two colored lights are represented by two points in a chromaticity diagram, the color of a mixture of those two lights will always lie on a straight line between those two points.

2. Any set of three lights specifies a triangle in the chromaticity diagram. Its corners are given by the chromaticity coordinates of the three lights. Any color within that triangle is realizable with a suitable mixture of the three lights. Figure 4.7 illustrates this with typical monitor *RGB* primaries.

3. The spectrum locus is the set of chromaticity coordinates of pure monochromatic (single-wavelength) lights. All realizable colors fall within the spectrum locus.

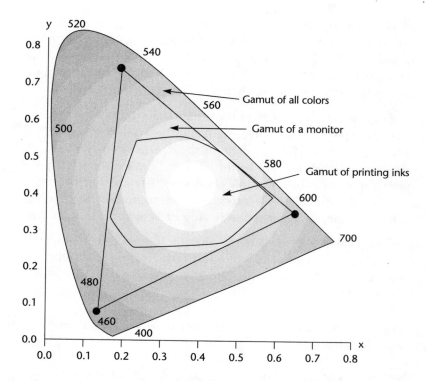

Figure 4.7   CIE chromaticity diagram with various interesting features added. The triangle represents the gamut of a computer monitor with long-persistence phosphors.

4. The *purple boundary* is the straight line connecting the chromaticity coordinates of the longest visible wavelength of red light, about 700 nm, to the chromaticity coordinates of the shortest visible wavelength of blue, about 400 nm.

5. The chromaticity coordinates of equal-energy white (light having an equal mixture of all wavelengths) are 0.333, 0.333. When a white light is specified for some application, what is generally required is one of the CIE standard illuminants. The CIE specifies a number that corresponds to different phases of daylight, and of these the most commonly used is D65. D65 was made to be a careful approximation to daylight with an overcast sky. It also happens to be very close to the mix of light that results when both direct sunlight and light from the rest of the sky fall on a horizontal surface. D65 also corresponds to a black-body radiator at 6500 degrees Kelvin. D65

has chromaticity coordinates $x = 0.313$, $y = 0.329$. Another CIE standard illuminant corresponds to the light produced by a typical incandescent tungsten source. This is illuminant A. Illuminant A has chromaticity coordinates $x = 0.448$, $y = 0.407$. This is considerably more yellow than normal daylight.

6. *Excitation purity* is a measure of the distance along a line between a particular pure spectral wavelength and the white point. Specifically, it is the value given by dividing the distance between the sample and the white point by the distance between the white point and the spectrum line (or purple boundary). This measure defines the vividness of a color. A less technical, but commonly used, term for this quantity is *saturation*. More saturated colors are more vivid.

7. The complementary wavelength of a color is produced by drawing a line between that color and white and extrapolating to the opposite spectrum locus. Adding a color and its complementary color produces white.

The set of chromaticity coordinates for two sets of typical monitor phosphors are the following:

| | *Short-Persistence Phosphor* | | | *Long-Persistence Phosphor* | | |
	Red	*Green*	*Blue*	*Red*	*Green*	*Blue*
x	0.61	0.29	0.15	0.62	0.21	0.15
y	0.35	0.59	0.063	0.33	0.685	0.063

The main difference between the two is that the long-persistence phosphor green is closer to being a pure spectral color than the short-persistence green. This makes the gamut larger.

When a CRT display is used, the CIE tristimulus values of a color formed from some set of red, green, and blue settings can be calculated from the following formula:

$$\begin{bmatrix} X \\ Y \\ Z \end{bmatrix} = \begin{bmatrix} \frac{x_R}{y_R} & \frac{x_G}{y_G} & \frac{x_B}{y_B} \\ 1 & 1 & 1 \\ \frac{z_R}{y_R} & \frac{z_G}{y_G} & \frac{z_B}{y_B} \end{bmatrix} \begin{bmatrix} Y_R \\ Y_G \\ Y_B \end{bmatrix} \tag{4.7}$$

where x_R, y_R, and z_R are the chromaticity coordinates of the particular monitor primaries and Y_R, Y_B, and Y_G are the actual luminance values produced from each phosphor for the particular color being converted. Notice that for a particular monitor the transformation matrix will be constant; only the Y vector will change.

To generate a particular color on a monitor that has been defined by CIE tristimulus values, it is only necessary to invert the matrix and create an appropriate voltage to each of the red, green, and blue guns. Naturally, to determine the actual value that must be specified, it is necessary to calibrate the monitor's red, green, and blue outputs in terms of luminance and apply gamma correction as described in Chapter 3. Once this is done, the monitor can be treated as a linear color creation device with a particular set of primaries, depending on its phosphors. For more on monitor calibration, see Cowan (1983).

Color Differences and Uniform Color Spaces

In a number of situations, it is useful to have a color space in which equal perceptual distances are equal distances in the space. Here are three applications.

The specification of color tolerances. When a manufacturer wishes to order a colored part from a supplier, such as a plastic molding for an automobile, it is necessary to specify the color tolerance within which the part will be accepted. It only makes sense for this tolerance to be based on perception, since ultimately it is the customer who decides whether the door trim matches the upholstery.

The specification of color codes. If we need a set of colors to code data, for example, different wires in a cable, we would normally like those colors to be as distinct as possible so that they will not be confused.

Pseudocolor sequences for maps. Many scientific maps use sequences of colors to represent ordered data values. This technique, called pseudocoloring, is widely used in astronomy, physics, medical imaging, and geophysics.

The CIE *XYZ* color space is very far from being perceptually uniform. However, in 1978 the CIE produced a set of recommendations on the use of two uniform color spaces that are transformations of the *XYZ* color space. These are called the *CIElab* and the *CIEluv* uniform color spaces. The reason that there are two, rather than one, has to do with the fact that different industries, such as the paint industry, had already adopted one standard or the other. Also, the two standards have somewhat different properties that make them useful for different tasks. Only the *CIEluv* formula is described here. It is generally held to be better for specifying large color differences. However, one measurement made using the *CIElab* color difference formula is worth noting. Using *CIElab*, Hill et al. (1997) estimated that there are between two and six million discriminable colors available within the gamut of a color monitor.

$$L^* = 116(Y/Y_n)^{1/3} - 16$$
$$u^* = 13L^*(u' - u'_n)$$
$$v^* = 13L^*(v' - v'_n)$$

$$(4.8)$$

where

$$u' = \frac{4X}{X + 15Y + 3Z} \qquad u'_n = \frac{4X_n}{X_n + 15Y_n + 3Z_n}$$
$$v' = \frac{9Y}{X + 15Y + 3Z} \qquad v'_n = \frac{9Y_n}{X_n + 15Y_n + 3Z_n}$$

$$(4.9)$$

u' and *v'* are a projective transformation of the *x, y* chromaticity diagram, designed to produce a perceptually more uniform color space. X_n, Y_n, and Z_n are the tristimulus values of a reference white. To measure the difference between colors ΔE^*_{uv}, the following formula is used:

$$\Delta E^*_{uv} = \sqrt{(\Delta L^*)^2 + (\Delta u^*)^2 + (\Delta v^*)^2}$$

$$(4.10)$$

The *CIEluv* system retains many of the useful properties of the *XYZ* tristimulus values and the *x, y* chromaticity coordinates.

The *u'v'* diagram is shown in Figure 4.8. Its official name is the CIE 1976 Uniform Chromaticity Diagram, or UCS diagram. Because *u'*, *v'* is a projective transformation, it retains the useful property that blends of two colors will lie on a line between the *u'*, *v'* chromaticity coordinates. It is worth noting that this is not a property of the *CIElab* uniform color space.

The *u**, *v** values change the scale of *u'*, *v'* with respect to the distance from black to white defined by the sample lightness *L** (recall from Chapter 3

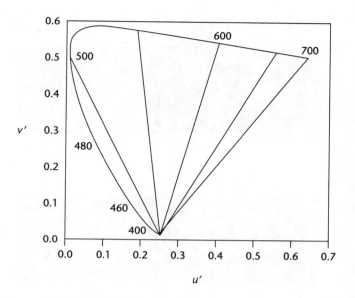

Figure 4.8   CIE *Lu'v'* UCS diagram. The lines radiating from the lower part of the diagram are tritanopic confusion lines. Colors that differ along these lines can still be distinguished by the great majority of color-blind individuals.

that L^* requires Y_n, a reference white in the application environment). The reason for this is straightforward: The darker the colors, the fewer we can see. At the limit there is only one: black.

A value of 1 for ΔE^*_{uv} is an approximation to a just noticeable difference (JND).

Although they are useful, uniform color spaces provide, at best, only a rough first approximation. Perceived color differences are influenced by many factors. Contrast effects can radically alter the shape of the color space. Small patches of light give different results from those of large patches. In general, we are much more sensitive to differences between large patches of color. When the patches are small, the perceived differences are smaller, and this is especially true in the yellow-blue direction. Ultimately, with very small samples, small-field tritanopia occurs; this is the inability to distinguish colors that are different in the yellow-blue direction. Figure 4.9 shows two examples of small patches of color on a white background and the same set of colors in larger patches on a black background. Both the white background and the small patches make the colors harder to distinguish.

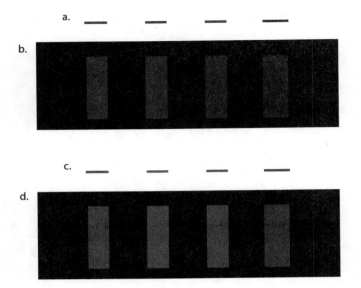

Figure 4.9   (a) Small samples of a yellow-to-blue sequence of colors on a
white background. (b) The same yellow-to-blue sequence with
larger samples on a black background. (c) Small samples of a
green-to-red sequence on a white background. (d) The same
green-to-red sequence with larger samples on a black
background. See also color plates.

Opponent Process Theory

Late in the nineteenth century, the German psychologist Ewald Hering proposed the theory that there are six elementary colors and these colors are
arranged perceptually as opponent pairs along three axes: black-white, red-
green, and yellow-blue (Hering, 1920). In recent years, this principle has
become a cornerstone of modern color theory, supported by a large variety
of experimental evidence (see Hurvich, 1981, for a review). Modern opponent process theory has a well-established physiological basis: The input
from the cones is processed into three distinct channels immediately after
the receptors. The luminance channel (black-white) is based on input from
all the cones. The red-green channel is based on the difference of long- and
middle-wavelength cone signals. The yellow-blue channel is based on the
difference between the short-wavelength cones and the sum of the other
two. These basic connections are illustrated in Figure 4.10.

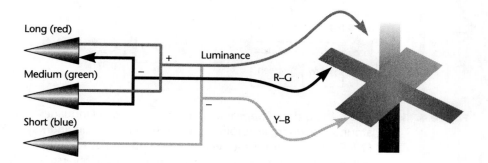

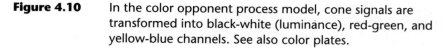

Figure 4.10   In the color opponent process model, cone signals are transformed into black-white (luminance), red-green, and yellow-blue channels. See also color plates.

There are many lines of scientific evidence for the opponent process theory. These are worth examining, because they illuminate a number of applications.

Naming

We often describe colors using combinations of color terms, such as "yellowish green" or "greenish blue." However, certain combination terms never appear. People never use "reddish green" or "yellowish blue," for example. Since these colors are polar opposites in the opponent color theory, these pairings should not occur (Hurvich, 1981).

Cross-Cultural Naming

In a remarkable study of more than 100 languages from many diverse cultures, anthropologists Berlin and Kay (1969) showed that primary color terms are remarkably consistent across cultures (Figure 4.11). In languages with only two basic color words, they are always black and white; if a third color is present, it is always red; the fourth and fifth are either yellow and then green, or green and then yellow; the sixth is always blue; the seventh is brown, followed by pink, purple, orange, and gray in no particular order. The key point here is that the first six terms define the primary axes of an opponent color model. This provides strong evidence that the neural basis for these names is innate. Otherwise, we might expect to find cultures where lime green or turquoise is a basic color term. The cross-cultural evidence strongly supports the idea that certain colors, specifically, red, green, yellow, and blue, are far more valuable in coding data than others.

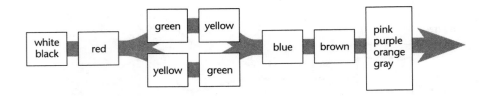

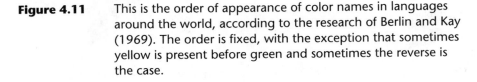

Figure 4.11   This is the order of appearance of color names in languages around the world, according to the research of Berlin and Kay (1969). The order is fixed, with the exception that sometimes yellow is present before green and sometimes the reverse is the case.

Unique Hues

There is something very special about yellow. If subjects are given control over a device that changes the spectral hue of a patch of light, and are told to adjust it until the result is a pure yellow, neither reddish nor greenish, they do so with remarkable accuracy. In fact, they are typically accurate within 2 nm (Hurvich, 1981).

Interestingly, there is good evidence for two unique greens. Most people set a pure green at about 514 nm, but about a third of the population sees pure green at about 525 nm (Richards, 1967). This may be why some people argue about the color turquoise; some people consider it to be a variety of green, while others consider it to be a kind of blue.

It is also significant that unique hues do not change a great deal when the overall luminance level is changed (Hurvich, 1981). This supports the idea that chromatic perception and luminance perception are really independent.

Neurophysiology

Neurophysiological studies have isolated classes of cells in the primary visual cortexes of monkeys that have exactly the properties of opponency that are required by the opponent process theory. Red-green and yellow-blue opponent cells exist, and other configurations do not appear to exist (deValois and deValois, 1975).

Categorical Colors

There is evidence that certain colors are canonical in a sense that is analogous to the philosopher Plato's theory of forms. Plato proposed that there are ideal objects, such as an ideal horse or an ideal chair, and that real horses and chairs can be defined in terms of their differences from the ideal. Something similar appears to operate in color naming. If a color is close to an ideal red or an ideal green, it is easier to remember. Colors that are not basic, such as orange or lime green, are not as easy to remember.

There is evidence that confusion between color codes is affected by color categories. Kawai et al. (1995) asked subjects to identify the presence or absence of a chip of a particular color. The subjects took much longer if the chip was surrounded by distracting elements that were of a different color but belonged to the same color category than if it was surrounded by distracting elements that were equally distinct but crossed a color category boundary.

Post and Greene (1986) carried out an extensive experiment on the naming of colors produced on a computer monitor and shown in a darkened room. They generated 210 different colors, each in a two-degree (of visual angle) patch with a black surround. Figure 4.12 illustrates the color areas that

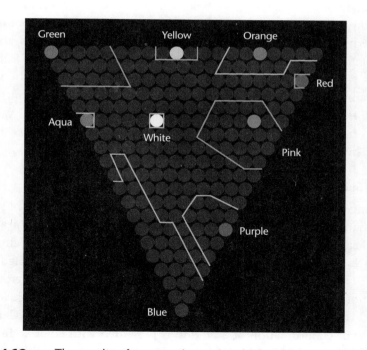

Figure 4.12   The results of an experiment in which subjects were asked to name 210 colors produced on a computer monitor. Outlined regions show the colors that were given the same name with better than 75% probability. See also color plates.

were given a specific name with at least 75% reliability. A number of points are worth noting:

- The pure monitor red was actually named orange most of the time.

- A true color red required the addition of a small amount from the blue monitor primary.

- The fact that only eight colors were consistently named, even under these highly standardized conditions, strongly suggests that only a very small number of colors can be used effectively as category labels.

Properties of Color Channels

From the perspective of data visualization, the different properties of the color channels have profound implications for the use of color. The most significant differences are between the two chromatic channels and the luminance channel, although the two color channels also differ from each other.

To display data on the luminance channel alone is easy; it is stimulated by patterns that vary only from black to white through shades of gray. But with careful calibration (which must be customized to individual subjects), patterns can be constructed that vary only for the red-green or the yellow-blue channel. In this way, the different properties of the color channels can be explored and compared with the luminance channel capacity. A key quality of such a pattern is that its component colors must not differ in luminance. This is called an *isoluminant* or *equiluminous* pattern.

Spatial Sensitivity

According to a study by Mullen (1985), the red-green and yellow-blue chromatic channels are each only capable of carrying about one-third the amount of detail carried by the black-white channel. Because of this, purely chromatic differences are not suitable for displaying any kind of fine detail. Figure 4.13 illustrates this problem with colored text on an equiluminous background. In the part of the figure where there is only a chromatic difference between the text and the background, the text becomes very difficult to read. Generally, when detailed information of any kind is presented with color coding, it is important that there be considerable luminance contrast in addition to color contrast, especially if the colored patterns are small.

It is very difficult to read text that is isoluminant with its background color. If clear text material is to be presented it is essential that there be substantial luminance contrast with the background color. Color contrast is not enough This particular example is especially difficult because the chromatic difference is in the yellow blue direction. The only exception to the

Figure 4.13   Yellow text on a blue gradient. Note how difficult the text is to read where luminance is equal, despite a large chromatic difference. See also color plates.

Stereoscopic Depth

It appears to be impossible, or at least very difficult, to see stereoscopic depth in stereo pairs that differ only in terms of the color channels (Lu and Fender, 1972; Gregory, 1977). Thus, stereo space perception is based primarily on information from the luminance channel.

Temporal Sensitivity

If a pattern is created that is equiluminous with its background and contains only chromatic differences, and that pattern is set in motion, something strange occurs. The moving pattern appears to slow down dramatically compared to a black-against-white pattern moving at the same speed (Anstis and Cavanaugh, 1983). Thus, motion perception appears to be primarily based on information from the luminance channel.

Form

We are very good at perceiving the shapes of surfaces based on their shading. However, when the shading is transformed from a luminance gradient into a purely chromatic gradient, the impression of surface shape is much reduced. Perception of shape and form appears to be processed mainly through the luminance channel (Gregory, 1977).

To summarize this set of properties, the red-green and yellow-blue channels are inferior to the luminance channel in almost every respect. The general implications for data display are clear. Purely chromatic differences should *never* be used for displaying object shape, object motion, or detailed information such as text. From this perspective, color would seem almost irrelevant and certainly a secondary method for information display. Nevertheless, when it comes to coding information, using color to display data categories is usually the best choice. To see why, we need to look beyond the basic processes that we have been considering thus far.

Color Appearance

The value of color (as opposed to luminance) processing, it would appear, is not in helping us to understand the shape and layout of objects in the environment. Color does not help us judge distances, so that the hunter can aim a stone accurately. Color does not help us remember the shape of the hills along a journey. Color does not help us see small objects at a distance. But color is useful to the gatherer. Food, in the forest or on the savannah, is often distinct because of its color. This is especially true of fruits and berries. Color creates a kind of visual attribute of objects: This is a red berry. That is a yellow door. Color names are used as adjectives because colors are perceived as attributes of objects. This suggests a most important role for color in visualization—namely, the coding of information. Visual objects can represent complex data entities, and colors can naturally code attributes of those objects. In the following section, we consider the way surface colors are perceived.

A major theme of the previous chapter was that the measured luminance of a patch of light has little or nothing to do with its appearance. The same can be said for color measurement. The *XYZ* tristimulus values of a patch of light physically define a color, but they do not tell us how it will look. Depending on the other surrounding colors in the environment and a whole host of spatial and temporal factors, the same physical color can look very different. If it is desirable that color appearance be preserved, it is important that close attention be paid to surrounding conditions. In a monitor-based display, a large patch of standardized reference white will help ensure that color appearance is preserved. When colors are reproduced on paper, viewing them under a standard kind of lamp will help preserve their appearance. In the paint and fabric industries, where color appearance is critical, standard viewing booths are used. These booths contain standard illumination systems that can be set to approximate daylight, or a standard indoor illuminant, such as a typical tungsten light bulb or a halogen lamp.

The mechanisms of surface lightness constancy, discussed at some length in Chapter 3, generalize to trichromatic color perception. Both chromatic adaptation and chromatic contrast occur and play a role in color constancy. Differential adaptation in the cone receptors helps us discount the color of the illumination in the environment. When there is colored illumination, different classes of cone receptors undergo independent changes in sensitivity. Thus, when the illumination contains a lot of blue light, the short-wavelength cones become relatively less sensitive than the others. The effect of this is to shift the neutral point at which the three receptor types are in equilibrium, such that more blue light will have to be reflected from a surface for it to seem white. This, of course, is exactly what is necessary for color constancy. That adaptation is effective in maintaining constancy is evident from the fact that not many people are aware how much yellower ordinary tungsten room lighting is than daylight.

Color Contrast

Chromatic contrast also occurs in a way that is similar to the lightness contrast effects discussed and illustrated in Chapter 3. Figure 4.14 shows a color contrast illusion. It has been shown that contrast effect can distort readings from color-coded maps (Cleveland and McGill, 1983; Ware, 1988). Contrast effects can be theoretically accounted for by activity in the color opponent channels (Ware and Cowan, 1982). However, as with lightness contrast, the ultimate purpose of the contrast-causing mechanism is to help us see surface colors accurately by revealing differences between colored patches and the background regions.

From the point of view of the monitor engineer and the user of color displays, the fact that colors are perceived relative to their overall context has the happy consequence of making the eye relatively insensitive to poor color balance. A visit to a television store will reveal that when television sets are viewed side by side, the overall color of the pictures can differ strikingly, yet when they are viewed individually, they are all acceptable. Of course, since the state of adaptation is governed by the light of the entire visual field, and a television screen takes up only part of the field, this adaptation will necessarily be incomplete.

Figure 4.14   A color contrast illusion. The "X" pattern is identical on both sides, but it seems more blue on the red background and more pink on the blue background. See also color plates.

Saturation

When describing color appearance in everyday language, people use many terms in rather imprecise ways. Besides using color names such as *lime green, mauve, brown, baby blue,* and so on, people also use adjectives such as *vivid, bright,* and *intense* to describe colors that seem especially pure. Because these terms are used so variably, scientists have created the technical term *saturation* to denote how pure colors seem to the viewer. A high-saturation color is vivid and a low-saturation color is close to black, white, or gray. Figure 4.15(a) shows a plot of equal saturation values in a CIE chromaticity diagram. It is clear that it is possible to obtain much more highly saturated red, green, and blue colors on a monitor than yellow, cyan, or purple values.

Brown

Brown is one of the most mysterious colors. Brown is dark yellow. While people talk about a light green or a dark green, a light blue or a dark blue, yellow is different. When colors in the vicinity of yellow and orange yellow are darkened, they turn to shades of brown and olive green. Unlike red, blue, and green, brown requires that there be a reference white somewhere in the vicinity for it to be perceived and brown appears qualitatively different to

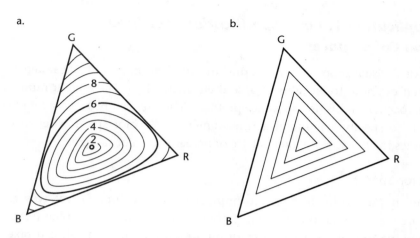

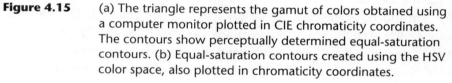

Figure 4.15   (a) The triangle represents the gamut of colors obtained using a computer monitor plotted in CIE chromaticity coordinates. The contours show perceptually determined equal-saturation contours. (b) Equal-saturation contours created using the HSV color space, also plotted in chromaticity coordinates.

orange yellow. There is no such thing as an isolated brown light in a dark room, but when a yellow or yellowish orange is presented with much brighter surrounding colors, brown appears. The relevance to visualization is that if color sets are being devised for the purposes of color coding—for example, a set of blues, a set of reds, and a set of greens—brown may not be recognized as belonging to the set of yellows.

Applications of Color in Visualization

Up to this point, this chapter has been mainly a presentation of the basic theory underlying color vision and color measurement. Now the emphasis shifts to applications of color, for which new theory will be introduced only as needed. Five different application areas are presented: color selection interfaces, color labeling, color sequences for map coding, color reproduction, and color for multidimensional discrete data display. Each of these presents a different set of problems and each benefits from an analysis in terms of the human perception of color.

Application 1: Color Specification Interfaces and Color Spaces

In data visualization programs, drawing applications, and CAD systems, it is often essential to let users choose their own colors. There are a number of approaches to this user interface problem. The user can be given a set of controls to specify a point in a three-dimensional color space, a set of color names to choose from, or a palette of predefined color samples.

Color Spaces

The simplest color interface to implement on a computer involves giving someone controls to adjust the amounts of red, green, and blue light that combine to make a patch of color on a monitor. The controls can take the form of sliders, or the user can simply type in three numbers. This provides access, in a straightforward way, to any point within the *RGB* color cube shown in Figure 4.5. However, although it is simple, many people find this kind of control confusing. For example, most people do not know that to get yellow you must add red and green. There have been many attempts to make color interfaces easier to use.

One of the most widely used color interfaces in computer graphics is based on the HSV color space (Smith, 1978). This is a simple transformation from hue, saturation, and value (HSV) coordinates to red, green, and blue (*RGB*) monitor coordinates. In Smith's scheme, hue represents an approximation to the visible spectrum by interpolating in sequence from red to yellow to green to blue and back to red. Saturation is the distance from monitor white to the purest hue possible. Figure 4.16 shows how hue and saturation can be laid out in two dimensions, with hue on one axis and saturation on the other, based on the HSV transformation of monitor primaries. As Figure 4.15(b) shows, HSV creates only the crudest approximation to perceptual equal-saturation contours. Value is the name given to the black-white axis. Some color specification interfaces based on HSV allow the user to control hue, saturation, and value variables with three sliders.

Color theory suggests that there are good reasons for separating a luminance (or lightness) dimension from the chromatic dimensions in an interface. A common method is to provide a single slider control for the black-white dimension and to lay out the two opponent color dimensions on a chromatic plane. The idea of laying out colors on a plane has a long history; for example, a color circle is a feature of a color textbook created for artists by Rood (1897). With the invention of computer graphics, it has

Figure 4.16   This plot shows hue and saturation, based on Smith's transformation (1978) of the monitor primaries. See also color plates.

become far simpler to create and control colors, and many ways of laying out colors are now available. Figure 4.17 illustrates a sampling of four different geometric color layouts, each of them embodying the idea of a chromatic plane.

Figure 4.17(a) shows a color circle with red, green, yellow, and blue defining opposing axes. Many such color circles have been devised over the past century. They differ mainly in the spacing of colors around the periphery.

Figure 4.17(b) shows a color triangle with the monitor primaries, red, green, and blue, at the corners. This color layout is convenient because it has the property that mixtures of two colors will lie on a line between them (assuming proper calibration).

Figure 4.17(c) shows a color square with the opponent color primaries, red, yellow, green, and blue, at the corners (Ware and Cowan, 1990).

Figure 4.17(d) shows a color hexagon with the colors red, yellow, green, cyan, blue, and magenta at the corners. This represents a plane through the single-hexcone color model (Smith, 1978). The hexagon representation has the advantage that it gives both the monitor primaries, red, green, and blue, and the print primaries, cyan, magenta, and yellow, prominent positions around the circumference.

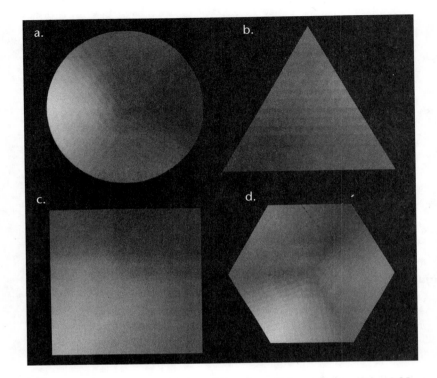

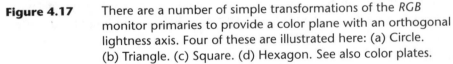

Figure 4.17   There are a number of simple transformations of the *RGB* monitor primaries to provide a color plane with an orthogonal lightness axis. Four of these are illustrated here: (a) Circle. (b) Triangle. (c) Square. (d) Hexagon. See also color plates.

To create a color interface using one of these color planes, it is necessary to allow the user to pick a sample from the color plane and adjust its lightness with a luminance slider. In some interfaces, when the luminance slider is moved, the entire plane of colors becomes lighter and darker according to the currently selected level. For those interested in implementing color interfaces, Foley et al. (1990) provides algorithms for a number of color geometries.

The problem of the best color selection interface is by no means resolved. Experimental studies have failed to show that one way of controlling color is substantially better than another (Schwarz et al., 1987; Douglas and Kirkpatrick, 1996). However, Douglas and Kirkpatrick have provided evidence that good feedback about the location of the color being adjusted in color space can help in the process.

Color Naming

The facts that there are so few widely agreed-on color names and color memory is so poor suggest that choosing colors by name will not be useful except for the simplest applications. Nevertheless, it is possible to remember a rather large number of color names and use them accurately under controlled conditions. Displays in paint stores generally have a standard illuminant and standard background for sample strips containing several hundred samples. Under these circumstances, the specialist can remember and use as many as 1000 color names. But many of the names are very idiosyncratic; the colors corresponding to "taupe," "fiesta red," and "primrose" are imprecisely defined for most of us. In addition, as soon as these colors are removed from the standard booth, they will change their appearance because of adaptation and contrast effects.

A standardized color naming system called the Natural Color System (NCS) has been developed based on Hering's opponent color theory (1920). NCS was developed in Sweden and is widely used in England and other European countries. In NCS, colors are characterized by the amounts of redness, greenness, yellowness, blueness, blackness, and whiteness that they contain. As shown in Figure 4.18, red, green, yellow, and blue lie at the ends

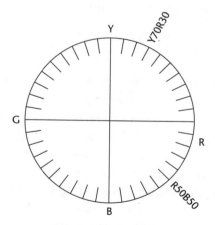

Figure 4.18   The Natural Color System (NCS) circle, defined midway between black and white. Two example color names are shown in addition to the "pure" opponent color primaries. One is an orange yellow and the other is purple.

of two orthogonal axes. Intervening "pure" colors lie on the circle circumference, and these are given numbers by sharing out 100 arbitrary units. Thus, a yellowish orange might be given the value Y70R30, meaning 70 parts yellow and 30 parts red. Colors are also given independent values on a black-white axis by allocating a blackness value between 0 and 100. A third color attribute, intensity (roughly corresponding to saturation), describes the distance from the gray-scale axis. For example, in NCS, the color "Spring Nymph" becomes 0030-G80Y20, which expands to blackness 00, intensity 30, green 80, and yellow 20 (Jackson et al., 1994). The NCS system combines some of the advantages of a color geometry with a reasonably intuitive and precise naming system.

In North America, other systems are more popular than NCS. The Pantone system is widely used in the printing industry and the Munsell system is an important reference for surface colors. The Munsell system is useful because it provides a set of standard color chips designed to represent equal perceptual spacing in a three-dimensional mesh. (Munsell color chips and viewing booths are available commercially as are Pantone products.) The NCS, Pantone, and Munsell systems were originally designed to be used with carefully printed paper samples providing the reference colors, but computer-based interfaces to these systems have been developed as part of illustration and design packages. Rhodes and Luo (1996) describe a software package that enables transformations between the different systems using the CIE as an intermediate standard.

Color Palette

Where the user wishes to use only a small set of standardized colors, providing a color palette is a good solution to the color selection problem. Often, color selection palettes are laid out in a regular order according to one of the color geometries defined above. It is useful to provide a facility for the user to develop a personal palette. This allows for consistency in color style across a number of visualization displays. Another valuable addition to a color user interface is a method for showing a color sample on differently colored backgrounds. This allows the designer to understand how contrast effects can affect the appearance of particular color samples.

Sometimes a color palette is based on one of the standard color sets used by the fabric industry or the paint industry. If this is the case, the monitor must be calibrated so that colors actually appear as specified. In addition, the proper lighting surrounding the monitor must be taken into account, as discussed in Chapter 3. Ideally, the monitor should be carefully set up with a standard monitor surround and little or no ambient light falling directly on the screen. This includes having a room light such that the standard white in the set of color samples on the screen closely matches the appearance of a standard white in the room environment.

Application 2: Color for Labeling

The technical name for labeling an object is *nominal information coding*. A nominal code does not have to be orderable; it simply has to be remembered and recognized. Color is often extremely effective as a nominal code. When we wish to make it easy for someone to classify visual objects into separate categories, giving the objects distinctive colors is often the best solution. One of the reasons that color is considered effective is that the alternatives are generally worse. For example, if we try to create gray-scale codes that are easily remembered and unlikely to be confused, we find that four is about the limit: white, light gray, dark gray, and black. Given that white will probably be used for the background and black is likely to be used for text, this leaves only two. In addition, using the gray scale as a nominal code may often be a mistake, because this may interfere with shape or detail perception. Chromatic coding can often be employed in a way that only minimally interferes with data presented on the luminance channel.

There are many perceptual factors to be considered in choosing a set of color labels.

1. **Distinctness.** A uniform color space, such as *CIEluv,* can be used to determine the degree of perceived difference between two colors that are placed close together. However, when we are concerned with the ability to *rapidly* distinguish a color from a set of other colors, different rules may apply. Bauer et al. (1996) showed that the target color should lie outside the convex hull of the surrounding colors in the CIE color space. This concept is illustrated in Figure 4.19. The issues related to coding for rapid target identification are discussed further in Chapter 5.

2. **Unique hues.** The unique hues, red, green, yellow, and blue, as well as black and white, are special in terms of the opponent process model. These colors are also special in the color vocabularies of the languages of the world. Clearly, these colors provide natural choices when a small set of color codes is required. In addition, work on

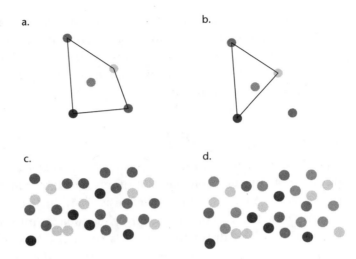

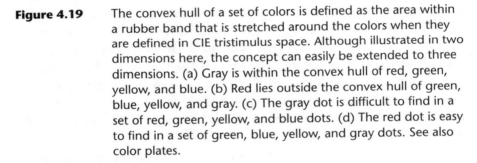

Figure 4.19   The convex hull of a set of colors is defined as the area within a rubber band that is stretched around the colors when they are defined in CIE tristimulus space. Although illustrated in two dimensions here, the concept can easily be extended to three dimensions. (a) Gray is within the convex hull of red, green, yellow, and blue. (b) Red lies outside the convex hull of green, blue, yellow, and gray. (c) The gray dot is difficult to find in a set of red, green, yellow, and blue dots. (d) The red dot is easy to find in a set of green, blue, yellow, and gray dots. See also color plates.

color confusion suggests that no two colors should be chosen from the same category, even through they may be relatively far apart in color space. We should avoid using multiple shades of green as codes, for example.

3. **Contrast with background.** In many displays, color-coded objects can be expected to appear on a variety of backgrounds. Simultaneous contrast with background colors can dramatically alter color appearance, making one color look like another. This is one reason why it is advisable to have only a small set of color codes. A method for reducing contrast effects is to place a thin white or black border around the color-coded object. This device is commonly used with signal lights; for example, train signals are displayed on large black background discs. In addition, we should never display codes using purely chromatic differences with the background. There should be a significant luminance difference in addition to the color difference.

4. Color blindness. Since there is a substantial color-blind population, it may be desirable to use colors that can be distinguished even by people who are color-blind. Recall that the majority of color-blind people cannot distinguish colors that differ in a red-green direction. Almost everyone can distinguish colors that vary in a yellow-blue direction, as shown in Figure 4.8. Unfortunately, this drastically reduces the design choices that are available.

5. Number. Although color coding is an excellent way of displaying category information, only a small number of codes can be rapidly perceived. Estimates vary between about five and ten codes (Healey, 1996).

6. Field size. Color-coded objects should not be very small; especially if the color differences are in a yellow-blue direction, at least half a degree of visual angle is probably a minimum size. Very small color-coded areas should not be used to avoid the small-field color blindness that is illustrated in Figure 4.9. In general, the larger the area that is color-coded, the more easily colors can be distinguished. Small objects that are color-coded should have strong, highly saturated colors for maximum discrimination. When large areas of color coding are used, for example, with map regions, the colors should be of low saturation and differ only slightly from one another. This enables small, vivid color-coded targets to be perceived against the background regions. When colors are used to highlight regions of black text, they should be light (minimum luminance contrast with the white paper) and also of low saturation (see Figure 4.20). This will minimize interference with the text.

7. Conventions. Color-coding conventions must sometimes be taken into account. Some common conventions are: red = hot, red = danger, blue = cold, green = life, green = go. However, it is important to keep in mind that these conventions do not necessarily cross cultural borders. In China, for example, red means life and good fortune, and green means death.

The following is a list of twelve colors recommended for use in coding. They are illustrated in Figure 4.21, and the reasons for choosing them are summarized below.

1. Red	**5.** Black	**9.** Gray
2. Green	**6.** White	**10.** Orange
3. Yellow	**7.** Pink	**11.** Brown
4. Blue	**8.** Cyan	**12.** Purple

```
import java.applet.Applet;
import java.awt.Graphics;
import java.awt.Color;

public class ColorText extends Applet
{
        public void init ( )
        {
            red = 100;
            green = 255;
            blue = 20;
        }

        public void paint (Graphics g)
        {
            Gr.setColor (new Color (red, green, blue));
            Gr.drawString ("Colored Text". 30, 50);
        }

        private int red;
        private int green;
        private int blue;

}
```

Figure 4.20   When large areas are color-coded, low-saturation light colors can be used on a white background. This interferes much less with detailed information in the text. See also color plates.

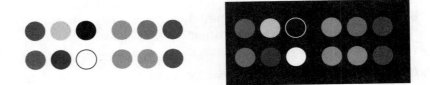

Figure 4.21   A set of twelve colors for use in labeling. The same colors are shown on a white and a black background. See also color plates.

These colors have widely agreed-upon category names and are reasonably far apart in color space. The first four colors, together with black and white, are chosen because they are the unique colors that mark the ends of the opponent color axes. The entire set corresponds to the eleven color names found to be the most common in the cross-cultural study carried out by Berlin and Kay, with the addition of cyan. The colors in the first set of six would normally be used before choosing any from the second set of six.

Application 3: Color Sequences for Maps

Pseudocoloring is the technique of representing continuously varying map values using a sequence of colors. Pseudocoloring is widely used for astronomical radiation charts, medical imaging, and many other scientific applications. For example, Figure 4.22 shows a map of gravitational variations over the North Atlantic, displayed with high-gravitation areas coded red and low-gravitation areas coded purple. Intermediate values are coded with a sequence of colors that roughly approximates the visible-light spectrum. Geographers use a well-defined color sequence to display height above sea level; lowlands are always green, which evokes images of vegetation, and the scale continues upward, through brown, to white at the peaks of mountains.

The most common coding scheme used by physicists is a color sequence that approximates the physical spectrum like that shown in Figure 4.22. Although this sequence has some useful properties, it is not a *perceptual* sequence. This can be demonstrated by the following test. Give subjects a series of gray paint chips and ask them to place these in order. They will happily comply with either a dark-to-light ordering or a light-to-dark ordering. Give the same subjects paint chips with the colors red, green, yellow, and blue and ask them to place them in order, and the result will be varied. For most people, the request will not seem particularly meaningful. They may even use an alphabetical ordering. This demonstrates that the whole spectrum is not perceptually ordered, although *parts* of it are. Figure 4.23 shows a

Figure 4.22   Gravitational variation over the North Atlantic is revealed using a spectrum-approximation pseudocolor sequence. See also color plates.

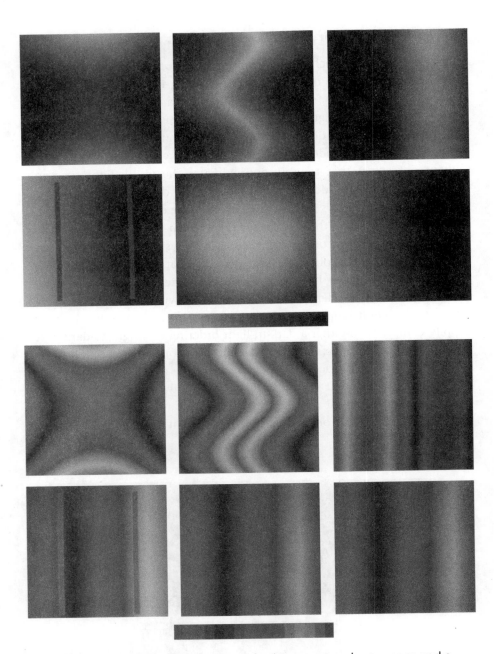

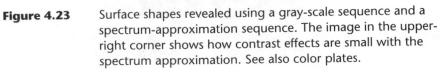

Figure 4.23   Surface shapes revealed using a gray-scale sequence and a spectrum-approximation sequence. The image in the upper-right corner shows how contrast effects are small with the spectrum approximation. See also color plates.

set of simple surface shapes displayed using both a spectrum approximation and a gray scale. As can be seen, where clearly identifiable ridges and valleys are perceived in the gray-scale version, only a set of stripes can be seen in the spectrum-approximation version. Thus, the spectrum pseudocolor sequence is not always a good way to reveal the form of a surface.

In pseudocoloring a map, there are generally two important issues. The first is perceiving the shape of features such as ridges, peaks, and valleys. The second is classification on the basis of color. A satellite image map might show wheat fields in green and forests in orange. It may be that wheat fields will be confused with hay fields, because they are a similar shade of green. In such cases, it is often useful to be able to read data values from the map using a map key. Unfortunately, it has been shown that errors resulting from simultaneous color and brightness contrast can be quite large in pseudocolored maps (Cleveland and McGill, 1983; Ware, 1988). We have shown (Ware, 1988) that if the spectrum-approximation sequence is used in a color sequence, the errors are smaller in magnitude. Thus, a sequence that is poor in revealing the form of the data is good in allowing values to be read from the map. We also obtained detailed evidence that the reason for the reduced errors with the spectrum sequence is that the contrast effects are more likely to cancel in the opponent channels.

What follows is a set of perceptual issues that are important when designing a pseudocolor sequence. Figure 4.24 shows a number of color sequences with different properties for you to consider while reading these guidelines.

- Some color sequences will not be perceived by people who suffer from the common forms of color blindness, protanopia and deuteranopia. Figure 4.24 shows some sequences that will be clear to these individuals. Meyer and Greenberg (1988) provide a detailed analysis of this problem.

- If a perceptually orderable sequence is required, a black-white, red-green, yellow-blue, or saturation (dull to vivid) sequence can be used. In general, a perceptually ordered sequence will result from a series of colors that monotonically increases or decreases with respect to one or more of the color opponent channels.

- Different sequences may be appropriate depending on the level of detail in the data. Rogowitz and Treinish (1996) suggest that when high levels of detail are to be displayed, the color sequence should be based mostly on luminance to take advantage of the capacity of

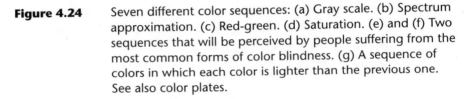

Figure 4.24   Seven different color sequences: (a) Gray scale. (b) Spectrum
approximation. (c) Red-green. (d) Saturation. (e) and (f) Two
sequences that will be perceived by people suffering from the
most common forms of color blindness. (g) A sequence of
colors in which each color is lighter than the previous one.
See also color plates.

this channel to convey high spatial frequencies. When there is little
detail, a chromatic sequence or a saturation sequence can be used.

- Uniform color spaces can be useful in generating color sequences
  (Robertson and O'Callaghan, 1988) in which equal perceptual steps
  correspond to equal metric steps. However, in some cases it may be
  desirable to deliberately exaggerate certain features in the data by
  using a perceptually nonuniform sequence (Guitard and Ware, 1990).

- When it is important to be able to read values back using a color
  key, the best color sequence for mimimizing errors due to contrast
  effect will be one that cycles through many colors; in this way, contrast effects will cancel each other.

- In many cases, the best color sequence may be a spiral in color
  space. The sequence can vary through a range of colors, but with
  each successive hue chosen to have higher luminance than the previous one (Ware, 1988). This may have the best characteristics both
  for perception of forms (because of the monotonically increasing
  luminance) and in terms of contrast errors (because the cyclic

pattern in color space reduces these effects). Figure 4.25 gives an example using the same gravity data displayed in Figure 4.22.

- Even if colors are created in a continuous, smooth sequence, we tend to perceive such a sequence as a set of discrete colors placed in order. This may be useful, but depending on where the color category boundaries occur, it may also lead us to miscategorize data.

- Since color is three-dimensional, it is possible to display two or even three dimensions using pseudocoloring. Indeed, this is commonly done in the case of satellite images, in which invisible parts of the spectrum are mapped to the red, green, and blue monitor primaries. Robertson and O'Callaghan (1986) discuss how uniform color spaces can be used to create optimally distinct bivariate coding schemes. However, it should be noted that bivariate color maps may be difficult to read (Wainer and Francolini, 1980), although they are effective for visual discrimination of regions.

- Pseudocoloring is only one way of revealing the shapes of surfaces. Often, shading the surface with an artificial light source using standard computer graphics techniques is a better alternative. Using shading to reveal map data is discussed in Chapter 7. Using shading in combination with chromatic pseudocoloring is often an effective way of revealing bivariate surfaces.

Figure 4.25   The same data shown in Figure 4.22, pseudocolored with a sequence that provides a kind of upward spiral in color space; each color is lighter than the preceding one. See also color plates.

Application 4: Color Reproduction

The problem of color reproduction is essentially one of transferring color appearances from one display device, such as a computer monitor, to another device, such as a sheet of paper. Because the colors that can be reproduced on a sheet of paper depend on such factors as illumination color and intensity, and because not all monitor colors can be reproduced within the range of printing inks, it is neither possible nor meaningful to reproduce colors directly using a standard measurement system such as the CIE *XYZ* tristimulus values.

As we have discussed, the visual system is built to perceive relationships between colors rather than absolute values. For this reason, the solution to the color reproduction problem lies in preserving the color relationships insofar as is possible, not the absolute values. It is also important to preserve the white point in some way, because of the role of white as a reference in judging other colors.

Stone et al. (1988) describe a process of gamut mapping designed to preserve color appearance in a transformation between one device and another. The set of all colors that can be produced by a device is called the gamut of that device. The gamut of a monitor is larger than that of a color printer, as shown in Figure 4.7. Stone et al. describe the following set of heuristic principles to create a good mapping from one device to another:

- The gray axis of the image should be preserved. What is perceived as white on a monitor should become whatever color is perceived as white on paper.
- Maximum luminance contrast (black to white) is desirable.
- Few colors should lie outside the destination gamut.
- Hue and saturation shifts should be minimized.
- An increase of color saturation is preferable to a decrease.

Figure 4.26 illustrates, in two dimensions, what is in fact a three-dimensional set of geometric transformations designed to accomplish the principles of gamut mapping. In this example, the process is a transformation from a monitor image to a paper hardcopy, but the same principles and methods apply to transformations between other devices.

1. **Calibration:** The first step is to calibrate the monitor and the printing device in a common reference system. Both can be characterized in terms of CIE tristimulus values. The calibration of the color printer must assume a particular illuminant.

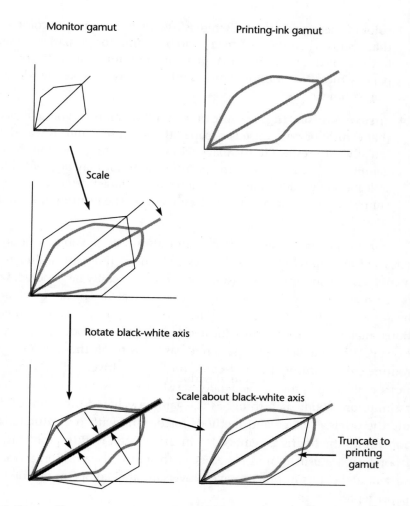

Figure 4.26   Illustration of the basic geometric operations in gamut mapping between devices as defined by Stone et al. (1988).

2. **Range scaling:** To equate the luminance range of the source and destination images, the monitor gamut is scaled about the origin until the white of the monitor has the same luminance as the white of the paper on the target printer.

3. **Rotation:** What we perceive as neutral white on the monitor and on the printed paper can be very different depending on the illumination. In general, in a printed image, the white is defined by the

color of the paper. Monitor white is usually defined by the color that results when the red, green, and blue monitor primaries are set to their maximum values. To equate the monitor white with the paper white, the monitor gamut is rotated so as to make the white axes collinear.

4. **Saturation scaling:** Because on a monitor colors can be achieved that cannot be reproduced on paper, the monitor gamut is scaled radially with respect to the black-white axis to bring the monitor gamut within the range of the printing gamut. It may be preferable to leave a few colors outside the range of the target device and simply truncate them to the nearest color on the printing-ink gamut boundary.

For a number of reasons, it may not always be possible to apply these rules automatically. Different images may have different scaling requirements; some may consist of pastel colors that can easily be handled, whereas others may have vivid colors that must be truncated. The approach adopted by Stone et al. is to design a set of tools that support the above transformations, making it easy for an educated technician to produce a good result. However, this elaborate process is not feasible with off-the-shelf printers and routine color printing. In these cases, the printer drivers will contain heuristics designed to produce generally satisfactory results. They will contain assumptions about such things as the gamma value of the monitor displaying the original image and methods for dealing with oversaturated colors. Sometimes the heuristics embedded in devices can lead to problems. In our laboratory, we usually find it necessary to start a visualization process with very muted colors in order to avoid oversaturated colors on videotape or in paper reproduction.

Another issue that is important in color reproduction is the ability of the output device to display smooth color changes. The visual system tends to amplify small artificial boundaries in smooth gradients of color. This sensitivity makes it difficult to display smoothly shaded images without artifacts. Because most output devices cannot reproduce the 16 million colors that can be created with a monitor, considerable effort has gone into techniques for generating a pattern of color dots to create the overall impression of a smooth color change. Making the dots look random is important to avoid aliasing artifacts (discussed in Chapter 2). Unless care is taken, artifacts of color reproduction can produce spurious patterns in scientific images.

Application 5: Color for Exploring Multidimensional Discrete Data

An interesting use of computer graphics is the task of exploratory data analysis. Visualization is a powerful tool in data mining, in which the problem is often a kind of general search for relationships and data trends. Sometimes a scientist or a data analyst approaches data with no particular theory to test. The goal is to explore the data for meaningful and useful information in masses of mostly meaningless numbers. Plotting techniques have long been tools of the data explorer. In essence, the process is to plot the data, look for a pattern, and interpret the findings. Thus, the critical step in the discovery process is an act of perception. For example, the four scatter plots in Figure 4.27 illustrate very different kinds of data relationships. In the first, there are two distinct clusters, perhaps suggesting distinct subpopulations of biological organisms. In the second, there is a clear negative linear relationship between two measured variables. In the third, there is a curvilinear relationship. In the fourth, there is an abrupt discontinuity. Each of these patterns will lead to a very different hypothesis about underlying causal relationships between variables. If any of the relationships were previously unknown, the researcher will be rewarded with a discovery.

Problems can arise in exploring data when more than two dimensions of data are to be displayed. It is possible to extend the scatter plot to three dimensions using the techniques for providing strong 3D spatial information, such as stereoscopic displays (see Chapter 8). What do we do, though, about data with more than three dimensions? For example, marketing experts often collect large amounts of data about individuals in potential

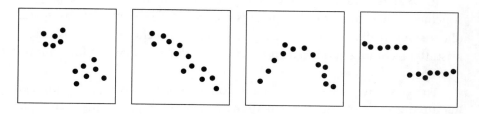

Figure 4.27   Visual exploratory data analysis techniques involve representing data graphically in order to understand relationships between data variables.

target populations. The variables that are collected might include age, income, educational level, employment category, tendency to purchase chocolate, and so on. If the marketer can identify a particular cluster of values in this population that are related to the likelihood of purchasing a product, this can result in better-targeted, more effective advertising. Each of the measured variables can be thought of as a data dimension. The task of finding particular market segments is one of finding distinct clusters in the multidimensional space that is formed by these many variables.

One solution for multidimensional data display is the generalized drafter's plot (Chambers et al., 1983). (See Figure 4.28(a).) In this technique, all pairs of variables are used to create two-dimensional scatter plots. Although the generalized drafter's plot can often be useful, it suffers from a disadvantage: It is very difficult to see data patterns that are present only when three or more data dimensions are taken into account.

Color mapping can be used to extend the number of displayable data dimensions to five or six in a single scatter plot, as shown in Figure 4.28(b). We developed a simple scheme for doing this (Ware and Beatty, 1988). The technique is to create a scatter plot in which each point is a colored patch rather than a black point on a white background. Up to five data variables can be mapped and displayed as follows:

Variable 1 → *x*-axis position

Variable 2 → *y*-axis position

Variable 3 → amount of red

Variable 4 → amount of green

Variable 5 → amount of blue

In a careful evaluation of cluster perception in this kind of display, we concluded that color display dimensions could be as effective as spatial dimensions in allowing the visual system to perceive clusters. For this task, at least, the technique produced an effective five-dimensional window into the data space.

There is a negative aspect of the color-mapped scatter plot. Although identifying clusters and other patterns can be easy using this technique, interpreting them can be difficult. A cluster may appear greenish because it is low on the red variable rather than high on the green variable. The use of color can help us identify the presence of multidimensional clusters and

a.

b.

c.

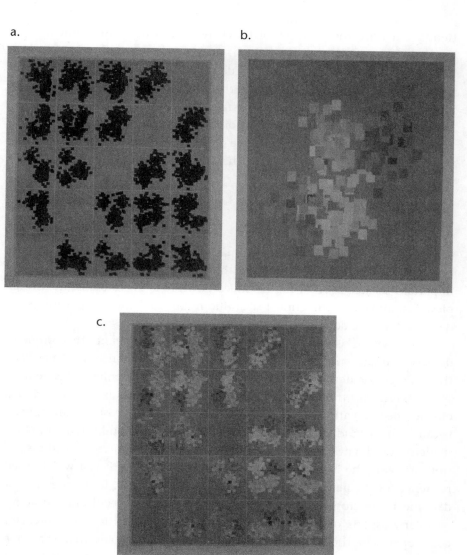

Figure 4.28   Five-dimensional data is presented in a generalized drafter's plot. (a) Without color dimension mapping. (b) A scatter plot with color dimension mapping. (c) The generalized drafter's plot can also be enhanced with color mapping. See also color plates.

trends, but once the presence of these trends has been ascertained, other methods are needed to analyze them. An obvious solution is to map data variables to the color opponent axes described earlier. However, our experiments with this practice showed us that the results were still not easy to interpret and that it was difficult to make efficient use of the color space.

Adding color is by no means the only way of extending a scatter plot to multiple dimensions, though it is one of the best techniques. In Chapter 5, we will consider other methods, which use shape and motion.

Conclusion

Color is a very broad topic. It encompasses a wide range of issues, from the physics of light to the esthetics of the artist. Nevertheless, much of the important science of color can be boiled down to a few fundamental principles. A summary of the critical scientific results and their implications for data display concludes this chapter.

Color vision is fundamentally three-dimensional, and this property derives ultimately from the three cone receptor types in our retinas. The three-dimensional nature of color is the basis of all color measurement systems; it means that just three numbers can be used to define a color. This chapter began with a brief introduction to color measurement theory, because understanding the CIE *XYZ* tristimulus system and the use of chromaticity coordinates is one of the basic tools needed for an informed discussion of color. The importance of the CIE system is that it is a widely used reference for the measurement and calibration of devices. It provides a standard means for cross-referencing the many other color specification systems.

Many aspects of color appearance can be explained in the context of color opponent theory. This well-established theory holds that the cone signals are transformed by neural mechanisms into three color opponent channels: a black-white channel (also called luminance), a red-green channel, and a yellow-blue channel. Sometimes the red-green and yellow-blue channels are called chromatic channels, to indicate their qualitative differences from the luminance channel.

The luminance and chromatic channels have very different properties. Luminance channel information dominates our perception of shape, space, and motion. It is essential that good luminance contrast be available in an image for any of these to be seen clearly. Luminance contrast is especially important when we are interpreting detailed information, especially small text. The chromatic channels have much lower spatial resolution and seem to be most useful for telling us about the surfaces of objects. The special nature of the colors red, green, yellow, blue, black, and white can be explained by opponent channel theory.

There are two very different classes of applications in which the use of color is important: those in which a small number of colors are needed and those in which many colors are needed. The color coding of graphical objects belongs in the first category. We can only use between six and twelve color codes reliably. This results partly from contrast effects that can alter the appearance of colors. As a rule, high-saturation colors should be used for labeling small objects and low-saturation colors should be used for labeling large areas.

The brain can distinguish among several million colors under optimal viewing conditions, and sometimes large numbers of colors are necessary because of this. The high-quality reproduction of smoothly varying colored images is one example. If not enough colors are available, discrete steps appear in parts of an image that should be smooth, and these artifacts can lead to errors of interpretation. Another application in which the availability of many colors is important is creating an enhanced scatter plot. In this case, one or more data variables are mapped to the colors of a set of enlarged data points. This enables us to see clusters and correlations that exist in a data space with as many as five dimensions. A third application involving the use of many colors is pseudocoloring data maps. When we are choosing a good pseudocolor sequence, it is better that a luminance variation be added to the chromatic variation in a color sequence, unless the data shows only low-frequency spatial variation.

There is much more to say about color than has been covered in this chapter. Chapter 5 places color in the context of methods for attracting attention and coding information. Other discussions related to the use of color are scattered through the remaining chapters.

Visual Attention and Information That Pops Out

Consider the eyeball as an information-gathering searchlight, sweeping the visual world under the guidance of the cognitive centers that control our attention. Information is acquired in bursts, a snapshot for each fixation. From an image buffer, the massively parallel machinery of early visual processing finds objects based on salient features of images. Once identified, complex objects are scanned in series, one after another, in a much slower process. Understanding the steps in this process can help us with many visualization tasks. Here are some examples.

Often a computer program should attract the user's attention. For example, most people sometimes want to be interrupted when an important email arrives. Such a user interruption is often achieved using sound, but it may also be accomplished visually.

A tactical map display used by a military strategist must simultaneously show many different kinds of information about resources, such as equipment and personnel, and environmental conditions that exist in the field.

151

Ideally, with such a display it should be possible either to attend to a single aspect of the data, such as the deployment of tanks, or, by an act of visual attention, to perceive the whole complex interwoven pattern. Understanding early vision is critical in understanding how to make information visually distinct or to make the integrated patterns stand out.

In a scatter plot, each plotted data point can be made to represent many different kinds of information by using a *glyph* instead of an undifferentiated circle. A glyph is a graphical object designed to convey multiple data values. For information about stocks on the stock exchange, the color of an information glyph might be used to show the price-to-earnings ratio, the size of the glyph to display the growth trend, and the shape of the glyph to represent the type of company—square for technology stocks, round for resources, and so on. But what makes a glyph stand out if it is displayed in this way? Such a graphical tool will only be useful if the interesting stocks can be made to stand out and catch the analyst's eye.

Visual search provides one of the great benefits of visualization. It is possible, in less than a second, to detect a single dark pixel in a 500-×-500 array of white pixels. This screen can be replaced every second by another, enabling a search of more than 15 million pixels in a minute. Clearly, this is an artificial example, since most search tasks are more complex. But it does highlight the incredible search capacity of the visual system. This chapter is about searching for, and rapidly identifying, information. A large body of vision research is related to this problem and in many cases this information can be translated, in a fairly direct way, into design guidelines for data visualization. We start by considering the eye movements controlled by the searchlight of attention.

Eye Movements

We constantly make eye movements to seek information. Moving our eyes causes different parts of the visual environment to be imaged on the high-resolution fovea, where we can see detail. These movements are frequent. For example, as you read this page, your eye is making between two and five jerky movements, called *saccades,* per second.

Here are the basic statistics describing three important types of eye movement.

1. **Saccadic movements** In a visual search, task the eye moves rapidly from fixation to fixation. The dwell period is generally between 200 and 600 msec and the saccade takes between 20 and 100 msec. The peak velocity of a saccade can be as much as 900 deg/sec (Hallett, P. E., 1986; Barfield et al., 1995).

2. **Smooth-pursuit movements** When an object is moving smoothly in the visual field, the eye has the ability to lock onto it and track it. This is called a smooth-pursuit eye movement. This ability also enables us to make head and body movements while maintaining fixation on an object of interest.

3. **Convergent movements** When an object moves toward us, our eyes converge. When it moves away, they diverge. Convergent movements can be either saccadic or smooth.

Saccadic eye movements are said to be *ballistic*. This means that once the brain decides to switch attention and make an eye movement, first the muscle signals for accelerating and decelerating the eye are programmed, and then the program is run to make the eye movement. The movement cannot be adjusted in mid-saccade. During the course of a saccadic eye movement, we are less sensitive to visual input than we normally are. This is called *saccadic suppression* (Riggs et al., 1974). The implication is that certain kinds of events can easily be missed if they occur while we happen to be moving our eyes. This is important when we consider the problem of alerting a computer operator to some event. Another implication of saccadic suppression is that it is reasonable to think of information coming into the visual system as a series of discrete snapshots. The brain is often processing rapid sequences of discrete images. This is a capacity that is being increasingly exploited in television advertising, in which several cuts per second of video have become commonplace.

Accommodation

When the eye moves to a new target, at a different distance from the observer, it must refocus, or *accommodate,* so that the target is clearly imaged on the retina. An accommodation response typically takes about 200 msec. The mechanisms controlling accommodation and convergent eye movements are neurologically coupled, and this can cause problems with virtual-reality displays. This problem is discussed in Chapter 8.

Visual Attention, Searching, and System Monitoring

Visual attention is largely tied to eye movements: We attend to what we fixate. Indeed, to do otherwise seems rather sneaky. We think of spies at spy school learning to attend to events out of the corners of their eyes.

Eye Movements, Attention, and the Useful Field of View

A searchlight is a useful metaphor for describing the interrelationship among eye movements, visual attention, and the useful field of view. In this metaphor, visual attention is like a searchlight used to seek information. We point our eyes at the things we want to attend to. The diameter of the searchlight beam (measured as a visual angle) describes the useful field of view. The direction of the searchlight beam is controlled by eye movements. Figure 5.1 illustrates the searchlight model of attention. (To avoid confusion, we must note at this point that there is another searchlight model that describes the scanning for visual objects independent of eye movements.)

Supervisory Control

The searchlight model has been developed mainly in the context of supervisory control systems to account for the way people scan instrument panels. *Supervisory control* is a term used for complex semiautonomous systems that are only indirectly controlled by human operators. Examples are sophisticated aircraft and power stations. In these systems, the operator has both a monitoring and a controlling role. Since the consequences of making an error during an emergency can be truly catastrophic, a good interface design is critical. Two Airbus passenger jets have crashed for reasons that are attributed to mistaken assumptions about the behavior of supervisory control systems (Casey, 1993). In some cases, operators of power grids have made the situation worse through inappropriate actions or lack of action. There are stories of pilots in fighter aircraft turning warning lights off because they are unable to concentrate in a tense situation.

A number of aspects of visual attention are related to supervisory control. One is creating effective ways for a computer to gain the attention

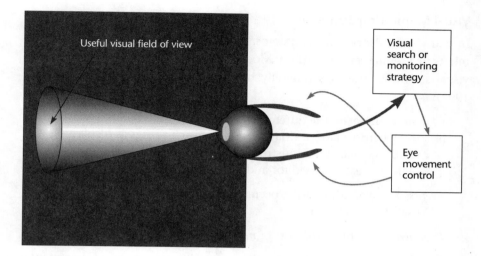

Figure 5.1　　　The searchlight model. The useful visual field of view depends on the area scanned. A visual search or monitoring strategy is used to guide eye movements that bring different areas into this region.

of a human—a human-interrupt signal. Sometimes a computer must alert the operator with a warning of some kind, or it must draw the operator's attention to a routine change of status. In other cases, it is important for an operator to become aware of *patterns* of events. For example, on a power grid, certain combinations of component failures can be indicative of a wider problem. Since the display panels for power grids can be very large, this may require the synthesis of widely separated visual information.

In many ways, the ordinary computer interface is becoming more like a supervisory control system. The user is typically involved in some foreground task, such as composing an email message, but at the same time this user may be monitoring activities occurring in other parts of the screen. The most common need for a user interrupt is email; as we have mentioned, some users like to be told unobtrusively that new mail has arrived. Another interrupt, which may soon become common, is the Internet search agent, having been hard at work searching for information on the Web, reporting back to a human user for further instruction.

Visual Monitoring Strategies

In many supervisory control systems, operators must monitor a set of instruments in a semirepetitive pattern. Models developed to account for operators' visual scanning strategies generally have the following elements (Wickens, 1992):

> *Channels:* These are the different ways in which the operator can receive information. Channels can be such things as display windows, dials on an instrument panel, or nonvisual inputs, such as speakers (used for auditory warnings).

> *Events:* These are the signals occurring on channels that provide useful information.

> *Expected Cost:* This is the cost of *missing* an event.

System operators base their monitoring of different channels on a mental model of system event probabilities and the expected costs of these (Moray and Rotenberg, 1989; Wickens, 1992). Charbonnell et al. (1968) and Sheridan (1972) proposed that monitoring behavior is controlled by two factors: the growth of uncertainty in the state of a channel (between samples) and the cost of sampling a channel. Sampling a channel involves fixating part of a display and extracting the useful information. The cost of sampling is inversely proportional to the ease with which the display can be interpreted. This model has been successfully applied by Charbonnell et al. (1968) to the fixation patterns of pilots making an instrument landing. A number of other factors may influence visual scanning patterns:

- Users may minimize eye movements. The cost of sampling is reduced if the points to be sampled are spatially close. Russo and Rosen (1975) found that subjects tended to make comparisons most often between spatially adjacent data (representing factors influencing decisions as to the most desirable car to purchase). If two indicators are within the same effective field of view, this tendency will be especially advantageous.

- There can be oversampling of channels on which infrequent information appears (Moray, 1981). This can be accounted for by short-term memory limitations. Human working memory has very limited capacity, and it requires significant cognitive effort to keep a particular task in mind. People can reliably monitor an information channel every minute or so, but they are much less reliable when asked to monitor an event every 20 minutes. One design solution is to build in visual or auditory reminders at appropriate intervals.

- Sometimes operators exhibit dysfunctional behaviors in high-stress situations. Moray and Rotenberg (1989) suggested that under crisis conditions, operators cease monitoring some channels altogether. In an examination of control-room emergency behavior, he found that under certain circumstances an operator's fixation became locked on a feedback indicator, waiting for a system response at the expense of taking other, more pressing actions. This is understandable; when a system is falling apart, operators naturally want to know for certain that actions they are taking are having some effect.

- Sometimes operators exhibit systematic scan patterns, such as the left-to-right, top-to-bottom one found in reading, even if these have no functional relevance to the task (Megaw and Richardson, 1979).

The Useful Field of View

Although the searchlight model is conceptually simple, it hides considerable complexity in the definition of the size of the searchlight beam. When we are reading fine print, we can read the words only at the exact point of fixation. But we can take in the overall shape of a larger pattern at a single glance. In the former case, the searchlight beam is as narrow as the fovea, whereas in the latter it is much wider. A concept called the *useful field of view* (UFOV) has been developed to define the size of the region from which we can rapidly take in information.

One design strategy that is implied by the UFOV concept is simply to scale down the display, thereby getting more information into the UFOV of the operator. However, in practice this does not work. The useful visual field varies greatly depending on the task and the information being displayed. Experiments using displays densely populated with targets reveal small UFOVs, from 1 to 4 degrees of visual angle (Wickens, 1992). But Drury and Clement (1978) have shown that for low character densities (less than one per degree of visual angle), the useful visual field can be as large as 15 degrees. Roughly, the UFOV varies with target density to maintain a constant number of targets in the attended region. With greater target density, the UFOV becomes smaller and attention is more narrowly focused; with a low target density, a larger area can be attended to.

Tunnel Vision and Stress

A phenomenon known as tunnel vision has been associated with operators working under extreme stress. In tunnel vision, the UFOV is narrowed so that only the most important information, normally at the center of the field of view, is processed. This phenomenon has been specifically associated with various kinds of nonfunctional behaviors that occur during problem handling in disaster situations. The effect can be demonstrated quite simply. Williams (1985) compared performance on a task that required intense concentration (high foveal load) to one that was simpler. The high-load task involved naming a letter drawn from six alternatives; the low-load task involved naming a letter drawn from two alternatives. There was a dramatic drop in performance, from 75% to 36% as load increased, when subjects were asked to respond to events occurring in the periphery of the visual field. The Williams data shows that we should not think of tunnel vision as strictly a response to disaster. It may generally be the case that as cognitive load goes up, the UFOV shrinks.

The Role of Motion in Attracting Attention

A study by Peterson and Dugas (1972) suggests that the useful visual field function can be far larger for detection of moving targets than for detection of static targets. They showed that subjects can respond in less than 1 second to targets 20 degrees from the line of sight, if they are moving. If static targets are used, performance falls off rapidly beyond about 4 degrees from fixation. (See Figure 5.2.) This implies a useful field of view at least 40 degrees across for the moving-targets task. However, this was merely the largest field that was measured. There is every reason to suppose that the useful visual field for moving targets is even larger; it may well encompass the entire visual field.

In real-time monitoring situations, it is important to consider how to attract a computer user's attention to events. Often a user is busy with a primary task, perhaps filling out forms, sending email, or interpreting incoming information, while at the same time events may be signaled on other parts of the display, demanding attention. For example, there may be an incoming message from a valued customer, a signal from a computer "agent" that has been out searching the Internet for information on visualization techniques, or an indication that a major computational task has been completed. As we have mentioned, we call this kind of message a "user interrupt" (Ware et al., 1992).

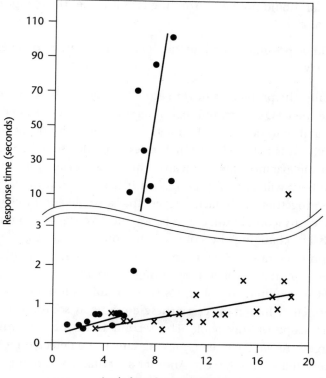

Figure 5.2　　Results of a study by Peterson and Dugas (1972). The task was to detect small symbols representing aircraft in a simulation display. The circles show the response times from the appearances of static targets. The crosses show response times from the appearances of moving targets. Note the two different scales.

There are four basic visual requirements for a user interrupt:

- A signal should be easily perceived even if it is outside of the area of immediate focal attention.

- If the user wishes to ignore the event while attending to another task, the signal should continue to remind the user that the event needs attention.

- The signal should not be so irritating that it makes the computer unpleasant to use.

- It should be possible to endow the signal with a variety of levels of urgency.

Essentially, the problem is how to attract the user's attention to information outside the UFOV. For a number of reasons, the options are limited. We have a low ability to detect small targets in the periphery of the visual field. Peripheral vision is color-blind, which rules out color signals. Saccadic suppression during eye movements means that some transitory event occurring in the periphery will generally be missed if it occurs during an eye movement. Taken together, these facts suggest that a single abrupt change in the appearance of an icon is unlikely to be an effective signal. Common examples of this are changing the color of an icon and causing the flag on a mailbox icon to be raised. Such events are likely to be missed unless the user includes the icon in an explicit monitoring schedule.

This set of requirements suggests two possible solutions. The first is to use auditory cues. In certain cases these are a good solution, but they are beyond the scope of this book. The second is to use blinking lights or moving targets. As we have seen, moving targets are detected more easily in the periphery than static targets. Another advantage of moving or blinking signals is that they can be persistent, unlike an instantaneous change in an icon, such as the raising of a mailbox flag, which will rapidly fade from attention. In a study that measured the eye movements made while viewing multimedia presentations, Faraday and Sutcliffe (1997) found that the onset of motion of an object generally produced a shift of attention to that object. They suggested that object motion can be effectively used to control attention and viewing order.

In a study involving shipboard alarm systems, Goldstein and Lamb (1967) showed that subjects were capable of distinguishing five flash patterns with approximately 98% reliability and that they responded with an average delay of approximately 2.0 seconds. Anecdotal evidence indicates that a possible disadvantage of flashing lights or blinking cursors is that users find them to be irritating.

To evaluate simple motion as a human interrupt, we (Ware et al., 1992) studied the use of icons that moved smoothly up and down to signal a background event requiring attention. Subjects were required to carry out the primary task of transcribing a document. What they typed appeared in a central window in the lower half of the screen. A secondary task was to monitor two icons and make a simple response when either started to move. Each icon consisted of a small vertical bar, which grew taller and shorter. In general, the results confirmed the utility of moving targets. When the target moved fast (48 mm per second), the mean response time was slightly under 2 seconds. When the target moved slowly (3 mm per second), the mean response time was more than 5 seconds. In addition, the response distribution was highly skewed, especially with the slowly moving targets. The probability of detecting the interrupt signal was highest in the first 4 seconds and became less and less likely in each successive time interval. In this study, we also gathered anecdotal evidence about the effectiveness of motion and came to the conclusion that degree of urgency could be effectively coded using motion velocity. A rapidly oscillating target is hard to ignore, and therefore demands immediate attention, while a slowly moving target can be ignored for a while.

Interestingly, more recent work has suggested that it may not be motion *per se* that attracts attention, but rather the *appearance* of a new object in the visual field (Hillstrom and Yantis, 1994). This seems right: After all, we are not constantly distracted in an environment of swaying trees or people moving about on a dance floor. It also makes ecological sense: When early man was outside a cave, intently chipping a lump of flint into a hand ax, or when early woman was gathering roots out on the grassland, awareness of emerging objects in the periphery of vision would have had clear survival value. Such a movement might signal an imminent attack of some kind. Of course, the evolutionary advantage goes back much further than this. Monitoring the periphery of vision for moving predators or prey would provide a survival advantage for most animals. Thus, the most effective reminder might be an object that moves into view, disappears, and then reappears every so often. Serendipitously, the icon that we designed for our experiment had somewhat similar properties. Since only the top of the bar moved up and down, it too had the property of appearing and disappearing.

Unfortunately, many Web page designers generate a kind of animated chart junk: Small animations with no functional purpose are often used to "jazz up" a page. The presence of these superfluous distractions interferes with our ability to make effective use of moving interrupts.

Reading from the Iconic Buffer

Figure 5.3 shows a collection of miscellaneous symbols. If we briefly flash such a collection of symbols on a screen—say, for one-tenth of a second—and then ask people to name as many of the symbols as they can, they typically produce a list of between three and seven items. There appears to be a short-lived visual buffer that allows us to hold the image for a second or two while we read the symbols into our short-term memory. We can get up to about seven before we run out of working memory capacity. This visual buffer is called iconic memory. Its properties were first described in a classic paper by Sperling (1960). See Humphreys and Bruce (1989) for a review. The limitation of seven items comes from three sources. The first is the decay of the iconic image. The second has to do with the rate at which items can be read from the visual buffer. The third is the capacity of short-term (working) memory, which can hold about seven items. For the task of counting the objects in a briefly presented display, the time is about 275 msec per item (Anderson et al., 1997).

This is an artificial example, but it has to do with a process that is very general. In each fixation between saccadic eye movements, an image of the world is captured. From each snapshot image of the world, the brain must identify objects, match them with objects previously perceived, and take information into working memory for symbolic analysis.

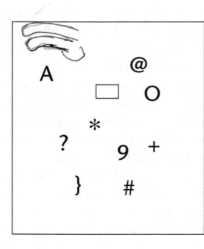

Figure 5.3   How many of these symbols can you remember after a glimpse one-tenth of a second long?

In the preceding sections, we have outlined a process whereby visual information is acquired by first pointing the fovea at regions of the visual field that are interesting, then using a scanning process whereby objects are read from an image buffer for more extensive processing. A useful model that integrates eye movements with cognitive task processing has been developed by Kieras and Mayer (1997). This can be used to predict quite accurately how long it will take to carry out tasks such as menu selection or scanning a display with well-defined layout and task requirements. The architecture of this model is given in Chapter 10 as a basis for a higher-level understanding of the interactive process of data visualization.

Pre-attentive Processing

We can do certain things to symbols to make it much more likely that they will be visually identified even after very brief exposure. Certain simple shapes or colors "pop out" from their surroundings. The theoretical mechanism underlying pop-out is called pre-attentive processing because logically it must occur prior to conscious attention. In essence, pre-attentive processing determines what visual objects are offered up to our attention. An understanding of what is processed pre-attentively is probably the most important contribution that vision science can make to data visualization.

Pre-attentive processing is best introduced with an example. To count the 3s in the table of digits given below, it is necessary to scan all the numbers sequentially.

```
8568972698468976268976435892226598659865548976892698988
0246299687402655762798678904567923276928546098677209
9083457980279075904709827908579084772908759082790875
9870985674906897578625984569024379047219079070981145
8568972698468976268976445892226598659865548976892698988
```

To count the **3**s in the next table, it is necessary only to scan the black digits. This is because lightness is pre-attentively processed.

```
856897269846897626897643589222659865986554897689269898
024629968740265576279867890456792327692854609867720
9083457980279075904709827908579084772908759082790875
987098567490689757862598456902437904721907907098114
8568972698468976268976445892226598659865548976892698988
```

The typical experiment that is conducted to find out whether something is pre-attentively processed involves measuring the response time to find a target in a set of "distractors"; for example, finding the 3s in a set of other numbers. If processing is pre-attentive, the time taken to find the target should be independent of the number of distractors. Thus, if time to find the target is plotted against number of distractors, the result should be a horizontal line. Figure 5.4 illustrates a typical pattern of results. The circles illustrate data from a visual target that is pre-attentively different from the distractors. The time taken to detect whether there is a dark digit in the array of digits shown above is independent of the number of gray digits. The Xs in Figure 5.4 show the results from processing a feature that is not pre-attentive. The time to respond depends on the number of distractors. The results of this kind of experiment are not always as perfectly clean-cut as Figure 5.4 would

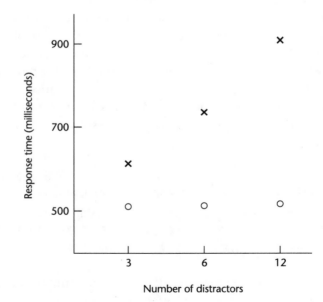

Figure 5.4   Typical results from a study of pre-attentive processing. The circles show time to perceive an object that is pre-attentively distinct from its surroundings. Time to process is independent of the number of irrelevant objects (distractors). The Xs show how time to process non-pre-attentively distinct targets depends on the number of distractors.

suggest. Sometimes there is a small, but still measurable, slope in the case of a feature that is thought to be pre-attentive. As a rule of thumb, anything that is processed at a rate that is faster than 10 msec per item is considered to be pre-attentive. Typical processing rates for non-pre-attentive features are 40 msec per item and more (Triesman and Gormican, 1988).

Why is this important? In displaying information, it is often useful to be able to show things "at a glance." If you want people to be able to instantaneously identify some mark on a map as being of type A, it should be differentiated from all other marks in a pre-attentive way.

There have been literally hundreds of experiments to test whether various kinds of features are processed pre-attentively. Figure 5.5 illustrates a few of the results: Orientation, size, basic shape, convexity, concavity, and an added box around an object are all pre-attentively processed. However, the junction of two lines is not pre-attentively processed; nor is the parallelism of pairs of lines, so it is harder to find the targets in the last two boxes in Figure 5.5.

The reason that pre-attentive processing has attracted so much attention among researchers is that it is thought to be a way of measuring the primitive features that are extracted in early visual processing (Triesman and Gormican, 1988). However, there is a risk of misinterpreting the findings of such studies. To take a single example, curved lines can be pre-attentively distinguished from straight lines. Despite this, it may be a mistake to think that there are curved-line detectors in early vision. It may simply be the case that cells responsive to long, straight line segments will not be strongly excited by the curved lines. Of course, it may actually be that early-vision curvature detectors do exist; it is just that the evidence must be carefully weighed. It is not a good idea to propose a new class of detector for everything that exhibits the pop-out effect. The scientific principle of finding the most parsimonious explanation (known as Occam's razor) applies here.

The features that are pre-attentively processed can be organized into a number of categories based on form, color, motion, and spatial position.

Form

- Line orientation
- Line length
- Line width
- Line collinearity
- Size
- Curvature
- Spatial grouping
- Added marks
- Numerosity

Color

- Hue
- Intensity

Motion

- Flicker
- Direction of motion

Spatial Position

- 2D position
- Stereoscopic depth
- Convex/concave shape from shading

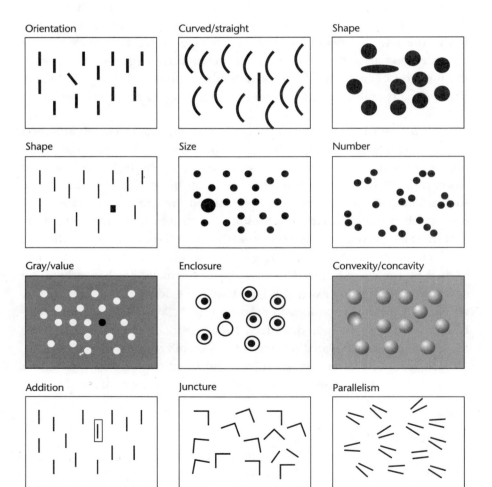

Figure 5.5   Most of the differences shown above are pre-attentively distinguished. Only juncture and parallelism are not.

The results of pre-attentive processing experiments can be directly applied in the design of symbols for information display. In some cases, it may be desirable that each of many symbols be pre-attentively distinct from all the others. For example, in the case of a map of the ocean environment, we might wish to be able to visually scan only for the scallop beds, only for the fish farms, only for the cod schools, or only for the fishing boats, assuming that we had all of this data. To make this possible, each type of symbol should be pre-attentively distinct from the others.

Figure 5.6 shows a set of seven symbols designed so that each of them is pre-attentively different from the others. The set can be easily extended—for example, by using blink coding, color coding, or motion coding, which are all pre-attentive. One thing that is clear from a cursory look at this example is that pre-attentive symbols become less distinct as the *variety* of distractors increases. It is easy to spot a single hawk in a sky full of pigeons, but if the sky contains a greater variety of birds, the hawk will be more difficult to see. A number of studies have shown that the immediacy of any pre-attentive cue declines as the variety of alternative patterns increases, even if all the distracting patterns are individually distinct from the target. For example, Chau and Yeh (1995) showed that segregation by stereoscopic depth decreased as the number of depth layers increased.

It is natural to ask which visual dimensions are pre-attentively stronger and therefore more salient. Unfortunately, this question cannot be answered, because it always depends on the strength of the particular feature and the context. For example, Callaghan (1989) compared color to orientation as a pre-attentive cue. The results showed that the pre-attentive strength of the

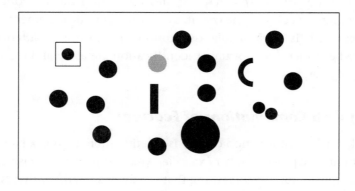

Figure 5.6   A set of symbols in which each of the seven symbol types is pre-attentively distinct from all the others.

color depended on the saturation (vividness) and size of the color patch as well as the degree of difference from surrounding colors. Similarly, line orientation depends on the length of the line, the degree to which it differs from surrounding lines, and the contrast of the line pattern with the background.

There are numerous studies that address various combinations of features. It would be impossible to describe all the interactions without writing a complete book on the subject. However, some generalizations are in order. Adding marks to highlight something is generally better than taking them away (Triesman and Gormican, 1988). Thus, it is better to highlight a word by underlining it than to underline all the words in a paragraph, except for the target word. It is also the case that simple numerosity is pre-attentively processed. We can see at a glance that there are one, two, three, or four objects in a group; this ability appears very early in human development (Dehaene, 1997). Once the number of objects increases beyond four, explicit counting is necessary.

That color is also pre-attentive has been well established, and the problem of defining a color that will be pre-attentively distinct from surrounding colors has already been discussed in Chapter 4. To restate a key finding, Bauer et al. (1996) showed that to be pre-attentively distinct, a color should lie outside the boundary of the region defined by all the other colors in the local part of the display (see Figure 4.19).

Rapid Area Judgments

Most work on pre-attentive processing has involved the detection of isolated targets. But other tasks can also benefit from rapid processing. In interpreting map data, a common task is to rapidly estimate the area of some region. Healey et al. (1998) showed that fast area estimation can be done on the basis of either the color or the orientation of the graphical elements filling a spatial region. It is a reasonable assumption that all the pre-attentive cues that have been identified for target identification are also valid for area estimation judgments.

Coding with Combinations of Features

A critical issue for information display is whether more complex patterns can be pre-attentively processed. For example, what happens if we wish to search for a gray square, not just something that is gray or something that is square? It turns out that this kind of search is slow if the surrounding objects are

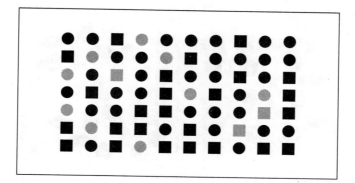

Figure 5.7   Searching for the gray squares is slow because they are identified by conjunction coding.

squares (but not gray ones) and other gray objects. We are forced to do a serial search of either the gray objects or the square objects. This is called a conjunction search, because it involves searching for the specific conjunction of gray-level and shape attributes. Figure 5.7 illustrates a conjunction search task in which the targets are represented by three gray squares. Conjunction searches are generally not pre-attentive, although there are a few very interesting exceptions.

Conjunctions with Spatial Dimensions

Although early research suggested that conjunction searches were never pre-attentive, it has emerged that there are a number of pre-attentive dimension pairs that do allow for conjunctive search. Searches can be pre-attentive when there is a conjunction of spatially coded information and a second attribute, such as color or shape. The spatial information can be position on the XY plane, stereoscopic depth, shape from shading, or motion.

Spatial grouping on the XY plane. Triesman and Gormican (1988) argue that pre-attentive search can be restricted by the identification of visual clusters. Attention can be directed to particular clusters of potential targets, making it possible to search, for example, for the color red in the upper left grouping of targets. This is a form of conjunction search, the conjunction of space and color. In Figure 5.8(b), we can rapidly search the conjunction of lower grouping and gray target. The fact that the target is also elliptical is irrelevant.

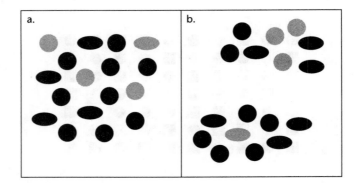

Figure 5.8   Spatial conjunction. The pattern on the left is a classic example of a pre-attentive conjunction search. To find the gray ellipses, either the gray things or the elliptical things must be searched. However, the example on the right shows that the search can be speeded up by spatial grouping. If attention is directed to the lower cluster, perceiving the gray ellipse is pre-attentive. This is a pre-attentive conjunction of spatial location and gray value.

Stereoscopic depth. Nakayama and Silverman (1986) showed that the conjunction of stereoscopic depth and color, or stereoscopic depth and movement, can be pre-attentively processed.

Convexity, concavity, and color. D'Zmura et al. (1997) showed that the conjunction of perceived convexity and color can be pre-attentively processed. In this case, the convexity is perceived through shape-from-shading information.

Motion. Driver et al. (1992) determined that motion and target shape can be pre-attentively scanned conjunctively. Thus, if the whole set of targets is moving, we do not need to look for nonmoving targets. We can pre-attentively find, for example, the red moving target.

An application in which pre-attentive spatial conjunction may be useful is found in geographic information systems (GISs). In these systems, data is often characterized as a set of layers: for example, a layer representing the topography of the surface, a layer representing the minerals, and a layer representing ownership patterns. It may be useful to differentiate such layers by means of differential-motion or stereoscopic-depth cues.

Designing a Symbol Set

One way of thinking about pre-attentive processing is that we can easily and rapidly perceive the "odd man out" in a particular part of visual space. If a set of symbols is to be designed to represent different classes of objects on a map display, they should be as distinct as possible. Military operational maps are an obvious example in which symbols can be used to represent many different classes of targets. (Targets are entities of operational importance that may be friendly or hostile.) A simplified example provides an interesting design exercise.

A tactical map might require the following symbols:

- Aircraft targets

- Tank targets

- Building targets

- Infantry position targets

In addition:

- Each of the target types can be classified as friendly or hostile.

- Targets exist whose presence is suspected but not confirmed.

Finally, there is a need to display features of the terrain itself. Roads, rivers, vegetation types, and topography are all important.

In this example, we encounter many of the characteristic problems of symbol set design. Even though this is a great simplification of the requirements of actual command and control displays, there are still a large number of different types of things to be represented. There is a need for various orthogonal classifications (friendly vs. hostile, tank vs. building). In some circumstances, conjunction search might be desirable (friendly tanks); in others, it would be useful if whole classes of objects could be rapidly estimated.

A solution to this simplified problem is illustrated in Figure 5.9. The actual symbols for the different target types have all been made pre-attentively distinct using shape. Color (represented here by gray value) has been used to pre-attentively classify the targets into friendly and hostile ones. Suspected targets are indicated by adding a thin rectangular box.

In this case, spatial grouping also helps to distinguish between friendly and hostile targets, but this would not always be the case.

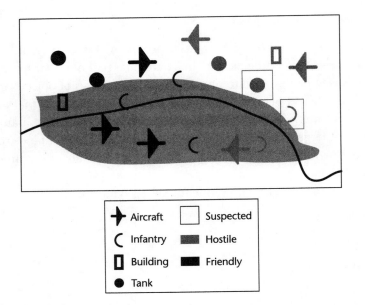

Figure 5.9   A set of symbols for a military command and control display.

Neural Processing, Graphemes, and Tuned Receptors

We now consider the same problem from a neurological perspective. Triesman and others claim that pre-attentive processing is due to *early* visual processing. What is the neurological evidence for this?

Visual information leaves the retina, passing up the optic nerve, through the neural junction at the lateral geniculate nucleus (LGN), and on to the much richer world of processing in the cortex. The first areas in the cortex to receive visual inputs are called, simply, Visual Area 1 and Visual Area 2. Most of the output from Area 1 goes on to Area 2, and together these two regions make up more than 40% of vision processing (Lennie, 1998). It is here that the elementary vocabularies of both vision and data display are defined. Figure 5.10 is derived from Livingstone and Hubel's diagram (1988) that summarizes both the neural architecture and the features processed in this area of the brain. A key concept in understanding this diagram is the tuned receptive field. In Chapter 3, we saw how single-cell recordings of cells in the retina and the LGN reveal cells with distinctive concentric receptive fields. Such cells are said to be *tuned* to a particular pattern of a white spot with a black surround or a black spot with a white surround. In general, a tuned filter is a device that responds strongly to a certain kind of pattern and responds much less, or not at all, to other patterns. In the early visual cortex, some cells respond only to elongated blobs with a particular position and orientation, others respond most strongly to blobs of a particular position moving in a particular direction at a particular velocity, and still others respond selectively to color.

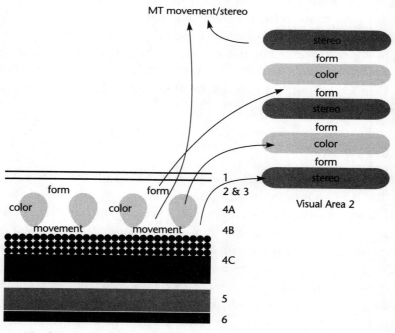

Figure 5.10   Architecture of primary visual areas. Adapted from Livingstone and Hubel (1988).

There are cells in Visual Areas 1 and 2 that are differentially tuned to each of the following properties:

- Orientation and size (with luminance)
- Color (two types of signal)
- Stereoscopic depth
- Motion

Moreover, all these properties are extracted for each point in the visual field. In this region and many other regions of the brain, neurons are arranged in the form of a spatial map of the retina. It is a somewhat distorted map, because the fovea is given more space than the periphery of vision. Nevertheless, for every point in Visual Area 1, there is a corresponding area of the visual field in a topographic relationship (adjacency is preserved between areas). It is a massively parallel system in which, for each point in visual space, there are tuned filters for many different orientations, many different kinds of color information, many different directions and velocities of motion, and many different stereoscopic depths. In general, the receptive fields are smaller for those cells that process information coming from the fovea than for cells that process information from peripheral regions of the visual field.

The Grapheme

It is useful to think of the things that are extracted by the early neural mechanisms like the "phonemes" of perception. *Phonemes* are the smallest elements in speech recognition, the atomic components from which meaningful words are made. In a similar way, we can think of orientation detectors, color detectors, and so on as "visual phonemes," the elements from which meaningful perceptual objects are constructed.

We use the term *grapheme* to describe a graphical element that is primitive in *visual* terms, the visual equivalent of a phoneme. The basis of the grapheme concept is that the pattern that most efficiently excites a neuron in the visual system is exactly the pattern that the neuron is tuned to detect (Ware and Knight, 1995). Thus, the most effective grapheme is one that matches the receptive field properties of some class of neurons. An orientation detector will be most strongly excited by a pattern whose light distribution is exactly the same as the sensitivity distribution of the cell. This is simply another way of saying that the detector is "tuned" to that particular pattern. Once we understand the kinds of patterns the tuned cells of the visual cortex respond to best, we can apply this information in creating efficient visual patterns. Patterns based on the receptive field properties of neurons should be rapidly understood and easily distinguished.

A number of assumptions are implicit in this concept. They appear to be plausible, and indeed they are implicit in much of the work that uses vision research to develop principles of information display, but they are worth examining critically. One basic assumption is that the rate at which single neurons fire is the key coding variable in terms of human perception. This assumption can certainly be questioned. It may be that what is important is the way in which groups of neurons fire, or perhaps the temporal spacing or synchronization of cell firings. In fact, there is evidence that these alternative information codings may be important, perhaps critical. Nevertheless, few doubt that neurons that are highly sensitive to color differences (in terms of their firing rates) are directly involved in the processing of color and that the same thing is true for motion and shape. Moreover, as we shall see, the behavior of neurons fits well with studies of how people perceive certain kinds of patterns. Thus, there is a convergence of lines of evidence.

We also assume that *early*-stage neurons are particularly important in determining how distinct things seem. We know that at higher levels of processing in the visual cortex, receptive fields are found that are much more complex; they respond to patterns that appear to be composites of the simple receptive field patterns found at earlier stages. The evidence suggests that the farther we go up the processing chain, the less immediate the perception is. These composite patterns are not, in general, processed as rapidly. It seems natural, then, to think of early-stage processing as forming the graphemes and of later-stage processing as forming the "words," or objects, of perception.

Much of the pre-attentive processing work already discussed in this chapter can be regarded as providing experimental evidence of the nature of graphemes. The following sections apply the concept to the perception of visual texture and show how knowledge of early mechanisms enables us to create rules for textures that are visually distinct.

The Gabor Model and Texture in Visualization

A number of electrophysiological and psychophysical experiments show that Visual Areas 1 and 2 contain large arrays of neurons that filter for orientation and size information at each point in the visual field. These neurons have both a preferred orientation and a preferred size (they are said to have spatial and orientation tuning). These particular neurons are not color-coded; they respond to luminance changes only.

A simple mathematical model that is widely used to describe the receptive field properties of these neurons is the Gabor function. This function is illustrated in Figure 5.11. It consists of the product of a cosine wave grating and a gaussian. Roughly, this can be thought of as a kind of fuzzy bar detector. It has a clear orientation, as shown in Figure 5.12, and it has an excitatory center, flanked by inhibitory bars. The opposite kind also exists, with an inhibitory center.

Many things about low-level perception can be explained by this model. Gabor-type detectors are used in theories of the detection of contours at the boundaries of objects (form perception), the detection of regions that have different visual textures, stereoscopic vision, and motion perception.

The Gabor function has two components, as illustrated in Figure 5.11: a cosine wave and a gaussian envelope. Multiply them together and the result is a Gabor function. Mathematically, a Gabor function has the following form (simplified for ease of explanation):

$$\text{Response} = C \cos\left(\frac{Ox}{S}\right) \exp\left(-\frac{(x^2 + y^2)}{S}\right)$$

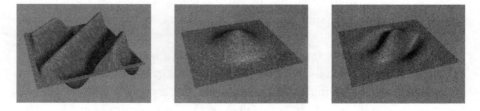

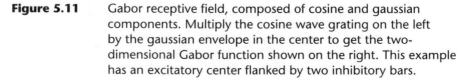

Figure 5.11   Gabor receptive field, composed of cosine and gaussian components. Multiply the cosine wave grating on the left by the gaussian envelope in the center to get the two-dimensional Gabor function shown on the right. This example has an excitatory center flanked by two inhibitory bars.

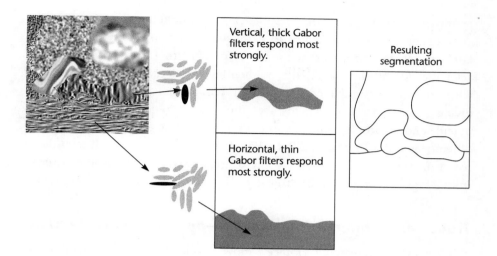

Figure 5.12   The texture segmentation model. Two-dimensional arrays of Gabor detectors filter every part of the image for all possible orientations and sizes. Areas exciting particular classes of detectors form the basis of visually distinct segments of the image.

The C parameter gives the amplitude or *contrast* value; S gives the overall *size* of the Gabor function by adjusting both the wavelength of the cosine grating and the rate of decay of the gaussian envelope. O is a rotation matrix that *orients* the cosine wave. Other parameters can be added to position the function at a particular location in space and adjust the ratio of the gaussian size to the sine wavelength; however, orientation, size, and contrast are most significant in modeling human visual processing.

Texture Segmentation

The first way we apply the Gabor model is in understanding how the visual system *segments* the visual world into regions of distinct visual texture. Suppose we wish to understand how people perceptually differentiate types of vegetation based on the visual textures in a black-and-white satellite image. A model based on Gabor filters provides a good description of the way people perform this kind of texture segmentation task (Bovik et al., 1990; Malik and Perona, 1990).

The segmentation model is illustrated in Figure 5.12. It has three main stages. In the first stage, banks of Gabor filters respond strongly to regions of texture where particular spatial frequencies and orientations predominate. In a later stage, the output from this early stage is low-pass-filtered. (This is a kind of averaging process that creates regions having the same general characteristic. At the final stage, the boundaries are identified between regions with strongly dissimilar characteristics.) This model predicts that we will divide visual space into regions according to the predominant spatial frequency and orientation information. A region with large orientation and size differences will be the most differentiated. Also, regions can be differentiated based on the texture contrast. A low-contrast texture will be differentiated from a high-contrast texture with the same orientation and size components.

Trade-Offs in Information Density—an Uncertainty Principle

A famous vision researcher, Horace Barlow, developed a set of principles that have become influential in guiding our understanding of human perception. The second of these, called "the second dogma" (Barlow, 1972), provides an interesting theoretical background to the Gabor model. In the second dogma, Barlow asserted that the visual system is simultaneously optimized in both spatial-location and spatial-frequency domains. John Daugman (1984) showed mathematically that Gabor detectors satisfy the requirements of the Barlow dogma. They optimally preserve a combination of spatial information (the location of the information in visual space) and oriented-frequency information. A single Gabor detector can be thought of as being tuned to a little packet of orientation and size information that can be positioned anywhere in space.

Daugman (1985) has also shown that a fundamental uncertainty principle is related to the perception of position, orientation, and frequency. Given a fixed number of detectors, resolution of size can be traded for resolution of orientation or position. We (Ware and Knight, 1995) have shown that same principle applies to the synthesis of texture for data display. A gain in the ability to precisely display orientation information inevitably comes at the expense of precision in displaying size information. Given a constant density of data, orientation or size can be specified precisely, but not both. Figure 5.13 illustrates this trade-off, expressed by changing the shape and size of the gaussian multiplier function with the same sinusoidal grating. When the gaussian is large, the spatial frequency is specified quite precisely, as shown by the small image in the Fourier transform. When the gaussian is small, the

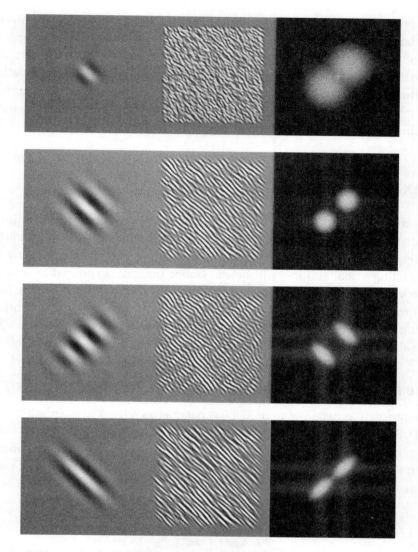

Figure 5.13 In the left-hand column, the same cosine pattern is paired with different gaussian multipliers. In the center column are textures created using each Gabor function by reducing the size by a factor of 5 and spattering it in the field. In the right-hand column are 2D Fourier transforms of the textures.

texton position is well specified but the spatial frequency is not, as shown by the large image in the Fourier transform. The lower two rows of Figure 5.13 show how the gaussian envelope can be stretched to specify either the spatial frequency or the orientation more precisely. Although a full mathematical treatment of these effects is beyond the scope of this book, the main point is that there are fundamental limits and trade-offs related to the ways texture can be used for information display.

Texture Coding Information

If texture perception can be modeled and understood using the Gabor function as a model of a detector, the same model should be useful in *producing* easily distinguished textures for information display. The ideal grapheme for generating visual textures will be the Gabor function expressed as a luminance profile, as shown in Figure 5.14. A neuron with a Gabor receptive field will respond most strongly to a Gabor pattern with the same size and orientation. Therefore, textures based on Gabor primitives should be easy to distinguish.

The Primary Perceptual Dimensions of Texture

A completely general Gabor model has parameters related to orientation, spatial frequency, contrast, and the size and shape of the gaussian envelope. However, in human neural receptive fields, the gaussian and cosine components tend to be coupled so that low-frequency cosine components have large gaussians and high-frequency cosine components have small gaussians (Caelly

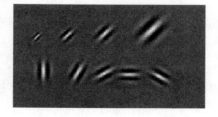

Figure 5.14   Gabor receptive fields shown as gray-scale images. Different sizes and orientations are represented for each part of the visual field.

and Moraglia, 1985). This allows us to propose a simple three-parameter model for the perception and generation of texture.

Orientation
O: the orientation of the cosine component

Scale
S: the size = 1/(spatial frequency component)

Contrast
C: an amplitude or contrast component

The Generation of Distinct Textures

With this simple model, it is straightforward to generate textures using Gabor functions as primitives. These textures can be varied in orientation, size (1/frequency), or contrast.

One method is to randomly splatter down Gabor functions whose orientation, size, and contrast have been determined by data values for the region in space where each splatter lands (Ware and Knight, 1995). When enough splatters have been accumulated in this way, we will have a continuous map that can represent up to three variables (a trivariate map). We can also map an additional variable to hue, producing a four-variable map.

Data value 1 → Orientation

Data value 2 → Size

Data value 3 → Contrast

Data value 4 → Hue

Figure 5.15 provides an example showing a magnetic field displayed using orientation and size manipulations. Color coding illustrates field strength.

Note that textures need not be made of Gabor patterns for the method or the theory to work. It is only necessary that texture graphons have a dominant orientation and spatial frequency. It is also important to note that the fundamental trade-offs in our ability to represent spatial information using texture are also independent of whether the Gabor model of texture perception is correct. To take a simple example, if we consider that textons can be made from small graphical shapes representing data, the number of such shapes that can be drawn per unit area is inversely proportional to their size. The location of the packet of information can be specified only to a precision determined by the size of the object representing that information.

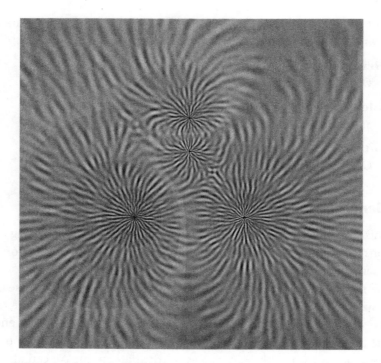

Figure 5.15   Magnetic field shown using Gabor textures. See also color
plates.

Spatial-Frequency Channels, Orthogonality, and Maps

Sometimes we may wish to display many different kinds of information in a
single map. For example, we might wish to show sea-surface temperature
and sea-surface salinity at the same time. Naturally, we would like the different sources of information not to interfere with one another. It would be
unfortunate if regions of high salinity appeared to have a greater apparent
temperature than they really have, due to visual "crosstalk" between the way
we display temperature and the way we display salinity. Thus, our goal is to
create display methods that are *perceptually independent.*

The concept of the visual processing "channel" can be taken directly
from vision research and applied to the independence problem. We have
already seen the concept of color channels in Chapter 4. Here, the same idea
is applied to spatial information. The idea is that information carried on one

channel should not interfere with information displayed on another. It is probably not the case that any of the perceptual channels we shall discuss are fully independent; nevertheless, it is certainly the case that some kinds of information are processed in ways that are more independent than others. A channel that is independent from another is said to be orthogonal to it. Here, the concept is applied to the spatial information carried by Gabor detectors.

A given Gabor-type neuron is broadly tuned with respect to orientation and size. The half width of the spatial tuning curve is approximately a period change (in the sinusoid) of a factor of 3, and the total number of spatial-frequency channels is about four. Wilson and Bergen (1979) determined these values using a masking technique, which essentially determines the extent to which one type of information interferes with another. The resulting estimation of spatial-frequency channels is illustrated in Figure 5.16.

Orientation tuning-in appears to be about ± 30 degrees (Blake and Holopigan, 1985). Therefore, textures that differ from one another by more than 30 degrees in orientation will be easily distinguished.

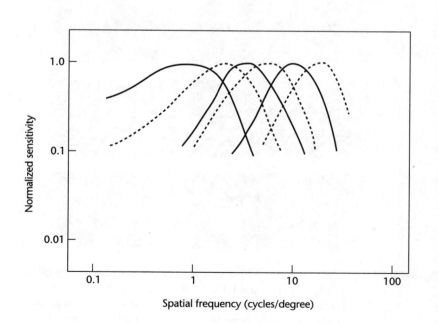

Figure 5.16   Wilson and Bergen spatial channels.

These experimental results can be applied to problems in information display. For textured regions to be visually distinct, the dominant spatial frequencies should differ by at least a factor of 3 or 4 and the dominant orientations should differ by more than 30 degrees, all other factors (such as color) being equal. In general, the more displayed information differs in spatial frequency and in orientation, the more distinct that information will be. In practical applications, this means that if we want different regions to be distinct because of their texture, the dominant orientations of the patterns should be made as different as possible. In Figure 5.17(a), only orientation is changed between different regions of the display, and although the word *TEXTURE* appears distinct from its background, it is weak. The difference appears much stronger when both the spatial frequency and the orientation differ between the figure and the background (Figure 5.17(b)). The third way that textures can be made easy to distinguish is by changing the contrast, as illustrated in Figure 5.17(c).

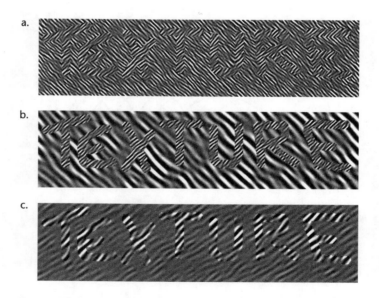

Figure 5.17   The word *TEXTURE* is visible only because of texture differences between the letters and the background; overall luminance is held constant. (a) Only texture orientation is altered. (b) Texture orientation and size are altered. (c) Texture contrast is altered.

Texture Resolution

The model of texture segmentation described above predicts performance when people are asked to rapidly classify regions of a display. However, if we ask how small a difference people can *resolve,* we need a different model. When people are allowed to stare at two regions of a display for as long as they like, they can resolve far smaller differences than those perceived in brief presentations.

The *resolvable* size difference for a Gabor pattern is a size change of about 9 percent (Caelli et al., 1983). The resolvable orientation difference is about 5 degrees (Caelli and Bevan, 1983). These resolutions are much smaller than the channel-tuning functions would predict. This implies that higher-level mechanisms are present to sharpen up the output from individual receptors. The mechanism is based on inhibition. If a neuron has an excitatory input from one neuron and an inhibitory input from another with a slightly differ-ent tuning, the resulting difference signal is much more sensitive to spatial tuning than either of the original signals. This kind of sharpening is common in neural systems; it appears in color systems, edge detection, and heading detection (for navigation). Figure 5.18 illustrates the concept. Neurons A and

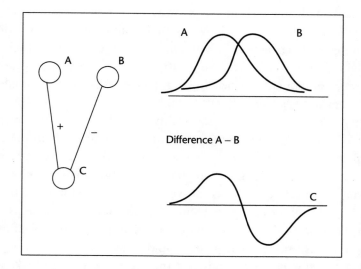

Figure 5.18   Differences between two signals are created by an excitatory and an inhibitory connection.

B both have rather broadly tuned and somewhat overlapping response functions to some input pattern. Neuron C has an excitatory input from A and an inhibitory input from B. The result is something that is highly sensitive to differences between the different kinds of signals at the crossover point.

Texture Contrast Effects

Texture/size/contrast illusions exist that are exactly analogous to the luminance/contrast illusions that were described earlier in this chapter. Thus, a given texture on a coarsely textured background will appear finer than the same texture on a finely textured background. This phenomenon is illustrated in Figure 5.19. The effect is predicted by higher-order inhibitory connections.

Other Dimensions of Visual Texture

Although there is considerable evidence to suggest that orientation, size, and contrast are the three dominant dimensions of visual texture, it is clear that the world of texture is much richer than this. The dimensionality of visual texture is very high, as a visual examination of the world around us attests. Think of the textures of wood, brick, stone, fur, leather, and other natural materials. Figure 5.20 shows some delightful examples of computer-generated textures that might be used in categorizing data. These examples clearly go beyond what can be generated by a simple Gabor-based model. However, there is no general agreement on what makes up the important higher-order perceptual dimensions of texture, once the dominant frequency, orientation, and contrast components are accounted for. One of the important additional texture dimensions is certainly randomness (Liu and Picard, 1994). Textures that are regular have a very different quality from that of random ones.

We would do well to learn to use texture more effectively in information display. The world of visual texture is arguably as rich and expressive as the world of color. Yet although there have been hundreds of experimental studies on the effective use of color, very few have investigated the use of texture in information display. This will inevitably change as texture mapping becomes a cheap and ubiquitous resource. In the meantime, we have good, robust models that predict rapid visual segmentation of patterns on the basis of texture, and because of this we know how to make textures visually distinct. We also have a good handle on the fundamental limitations of texture coding.

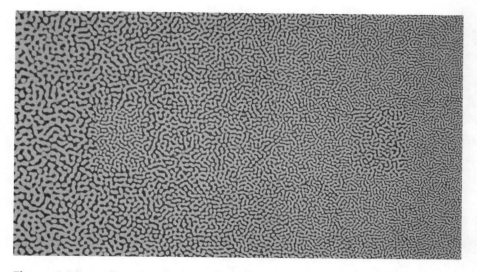

Figure 5.19 Texture contrast effect. The two patches left of center and right of center have the same texture granularity, but texture contrast makes them appear different.

Figure 5.20 Textures from Witkin and Kass (1991). See also color plates.

Glyphs and Multivariate Discrete Data

In the previous section, we saw how texture could be used to represent continuous map data. In Chapter 4 it was shown that color could be used in a similar way. However, sometimes multivariate *discrete* data is the subject of interest. For example, a marketing specialist may have data for every person in a particular geographical area, including estimates of income, educational level, employment category, and location of residence. The marketer would like to see each person on a map in such a way that the concentrations of individuals with particular sets of attributes could be easily seen. In this way, neighborhoods to be blanketed with flyers might be selected most effectively.

One way of representing multivariate discrete data is by using a glyph. A glyph is a single graphical object that represents a multivariate data object. To create a glyph, multiple data attributes are mapped in a systematic way to show the different aspects of the appearance of the graphical object. In the above example, income might be mapped to the glyph's size, education level to its color, employment category to the shape, and geographic location to the *x,y* location where the glyph is plotted. All the results discussed previously, related to pre-attentive detection of size orientation and color coding of data, apply to the design of glyphs. Another body of theory that is relevant is the theory of *integral* and *separable* dimensions, developed by Garner (1974).

The kind of multidimensional coding that occurs in the use of glyphs raises questions about the perceptual independence of the display dimensions. Will the color-coding scheme interfere with our perception of glyph size and therefore distort perceived income level? What if we use both color and size to represent a single variable? Will this make the information clearer?

The concept of integral versus separable visual dimensions is related to situations in which one display attribute (e.g., color) will be perceived independently from another (e.g., size).

With *integral* display dimensions, two or more attributes of a visual object are perceived holistically. An example is a rectangular shape, perceived as a holistic combination of the rectangle's width and height. Another is the combination of green light and red light; this is seen holistically as yellow light.

With *separable* dimensions, people tend to make judgments about each graphical dimension separately. This is sometimes called *analytic processing*. Thus, if the display dimensions are the diameter of a ball and the color of a ball, these will be processed relatively independently. It is easy to respond independently to ball size and ball color.

Integral and separable dimensions have been experimentally determined in a number of ways. We will now discuss three of them. They are all related to interactions between pairs of variables. Very little work has been done on interactions among three or more display variables.

Restricted Classification Tasks

In restricted classification tasks, observers are shown sets of three glyphs that are constructed according to the diagram shown in Figure 5.21. Two of the glyphs (A and B) are made the same on one of the variables. A third glyph (C) is constructed so that it is closer to glyph B in feature space, but this glyph differs from the other two on both of the graphical dimensions. Subjects are asked to group the two glyphs that they think go together best. If the dimensions are integral, A and C are grouped together because they are closest in the feature space. If they are separable, A and B are grouped together because they are identical on one of the dimensions (analytic mode). The clearest example of integral dimensions is color space dimensions. If dimension X is the red-green dimension and dimension Y is the yellow-blue dimension of color space, subjects tend to classify objects (roughly) according to the Euclidean distance between the colors (defined according to one of the uniform color

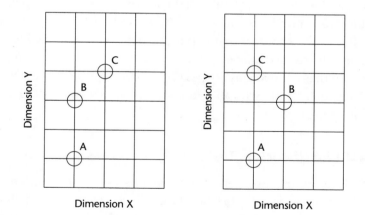

Figure 5.21   When we are considering integral and separable visual dimensions, it is useful to consider a space defined by two display dimensions. One might be size; the other might be color. Or one might be hue and the other might be saturation, both defined in color space.

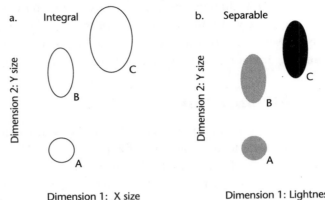

Figure 5.22   (a) The width and height of an ellipse are perceived integrally; therefore, B and C are perceived as more similar. (b) The gray value and the height of an ellipse are perceived as separable; therefore, A and B, which have identical lightness, are perceived as more similar.

spaces discussed in Chapter 4). Note that even this is not always the case, as the evidence of color categories (also discussed in Chapter 4) shows.

The X and Y size of an ellipse creates an integral perception of shape. Thus, in Figure 5.22(a), the ellipses B and C appear to be more similar to each other than to the circle A, even though the width of B matches the width of A.

If the two dimensions are separable, subjects act in a more analytic manner and react to the fact that two of the objects are actually identical on one of the dimensions. Shape and gray value are separable. Thus, in Figure 5.22(b), either the two gray shapes or the two elliptical shapes will be categorized together. With separable dimensions, it is easy to attend to one dimension or the other.

Speeded Classification Tasks

Speeded classification tasks tell us how glyphs can visually interfere with each other. In a speeded classification task, subjects are asked to rapidly classify visual patterns according to only one of the visual attributes of a glyph. The other visual attribute can be set up in two different ways. It can be given random values (interference condition), or it can be coded in the same way as the first dimension (redundant coding). If the data dimensions are integral, substantial interference occurs in the first case. With redundant coding, classification is generally speeded for integral dimensions. With separable codes, the results are different. There is little interference from the irrelevant graphical dimension, but there is also little advantage in terms of speeded classification when redundant coding is used. Of course, in some cases, using redundant separable codes may still be desirable. For example, if both color and shape are used for information coding, color-blind individuals will still have access to the information. Figure 5.23 gives examples of the kinds of patterns that are used in experiments.

The lessons to be learned from integral-separable dimension experiments are straightforwardly applied to cases in which each data entity has

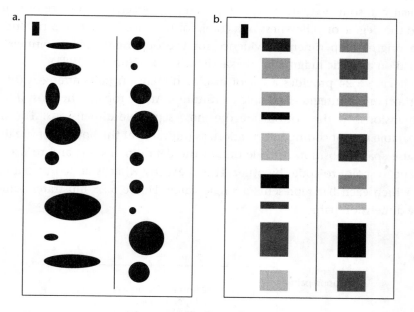

Figure 5.23   Patterns for a speeded classification task. Subjects are required to respond positively only to those glyphs that have the same height as the black bar in the upper-left corner. (a) Integral dimensions. In the first column, a second integral dimension is randomly coded by horizontal size (interference condition). In the second column, width information is redundantly coded with height information. (b) Separable dimension. In the first column, gray information is not correlated with height. In the second column, gray level is a redundant code.

two attributes. If we want people to respond holistically to a combination of two variables, using integral dimensions will be better. If we want people to respond analytically, making judgments on the basis of one variable or the other, using separable dimensions will be better.

Integral-Separable Dimension Pairs

The above analysis has presented integral and separable dimensions as if they were qualitatively distinct. This overstates the case; a continuum of integrality-separability more accurately represents the facts. There is always some interference between different data values presented using different graphical attributes of a single visual object, even between the most separable dimensions. Likewise, the most integral dimensions can be regarded analytically to some extent. We can, for example, perceive the degree of redness and the degree of yellowness of a color, for instance, orange or pink. Indeed, the original experimental evidence for the opponent color channels was based on analytic judgments of exactly this type (Hurvich, 1981).

Figure 5.24 provides a list of display dimension pairs arranged (by the author) on an integral-separable continuum. At the top are the most integral dimensions. At the bottom are the most separable dimensions. The most separable way of coding information, as indicated at the bottom of the list, is to use spatial position to code one of the data dimensions and to use size, shape, or color to code the other. This is exactly what is done in a bar chart in which each bar represents a single value. Figure 5.25 illustrates some of the dimension pairs.

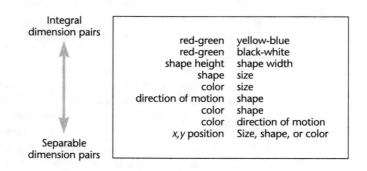

Figure 5.24   This table lists some of the display dimension pairs ranked in order from highly integral to highly separable.

Dimensions

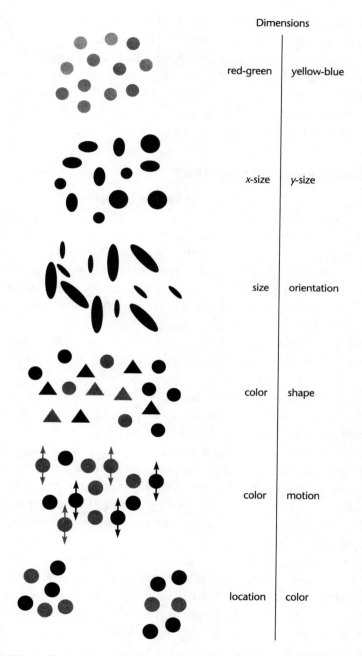

red-green	yellow-blue
x-size	y-size
size	orientation
color	shape
color	motion
location	color

Figure 5.25 Examples of glyphs coded according to two display attributes. At the top are more integral coding pairs. At the bottom are more separable coding pairs. See also color plates.

As a theoretical concept, the notion of integral and separable dimensions is undoubtedly simplistic; it lacks mechanism and fails to account for a large number of exceptions and asymmetries that have been experimentally discovered. Eventually, it is to be expected that a more complete body of theory will emerge to account for the ways in which different kinds of visual information are combined. The beauty of the integral-separable distinction lies in its simplicity as a design guideline.

Multidimensional Discrete Data

This is a good place to step back and look at the general problem of multivariate discrete data display in light of the concepts that have been presented here and in the previous chapter. It is worth restating this problem in general terms. We are provided with a set of entities, each of which has values on a number of attribute dimensions. For example, we might have 1000 beetles, each measured on 30 anatomical characteristics, or 500 stocks, each described by 20 financial variables. The reason for displaying such data graphically is often a form of data exploration. We hope to find meaning in the diversity. In the case of the beetles, the meaning might be related to their ecological niches. In the case of the stocks, the meaning is likely to lie in opportunities for profit.

If we decide to use a glyph display, each entity becomes a graphical object and data attributes are mapped to graphical attributes of each glyph. The problem is one of mapping data dimension to the graphical attributes of the glyph. The work on pre-attentive processing, early visual processing, and integral and separable dimensions suggests that a rather limited set of visual attributes are available to us if we want to understand the values easily. Figure 5.26 is a list of the most interesting graphical attributes that can be applied to glyph design, with a few summary comments about the number of dimensions available.

Many of these display dimensions are not independent of one another. To display texture, we must use at least one color dimension to make the texture visible. Blink coding will certainly interfere with motion coding. Overall, we will probably be fortunate to display eight-dimensional data clearly, using color, shape, spatial position, and motion to create the most differentiated set possible.

There is also the issue of how many resolvable steps are available on each dimension, and the number here is also small. When we require rapid pre-attentive processing, no more than eight colors are available. The number of

Visual variable	Dimensionality	Comment
Spatial position of glyph	3 dimensions: *X, Y, Z.*	
Color of glyph	3 dimensions: defined by color opponent theory.	Luminance contrast is needed to specify all other graphical attributes.
Shape	2–3? Dimensions unknown.	The dimensions of shape that can be rapidly processed are unknown. However, evidence suggests that size and degree of elongation are two primary ones.
Orientation	3 dimensions: corresponding to orientation about each of the primary axes.	Orientation is not independent of shape. One object can have rotation symmetry with another.
Surface texture	3 dimensions: orientation, size, and contrast.	Not independent of shape or orientation. Uses up one color dimension.
Motion coding	2–3? Dimensions largely unknown, but phase may be useful.	
Blink coding: The glyph blinks on and off at some rate.	1 dimension.	Motion and blink coding are highly interdependent.

Figure 5.26   Graphical attributes that may be used in glyph design.

orientation steps that we can easily distinguish is probably about four. The number of size steps that we can easily distinguish is no more than four, and the values for the other data dimensions are also in the single-digit range. It is reasonable, therefore, to propose that we can represent about 2 bits of information for each of the eight graphical dimensions. If the dimensions were truly independent, this would yield 16 displayable bits per glyph (64,000 values). Unfortunately, conjunctions are generally not pre-attentive. If we allow no conjunction searching, we are left with four alternatives on each of eight channels, yielding only thirty-two rapidly distinguishable alternatives, a far smaller number. Anyone who has tried to design a set of easily distinguishable glyphs will recognize this number to be more plausible.

Stars, Whiskers, and Other Glyphs

There is a family of glyph designs for multidimensional discrete data displays that is interesting to analyze from a perception perspective. In the whisker plot, each data value is represented by a line segment radiating out from a central point (Figure 5.27(a)). The length of the line segment denotes the value of the corresponding data attribute.

A variant of the whisker plot is the star plot (Chambers et al., 1983). This is the same as the whisker plot, but with the ends of the lines connected as in Figure 5.27(b).

A related plot is produced by the Exvis tool, which maps data values to various attributes of stick-figure icons such as that shown in Figure 5.27(c) (Pickett and Grinstein, 1988). This package has many display options, which include changing the angles of line segments relative to each other, or relative to a reference orientation, and changing the line segment widths. Although the Exvis development team implemented the capability to map data to icon colors, they have worked mostly with angles (Pickett et al., 1995).

When large numbers of glyphs are present in a display, in effect, the glyph field becomes a texture field and the psychophysical theory of orientation and size channels, discussed earlier in this chapter, can be applied. This theory suggests that glyph element orientations should be separated by at least 30 degrees and because a line-oriented segment will be confused with an

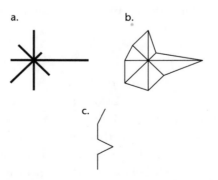

Figure 5.27   Three glyph designs: (a) The whisker or fan plot. (b) A star plot. (c) An Exvis stick icon.

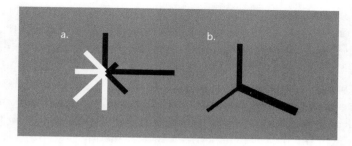

Figure 5.28   (a) It may be possible to increase the number of distinct orientations in a glyph display by changing the luminance polarity of half the line segments. (b) Changing the widths as well as the lengths of segments may also be effective.

identical segment rotated through 180 degrees, this means that fewer than six orientations can be rapidly distinguished. It is also important that different data dimensions not be represented through collinear or parallel line segments, because these line segments will be visually confounded. This occurs in all three examples shown in Figure 5.27. In any case, it is unreasonable to expect that the 12 or more whiskers displayed by Chambers et al. (1983) will be easily interpreted.

In general, it is better to use only a very small number of orientations, perhaps only three, for really rapid classification of glyphs (Figure 5.28(b)). But it may be possible to increase the number of rapidly distinguishable orientations by inverting the luminance polarity of half of the bars (Figure 5.28(a)). Color and position in space can be used to display other data dimensions. If we map three data dimensions to the position of each glyph and two dimensions to the color of the glyph, we can represent eight-dimensional data clearly and effectively. It may also be useful to change the amount of "energy" in glyph segments by altering the line width as well as the length of the line.

Polarity of Visual Attributes

Some visual attributes have a natural polarity. For example, in a 3D data space, the "up" direction is defined by gravity. The axis representing direction "toward" and "away from" the viewpoint is similarly well defined, but the left and right directions do not have as clear a polarity. (This issue will be discussed further in Chapter 8 in the context of space perception.) For representing simple quantity, an increase in any of the following attributes will be effective: size, lightness (on a dark background), darkness (on a light background), or vertical height above the ground plane. If we wish to display an increasing trend, then increasing size, increasing luminance, and positioning higher in the data space will all be interpreted correctly, whereas an inverse mapping will lead to confusion.

Some visual attributes have no visual polarity. Orientation is one. It is meaningless to say that one orientation is greater or less than another. The same is true of the phase angle between two oscillating objects. As the phase difference is increased, they first appear to move in opposite directions, but as the phase difference continues to increase, the objects appear to move together again. Phase is cyclic, just as line orientation is cyclic. Hue also lacks polarity: There is no sense that one hue is more or less than another; they are just different.

Conclusion

This chapter has provided an introduction to the early stages of vision, in which massively parallel processes extract elementary aspects of form, color, texture, motion, and stereoscopic depth with arrays of specialized cells. The fact that this processing is done for each point of the visual field means that objects differentiated in terms of these simple low-level features "pop out" and can be easily attended to. Understanding such pre-attentive processes is the key to designing elements of displays that must be rapidly attended to. Making an icon or a symbol significantly different from its surroundings on one of the pre-attentive dimensions ensures that it can be detected without effort and at high speed by a viewer.

An important aspect of pre-attentive processing is the theory of visual processing channels and the degree of independence between them. If we want an information-carrying object to stand out from its surroundings, the display variable must be robust in its resistance to visual noise: Irrelevant information that is also visually coded should not interfere. Independence between information channels can be achieved, to some extent, by using different visual channels. Thus, for example, if a particular kind of information is graphically coded using color, it will still stand out if irrelevant information is presented using blink coding. On the other hand, if we use color for the first dimension and luminance for the second, considerable interference can be expected.

We have arrived at a transition point in this book, between the consideration of the low-level feature processing of early vision and that of the more complex objects of later vision. Thus far, we have mostly discussed the massively parallel processing of simple features, but in the following chapters, we consider the way the brain extracts a few complex objects from this elemental information and subjects them to a much more sophisticated analysis. Rather than concerning ourselves with the elementary coding of information, we turn our attention to finding more elaborate patterns in data, and eventually to the ways in which information should be integrated and displayed for solving complex problems.

Figure 2.6
(a) Lambertian shading only. (b) Lambertian shading with specular and ambient shading. (c) Lambertian shading with specular, ambient, and cast shadows.

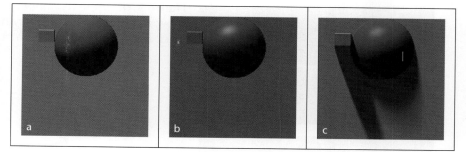

Figure 2.7 Glossy leaves. Note that the highlights are the color of the illuminant.

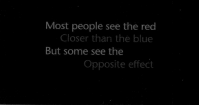

Most people see the red
Closer than the blue
But some see the
Opposite effect

Figure 2.14 Chromostereopsis. For most people, the red advances and the blue recedes.

Figure 3.14 These two pieces of paper are illuminated by a desk lamp just to the right of the picture.

a.

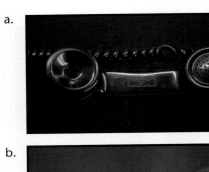

b.

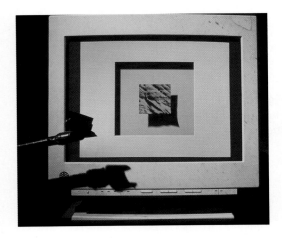

Figure 3.16 These two photographs show scenes in which (a) everything is black and (b) everything is white.

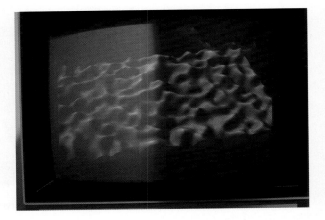

Figure 3.18 A monitor with a shadow falling across its face. Under normal viewing conditions, a significant proportion of the light coming from the screen is reflected ambient room illumination.

Figure 3.20 A projector was set up containing a mask especially designed so that no light actually fell on the portion of the monitor screen containing the image. In this way, the illumination in the virtual environment displayed on the monitor was made to closely match the illumination falling on the monitor and surrounding region.

Figure 4.1 Finding the cherries among the leaves is much easier if we have color vision.

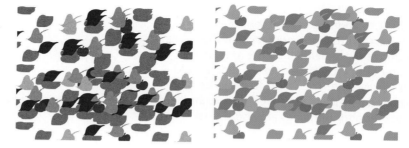

Figure 4.4
A color-matching setup. (a) When the light from three projectors is combined, the results are as shown. Yellow light is a mixture of red and green. Purple light is a mixture of red and blue. Cyan light is a mixture of

a.

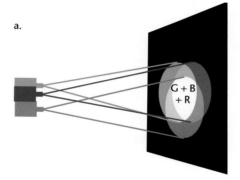

b.

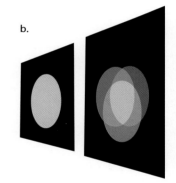

blue and green. White light is a mixture or red, green, and blue. (b) Any other color can be matched by adjusting the proportions of red, green, and blue light.

Figure 4.6
The X, Y, and Z axes represent the CIE
standard virtual primaries. Within the
positive space defined by the axes, the
gamut of perceivable colors is represented
as a gray solid. The colors that can be
created by means of the red, green, and
blue monitor primaries are also shown.

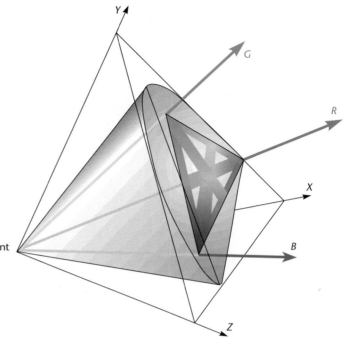

Figure 4.9 (a) Small samples of a yellow-
to-blue sequence of colors on a white
background. (b) The same yellow-to-blue
sequence with larger samples on a black
background. (c) Small samples of a green-
to-red sequence on a white background.
(d) The same green-to-red sequence with
larger samples on a black background.

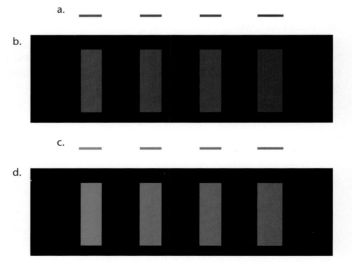

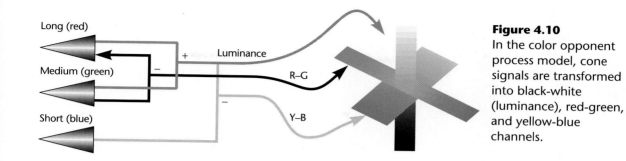

Figure 4.10
In the color opponent process model, cone signals are transformed into black-white (luminance), red-green, and yellow-blue channels.

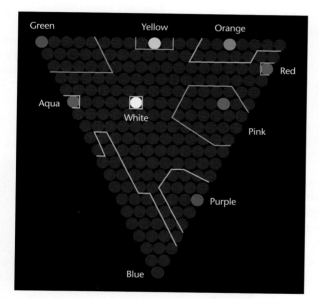

Figure 4.12 The results of an experiment in which subjects were asked to name 210 colors produced on a computer monitor. Outlined regions show the colors that were given the same name with better than 75% probability.

Figure 4.13 Yellow text on a blue gradient. Note how difficult the text is to read where luminance is equal, despite a large chromatic difference.

It is very difficult to read text that is isoluminant with its background color. If clear text material is to be presented it is essential that there be substantial luminance contrast with the background color. Color contrast is not enough. This particular example is especially difficult because the chromatic difference is in the yellow-blue direction. The only exception to the requirement for luminance contrast is when the purpose is artistic effect and not clarity.

Figure 4.14 A color contrast illusion. The "X" pattern is identical on both sides, but it seems more blue on the red background and more pink on the blue background.

Figure 4.16 This plot shows hue and saturation, based on Smith's transformation (1978) of the monitor primaries.

Figure 4.17 There are a number of simple transformations of the *RGB* monitor primaries to provide a color plane with an orthogonal lightness axis. Four of these are illustrated here: (a) Circle. (b) Triangle. (c) Square. (d) Hexagon.

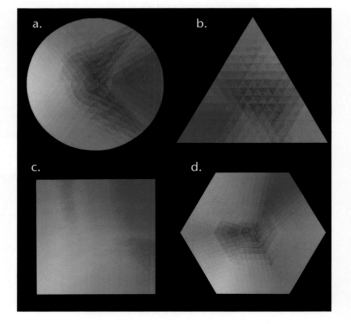

Figure 4.19
The convex hull of a set of colors is defined as the area within a rubber band that is stretched around the colors when they are defined in CIE tristimulus space. Although illustrated in two dimensions here, the concept can easily be extended to three dimensions. (a) Gray is within the convex hull of red, green, yellow, and blue. (b) Red lies outside the convex hull of green, blue, yellow, and gray. (c) The gray dot is difficult to find in a set of red, green, yellow, and blue dots. (d) The red dot is easy to find in a set of green, blue, yellow, and gray dots.

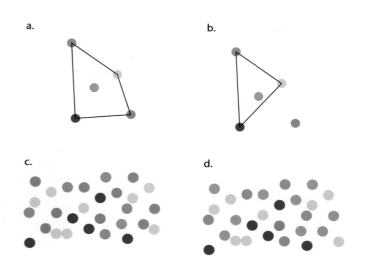

a.

b.

c.

d.

Figure 4.20
When large areas are color-coded, low-saturation light colors can be used on a white background. This interferes much less with detailed information in the text.

```java
import java.applet.Applet;
import java.awt.Graphics;
import java.awt.Color;

public class ColorText extends Applet
{
        public void init ( )
        {
                red = 100;
                green = 255;
                blue = 20;
        }

        public void paint (Graphics g)
        {
                Gr.setColor (new Color (red, green, blue));
                Gr.drawString ("Colored Text". 30,50);
        }

        private int red;
        private int green;
        private int blue;
}
```

Figure 4.21 A set of twelve colors for use in labeling. The same colors are shown on a white and a black background.

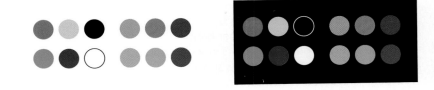

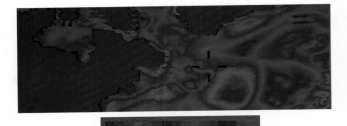

Figure 4.22 Gravitational variation over the North Atlantic is revealed using a spectrum-approximation pseudocolor sequence.

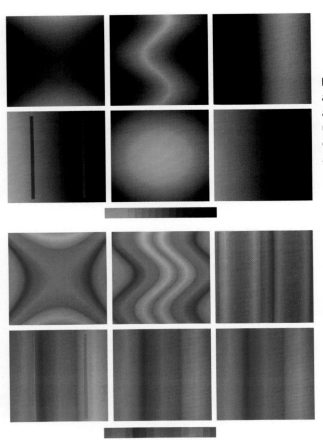

Figure 4.23 Surface shapes revealed using a gray-scale sequence and a spectrum-approximation sequence. The image in the upper-right corner shows how contrast effects are small with the spectrum approximation.

Figure 4.24
Seven different color sequences:
(a) Gray scale. (b) Spectrum
approximation. (c) Red-green.
(d) Saturation. (e) and (f) Two
sequences that will be perceived
by people suffering from the
most common forms of color
blindness. (g) A sequence of
colors in which each color is
lighter than the previous one.

Figure 4.25 The same data shown in
Figure 4.22, pseudocolored with a sequence
that provides a kind of upward spiral in color
space; each color is lighter than the preceding
one.

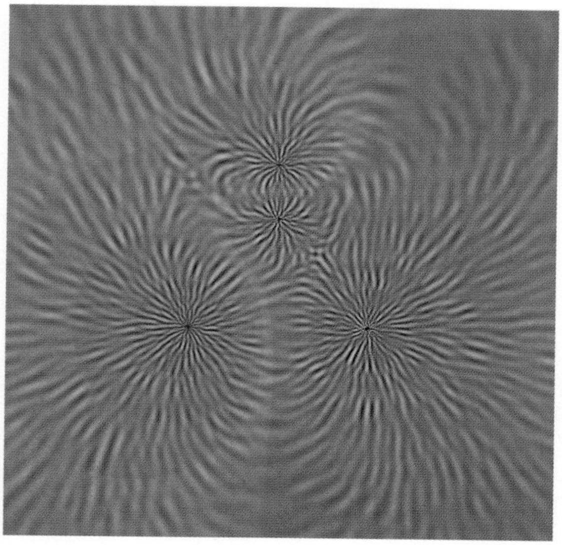

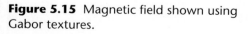

Figure 5.15 Magnetic field shown using
Gabor textures.

Figure 5.20 Textures from Witkin and Kass (1991).

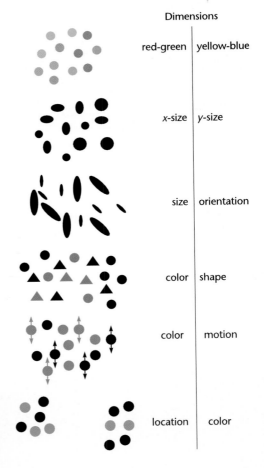

Figure 5.25 Examples of glyphs coded according to two display attributes. At the top are more integral coding pairs. At the bottom are more separable coding pairs.

Dimensions

red-green	yellow-blue
x-size	y-size
size	orientation
color	shape
color	motion
location	color

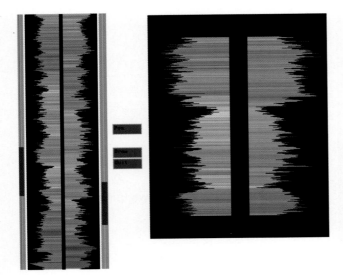

Figure 6.11 An application designed to allow users to recognize similar patterns in different time-series plots. The data represents a sequence of measurements made on deep ocean drilling cores. Two subsets of the extended sequences are shown on the right.

Figure 7.12 (a) A geon diagram constructed using a subset of Biederman's geon primitives. The primitive elements can also be color-coded and textured. (b) A Unified Modeling Language (UML) equivalent.

a.

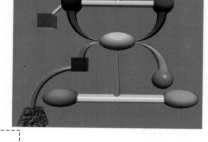

b.

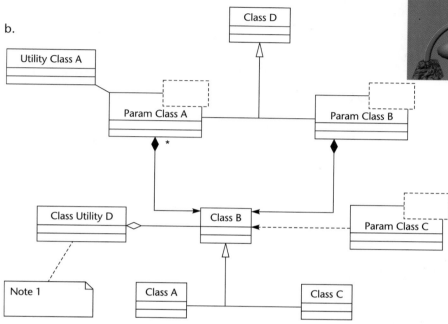

Figure 7.13 A shaded representation of San Francisco Bay, shown as if the water had been drained out of it. Data courtesy of Jim Gardiner, U.S. Geological Survey. Image constructed using IVS Fledermaus software.

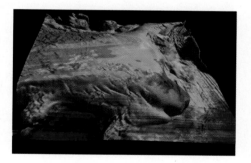

Figure 7.24 A bivariate map showing part of the Stellwagen Bank National Marine Sanctuary (Mayer et al., 1997). One variable shows angular response of sonar backscatter, color-coded and draped on the depth information given through shape-from-shading.

Figure 8.21 The structure of object-oriented software code is represented as a graph in 3D.

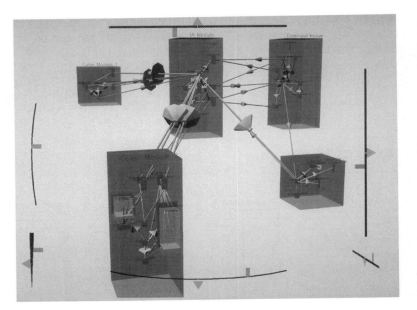

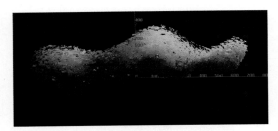

Figure 8.25 A cloud of discrete points is represented by oriented particles. The orientation is determined by using an inverse-square law of attraction between the particles. When the cloud is artificially shaded, its shape is revealed (Li, 1997).

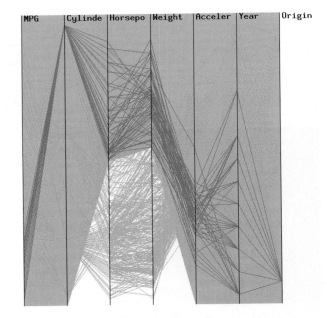

Figure 10.16 In a parallel-coordinates plot, each data dimension is represented by a vertical line. This example illustrates brushing. The user can interactively select a set of objects by dragging the cursor across them. (Courtesy of Matthew Ward)

Static and Moving Patterns

Data mining is about finding patterns that were previously unknown or patterns that depart from the norm. The stock market analyst looks for any pattern of variables that may predict a future change in price or earnings. The marketing analyst is interested in perceiving trends and patterns in a customer database. Seeing a pattern can often lead to a key insight, and this is the most compelling reason for visualization.

Here are some of the perceptual questions addressed in this chapter: What does it take for us to see a group? How can 2D space be divided into perceptually distinct regions? Under what conditions are two patterns recognized as similar? When do different elements in a display appear to be related? Answers to these questions are central to visualization, because most data displays are two-dimensional and pattern perception deals with the extraction of structure from 2D space.

Object perception is generally thought of as occurring in several stages (illustrated in Figure 6.1). At the early feature abstraction stages, the visual

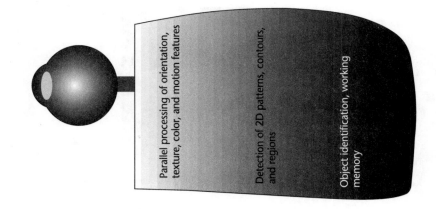
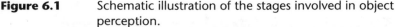

Figure 6.1   Schematic illustration of the stages involved in object perception.

image is analyzed in terms of primitive elements of form, motion, color, and stereo depth. At the next 2D pattern perception stage, the contours forming the boundaries of objects are discovered and the visual world is segmented into distinct regions, based on these same primitives. Next, the structures of objects and scenes are discovered using information about the connections between component parts, shape-from-shading information, and so on. Finally, objects are identified by means of a process that matches them with a stored representation, a memory trace. Thus, pattern perception is a set of intermediate 2D processes occurring between feature analysis and full object perception. As such, pattern perception provides a level of abstraction that can tell us much about how we should organize data so that important structures will be perceived.

There are also radical changes in the kinds of processing that occur at the different stages. In the early stages, massively parallel processing of the entire image occurs. But object recognition is a process whereby a small number of entities are analyzed in terms of their structures and shapes. Instead of millions of parallel operations, we are dealing with systems that can handle only a much smaller number of objects in a sequential fashion. When the theorists discuss higher-order processes leading to object perception, their language is full of rules. There are rules for the kinds of components that make up the letters of the alphabet and rules for the detection of separate regions in space or overlapping objects. Pattern perception is the middle ground where objects are extracted from patterns of features. Active processes of object perception reach down into the pattern space to keep track of those objects and to analyze them for particular tasks. It is in pattern space that the essentially bottom-up processing of feature primitives meets the top-down processes of cognitive perception.

It should be borne in mind that this picture of a simple linear set of stages, although useful, is certainly an oversimplification. There are feedback loops. There is overwhelming evidence that what are usually considered to be higher-level processes are influencing lower-level processes. For example, once we have identified an object, it becomes much easier to identify the same object on subsequent appearance anywhere in the visual field (Biederman and Cooper, 1992).

The first serious attempt to understand pattern perception was undertaken by a group of German psychologists who founded what is known as the Gestalt School.

Gestalt Laws

The Gestalt School of Psychology was founded in 1912 to investigate the way we perceive form. The group consisted principally of Max Westheimer, Kurt Koffka, and Wolfgang Kohler (see Koffka, 1935, for an original text). The word *gestalt* simply means *pattern* in German. The work of the Gestalt psychologists is still valued today because they provided a clear description of many basic perceptual phenomena. They produced a set of Gestalt "laws" of pattern perception. These are robust rules that describe the way we see patterns in visual displays, and although the actual mechanisms proposed by these researchers have not withstood the test of time, the laws themselves have proven to be of enduring value. The Gestalt laws easily translate into a set of design principles for information displays. Seven Gestalt laws and related design principles are presented below.

Proximity

Spatial proximity is clearly one of the most powerful perceptual organizing principles and one of the most useful in design. Things that are close together are perceptually grouped together. Figure 6.2 shows two arrays of dots that illustrate the proximity principle. Only a small change in spacing causes us to change what is perceived from a set of rows (6.2(a)) to a set of columns (6.2(b)). In 6.2(c), the existence of two groups is perceptually inescapable.

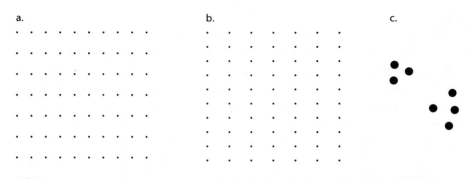

a.   b.   c.

Figure 6.2   Spatial proximity is a powerful cue for perceptual organization.
                      A matrix of dots is perceived as rows on the left (a) and
                      columns on the right (b). In (c), because of proximity
                      relationships, we perceive two groupings of three dots.

Proximity is not the only factor in predicting perceived groups. In Figure 6.3,
the dot labeled x is perceived to be part of cluster a rather than cluster b, even
though it is as close to the other points in cluster b as they are to each other.
Slocum (1983) called this the spatial concentration principle. According to
this principle, we perceptually group regions of similar element density.

The application of the proximity law in display design is straightforward:
The simplest and most powerful way of emphasizing the relationships between different data entities is to place them in proximity in a display.

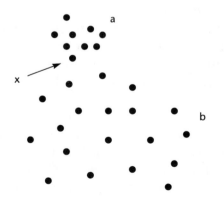

Figure 6.3   The principle of spatial concentration. The dot labeled x is
                      perceived as part of group a rather than group b.

Similarity

The shapes of individual pattern elements can also determine how they are grouped. Similar elements tend to be grouped together. In both Figure 6.4(a) and 6.4(b), the similarity of the elements causes us to see the rows most clearly.

We can combine the similarity principle with lessons from the concept of integral and separable dimensions that was discussed in Chapter 5. In Figure 6.5(a), shape is used to delineate columns and gray color is used to delineate rows. These are separable dimensions and the result is a pattern that can

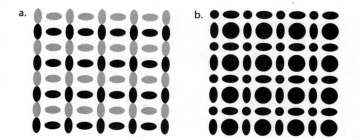

Figure 6.4   According to the Gestalt psychologists, similarity between the elements in alternate rows causes the row percept to dominate.

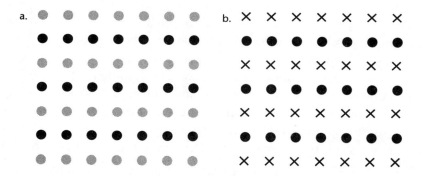

Figure 6.5   (a) Separable dimensions are used to delineate rows and columns. (b) Integral dimensions are used, and the result is that the overall pattern emerges more strongly.

be visually segmented either by rows or by columns. This can be useful if we are designing a table with graphical symbols and wish to make it easy for users to attend either to rows or to columns. In Figure 6.5(b), the integral dimensions of the horizontal and vertical measures of an ellipse are applied. The result is an overall square pattern that is more distinct than either rows or columns.

Continuity

The Gestalt principle of continuity states that we are more likely to construct visual entities out of visual elements that are smooth and continuous, rather than ones that contain abrupt changes in direction. (See Figure 6.6.)

The principle of good continuity can be applied to the problem of drawing diagrams consisting of networks of nodes and the links between them. It should be easier to identify the sources and destinations of connecting lines if they are smooth and continuous. This point is illustrated in Figure 6.7.

Continuity assumes connectedness, and Palmer and Rock (1994) argue that connectedness is a more fundamental organizing principle that the Gestalt psychologists overlooked. The demonstrations in Figure 6.8 show that connectedness can be a more powerful grouping principle than proximity, color, size, or shape.

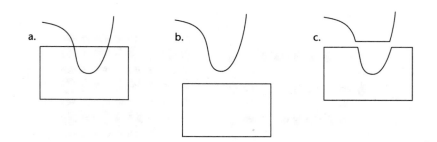

Figure 6.6   The pattern on the left (a) is perceived as a curved line overlapping a rectangle (b) rather than as the more angular components shown in (c).

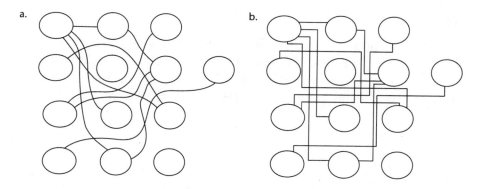

Figure 6.7   In (a), smooth continuous contours are used to connect the elements, while in (b), lines with abrupt changes in direction are used. It is much easier to perceive connections when contours connect smoothly.

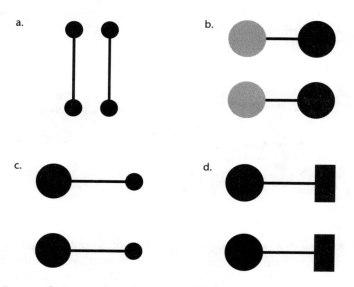

Figure 6.8   Connectedness is a powerful grouping principle that is stronger than (a) proximity, (b) color, (c) size, and (d) shape.

Symmetry

Symmetry can provide a powerful organizing principle. Figures 6.9 and 6.10 provide two examples. The symmetrically arranged pairs of lines in Figure 6.9 are perceived much more strongly as forming a visual whole than the pair of parallel lines. In Figure 6.10(a), symmetry may be the reason why the cross

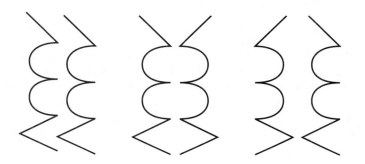

Figure 6.9   The pattern on the left consists of two identical parallel contours. In each of the other two patterns, one of the contours has been reflected about a vertical axis, producing bilateral symmetry. The result is a much stronger sense of a holistic figure.

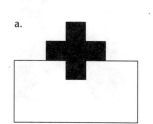
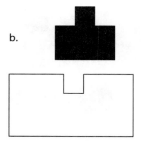

a.

b.

Figure 6.10   We interpret pattern (a) as a cross in front of a rectangle. The two objects shown in (b) are not perceived as components even though the black shape behind the white shape would be an equally simple interpretation. The cross on the rectangle interpretation has greater symmetry (about horizontal axes) for both of the components.

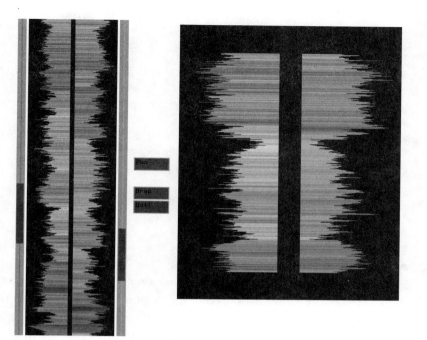

Figure 6.11   An application designed to allow users to recognize similar patterns in different time-series plots. The data represents a sequence of measurements made on deep ocean drilling cores. Two subsets of the extended sequences are shown on the right. See also color plates.

shape is perceived, as opposed to shapes in 6.10(b), even though the second option is not more complicated. A possible application of symmetry is in tasks in which data analysts are looking for similarities between two different sets of time-series data. It may be easier to perceive similarities if these time series are arranged using vertical symmetry, as shown in Figure 6.11, rather than using the more conventional parallel plots.

Closure

A closed contour tends to be seen as an object. The Gestalt psychologists argued that there is a perceptual tendency to close contours that have gaps in them. This can help explain why we see Figure 6.12 as a complete circle and a rectangle rather than as a circle with a gap in it.

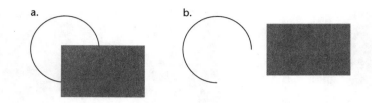

Figure 6.12   The Gestalt principle of closure holds that neural mechanisms operate to find perceptual solutions involving closed contours. Hence in (a), we see a rectangle behind a circle, not a broken ring as in (b).

Wherever a closed contour is seen, there is a very strong perceptual tendency to divide regions of space into "inside" or "outside" the contour. A region enclosed by a contour becomes a *common region* in the terminology of Palmer (1992). He showed that common region to be a much stronger organizing principle than simple proximity. This, presumably, is the reason why the Venn diagram is such a powerful device for displaying the interrelationships among sets of data. In a Venn diagram, we interpret the region inside a closed contour as defining a set of elements. Multiple closed contours are used to delineate the overlapping relationships among different sets. The two most important perceptual factors in this kind of diagram are closure and continuity. A fairly complex structure of overlapping sets is illustrated in Figure 6.13, using a Venn diagram. This kind of diagram is almost always used in teaching introductory set theory, and this in itself is evidence for its effectiveness. Students easily understand the diagrams, and they can transfer this understanding to the more difficult formal notation. Stenning and Oberlander (1994) theorize that the ease with which Venn diagrams can be understood results specifically from the fact that they have limited expressive power, unlike fully abstract formal notation.

Closed contours are extremely important in segmenting the monitor screen in "windows"-based interfaces. The rectangular overlapping boxes provide a strong segmentation cue, dividing the display into different regions. In addition, rectangular frames provide "frames of reference": The position of every object within the frame tends to be judged relative to the enclosing frame. (See Figure 6.14.)

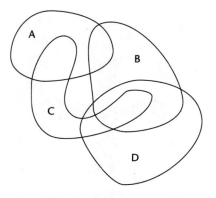

Figure 6.13   A Venn diagram. This diagram tells us (among other things) that entities can simultaneously be members of sets A and C but not of A, B, and C. Also, anything that is a member of both B and C is also a member of D. These rather difficult concepts are clearly expressed and understood by means of closed contours.

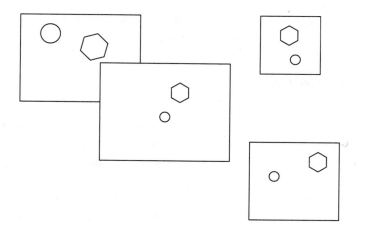

Figure 6.14   Closed rectangular contours strongly segment the visual field. They also provide reference frames. Both the positions and the sizes of enclosed objects are, to some extent, interpreted with respect to the surrounding frame.

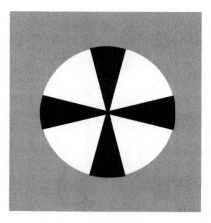

Figure 6.15   The black areas are smaller, and therefore more likely to be perceived as an object. It is also easier to perceive patterns that are oriented horizontally and vertically as objects.

Relative Size

In general, smaller components of a pattern tend to be perceived as objects. In Figure 6.15, a black propeller is seen on a white background, as opposed to the white areas being perceived as objects.

Figure and Ground

Gestalt psychologists were also interested in what they called *figure-ground* effects. A *figure* is something object-like that is perceived as being in the foreground. The *ground* is whatever lies behind the figure. The perception of figure as opposed to ground can be thought of as the fundamental perceptual act of identifying objects. All the Gestalt laws contribute, along with other factors that the Gestalt psychologists did not consider, such as texture segmentation (see Chapter 5). Closed contour, symmetry, and the surrounding white area all contribute to the perception of the shape in Figure 6.16 as figure, as opposed to a cut-out hole, for example.

Figure 6.17 shows the classic Rubin's Vase figure, in which it is possible to perceive either two faces, nose to nose, or a black vase centered in the display. The fact that the two percepts tend to alternate suggests that competing active processes may be involved in trying to construct figures from the pattern.

Figure 6.16   Symmetry, surrounding white space, and a closed contour all contribute to the strong sense that this shape is figure, rather than ground.

Figure 6.17   Rubin's Vase. The cues for figure and ground are roughly equally balanced, resulting in a bistable percept of either two faces or a vase.

More on Contours

A contour is a continuous perceived boundary between regions of a visual image. A contour can be defined by a line, by a boundary between regions of different color, by stereoscopic depth, by motion patterns, or by texture. Contours can even be perceived where there are none. Figure 6.18 illustrates an *illusory contour*: Ghostly boundaries of a blobby shape are seen even where none are physically present. There is extensive literature on illusory contours (see Kaniza, 1976, for an early review).

Since the process that leads to the identification of contours is seen as fundamental to object perception, contour detection has received considerable attention from vision researchers. There are a number of detailed neurophysiological models designed to explain how contours can be extracted from the visual image, based on what is known about early visual processing. See Marr (1982), for example.

Higher-order neurophysiological mechanisms of contour perception are not well understood. However, one result is intriguing. Gray, Konig, Engel, and Singer (1989) found that cells with collinear receptive fields tend to fire in synchrony. Thus, we do not need to propose higher-order feature detectors, responding to more and more complex curves, to understand the neural encoding of contour information. Instead, it may be that groups of cells firing in synchrony may be the way that the brain holds related pattern elements in mind. Theorists have suggested a kind of fast enabling link, a kind of rapid feedback system, to achieve the firing of cells in synchrony. For a review, see Singer and Gray (1995).

Fortunately, since a theoretical understanding is only just emerging, the exact mechanisms involved in contour detection are less relevant to the purpose of designing visualizations than are the circumstances under which we perceive contours. A set of experiments by Field et al. (1993) places the Gestalt notion of "good continuation" on a firmer scientific basis. In their experiment, subjects had to detect the presence of a continuous path in a field of 256 randomly oriented Gabor patches (see Chapter 5 for a discussion of Gabor functions). The setup is illustrated schematically in Figure 6.19. The results show that subjects were very good at perceiving a smooth path through a sequence of patches. Unsurprisingly, continuity between Gabor patches oriented in straight lines was the easiest to perceive. More interesting, even quite wiggly paths were readily seen if the Gabor elements were aligned as shown in Figure 6.19(b).

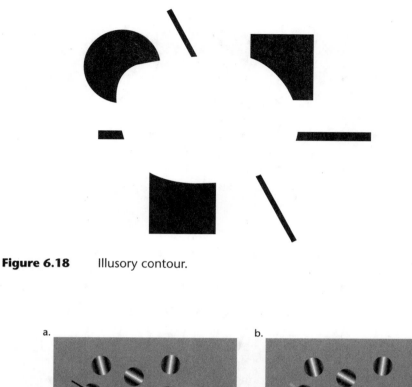

Figure 6.18   Illusory contour.

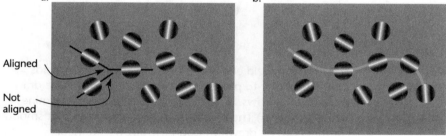

Figure 6.19   A schematic diagram illustrating the experiments conducted by Field et al. (1993). If the elements were aligned as shown in (a) so that a smooth curve could be drawn through some of them, the curve shown in (b) was perceived. In the actual experiments, Gabor patches were used.

There are direct applications of this result in displaying vector field data. A common technique is to create a regular grid of oriented arrows such as the one shown in Figure 6.20. When the arrows are displaced so that smooth contours can be drawn between them, the flow pattern is much easier to see.

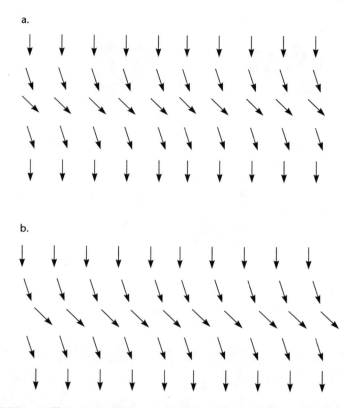

Figure 6.20   The results of Field et al. (1993) suggest that vector fields should be easier to perceive if smooth contours can be drawn through the arrows. (a) A regular grid is used to determine arrow layout. (b) The arrows have been shifted so that smooth contours can be drawn through the arrows. As theory predicts, the latter is more effective.

Perceiving Direction: Representing Vector Fields

The perception of contour leads us naturally into considering the perceptual problem of representing vector fields. This problem can be broken down into two components: the representation of orientation and the representation of magnitude. Some techniques display one component but not both.

Instead of using little arrows, one obvious and effective way of representing vector fields is through the use of continuous contours; a number of effective algorithms exist for this purpose. Figure 6.21 shows an example

Figure 6.21   Vector field streamlines are an effective way of representing vector field data. However, the direction is ambiguous and the magnitude is not clearly expressed. (Turk and Banks, 1996)

from Turk and Banks (1996). However, although this effectively illustrates the direction of the vector field, it is ambiguous in the sense that for a given contour there can be two directions of flow. Arrowheads can be added as in Figure 6.20, but this is a conventional device and the result is visual clutter. In addition, although the magnitudes of the vectors are given by line density and inverse width in Figure 6.21, this is not easy to read.

An interesting way to resolve the flow direction ambiguity is provided in a seventeenth-century vector field map of North Atlantic wind patterns by Edmund Halley (discussed in Tufte, 1983). Halley's elegant pen strokes (illustrated in Figure 6.22) are shaped like long, narrow airfoils oriented to the flow, with the wind direction given by the blunt end. Interestingly, Halley also arranges his strokes along streamlines. We experimentally verified that strokes like those of Halley are unambiguously interpreted with regard to direction (Fowler and Ware, 1989).

We also developed a new method for creating an unambiguous sense of vector field direction that involves varying the color along the length of a stroke. This is illustrated in Figure 6.23. There was a strong interaction between the direction of color change and the background color. If one end of the stroke was given the background color, the stroke direction was perceived to be in the direction of color change away from the background color. In our experiments, the impression of direction produced by color change completely dominated that given by shape.

Figure 6.22　　　Drawing in a style based on the pen strokes used by Edmund Halley (1696), discussed in Tufte (1983), to represent the trade winds of the North Atlantic. Halley described the wind direction as being given by "the sharp end of each little stroak pointing out that part of the Horizon, from whence the wind continually comes."

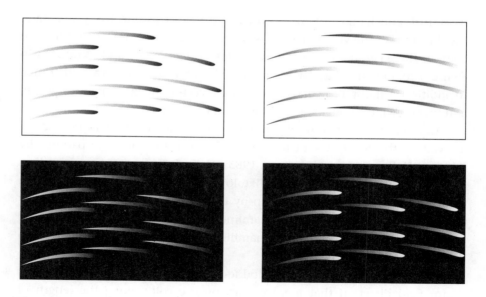

Figure 6.23　　　Vector direction can be unambiguously given by means of color change relative to the background.

Figure 6.24   Three-dimensional streamlines made using tubes. Shading provides better information about the orientation of the tubes. (Schroeder et al., 1997)

When we are rendering vector fields in 3D space, shape from shading and geometric depth cues can be used to good effect. For example, Figure 6.24 shows the three-dimensional orientation of streamlines in 3D far more effectively than simple colored lines. Three-dimensional shading and other spatial cues are discussed in Chapter 8.

Perception of Transparency: Overlapping Data

In many visualization problems, it is desirable to present data that has a layered form. This is especially common in geographical information systems (GISs). Sometimes a useful technique is to present one layer of data as if it were a transparent layer over another. However, there are many perceptual pitfalls in doing this. The contents of the different layers will always interfere with each other to some extent, and sometimes the two layers will fuse perceptually so that it is not possible to determine to which layer a given object belongs.

In simple displays such as those shown in Figure 6.25(a), the two main determinants of perceived transparency are good continuity (see Beck and Ivry, 1988) and the ratio of colors or gray values in the different pattern elements. A reasonably robust rule for transparency to be perceived is $x < y < z$ or $x > y > z$ or $y < z < w$ or $y > z > w$, where x, y, z, and w refer to gray values arranged in the pattern shown in Figure 6.25(b) (Masin, 1997). Readers who are interested in perceptual rules of transparency should also consult Metelli (1974).

Another way of representing layers of data is to show each layer as a see-through texture or screen pattern (Figure 6.26). Watanabe and Cavanaugh (1996) explored the conditions under which people perceive two distinct overlapping layers, as opposed to a single fused composite texture. In Figure 6.26(a) and (b), two different overlapping squares are clearly seen, but in (c), only a single textured patch is perceived. In (d) the percept is bistable. Sometimes it looks like two overlapping squares containing patterns of "–" elements; sometimes a central square containing a pattern of "+" elements seems to stand out as a distinct region.

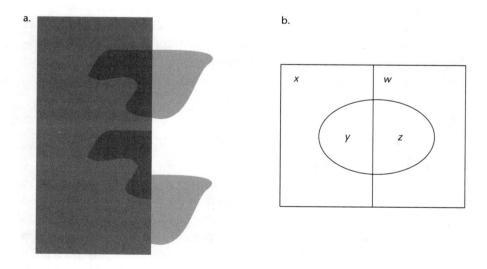

Figure 6.25   In (a), transparency is perceived only when good continuity is present and when the correct relationship of the colors is present. (See text for an explanation of (b).)

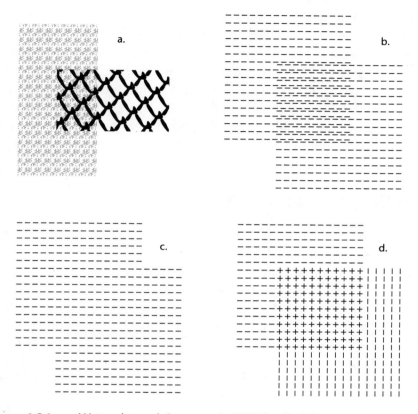

Figure 6.26   Watanabe and Cavanaugh (1996) called the texture equivalent of transparency "laciness." This figure is based on their work. (See text for an explanation.)

In general, when we present layered data, we can expect the basic rules of perceptual interference, discussed in Chapter 5, to apply. Similar patterns interfere with one another. Graphical patterns that are similar in terms of color, spatial frequency, motion, and so on tend to interfere more with one another than do those with dissimilar components.

One possible application of transparency in user interfaces is to make pop-up menus transparent so that they do not interfere with information located behind them. Harrison and Vincente (1996) investigated the interference between background patterns and foreground transparent menus. They found that it took longer to read from the menu with text or wireframe drawings in the background than with continuously shaded images in the background. This is exactly what would be expected from an interference model. Since a continuously shaded image lacks the high-frequency detail of a wireframe image or text, there will be less interference. The advantages of transparent layered displays must be weighed against the perceptual interference between the layers. In the designing of layers, textures, colors, and forms can be chosen for minimal interference by maximizing the factors differentiating the patterns on each of the channels described in Chapter 5.

The Perceptual Syntax of Diagrams

Diagrams are always hybrids of the conventional and the perceptual. Diagrams contain conventional elements, such as abstract labeling codes, that are difficult to learn but formally powerful. They also contain information that is coded according to perceptual rules, such as Gestalt principles. Arbitrary mappings may be useful, as in the case of mathematical notation, but it is important that a good diagram take advantage of basic perceptual mechanisms evolved to perceive structure in the environment. By presenting examples, the following sections describe the visual grammar of two different kinds of diagrams: node-link diagrams and the layered maps used in geographical information systems.

The Grammar of Node-Link Diagrams

There is a very large class of diagrams that we can call node-link diagrams. The essential characteristic of these diagrams is that they consist of nodes, representing various kinds of entities, and links, representing relationships between the entities. Literally dozens of different diagrams have this basic form, including software structure diagrams, data flow diagrams, organization charts, and software modeling diagrams. Figure 6.27 provides four examples commonly used in software engineering.

One set of abstractions common to node-link diagrams is so close to ubiquitous that it can be called a visual grammar. The nodes are almost always outline boxes or circles, usually representing the entities in a system. The connecting lines generally represent different kinds of relationships, transitions, or communication paths between nodes. Experimental work shows that visualizing *interdependencies* between program elements helps program understanding (Linos et al., 1994).

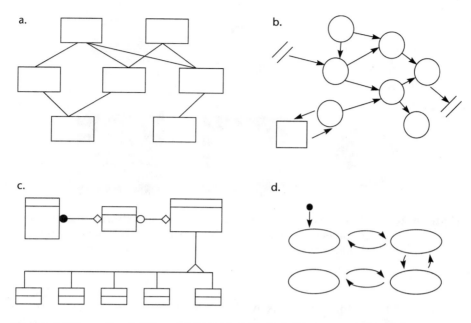

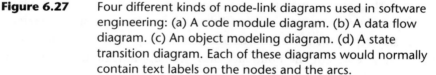

Figure 6.27   Four different kinds of node-link diagrams used in software engineering: (a) A code module diagram. (b) A data flow diagram. (c) An object modeling diagram. (d) A state transition diagram. Each of these diagrams would normally contain text labels on the nodes and the arcs.

The various reasons that we may be justified in calling these graphical codes *perceptual* are distributed throughout this book, but are mostly in this chapter and Chapter 7. The fundamental argument is that closed contours are basic in defining visual objects. Thus, although a circular line may be only a mark drawn on paper, at some level in the visual system it is object-like. Similarly, two objects can be connected by a line, and this visual connection can create a link that can represent any of a number of relationships.

Although lines get their expressive power from neural mechanisms designed to interpret objects, they are fundamentally ambiguous. Kennedy (1974) has elucidated many ways in which contours (lines) can represent aspects of the environment. Some of them are illustrated in Figure 6.28. A circle can represent a ring, a flat disk, a ball, a hole, or the boundary between two objects (a disk in a hole). This nicely illustrates the mixture of perception and convention that is common to diagrams. Our visual systems are capable of interpreting a line contour in any of these ways. In real-world

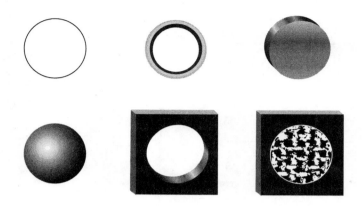

Figure 6.28   The line circle shown at the top left can represent many kinds of objects: a wire ring, a disk, a ball, a cut-out hole, or the boundary between a disk and the hole in which it resides.

scenes, additional information is available to clarify ambiguous contours. In a diagram, the contour may remain perceptually ambiguous and some convention may be necessary to remove the ambiguity. In one kind of diagram, a circle may represent an object; in another, it may represent a hole; in a third, it may represent the boundary of a geographic region. The diagram convention tells us which interpretation is correct.

The most general data model that is expressed by node-link diagrams is the entity-relationship model. It is widely used in computer science and business modeling (Chen, 1976). In entity relationships, modeling entities can be objects and parts of objects, or more abstract things such as parts of organizations. Relationships are the various kinds of connections that can exist between entities. For example, an entity representing a wheel will have a part-of relationship to an entity representing an automobile. A person may have a customer relationship to a store. Both entities and relationships can have attributes. Thus, a particular customer might be a *preferred* customer. An attribute of an organization might be the number of its employees. There are standard diagrams for use in entity-relationship modeling, but we are not concerned with these here. We are more interested in the way diagrams can be constructed that represent entities, relationships, and attributes in an easily perceived manner.

The following list is a description of the general ways in which entities and relationships can be expressed using node-link diagrams. This can be regarded loosely as a visual syntax. Each of the elements in the list has a perceptual, rather than conventional, basis for the way in which it conveys meaning. Most of these elements are discussed more extensively elsewhere in this book. Figure 6.29 provides a set of matching illustrations.

1. A closed contour in a node-link diagram generally represents an entity of some kind. It can be part of a body of software, or a person in an organization.

2. The shape of the closed contour is frequently used to represent an entity type (an attribute of the entity).

3. The color of an enclosed region represents an entity type (an attribute).

4. The size of an enclosed region can be used to represent the magnitude of an entity (a scalar attribute).

5. Lines that partition a region within a closed contour can delineate subparts of an entity. This may correspond to a real-world multipart object.

6. Closed-contour regions may be aggregated by overlapping them. The result is readily seen as a composite entity.

7. A number of closed-contour regions within a larger closed contour can represent conceptual containment.

8. Placing closed contours spatially in an ordered sequence can represent conceptual ordering of some kind.

9. A linking line between entities represents some kind of relationship between them.

10. A line linking closed contours can have different colors, or other graphical qualities such as waviness, and this effectively represents an attribute or type of a relationship.

11. The thickness of a connecting line can be used to represent the magnitude of a relationship (a scalar attribute).

12. A contour can be shaped with tabs and sockets that can indicate which components have particular relationships.

13. Proximity of components can represent groups.

The vast majority of node-arc diagrams currently in use are very simple in comparison with real-world environments. For the most part, these diagrams

Graphical Code	Visual Instantiation	Semantics
1. Closed contour.		Entity, object, node.
2. Shape of closed region.	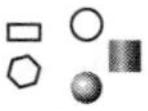	Entity type.
3. Color of enclosed region.		Entity type.
4. Size of enclosed region.		Entity value. Larger = more.
5. Partitioning lines within enclosed region.		Entity partitions are created, e.g., TreeMaps.
6. Attached shapes.		Attached entities. Part_of relations.
7. Shapes enclosed by contour.	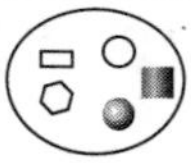	Contained entities.
8. Spatially ordered shapes.		A sequence.
9. Linking line.	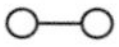	Relationship between entities.
10. Linking-line quality.	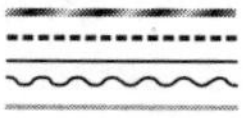	Type of relationship between entities.
11. Linking-line thickness.		Strength of relationship between entities.
12. Tab connector.		A fit between components.
13. Proximity.		Groups of components.

Figure 6.29   The visual grammar of diagram elements (node-link diagrams).

use identical rectangular or circular nodes and constant-width lines like those shown in Figure 6.27. While generic node-link diagrams are very effective in conveying patterns of structural relationships among entities, they are often poor at showing the types of entities and the types of relationships. Attributes, when they are shown, are often provided in the form of text labels attached to the boxes and lines, although occasionally dashed lines and other variations are used to denote types. Clearly, there are ways of extending this vocabulary that are perceptually sound. Chapter 7 introduces the concept of a geon diagram as a graphical device that uses 3D objects, with surface texture and color, to represent entities and relationships. However, there is a range of possibilities between the rectangular box and line diagram and fully rendered, colored, and textured 3D objects. We can make diagram boxes that are more object-like, with shape and texture denoting various attributes, and we can depict relationships that are more thread-like. Most of the different ways of representing attributes shown in Figure 6.29 are rarely used, although they are relatively easy to implement with modern computer graphics.

The Grammar of Maps

A second visual grammar can be found in the way maps are designed and interpreted. Only three basic kinds of graphical marks are common to most maps—areas, line features, and point features (Mark and Franck, 1996). Figure 6.30 illustrates this basic grammar of maps and shows how these three elements can work both in isolation and in combination.

1, 2, 3) Geographical areas are usually denoted by closed contours, tinted areas, or textured areas. Often, in a map, all three methods can be used; for example, lines may be used to represent county boundaries, texture may be used to represent vegetation, and color coding may be used to represent climate.

4) Geographical linear features represent either boundaries or elongated geographical regions. The difference between geographical areas and linear features is sometimes related to scale. At a small scale, a river will be represented by a thin line of constant width; at a larger scale, it can become an extended geographical area.

5) Dots or other small symbols are used to represent "point features," although whether or not something is a point feature

depends on the scale. At a large scale, an entire city may be represented by a single dot; at a small scale, a dot might be used to show the locations of churches, schools, or tourist attractions.

6) A dot on a line means that the entity denoted by the point feature is on, or attached to, the entity denoted by the linear feature. For example, a city is "on" a river.

Graphical Code	Visual Instantiation	Semantics
1. Closed contour.		Geographic region.
2. Colored region.		Geographic region.
3. Textured region.		Geographic region.
4. Line.		Linear map features such as rivers, roads, etc. Depends on scale.
5. Dot.	•	Point features such as town, building. Depends on scale.
6. Dot on line.		Point feature such as town on linear feature such as road.
7. Dot in closed contour.		Point feature such as town located within a geographic region.
8. Line crosses closed-contour region.		Linear feature such as river crossing geographic region.
9. Line exits closed-contour region.		A linear feature such as a river terminates in a geographic region.
10. Overlapping contour, colored regions, textured regions.		Overlapping geographically defined areas.

Figure 6.30   The visual grammar of map elements.

7) A dot within a closed contour means that the entity denoted by the point feature lies within the boundaries of the area feature. For example, a town is within a province.

8) A line crossing a closed-contour region means that a linear feature traverses an area feature. For example, a road passes through a county.

9) A line that ends in a closed-contour region means that a linear feature ends or starts within an area feature. For example, a river flows out of a park.

10) Overlapping contour regions denoted by contour, color, or texture denote overlapping spatial entities. For example, a forested region may overlap a county boundary.

Maps need not be used only for geographical information. Johnson and Schneiderman (1991) developed a system for viewing abstract data that they called TreeMaps, for displaying information about the tree data structures commonly used in computer science. (Other representations of trees are discussed in Chapter 8.) Figure 6.31 shows an example of a tree data structure presented in TreeMap form and in a conventional node-link diagram. With the TreeMap, the area of each leaf on the tree corresponds to the amount of information that is stored there. The great advantage of this technique over

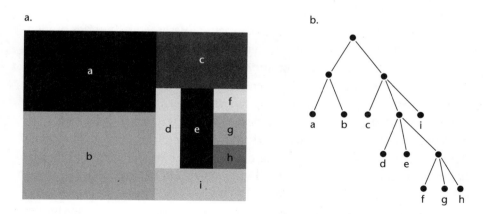

Figure 6.31 (a) A TreeMap representation of hierarchical data. Areas represent the amount of data stored in parts of the tree data structure. (b) The same tree, represented using a node-link diagram.

conventional tree views is that the amount of information on each branch of the tree can be easily visualized. The disadvantage is that the hierarchical structure is not as clear.

Of course, with interactive 3D graphics and virtual-reality displays, a map need no longer be a two-dimensional schematic diagram. It can be a much more complete visual reconstruction of part of an environment. The perceptual issues related to perceiving 3D spaces and navigating through them are discussed in Chapters 8 and 10.

Patterns in Motion

To this point, we have mainly discussed the use of static patterns to represent data, even though that data is sometimes dynamic—as in the case of a vector field representing a pattern of moving liquid or moving gas. We can also use motion as a display technique to represent data that is either static or dynamic. The perception of dynamic patterns is less well understood than the perception of static patterns. But we are very sensitive to patterns in motion and, if we can learn to use motion effectively, it may be a very good way of displaying certain aspects of data.

We start by considering the problem of how to represent data communications with computer animation. One way of doing this is to use a graphical object to represent each packet of information and then to animate that package from the information source to its destination.

First we consider the simplest case—data represented by a series of identical and equally spaced graphical elements, as shown in Figure 6.32. In this case, there is a fundamental limitation on the throughput that can be represented. In a computer animation sequence, the basic process is a loop that involves drawing the animated object, displaying it, moving it, and then redrawing it. When this cycle is repeated fast enough, a sequence of static pictures is seen as a smoothly moving image. The limitation on perceived data throughput arises from the amount that a given object can be moved before it becomes confused with another object on the next frame—this is called the correspondence problem.

If we define the distance between pattern elements as λ, we are limited to a maximum displacement of $\frac{\lambda}{2}$ on each frame of animation before the pattern is more likely to be seen as moving in the reverse direction from that desired. The problem is illustrated in Figure 6.32(a). When all the elements are

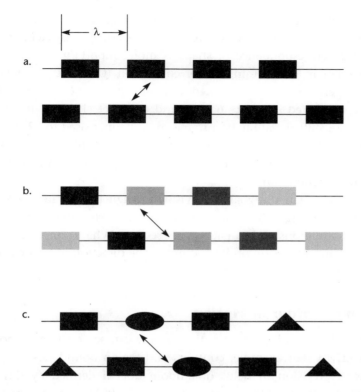

Figure 6.32   If motion is represented using a regular sequence of identical and equally spaced elements, there is a strict limit on the throughput that can be perceived. This limit can be extended by varying the sizes and shapes of the graphical elements.

identical, the brain constructs correspondences based on object proximity in successive frames. This is sometimes called the "wagon-wheel effect," because of the tendency of wagon wheels in Western movies to appear to be rotating in the wrong direction. Experiments by Fleet (1998) suggest that the maximum change per frame of animation for motion to reliably be seen in a particular direction is about ⅔ for the basic representation shown in Figure 6.32(a). Given an animation frame rate of 60 frames per second, this establishes an upper bound of 20 messages per second that can be represented.

There are many ways in which the correspondence limitation can be overcome by giving the graphical elements a different shape, orientation, or color. Two possibilities are illustrated in Figure 6.32(b) and (c). In one, the gray values of the elements are varied from message to message, and in the other, the shapes of the elements are varied. Research with element shapes suggests that correspondence of shape is more important than correspondence of color in determining perceived motion (Caelli et al., 1993). In a series of experiments that examined a variety of enhanced representations like those illustrated in Figure 6.32(b) and (c), Fleet (1998) found that the average phase shift per animation frame could be increased to 3λ before correspondence was lost. Given an animation frame rate of 60 frames per second, this translates to an upper bound of 180 messages per second that can be represented using animation.

Of course, when the goal is to visualize high traffic rates, there is no point in representing individual messages in detail. Most digital communications transfer millions of data packets per second. What is important at high data rates is an impression of data volumes, the direction of traffic flow, and large-scale patterns of activity in general.

Form and Contour in Motion

A number of studies have shown that people can see relative motion with great sensitivity. For example, contours and region boundaries can be perceived with precision in fields of random dots if defined by differential motion alone (Regan, 1989; Regan and Hamstra, 1991). Human sensitivity to such motion patterns rivals our sensitivity to static patterns; this suggests that motion is an underutilized method for displaying patterns in data.

For purposes of data display, we can treat motion as an attribute of a visual object much as we consider size, color, and position as object attributes. We (Limoges et al., 1989) evaluated the use of simple sinusoidal motion in enabling people to perceive correlations between variables. We enhanced a conventional scatter plot representation by allowing the points to oscillate sinusoidally, either horizontally or vertically (or both) about a center point. An experiment was conducted to discover whether the frequency, phase, or amplitude of point motion was the most easily "read." The task was to distinguish a high correlation from a low one. A comparison was made with more conventional graphical techniques, including using point size, gray value, and x,y position in a conventional scatter plot. The results showed that data mapped to *phase* was perceived best; in fact, it was as effective as most of the more conventional techniques, such as the use of point size or gray value. In informal studies, we also showed that motion appears to be effective in revealing clusters of distinct data points in a multidimensional data space

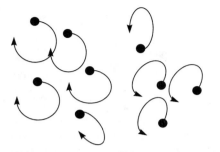

Figure 6.33   An illustration of the elliptical motion paths that result when
variables are mapped to the relative phase angles of oscillating
dots. The result is similar elliptical motion paths for points that
are similar. In this example, two distinct groups of oscillating
dots are clearly perceived.

(see Figure 6.33). Related data shows up as clouds of points moving together
in elliptical paths, and these can be easily differentiated from other clouds of
points.

Moving Frames

Perceived motion is highly dependent on its context. Johansson (1975) has
demonstrated a number of grouping phenomena that show that the brain
has a strong tendency to group moving objects in a hierarchical fashion. One
of the effects he investigated is illustrated in Figure 6.34. In this example,
three dots are set in motion. The two outer dots move in synchrony in a horizontal direction. The third dot, located between the other two, also moves in
synchrony but in an oblique direction. However, the central dot is not perceived as moving along an oblique path. Instead, what is perceived is illustrated in 6.34(b). An overall horizontal motion of the entire group of dots is
seen, and within this group the central dot appears to move vertically.

A rectangular frame provides a very strong contextual cue for motion
perception. It is so strong that if a bright frame is made to move around a
bright static dot in an otherwise completely dark environment, it is often the
static dot that is seen to move (Wallach, 1959). Wallach also showed that the
effect works in a hierarchical fashion. Thus, the motion of the dot in Figure 6.35(b) is strongly influenced by the surrounding square frame, but is not
influenced by the motion of the circle that is outside the square. The square
frame is perceived to move within the context of the surrounding circle.

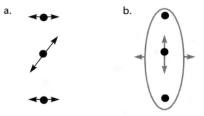

Figure 6.34   When dots are set in sychronized motion as shown in (a), what is actually perceived is shown in (b): The entire group of dots moves horizontally, while the central dot moves vertically within the group.

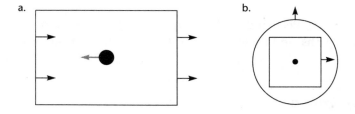

Figure 6.35   When a stationary dot is placed within a moving frame in a dark room, it is the dot that is perceived to move in the absence of other cues.

Computer animation is often used in a straightforward way to display dynamic phenomena, such as a particle flow through a vector field, and in these applications the main goal from a perceptual point of view is to bring the motion into the range of human sensitivities. The issue is the same for viewing high-speed or single-frame movie photography. The motions of flowers blooming or bullets passing through objects are speeded up and slowed down, respectively, so that we can perceive the dynamics of the phenomena. Humans are reasonably sensitive to motion ranging from a few millimeters per second to a few hundred millimeters per second for objects viewed at normal screen distances. Generally, the data animator should aim for motion in the midrange of a few centimeters per second. (See Chapter 2 for some of the basic issues related to motion sensitivity.)

The use of motion to help us distinguish patterns in abstract data is at present only a research topic, albeit a very promising one. One application of the research results is the use of frames to examine dynamic flow field animations. Frames can be used as an effective device for highlighting local relative motion. If we wish to highlight the local relative motion of a group of particles moving through a fluid, a rectangular frame that moves along with the group will create a reference area within which local motion patterns can emerge.

Another way in which motion patterns are important is in helping us to perceive visual space and rigid 3D shapes. This topic is covered in Chapter 8 in the context of the other mechanisms of space perception.

Expressive Motion

Using moving patterns to represent motion on communication channels, or in vector fields, is a rather obvious use of motion for information display, but there are other, more subtle uses. There appears to be a vocabulary of expressive motion comparable in richness and variety to the vocabulary of static patterns explored by the Gestalt psychologists. In the following sections, some of the more provocative results are discussed, together with their implications for data visualization.

Perception of Causality

When we see a billiard ball strike another and set the second ball in motion, we perceive that the motion of the first ball *causes* the motion of the second, according to the work of Michotte (translated 1963). Michotte conducted detailed studies of the perception of interactions between two patches of light and came to the conclusion that the perception of causality can be as direct and immediate as the perception of simple form. In a typical experiment, illustrated in Figure 6.36, one rectangular patch of light moved from left to right until it just touched a second patch of light, then stopped. At this point, the second patch of light would start to move. This was before the advent of computer graphics and Michotte conducted his experiments with an apparatus that used little mirrors and beams of light. Depending on the temporal relationships between the moving-light events and their relative velocities, observers reported different kinds of causal relationships, variously described as "launching," "entraining," or "triggering." Precise timing

Figure 6.36   Michotte studied the perception of causal relationships between two patches of light that moved always along the same line but with a variety of velocity patterns.

is required to achieve perceived causality. For example, Michotte found that for the effect he called launching to be perceived, the second object had to move within 70 milliseconds of contact; after this interval, subjects still perceived the first object as setting the second object in motion, but the phenomenon was qualitatively different. He called it delayed launching. Beyond about 160 milliseconds, there was no longer an impression that one event caused the other; instead, unconnected movements of the two objects were perceived. Figure 6.37 provides a reproduction of some of his results. For causality to be perceived, visual events must be synchronized within at least one-sixth of a second. Given that virtual-reality animation often occurs at only about 10 frames per second, events should be frame-accurate for clear causality to be perceived.

Michotte's book *The Perception of Causality* is a compendium of dozens of experiments, each showing how variations in the basic parameters of velocity and event timing can radically alter what is perceived. For example, if an object makes contact with another and that second object moves off at a much greater velocity, a phenomenon that Michotte called "triggering" is perceived. The first object does not seem to cause the second object to move by imparting its own energy; rather, it appears that contact triggers propelled motion in the second object.

More recent developmental work by Leslie and Keeble (1987) has shown that infants at only 27 weeks of age can perceive causal relations such as launching. This would appear to support the contention that such percepts are in some sense basic to perception.

The significance of Michotte's work for data visualization is that it provides a way to increase the expressive range beyond what is possible with static diagrams. In a static visualization, the visual vocabulary for representing relationships is quite limited. To show that one visual object is related to another, we can draw lines between them, we can color or texture groups of objects, or we can use some kind of simple shape coding. The only way of

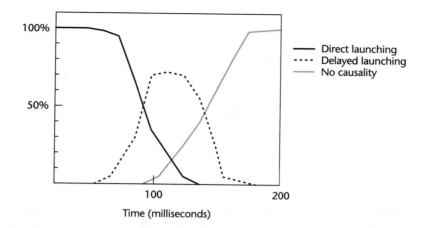

Figure 6.37   From Michotte (1963). When one object comes into contact with another, and the second moves off, the first motion may be seen to cause the second if the right temporal relationships exist. The graph shows how different kinds of phenomena are perceived depending on the delay between the arrival of one object and the departure of the other.

showing a causal link between two objects is using some kind of a conventional code, such as a labeled arrow. However, such codes owe their meaning more to our ability to understand coded language symbols than to anything essentially perceptual. This point about the differences between language-based and perceptual codes is elaborated in Chapter 9. What Michotte's work gives us is the ability to significantly enrich the vocabulary of things that can be immediately and directly represented in a diagram.

Perception of Animate Motion

In addition to the fact that we can perceive causality using simple animation, there is evidence that we are highly sensitive to motion that has a biological origin. In a series of now-classic studies, Gunnar Johansson attached lights to the limb joints of actors (Johansson, 1973). He then produced moving pictures of the actors carrying out certain activities such as walking and dancing. These pictures were made so that only the points of light were visible and in any given still frame, all that was perceived was a rather random-looking collection of dots (see Figure 6.38(a)). A remarkable result

a.   b.

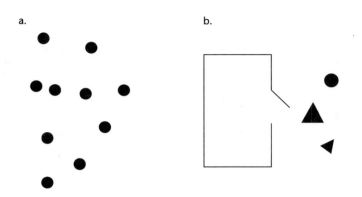

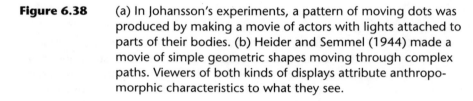

Figure 6.38   (a) In Johansson's experiments, a pattern of moving dots was
produced by making a movie of actors with lights attached to
parts of their bodies. (b) Heider and Semmel (1944) made a
movie of simple geometric shapes moving through complex
paths. Viewers of both kinds of displays attribute anthropo-
morphic characteristics to what they see.

from Johansson's studies was that viewers of the animated movies were
immediately conscious of the fact that they were watching human motion.
In addition, they could identify the genders of the actors and the tasks they
were performing. Some of these identifications could be made after exposures lasting only a small fraction of a second.

Another experiment pointing to our ability to recognize form from
motion was a study by Heider and Semmel (1944). In this study, an animated movie was produced incorporating the motion of two triangles and a
circle, as shown in Figure 6.38(b). People viewing this movie readily attributed human characteristics to the shapes; they would say, for example, that a
particular shape was angry, or that the shapes were chasing one another.
Moreover, these interpretations were consistent across observers. Since the
figures were simple shapes, the implication is that patterns of motion were
conveying the meaning. Other studies support this interpretation. Rimé et
al. (1985) did a cross-cultural evaluation of simple animations using European, American, and African subjects, and found that motion could express
such concepts as kindness, fearfulness, or aggressiveness, and there was considerable similarity in these interpretations across cultures, suggesting some
measure of universality.

Enriching Diagrams with Simple Animation

The research findings of Michotte, Johansson, Rimé, and others suggest that the use of simple motion can powerfully express certain kinds of relationships in data. Animation of abstract shapes can significantly extend the vocabulary of things that can be conveyed naturally beyond what is possible with a static diagram. The key result, that motion does not require the support of complex depictive representations (of animals or people) to be perceived as animate, means that simplified motion techniques may be useful in multimedia presentations. The kinds of animated critters that are starting to crawl and hop over Web pages are often unnecessary and distracting. Just as elegance is a virtue in static diagrams, so it is a virtue in diagrams that use animation. A vocabulary of simple expressive animation requires development, but the research results strongly suggest that this will be a productive and worthwhile endeavor. The issue is pressing, because animation tools are becoming more widely available for information display systems. More design work and more research are needed.

Conclusion

The brain is a powerful pattern-finding engine; indeed, this is the fundamental reason that visualization techniques are becoming important. There is no other way of presenting information so that structures, groups, and trends can be discovered among hundreds of data values. If we can transform data into the appropriate visual representation, its structure may be revealed. However, not all patterns are equally easy to perceive. The brain appears to be especially good at discovering linear features and distinct objects, so much so that the discovery of spurious patterns should always be a concern. Since the brain is a pattern-finding engine, patterns may be perceived even where there is only visual noise.

Much of the material presented in this chapter, especially the Gestalt laws of pattern perception, leads to rules that seem obvious to any visual designer. Nevertheless, it is surprising how often these design rules are violated. Objects that should be grouped together are commonly placed far apart in displays. Closed contours are used in ways that visually segment a display into regions that actually make it difficult, rather than easy, to comprehend related information. A common example of this is a windows display in which related information is placed in separate rectangular boxes. The very strong framing effect tends to prohibit between-window comparisons.

For the researcher and for those interested in finding novel display techniques, the effective use of motion is suggested as a fertile area for investigation. Patterns in moving data points can be perceived easily and rapidly. Given the computing power of modern personal computers, the opportunity exists to make far greater use of animation in visualizing information.

In considering pattern perception, we should always bear in mind that the perception of abstract patterns is probably not a primary purpose of visual perception. Rather, pattern-finding mechanisms are part of the neural machinery that divides the world into visual objects. For example, the reason that closed contours are so compelling in segmenting space is that they normally define objects in our environment, not that in and of themselves they have any special significance. In the next chapter, we consider ways in which 3D objects are perceived and ways in which object displays can be used to organize information.

Visual Objects and Data Objects

For our present purposes, an object can be thought of as any identifiable, separate, and distinct part of the visual world. Information about visual objects is cognitively stored in a way that ties together critical features, such as oriented edges and patches of color and texture, so that they can be identified, visually tracked, and remembered. Because visual objects cognitively group visual attributes, if we can represent data values as visual features and group these features into visual objects, we will have a very powerful tool for organizing related data. The object metaphor is pervasive in the way we think about abstract data. Object-oriented programming is but one example; the body politic is another. Object-related concepts are also basic in modern systems design. A modular system is one that has easily understood and easily replaced components. Good modules are "plug-compatible" with one another; they are discrete and separate parts of a system. In short, the concept of a module has a lot in common with the perceptual and cognitive structures that define visual objects. This suggests that visual objects may be an excellent way of representing modular system components. A visual object provides a useful metaphor for encapsulation and cohesiveness, both important concepts in defining modular systems.

Two radically different theories have been proposed to explain object recognition. The first is image-based. It proposes that we recognize an object by matching the visual image with something roughly like a snapshot stored in memory. The second type of theory is structure-based. The visual image is analyzed in terms of primitive 3D forms and the structural interrelationships between them. Both of these models have much to recommend them, and it is entirely plausible that each is correct in some form. It is certainly clear that the brain has multiple ways of analyzing visual input. Certainly, both models provide interesting insights about how to display data effectively.

Image-Based Object Recognition

We begin with some evidence related to picture and image perception. People have a truly remarkable ability to recall pictorial images. In an arduous experiment, Standing et al. (1970) presented subjects with a list of 2560 pictures at a rate of one every 10 seconds (the process took them more than seven hours spread over a four-day period). When subsequently tested, subjects were able to distinguish pictures from others not previously seen, with better than 90% accuracy. People can also recognize objects in images that are presented very rapidly. For example, Pavio and Csapo (1969) found that subjects were able to identify objects in pictures presented at the very rapid rate of 16 per second.

It is useful to make a distinction between recognition and recall. We have a great ability to recognize information that we have encountered before, as the picture memory experiment of Standing et al. shows. However, if we are asked to reconstruct visual scenes—for example, to recall what happened at a crime scene—our performance is much worse. Recognition is much better than recall. This suggests that a major use of visual images can be as an aid to memory. An image that we recognize can help us remember events or other information related to that image. This is why icons are so effective in user interfaces; they help us recall the functionality of computer programs.

Although most objects can easily be recognized independent of the size of the image on the retina, image size does have some effect. Figure 7.1 illustrates this. When the picture is seen from a distance, the image of the Mona Lisa

Figure 7.1   When the image of the Mona Lisa is viewed from a distance, the face dominates. But look at it from 30 cm and the gremlin hiding in the shadows of the mouth and nose emerges. When component objects have a size of about 4 degrees of visual angle, they become maximally visible. Adapted from the work of the Tel Aviv artist Victor Molev.

face dominates; when it is viewed up close, smaller objects become dominant: a gremlin, a bird, and a claw emerge. Experimental work by Biederman and Cooper (1992) suggests that the optimal size for recognizing a visual object is about 4 to 6 degrees of visual angle. This gives a useful rule of thumb for the optimal size for rapid presentation of visual images so that we can best see the visual patterns contained in them.

Another source of evidence for image-based object recognition comes from priming effects. The term *priming* refers to the fact that people can more easily identify objects if they are given prior exposure to some relevant information. Most priming studies have been carried out using verbal information, but Kroll and Potter (1984) showed that *pictures* of related objects, such as a cow and a horse, have a mutually priming effect. This is similar to the priming effect between the words *cow* and *horse*. However, they found little cross-modality priming; the word *cow* provided only weak priming for a picture of a horse. It is also possible to prime using purely visual information, that is, information with no semantic relationship. Lawson et al. (1994) devised a series of experiments in which subjects were required to identify a specified object in a series of briefly presented pictures. Recognition was much easier if subjects had been primed by visually similar images. They argued that this should not be the case if objects are recognized on the basis of a high-level, 3D structural model of the kind that we will discuss later in this chapter; only image-based storage can account for these results.

Priming effects can occur even if information is not consciously perceived. Bar and Biederman (1998) showed pictorial images to subjects, so briefly that it was impossible for them to identify the objects. They used what is called a masking technique, a random pattern shown immediately after the target stimulus to remove it from the iconic store, and they rigorously tested to show that subjects performed at chance levels when reporting what they had seen. Nevertheless, 15 minutes later, this unperceived exposure substantially increased the chance of recognition on subsequent presentation. Although the information was not consciously perceived, exposure to the particular combination of image features apparently primed the visual system to make subsequent recognition easier. They found that the priming effect decreased substantially if the imagery was translated by a few degrees. They conclude that the mechanism of priming is highly image-dependent and not based on high-level semantic information.

Palmer, Rosh, and Chase (1981) showed that not all views of an object are equally easy to recognize. They found that many different objects have something like a "canonical view" from which they are most easily identified. From this and other evidence, a theory of object recognition has been developed, proposing that we recognize objects by matching the visual information with internally stored viewpoint-specific exemplars, or "prototypes" (Edelman and Buelthoff, 1992; Edelman, 1995). According to this theory, the brain stores a number of key views of objects. These views are not simple snapshots; they allow recognition despite simple geometric distortions of the image that occur in perspective transformation. This explains why object perception appears to be robust against the kinds of geometric distortions that occur when a picture is viewed and tilted with respect to the observer. However, there are strict limits on the extent to which we can change an image before recognition problems occur. For example, numerous studies show that face recognition is considerably impaired if the faces are shown upside down (Rhodes, 1995).

Adding support to the multiple-view, image-based theory of object recognition is neurophysiological data from recordings of single cells in the inferotemporal cortexes of monkeys. Perett et al. (1991) discovered cells that respond preferentially to particular views of faces. Figure 7.2 shows some of their results. One cell (or cell assembly) responds best to a three-quarter view of a face; another, to profiles, either left or right; still another responds to a view of a head from any angle. We can imagine a kind of hierarchical structure, with the cell assemblies that respond to particular views feeding into higher-level cell assemblies that respond to any view of the object.

Applications of Images in User Interfaces

The fact that visual images are easily recognized after so little exposure suggests that icons in user interfaces should make excellent memory aids, helping us recall the functionality of parts of complex systems. Icons that are readily recognized may trigger activation of related concepts in the semantic network of long-term memory. Icons are also helpful because to some extent they can pictorially represent the things they are used to reference.

Priming may be useful in helping people search for particular patterns in data. The obvious way of doing this is to provide sample images of the kind of pattern being looked for and repeating the samples at frequent intervals during the search process. An example would be the use of images of sample viruses in a medical screening laboratory.

Searching an Image Database

Presenting images rapidly in sequence may be a useful way of allowing users to scan picture databases. The fact that people can rapidly search for an image in a sequence of 16 pictures per second suggests that presenting images in a rapid sequence, or *burst,* all in the same position may be efficient. Contrast this with the usual method of presenting image collections in a regular grid of small "thumbnail" images. If it is necessary to make an eye movement to fixate each thumbnail, it will not be possible to scan more than 3 to 4 images per second. Once a likely candidate image is identified as being present in a sequence using the burst method, the image set has to be fanned out in a conventional thumbnail array to confirm that candidate's presence.

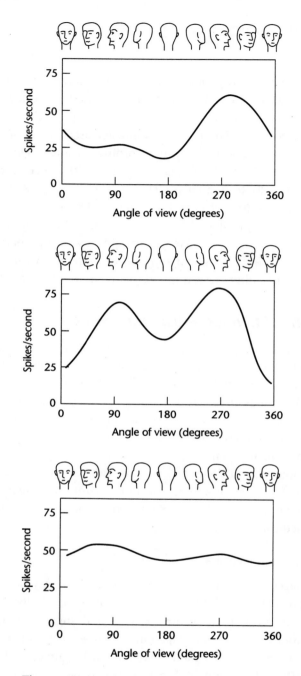

Figure 7.2 The responses of three cells in the temporal cortex of a monkey to faces in different orientations. At the top is a cell most sensitive to a left profile. In the middle is a cell that responds well to either profile. The cell at the bottom responds well to a face irrespective of orientation. Adapted from Perrett et al. (1991).

Personal Image Memory Banks

Based on straightforward predictions about the declining cost and increasing capacity of computer memory, it will shortly be possible to have a personal memory data bank containing video and sound data collected during every waking moment of a person's lifetime. This supplementary memory can be achieved with an unobtrusive miniature camera, perhaps embedded in a pair of eyeglasses, and, assuming continuing progress in solid-state storage devices, may be stored in a device weighing a few ounces and costing a few hundred dollars. Storing speech information will be even more straightforward. The implications of such a device are staggering. Among other things, it would be the ultimate memory aid—the possessor would never have to forget anything. However, a personal visual memory device of this kind would need a good user interface to be useful. One way of searching the visual content might be by viewing a rapidly presented sequence of selected frames from the video sequence. Perhaps 100 per day would be sufficient to jog the user's memory about basic events. Video data compressed in this way might make it possible to review a day in a few seconds, and a month in a few minutes.

Structure-Based Object Recognition

Image-based theories of object recognition imply a rather superficial level of analysis of visual objects. However, there is evidence that a much deeper kind of structural analysis must also occur. Figure 7.3 shows two novel objects, probably never seen by the reader before. Yet despite the fact that the *images* of these two objects are very different from one another, they can be rapidly recognized as representations of the same object. No image-based theory can account for this result.

Figure 7.3   These two objects are rapidly recognized as identical, or at least very similar, despite the very different visual images they present.

Geon Theory

Figure 7.4 provides a somewhat simplified overview of a neural-network model of structural object perception, developed by Hummel and Biederman (1992). This theory proposes a hierarchical set of processing stages leading to

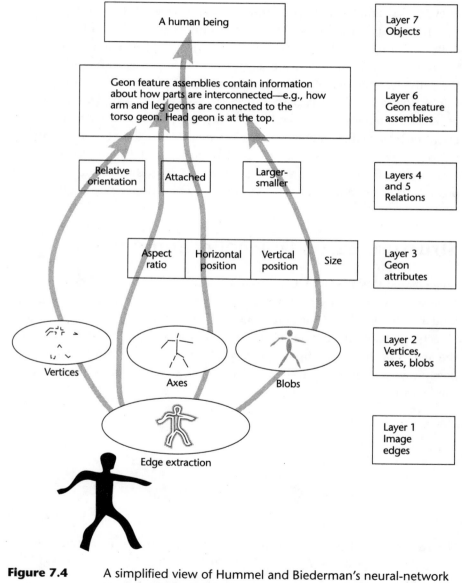

Figure 7.4   A simplified view of Hummel and Biederman's neural-network model of form perception.

Figure 7.5   According to Biederman's geon theory, the visual system interprets 3D objects by identifying 3D component parts called geons.

object recognition. Visual information is decomposed first into edges, then into component axes, oriented blobs, and vertices. At the next layer, three-dimensional primitives such as cones, cylinders, and boxes (called geons) are identified. A selection is illustrated in Figure 7.5. Next, the structure is extracted that specifies how the geon components interconnect; for example, for a human figure, the arm cylinder is attached near the top of the torso cylinder. Finally, object recognition is achieved.

Silhouettes

Silhouettes appear to be especially important in determining how we perceive the structure of objects. The fact that simplified line drawings are often silhouettes may, in part, account for our ability to interpret them. At some level of perceptual processing, the silhouette boundaries of objects and the simplified line drawings of those objects excite the same neural contour-extraction mechanisms. Halverston (1992) noted that modern children tend to draw objects on the basis of the most salient silhouettes, as did early cave artists. Many objects have particular silhouettes that are easily recognizable; think of a teapot, a shoe, a church, a person, or a violin. These *canonical* silhouettes are based on a particular view of an object, often from a point at right angles to a major plane of symmetry. Figure 7.6 illustrates canonical views of a teapot and a person.

David Marr suggested ways in which the brain might use silhouette information to extract the structures of objects (Marr, 1982). He argued that "buried deep in our perceptual machinery" (p. 219) are mechanisms that contain constraints determining how silhouette information is interpreted. Three rules are embedded in this perceptual machinery:

1. Each line of sight making up a silhouette grazes the surface exactly once. The set of such points is the contour generator.

2. Nearby points on the contour of an image arise from nearby points on the contour generator of the viewed object.

3. All the points on the contour generator lie on a single plane.

The idea of the contour generator is illustrated in Figure 7.7.

Under Marr's default assumptions, contour information is used in segmenting an image into its component solids. Marr and Nishihara (1978) suggested that concave sections of the silhouette contour are critical in defining the ways different solid parts are perceptually defined. Figure 7.8 illustrates a crudely drawn animal that we nevertheless readily segment into head, body, neck, legs, and so on. Marr and Nishihara also suggested a mechanism whereby the axes of the parts become cognitively connected to form a structural skeleton.

Figure 7.6   Many objects have canonical silhouettes, defined by the viewpoints from which they are most easily recognized. In the case of the man, the overall posture is unnatural, but the component parts—hands, feet, head, and so on—are all given in canonical views.

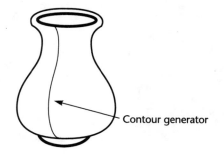

Figure 7.7 According to Marr, the perceptual system makes assumptions that occluding contours are smoothly connected and lie in the same plane. Adapted from Marr (1982).

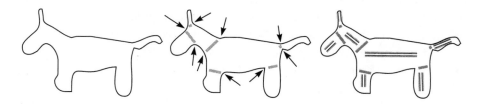

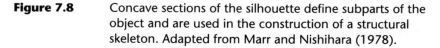

Figure 7.8 Concave sections of the silhouette define subparts of the object and are used in the construction of a structural skeleton. Adapted from Marr and Nishihara (1978).

One of the consequences of structural theories of perception is that certain simplified views should be easier to read. There are practical advantages to this. For example, a clear diagram may sometimes be more effective than a photograph. This is exactly what Ryan and Schwarz (1956) showed when they found that a hand could be perceived more rapidly in the form of a simplified line drawing than in the form of a photograph (see Figure 7.9).

But this result should not be overgeneralized. Other studies have shown that time is required for detailed information to be perceived (Price and Humphreys, 1989; Venturino and Gagnon, 1992). Simplified line drawings may be most appropriate only where rapid responses are required.

Although image-based theories and structure-based theories of object recognition are usually presented as alternatives, it may be that both kinds of processes occur. If geons are extracted based on concavities in the silhouette, certain views of a complex object will be much easier to recognize. Further, it

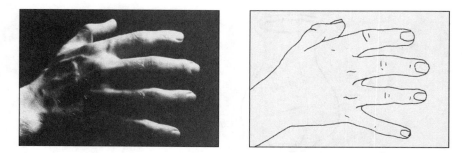

Figure 7.9   A photograph of a hand and a simplified line drawing of the hand. Ryan and Schwarz (1956) showed that a cartoon image was recognized more rapidly than a photograph.

may well be that viewpoint-dependent aspects of the visual image are stored in addition to the 3D structure of the object. Indeed, it seems likely that the brain is capable of storing many kinds of information about an object or scene if they have some usefulness. The implication is that even though 3D objects in a diagram may be more effective in some cases, care should be taken to provide a good 2D layout.

The Object Display and Object-Based Diagrams

Wickens (1992) is primarily responsible for the concept of an *object display* as a graphical device employing "a single contoured object" to integrate a large number of separate variables. Wickens theorized that mapping many data variables onto a single object will guarantee that these variables are processed together, in parallel. This approach, he claimed, has two distinct advantages. The first is that the display can reduce visual clutter by integrating the variables into a single visual object. The second is that the object display makes it easier for an operator to integrate multiple sources of information.

Among the earlier examples of object displays are Chernoff Faces, named after their inventor, Chernoff (1973). In this technique, a simplified image of a human face is used as a display. Examples are shown in Figure 7.10. To turn a face into a display, data variables are mapped to different facial features such as the length of the nose, the curvature of the mouth, the size of the

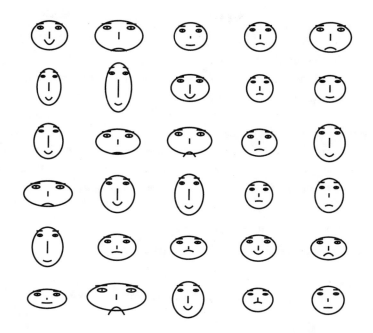

Figure 7.10   Chernoff Faces. Different data variables are mapped to the sizes and shapes of different facial features.

eye, the shape of the head, and so on. There are good psychological reasons for choosing what might seem to be a rather whimsical display object. Faces are probably the most important class of objects in the human environment. Even newborn babies can rapidly distinguish faces from nonfaces with scrambled features, suggesting that we may have special neural hardware for dealing with faces. Jacob et al. (1976) carried out a classification task using a series of displays that were progressively more object-like. The displays included Chernoff Faces, tables, star plots, and the whisker plots described in Chapter 5. They found that the more object-like displays, including Chernoff Face plots, enabled faster, more accurate classification.

Chernoff Faces have not generally been adopted in practical visualization applications. The main reason for this may be the idiosyncratic nature of faces. When data is mapped to faces, many kinds of perceptual interactions can occur. Sometimes the combination of variables will result in a particular stereotypical face, perhaps a happy face or a sad face, and this will be identified more readily. In addition, there are undoubtedly great differences in our sensitivity to the different features. We may be more sensitive to the curvature of the mouth than to the height of the eyebrows, for example. This means that the perceptual space of Chernoff Faces is likely to be extremely nonlinear. In addition, there are almost certainly many uncharted interactions between facial features, and these are likely to vary from one viewer to another.

Often, object displays will be most effective when the components of the objects have a natural or metaphorical relationship to the data being represented. For example, Figure 7.11 illustrates how a storage vessel in a chemical plant might be represented using both a conventional bar chart and a customized object display. The variables in the object diagram are represented as follows:

- Size of cylinder represents tank capacity
- Height of liquid represents volume of material stored
- Texture of liquid represents the chemical composition
- Color of liquid represents liquid temperature
- Diameter of pipe represents outflow capacity
- Status of the valve and thickness of the outgoing fluid stream represent rate at which liquid is being drawn from the tank

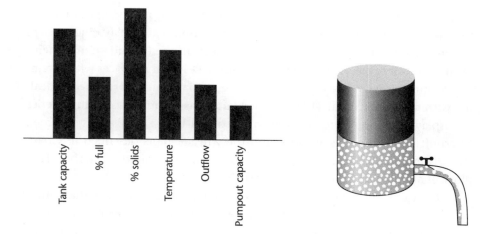

Figure 7.11   Two representations of the same data. The object diagram on the right combines six variables in an easily interpreted, cohesive representation.

In this example, the object display has a number of clear advantages. It can reduce accidental misreadings of data values. Mistakes are less likely because components act as their own descriptive icons. In addition, the structural architecture of the system and the connections between system components are always visible and this may help in diagnosing the causes and effects of problems. Conversely, the disadvantage of object displays is that they lack generality. Each display must be custom-designed for the particular application, and ideally should be validated with a user population to ensure that the data representation is clear and properly interpreted. This requires far more effort than displaying data as a table of numbers or a simple bar chart.

The Geon Diagram

Biederman's geon theory, outlined earlier, can be applied directly to object display design. If cylinders and cones are indeed perceptual primitives, it will make sense to construct diagrams using these geon elements. This should make them easy to interpret if a good mapping can be found from the data to a geon structure. The geon diagram concept is illustrated in Figure 7.12(a). Geons are used to represent the major components of a compound data object, while the architecture of the data object is represented by the structural skeleton linking the geons. The size of a geon becomes a natural metaphor for the relative importance of a data entity, or its complexity, or its relative value. The strength of the connections between the components is given by the neck-like linking structures. Additional attributes of entities and relationships can be coded by coloring and texturing them.

We (Irani and Ware, 1999) evaluated the geon diagram concept in a comparison with Unified Modeling Language (UML) diagrams. UML is a widely used, standardized diagramming notation for representing complex systems. Equivalent diagrams were constructed by matching geon elements to UML elements (see Figure 7.12). We found that when the task involved rapid identification of substructures in a larger diagram, participants performed both faster and with only half the errors using the geon diagrams. Another experiment showed that geon diagrams were easier to remember.

In Biederman's theory, surface properties of geons, such as their colors and textures, are secondary characteristics. This makes it natural to use the surface color and texture of the geon to represent data attributes of a data

a.

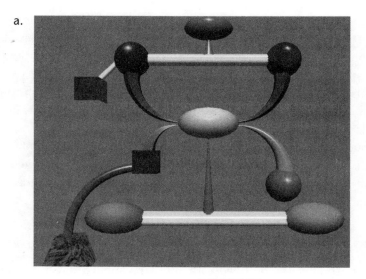

b.

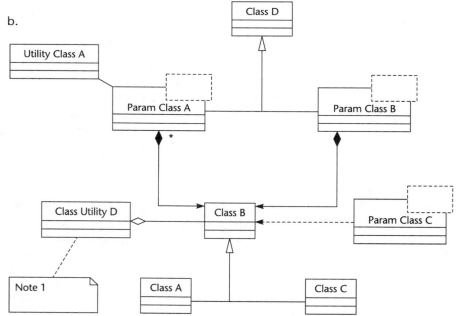

Figure 7.12   (a) A geon diagram constructed using a subset of Biederman's geon primitives. The primitive elements can also be color-coded and textured. (b) A Unified Modeling Language (UML) equivalent. See also color plates.

object. The important mappings between data and a geon diagram are as follows:

Major components of → Geons.
a complex data object

Architectural links → Limbs consisting of elongated geons.
between data object Connections between limbs reflect
components architectural structure of data.

Minor subcomponents → Geon appendices—small geon
components attached to larger geons.

Component attributes → Geon color, texture, and symbology
mapped onto geons.

Although the geon diagram is a 3D representation, there are reasons to pay special attention to the way it is laid out in 2D in the *x,y* plane. As discussed earlier, some silhouettes are especially effective in allowing the visual system to extract object structure. Thus, a common sense design rule is to lay out structural components principally on a single plane. A diagramming method resembling the bas-relief stone carvings common in classical Rome and Greece may be optimal. Such carvings contain careful 3D modeling of the component objects, combined with only limited depth and a mainly planar layout.

Perceiving the Surface Shapes of Objects

Not all things in the world are made up of closed discrete components like geons. For example, there are undulating terrains that have no clearly separable components. Although to some extent we can decompose such a landscape into features such as hills and valleys, these are not essential to perceiving the shape of any given area of the surface. Examples of continuous surfaces that are important in visualization include digital elevation maps representing the topography of the land or the ocean floor, maps of physical properties of the environment, such as pressure and temperature, and maps representing mathematical functions that are only distantly related to the raw data. The general terms for this class of data object are *two-dimensional scalar fields* and *univariate maps.* The two traditional methods for displaying scalar-field information are the contour map, which originated in cartography, and the pseudocolor map discussed in Chapter 4.

Spatial Cues for Representing Scalar Fields

From a Gibsonian point of view, the obvious way of representing a univariate map is to make it into a physical surface in the environment. Some researchers occasionally do just this; they construct plaster or foam models of data surfaces. But the next-best thing may be to use computer graphics techniques to shade the data surface with a simulated light source and give it a simulated color and texture to make it look like a real physical surface. Such a simulated surface can be viewed using a stereoscopic viewing apparatus, by creating different perspective images, one for each eye. These techniques have become so successful that the auto industry is using them to design car bodies in place of the full-sized clay models that were once constructed by hand to show the curves of a design. The results have been huge cost savings and a considerably accelerated design process.

An important issue in the creation of univariate maps is determining how to represent surface shape most effectively. Four principal sets of visual cues for surface shape perception have been studied: shading models, surface texture, stereoscopic depth, and motion parallax.

Shading Models

The basic shading model used in computer graphics to represent the interaction of light with surfaces has already been discussed in Chapter 2. The reader should refer back to it at this point, and recall that it has four basic components, as follows:

Lambertian shading: light reflected from a surface equally in all directions.

Specular shading: the highlights reflected from a glossy surface.

Ambient shading: light coming from the surrounding environment.

Cast shadows: shadows cast by an object, either on itself or on other objects.

Figure 7.13 illustrates the shading model, complete with cast shadows, applied to a digital elevation map of San Francisco Bay. As can be seen, even this simplified model is capable of producing a dramatic image of a surface

Figure 7.13   A shaded representation of San Francisco Bay, shown as if the water had been drained out of it. Data courtesy of Jim Gardiner, U.S. Geological Survey. Image constructed using IVS Fledermaus software. See also color plates.

topography. A key question in choosing a shading model for data visualization is not its degree of realism, but how well it reveals the surface shape. There is some evidence to support the idea that more sophisticated lighting may be harmful in representing surfaces. Experiments by Ramarchandran (1988) suggest that the brain assumes a *single* light source from *above* in determining whether a particular shaded area is a bump or a hollow. (See Figure 7.14.) The kinds of complex shadows that result from multiple light sources and radiosity modeling may be visually confusing rather than helpful. Chapter 8 presents additional evidence that cast shadows can provide spatial information relevant to the layout of objects in space rather than their surface shapes.

Surface Texture

Surfaces in nature are generally textured. Gibson (1986) took the position that surface texture is an essential property of a surface. A nontextured surface, he said, is merely a patch of light. The way in which textures become wrapped around surfaces can provide valuable information about surface shape.

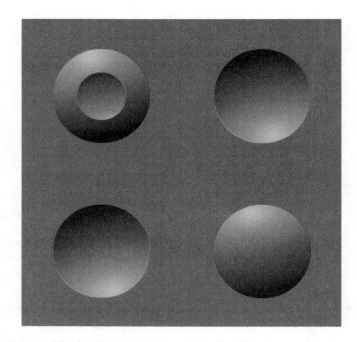

Figure 7.14   The brain generally assumes that lighting comes from above. The bumps in this image become hollows when the picture is turned upside down.

Texturing surfaces is especially important when they are viewed stereoscopically. This becomes obvious if we consider that a uniform nontextured polygon contains no *internal* stereoscopic information about the surface it represents. Under uniform lighting conditions, such a surface also contains no orientation information. When a polygon is textured, every texture element provides stereoscopic depth information relative to neighboring points. Figure 7.15 shows a stereo pair representing a textured surface.

Without texture, it is usually impossible to distinguish one transparent curved surface from another transparent curved surface lying beneath it. Figure 7.16 shows an illustration from Interrante et al. (1997) containing experimental see-through textures designed to reveal one curved surface lying above another. The concept of "laciness," discussed in Chapter 6, is relevant here, because it tells us something about how to make layers visually distinct.

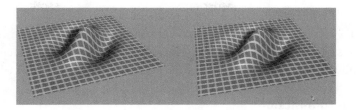

Figure 7.15   A stereo pair showing a textured surface.

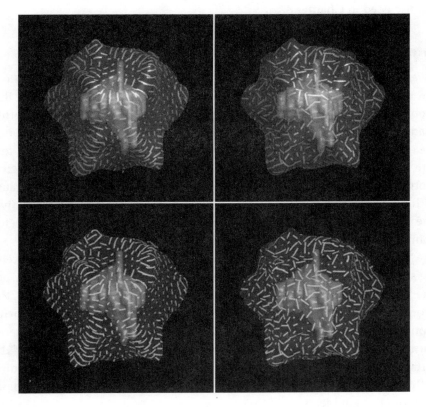

Figure 7.16   Texture designed to reveal surface shape. From Interrante et al. (1997).

Stereoscopic Viewing

The visual system can extract spatial information from differences between the images present in the two eyes. We will discuss the basis of stereoscopic depth and the perception of surfaces under stereoscopic viewing in Chapter 8.

Structure-from-Motion

When objects move, or when we move through the environment, the shapes that appear on the retina change correspondingly. The brain can use these moving patterns to infer spatial layout. When surfaces are in motion, we can perceive their shapes more accurately. Structure-from-motion has two forms: the kinetic depth effect and motion parallax. These strong spatial cues are discussed in Chapter 8.

Integration of Cues for Surface Shape

Given the many factors that may be involved in surface shape perception, the question arises as to which of them are most helpful. To study this problem, Norman et al. (1995) used computer graphics to render smoothly shaded rounded objects like that shown in Figure 7.17. They manipulated the entire list of variables given above (specular and lambertian shading, texture, stereo, and motion parallax) in a multifactor experiment. Stereo and motion were studied only in combination with the other cues because without shading or texture, neither stereo nor motion cues can be effective. The subjects' task was to indicate surface orientation at a number of selected points by manipulating the 3D glyph shown in Figure 7.18.

Norman et al. found *all* of the cues they studied to be useful in perceiving surface orientation, but the relative importance of the cues differed from one subject to another. For some subjects, motion appeared to be the stronger cue; for others, stereo was stronger. A summary of their results with motion and stereo data combined is given in Figure 7.19. Motion and stereo both reduced errors dramatically when used in combination with *any* of the surface representations. Overall, the combination of lambertian shading with either stereo or motion was either the best or nearly the best combination for all the subjects.

There have been other studies of the relative importance of different cues to the perception of surface shape. Todd and Mingolla (1983) found surface texture to be more effective in determining surface shape than either lambertian shading or specular shading. However, because of the lack of a

Figure 7.17   Textured shaded irregular objects used by Norman et al. (1995) in experiments to determine which visual information contributes most to the perception of surface shape.

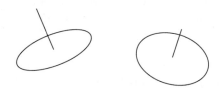

Figure 7.18   Interactive glyph used by Norman et al. (1995) to measure perception of surface orientation.

convincing general theory for the combination of spatial cues, it is difficult to generalize from experiments such as this. Many of the results may be valid only for specific textures used, for example, and the fact that there are large individual differences is another barrier to reaching general conclusions. Random textures, such as those used by Norman et al. (1995), may not be as effective in revealing shape as regular textured surface shape (Interrante et al., 1997). For these reasons, it is not meaningful to make general statements such as "Lambertian shading is more useful than texture." The values of the

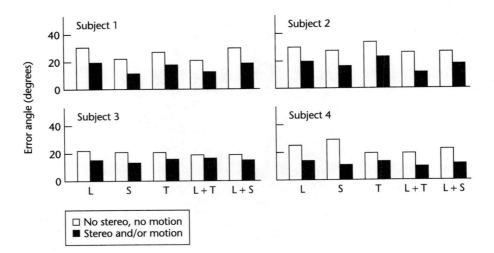

Figure 7.19   Results for the study of shape perception by Norman et al. (1995). The average errors in adjusted orientation are shown for five different surface representations. The different representations are labeled as follows: lambertian shading (L), texture with no shading (T), specular highlight shading (S), lambertian shading with texture (L+T), and lambertian shading with specular highlights (L+S). The four sets of histograms represent results from four different subjects.

different cues will also depend on the specific task. For example, specular highlights can be extremely useful in revealing fine surface details, as when a light is used to show scratches on glass. At other times, highlights will obscure patterns of surface color.

Interaction of Shading and Contour

The boundary contours of objects can interact with surface shading to dramatically change perception of surface shape. Figure 7.20 is adapted from Ramarchandran (1988). It shows two shapes that have exactly the same shading, but have different silhouette contours. The combination of silhouette contour information with shading information is convincing in both cases, but the surface shapes that are perceived are very different. This tells us that shape-from-shading information is inherently ambiguous; it can be interpreted in different ways depending on the contours.

Contours that are drawn on a shaded surface can also drastically alter the perceived shape of that surface. Figure 7.21 has added shaded bands that provide internal contour information. As in Figure 7.20, the actual pattern of shading within each of the two images, and within the bands, is the same. It

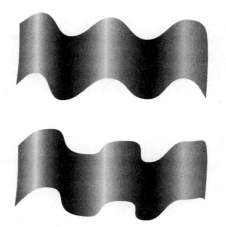

Figure 7.20   When scanned from left to right, the sequences of gray values in these two patterns are identical. The external contour interacts with the shading information to produce the perception of two very differently shaped surfaces.

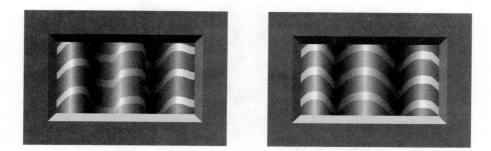

Figure 7.21   The left-to-right sequence in these patterns is also identical. The internal contours interact with the shading information to produce the perception of two very differently shaped surfaces.

is the contour information that makes one surface shape appear so different from the other. This technique can be used directly in displaying shaded surfaces to make a shape easier to perceive.

One of the most common ways of representing surfaces is using a contour map. A contour map is a plan view representation of a surface with isoheight contours, usually spaced at regular intervals. Conceptually, each contour can be thought of as the line of intersection of a horizontal plane with a particular value in a scalar height field, as illustrated in Figure 7.22. Although reading contour maps is a skill that requires practice and experience, contour maps should not necessarily be regarded entirely as arbitrary graphical conventions. Contours are visually ambiguous with respect to such things as degree of slope and direction of slope; this information is given only in the printed labels that are attached to them. However, it is likely that the contours in contour maps get at least some of their expressive power because they provide a limited perceptual code. As we have seen, both occluding (silhouette) contours and surface contours are effective in providing shape information. Also, although contour-map contours are not silhouettes, they obey one of the cognitive restrictions that Marr (1982) proposed for occluding contours, namely, that contours are assumed to be planar. They also provide texture gradient information. Thus, contour maps are a good example of a hybrid code; they make use of a perceptual mechanism, and they are also partly conventional.

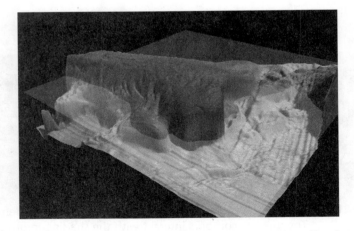

Figure 7.22   How a contour is created by the intersection of a plane with a scalar field.

Saito and Takahashi (1990) developed techniques for combining naturally shaded representations with artificial techniques such as contouring to render digital terrains more effectively. Figure 7.23, from Saito and Takahashi (1990), shows a number of illustrations of the same digital landscape enhanced by silhouette information, shading, and contour information.

(sh) shaded image

(mx3) combination of three enhanced images

(cn) contour image

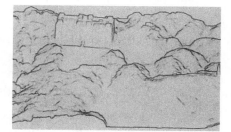

(pr) profile image

(mx2) combination of (pr) and (sh)

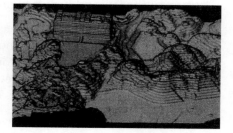

(mx4) combination of four enhanced images

Figure 7.23   A landscape with enhanced silhouettes, horizontal contours, color coding by height, and shading. (Saito and Takahashi, 1990. Reproduced with permission.)

Guidelines for Displaying Surfaces

Taken together, the evidence suggests that it may be possible to do better than simply create a photorealistic rendering of a scene using the most sophisticated techniques of computer graphics. A simplified lighting model— for example, a single light source located at infinity—may be more effective than complex rendering using multiple light sources. The importance of contours and the easy recognizability of cartoon representation suggest that an image may be enhanced for display purposes by using techniques that are nonrealistic.

Taking all the above caveats into consideration, some simple guidelines may be useful for the typical case:

1. A simple lighting model, based on a single light source, should normally be used. The light source should be from above and to one side and infinitely distant.

2. Both lambertian and moderate specular surface reflection should be modeled. More sophisticated lighting modeling, such as the inter-reflection of light between surfaces, should be avoided for reasons of clarity.

3. Specular reflection is especially useful in revealing fine surface detail. Because of its dependence on both the viewpoint and the position of the light source, the user should be given interactive controls to specify where the highlights will appear.

4. Cast shadows should be used if possible, but only if the shadows do not interfere with other displayed information. The shadows should be computed to have blurred edges to make a clear distinction between shadow and surface pigment changes.

5. Surfaces should be textured, especially if they are to be viewed in stereo. However, the texturing should ideally be low-contrast so as not to interfere with shading information. Textures that have linear components are more likely to reveal surface shape than are randomly stippled patterns.

6. Where appropriate hardware is available, both structure-from-motion (by rotating the surface) and stereoscopic viewing will enhance the user's understanding of 3D shape. These may be especially useful where one textured transparent surface overlays another.

Bivariate Maps: Lighting and Surface Color

In many cases, it is desirable to represent more than one continuous variable over a plane. This representation is called a bivariate or multivariate map. From the ecological optics perspective discussed in Chapter 1, the obvious bivariate map solution is to represent one of the variables as a shaded surface and the other as color coding on that surface. A third variable might use variations in the surface texture. These are the patterns we have evolved to perceive. An example is given in Figure 7.24, where one variable is a height map of the ocean floor and the surface color represents sonar backscatter strength. In this case, the thing being visualized is actually a physical 3D surface. However, the technique also works when both variables are abstract. For example, a radiation field can be expressed as a shaded height map and a temperature field can be represented as the surface color.

If this colored and shaded surface technique is used, some obvious trade-offs must be observed. Since luminance is used to represent shape-from-shading by artificially illuminating the surface, we should not use luminance (at least not much) in coloring the surface. Therefore, the surface coloring must be done mainly using the chromatic opponent channels discussed in Chapter 4. But because of the inability of color to carry high-spatial-frequency

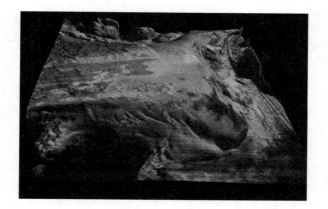

Figure 7.24　A bivariate map showing part of the Stellwagen Bank National Marine Sanctuary (Mayer et al., 1997). One variable shows angular response of sonar backscatter, color-coded and draped on the depth information given through shape-from-shading. See also color plates.

information, only rather gradual changes in color can be perceived. Therefore, in designing a multivariate surface display, rapidly changing information should always be mapped to luminance. For a more detailed discussion of these spatial trade-offs, see Robertson (1988), Rogowitz and Treinish (1996), and Chapter 4 of this book.

A similar set of constraints applies to the use of visual texture. Normally it is advisable to use luminance contrast in displaying texture, but this will also tend to interfere with shape-from-shading information. Thus, if we use texture to convey information, we have less available visual bandwidth to express surface shape and surface color. We can gain a relatively clear and easily interpreted trivariate map, but only so long as we do not need to express a great deal of detail. Using color, texture, and shape-from-shading to display different continuous variables does not increase the total amount of information that can be displayed per unit area, but it does allow multiple map variables to be independently perceived.

Integration

In this chapter, we have seen a number of ways in which different spatial variables interact to help us recognize objects, their object structures, and their surfaces. However, nothing has been presented on how the brain organizes these different kinds of information. What is the method by which the shape, color, size, texture, structure, and other attributes of an object are stored and indexed? Unfortunately, this is still largely an open question. Only some highly speculative theories exist.

One suggestion is the theoretical concept of the object file, introduced by Kahneman and Henik (1981) to account for human perceptual organization. An object file is a temporary cognitive structure that stores or indexes all aspects of an object: its color, size, orientation, and texture, and even its name and other semantic links (Kahneman et al., 1992). An object file can be thought of as a cognitive object data structure that maintains links to all the attributes of an object that is being perceived. An object file allows us to keep track of objects in the visual field, both when they disappear behind other objects and from one fixation to the next. Work by Pylyshyn and Storm (1988) and Yantis (1992) suggests that only a small number of visual objects, somewhere between two and four, can be maintained simultaneously in this way. Because of this, the display designer should drastically restrict the number of complex objects that are required simultaneously for any complex decision-making task.

Since linguistic as well as visual information is included in the object file, it explains a number of well-known psychological effects. One effect is that almost any information about an object, either visual or verbal, can be used to prime for that object. *Priming* is the term used to refer to the way that prior "priming cues" make an object more easily and more rapidly recognized. If there were a strong separation between visual and verbal information, we would not expect a verbal priming cue, the word *bark,* to make it easier to identify a picture of a dog. But in fact, verbal priming does improve object recognition, at least under certain circumstances. Although, as discussed early in this chapter, there are also many priming effects that are strongest within a sensory modality and this is part of the evidence for separate verbal and visual processing centers. The concept of the object data structure also accounts for interference effects. In the Stroop effect, subjects read a list of color words such as *red, yellow, green,* and *blue* (Stroop, 1935). If the words are themselves printed with colored inks and the colors do not match the word meanings—for example, the word *blue* is colored red—people read more slowly. This shows that visual and verbal information must be integrated at some level, perhaps in something like Kahneman and Henik's object file.

Speculating further, the cognitive object file also provides an explanation of why object displays can be so effective. Essentially, the object display is the graphical analog of a cognitive object file. However, the strong grouping afforded by an object display can be a double-edged sword. A particular object display may suit one purpose but be counterproductive for another. Object-based displays are likely to be most useful when the goal is to give an unequivocal message about the relationship of certain data variables. For example, when the goal is to represent a number of pieces of information related to a part of a chemical plant, the object display can be clear and unambiguous. Conversely, when the goal is information discovery, the object display may not be useful because it will be strongly biased toward a particular structure. Other, more abstract methods, such as the multidimensional plotting techniques discussed in previous chapters, are likely to be more suitable. Chapter 9 offers more discussion of the relationship between verbal and visual information and presents a number of rules for integrating the two kinds of information.

Conclusion

The notion of a visual object is central to our understanding of the higher levels of visual processing. In a sense, the object can be thought of as the point where the image becomes thought. Objects are units of cognition as well as things that are recognized in the environment.

There is strong evidence to support both viewpoint-dependent recognition of objects and the theory that the brain creates 3D structural models of objects. Therefore, in representing information as objects, both kinds of information should be taken into account. Even though data may be represented as a 3D structure, it is critical that this structure be laid out in such a way that it presents a clear 2D image. Special attention should be paid to silhouette information, and if objects are to be rapidly recognized, they should be presented in a familiar orientation.

Visual processing of objects is very different from the massive processing of low-level features described in Chapter 5. Only a very small number of complex visual objects, perhaps only one or two, can be held in mind at any given time. This makes it difficult to find novel patterns that are distributed over multiple objects. However, there is a kind of parallelism in object perception. Although only one visual object may be processed at a time, all the features of that object are processed together. This makes the object display into the most powerful way of grouping disparate data elements together. Such a strong grouping effect may not always be desirable; it may inhibit the perception of patterns that are distributed across multiple objects. However, where strong visual integration is a requirement, the object display is likely to be the best solution.

Once we choose to represent visual objects in a data display, we encounter the problem of the degree of abstraction, or the realism, that should be employed. There is a trade-off between literal realism, which leads to unequivocal object identification, and abstraction, which leads to more general-purpose displays. Most interesting is the possibility that we can create a kind of hyperrealism through our understanding of the mechanisms of perception. By the use of simplified lighting models and enhanced contours, together with carefully designed colors and textures, the important information in our data may be brought out with optimal clarity.

Space Perception and the Display of Data in Space

We live in a three-dimensional world, actually four dimensions if time is included. In the short history of visualization research, most graphical display methods have required that data be plotted on sheets of paper, but computers have evolved to the point where this is no longer necessary. Now we can create the illusion of 3D space behind the monitor screen, changing over time if we desire. The big question is why we should do this. There are clear advantages to conventional 2D techniques such as the bar chart and the scatter plot. Designers already know how to draw diagrams and represent data effectively in two dimensions, and the results can easily be included in books and reports. Of course, one compelling reason for an interest in 3D space perception is the explosive advance in 3D computer graphics. It has recently become cheap to display data in an interactive 3D virtual space and so people are doing it, often for the wrong reasons. It is inevitable that there is now much ill-conceived 3D design, just as the advent of desktop publishing brought much poor use of typography and the advent of cheap color brought much ineffective use of color. Through an understanding of space perception, we hope to reduce the amount of poor 3D design and clarify those instances in which 3D representation is really useful.

The first half of this chapter presents an overview of the different factors involved in the perception of 3D space. The second half gives a task-based analysis of the ways in which different kinds of spatial information are used in performing seven different tasks, ranging from tracing paths in 3D networks to judging the morphology of surfaces to appreciating an esthetic impression of spaciousness. The way we use spatial information differs greatly, depending on whether we are docking one object with another or trying to trace a path in a tangled web of virtual wires.

Depth Cue Theory

The visual world provides many different sources of information about 3D space. These sources are usually called *depth cues* and a large body of research is related to the way the visual system processes depth cue information to provide the accurate perception of space. Here is a list of the more important depth cues. It is common to divide these into categories according to whether they can be reproduced in a static picture (monocular static) or a moving picture (monocular dynamic) or require two eyes (binocular).

Monocular Static (Pictorial):
- Linear perspective
- Texture gradient
- Size gradient
- Occlusion
- Depth of focus
- Cast shadows
- Shape-from-shading

Monocular Dynamic (Moving Picture):
- Structure-from-motion (kinetic depth, motion parallax)

Binocular:
- Eye convergence
- Stereoscopic depth

Shape-from-shading information has already been discussed in Chapter 7. The other types are discussed in this chapter. More attention is devoted to stereoscopic depth perception than to the other depth cues, not because it is the most important, but because it is relatively complex and because it is difficult to use stereoscopic depth effectively.

Perspective Cues

Figure 8.1 shows how perspective geometry can be described for a particular viewpoint and a picture plane. The position of each feature on the picture plane is determined by extending a ray from the viewpoint to that feature in the environment. If the resulting picture is subsequently scaled up or down, the correct viewpoint is specified by similar triangles, as shown. If the eye is placed at the specified point with respect to the picture, the result is a correct perspective view of the scene. A number of the depth cues are direct results of the geometry of perspective. These are illustrated in Figures 8.2 and 8.3.

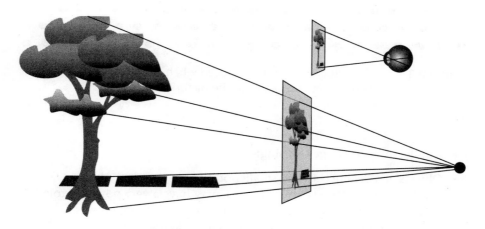

Figure 8.1 The geometry of linear perspective is obtained by sending a ray from each point in the environment through a picture plane to a single fixed point. Each point on the picture plane is colored according to the light that emanates from the corresponding region of the environment. The result is that objects vary in size on the picture plane in inverse proportion to their distance from the fixed point. If an image is created according to this principle, the correct viewpoint is determined by similar triangles, as shown in the upper right.

Figure 8.2   Perspective cues arising from perspective geometry include the convergence of lines and the fact that more distant objects become smaller on the picture plane.

Figure 8.3   A texture gradient is produced when a uniformly textured surface is projected onto the picture plane.

- Parallel lines converge to a single point.

- Objects at a distance appear smaller on the picture plane than do nearby objects. Objects of known size may have a very powerful role in determining the perceived size of adjacent unknown objects. Thus, if an image of a person is placed in a picture of otherwise abstract objects, this gives a scale to the entire scene.

- Uniformly textured surfaces result in texture gradients in which the texture elements become smaller with distance.

The fact that in the real world we generally perceive the actual size of objects rather than the size at which they appear on a picture plane (or on the retina) is called size constancy. The degree to which size constancy is obtained is a useful measure of the relative effectiveness of depth cues. However, when we perceive pictures of objects, we enter a kind of dual perception mode. To some extent, we have a choice between accurately perceiving the size of the depicted object as though it were in a 3D space and accurately perceiving the size of the object as it covers the picture plane (Hagen, 1974). The amount and effectiveness of the depth cues that are used will to some extent make it easy to see in one mode or the other. The picture-plane sizes of objects in a very sketchy schematic picture are easy to perceive. Conversely, the 3D sizes of objects will be more readily perceived with a highly realistic moving picture, but large errors will be made in estimating picture-plane sizes.

Pictures Seen from the Wrong Viewpoint

It is an obvious fact that most pictures are not viewed from their correct centers of perspective. In a movie theatre, only one person can occupy this optimal viewpoint (determined by the focal length of the original camera and the scale of the final picture). When a picture is viewed from an incorrect viewpoint, the laws of geometry suggest that significant distortions should occur. Figure 8.4 illustrates this. If the mesh shown in Figure 8.4 is projected on a screen with a geometry based on viewpoint a, but it is actually viewed from position b, it should be perceived to stretch along the line of sight as shown (if the visual system were a simple geometry processor). However, while people report seeing some distortion initially when looking at moving pictures from the wrong viewpoint, they become unaware of the distortion after a few minutes. Kubovy (1986) calls this the robustness of linear perspective. Apparently the human visual system overrides some aspects of perspective in constructing the 3D world that we perceive. One of the mechanisms that can account for this lack of perceived distortion may be based on a built-in perceptual assumption that objects in the world are rigid. Suppose that the mesh in Figure 8.4 is smoothly rotated about a vertical axis, projected assuming viewpoint a but viewed from point b. It should appear as a nonrigid, elastic body. But perceptual processing is constrained by a rigidity assumption and this causes us to see a stable, nonelastic three-dimensional object.

Under extreme conditions, some distortion is still seen with off-axis viewing of moving pictures. Hagen and Elliott (1976) showed that this residual distortion is reduced if the projective geometry is made more parallel. This can be done by simulating long-focal-length lenses, which may be a useful technique if displays are intended for off-axis viewing.

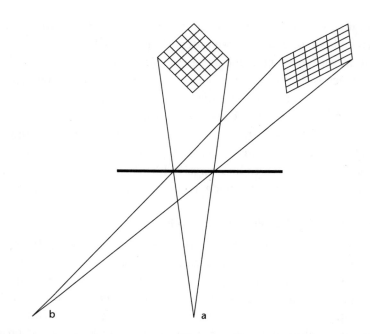

Figure 8.4   When a perspective picture is seen from the wrong viewpoint, simple geometry predicts that large distortions should be seen. However, they are generally not seen or, when seen, are minimal.

Various technologies exist that can track a user's head position with respect to a computer screen and thereby estimate the position of the eye(s). With this information, a 3D scene can be computed and viewed so that the perspective is "correct" at all times by adjusting the viewpoint parameters in the computer graphics software (Deering, 1992; Ware et al., 1993). There are two reasons why this might be desirable, despite the fact that incorrect perspective viewing of a picture seems generally unimportant. The first reason is that as an observer changes position, the perspective image will change accordingly, resulting in motion parallax. Motion parallax is itself a depth cue, as discussed below in the structure-from-motion section. The second reason is that in some virtual-reality systems, it is possible to place the subject's hand in the same space as the virtual computer graphics imagery. When we make visually guided hand movements toward some object in the world, we are constantly correcting our movements based on visual feedback. If this is done using computer graphics imagery to represent a virtual object and a virtual image of the subject's hand, head-coupled perspective may be neces-sary to keep the subject's body sense (kinesthetic feedback) of hand position aligned with that person's visual feedback. An example of an experimental setup is shown in Figure 8.5. However, research has shown that as long as continuous visual feedback is provided, *without excessive lag,* people can rapidly adjust to simple changes in the eye-hand relationship (Held et al., 1966). The effects of lag on performance are discussed further in Chapter 10.

When virtual-reality head-mounted displays are used, it is essential that the perspective be coupled to a user's head movement, since the whole point is to allow users to change viewpoint in a natural way. Experimental evidence supports the idea that head-coupled perspective enhances the sense of "presence" in virtual spaces more than stereoscopic viewing (Arthur et al., 1993; Pausch et al., 1996).

Figure 8.5   A user is attempting to trace 3D blood vessels in an interface that puts his hand in the same space as the virtual computer graphics imagery (from Serra et al., 1997).

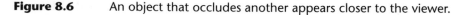

Figure 8.6   An object that occludes another appears closer to the viewer.

Occlusion

If one object overlaps or occludes another, it appears closer to the observer. (See Figure 8.6.) This is probably the strongest depth cue, but it provides only binary information. An object is either behind or in front of another; no information is given about the distance between them. A kind of partial occlusion occurs when one object is transparent or translucent. In this case, there is a color difference between the parts of an object that lie behind the transparent plane and the parts that are in front of it. This can be useful in positioning one object inside another (Zhai et al., 1994).

Depth of Focus

As we look around the world, our eyes change focus to bring the images of fixated objects into sharp focus on the fovea. As a result, the images of both nearby and more distant objects become blurred. The equations that determine depth of focus are presented in Chapter 2. Focus effects are important in separating foreground objects from background objects, as shown in Figure 8.7. Perhaps because of its role as a depth cue, simulating depth of focus is an excellent way of highlighting information by blurring everything except that which is critical. Unfortunately, the technique is computationally expensive and thus currently limited in utility.

Focus can be considered a pictorial depth cue only if the object of fixation can be predicted. In normal vision, our attention shifts and our eyes refocus dynamically depending on the distance of the object fixated. Chapter 2 describes a system designed to change focus information based on measured point of fixation in a virtual environment.

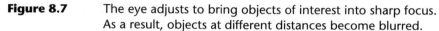

Figure 8.7   The eye adjusts to bring objects of interest into sharp focus. As a result, objects at different distances become blurred.

Cast Shadows

Cast shadows are a very potent cue to the *height* of an object above a plane, as illustrated in Figure 8.8(a). Thus, they can function as a kind of indirect depth cue—the shadow locates the object with respect to some surface in the environment, and cues from the surface, such as perspective and texture gradients, give the actual distance. In a multifactor experiment, Wanger et al. (1992) found that shadows provided the strongest "depth" cue when compared to texture, projection type, frames of reference, and motion. But it should be noted that they used a strong checkerboard as a base plane to provide the actual distance information.

Since shadows are most effective when cast onto a nearby surface, they can be very useful in distinguishing information that is layered a small distance above a planar surface. This is illustrated in Figure 8.9.

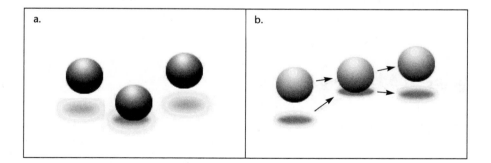

Figure 8.8   (a) Shadows can provide a strong cue for the relative height of objects above a plane. The effect becomes even stronger with motion. In (b), the ball actually appears to bounce when the ball and shadow are animated to follow the trajectories shown.

Figure 8.9   Cast shadows can be useful in making data appear to stand out above an opaque plane.

Kersten et al. (1997) showed that cast shadows are especially powerful when objects are in motion. One of their demonstrations is illustrated in Figure 8.8(b). In this case, the apparent trajectory of a ball moving in 3D space is caused to change dramatically depending on the path of the *shadow* of the object. The image of the ball actually travels in a straight line, but the ball appears to bounce because of the way the shadow moves. In this study, shadow motion was shown to be a stronger depth cue than change in size with perspective.

It seems likely that shadows can be correctly interpreted without being realistic. Kersten et al. (1996) found no effect of shadow quality in their results. However, one of the principal cues in distinguishing shadows from nonshadows in the environment is the lack of sharpness in shadow edges. Fuzzy shadows are likely to lead to less confusing images.

Shape-from-Shading

See Chapter 7 for a discussion of the perception of surface shape-from-shading information.

Structure-from-Motion

When an object is in motion or when we ourselves move through the environment, the result is a dynamically changing pattern of light on the retina. Structure-from-motion information is generally divided into two different classes: motion parallax and the kinetic depth effect.

An example of motion parallax occurs when we look sideways out of a car or train window. Things nearby appear to be moving very rapidly, while objects close to the horizon only appear to move gradually. Overall, there is a velocity gradient, as illustrated in Figure 8.10(a). When we move forward through a cluttered environment, the result is a very different expanding pattern of motion, like that shown in Figure 8.10(b). Wann et al. (1995) showed that subjects were able to control their headings with an accuracy of 1 to 2 degrees when they were given feedback from a wide-screen field of dots through which they had to steer. There is also evidence for specialized neural mechanisms sensitive to the time to contact with visual moving targets. These may enable animals to become aware of objects on a collision course (Wang and Frost, 1992).

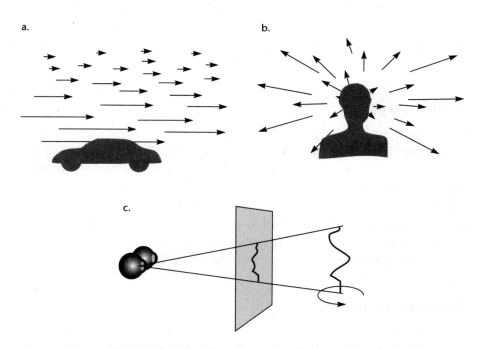

Figure 8.10 Three different kinds of structure-from-motion information. (a) The velocity gradient that results when the viewer is looking sideways out of a moving vehicle. (b) The velocity field that results when the viewer is moving forward through the environment. (c) The kinetic depth information that results when a rotating rigid object is projected onto a screen.

The kinetic depth effect can be demonstrated with a wire bent into a complex 3D shape and projected onto a screen, as shown in Figure 8.10(c). Casting the shadow of the wire will suffice for the projection. The result is a two-dimensional line, but if the wire is rotated, the three-dimensional shape of the wire immediately becomes apparent (Wallach and O'Connell, 1953). The kinetic depth effect dramatically illustrates a key concept in understanding space perception. The brain generally assumes that objects are rigid in 3D space, and the mechanisms of object perception incorporate this constraint. Although the shadow of the line is continuously changing on the screen, what is perceived is a rigid 3D object. It is easy to simulate this in a computer graphics system by creating an irregular line, rotating it about a vertical axis, and displaying it using standard graphics techniques.

In general, structure-from-motion information is at least as important as stereoscopic depth in providing us with information about the spatial layout of objects in space (Rogers and Graham, 1979). It helps us determine both the 3D shapes of objects and the large-scale layout of objects in space. Structure-from-motion is the reason for the effectiveness of fly-through animated movies that take an observer through a data space.

Eye Convergence

When we fixate an object with both eyes, they must converge to a degree dictated by the distance of the object. This *vergence* angle is illustrated in Figure 8.11. Given the two line-of-sight vectors, it is a matter of simple trigonometry to determine the distance to the fixated object. However, the evidence suggests that the human brain is not good at this geometric computation in an absolute sense, although relative vergence may be used. The vergence sensing system appears capable of quite rapid recalibration in the presence of other spatial information (Fisher and Cuiffreda, 1990).

Stereoscopic Depth

There is a common, often-expressed opinion that stereoscopic displays allow "truly" three-dimensional images. In advertising literature, potential buyers are urged to buy stereoscopic display equipment and "see it in 3D." As should be plain from this chapter, stereoscopic disparity is only one of many depth cues that the brain uses to analyze 3D space, and it is by no means the most

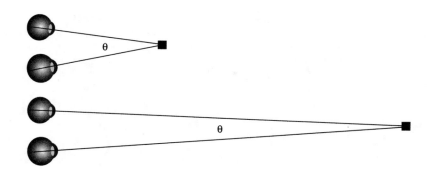

Figure 8.11   The vergence angle θ varies as the eyes fixate near and far objects.

useful one. If fact, as many as 20% of the population may be stereo-blind, yet they function perfectly well and in fact are often unaware that they have a disability. Nevertheless, stereoscopic displays can provide a particularly compelling sense of a three-dimensional virtual space, and for certain tasks they can be extremely useful.

The basis of stereoscopic depth perception is forward-facing eyes with overlapping visual fields. On average, human eyes are separated by about 6.4 centimeters; this means that the brain receives slightly different images, which can be used to compute relative distances of pairs of objects. Stereoscopic depth is a technical subject, and we therefore begin by defining some of the terms.

Figure 8.12 illustrates a simple stereo display. Both eyes are fixated on the vertical line a,c. A second line d in the left eye's image is fused with b in the right eye's image. The brain resolves the discrepancy in line spacing by perceiving the lines as being at different depths, as shown.

Angular disparity is the difference between the angular separation of a pair of points imaged by the two eyes (disparity = $\alpha - \beta$). *Screen disparity* is the distance between parts of an image on the screen (screen disparity = (c − d) − (a − b)).

If the disparity between the two images becomes too great, *diplopia* occurs. Diplopia is the appearance of the doubling of part of a stereo image when the visual system fails to fuse the images. The 3D area within which objects can be fused and seen without double images is called *Panum's fusional area*. In the worst case, Panum's fusional area has remarkably little

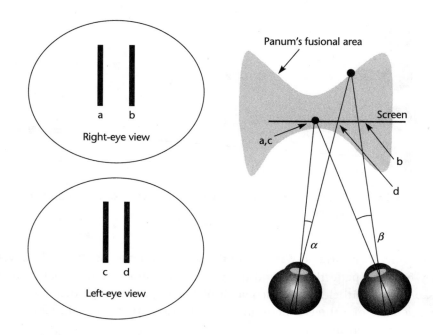

Figure 8.12   A simple stereo display. Different images for the two eyes are shown on the left. On the right a top-down view shows how the brain interprets this display. The vertical lines a and b in the right-eye image are perceptually fused with c and d in the left-eye image.

depth. At the fovea, the maximum disparity before fusion breaks down is only $\frac{1}{10}$ degree, whereas at 6 degrees eccentricity (of the retinal image from the fovea), the limit is $\frac{1}{3}$ degree (Patterson and Martin, 1992).

It is worthwhile to consider what these numbers imply for monitor-based stereo displays. A screen with 30 pixels/cm, viewed at 57 cm, will have 30 pixels per degree of visual angle. The $\frac{1}{10}$-degree limit on the visual angle before diplopia occurs translates into about three pixels of screen disparity. This means that we can only display three whole-pixel-depth steps before diplopia occurs, either in front of or behind the screen. It also means that in the worst case, it will only be possible to view a virtual image that extends in depth a fraction of a centimeter from the screen (assuming an object on the screen is fixated). However, it is important to emphasize that this is a worst-case scenario. It is likely that antialiased images will allow better-than-pixel resolution, for exactly the same reason that vernier acuities can be achieved to better-than-pixel resolution (discussed in Chapter 2). In addition, the size of Panum's fusional area is highly dependent on a number of visual display parameters, such as the exposure duration of the images and the size of the targets. Both moving targets and blurred images can be fused at greater disparities, and the fusional area becomes larger, with lateral separation of the image components (Patterson and Martin, 1992). Depth judgments can also be made outside the fusion area, although these are less accurate.

Problems with Stereoscopic Displays

It is common for users of 3D visualization systems with stereoscopic display capabilities to disable stereo viewing once the novelty has worn off, and view the data using a monocular perspective. There are a number of reasons that stereoscopic displays are disliked. Double-imaging problems tend to be much worse in stereoscopic computer displays than in normal viewing of the 3D environment. One of the principal reasons for this is that in the real world, objects farther away than the one fixated are out of focus on the retina. Since we can fuse blurred images more easily than sharply focused images, this reduces diplopia problems in the real world. In addition, focus is linked to attention and foveal fixation. Double images of nonattended peripheral objects generally will not be noticed. Unfortunately, in present-day computer graphics systems, particularly those that allow for real-time interaction, depth of focus is never simulated. All parts of the computer graphics image are therefore equally in focus, even though some parts of the image may have large disparities. Thus, the double images that occur in stereoscopic computer graphics displays are very obtrusive.

Frame Cancellation

Valyus (1966) coined the phrase *frame cancellation* to describe a common problem with stereoscopic displays. If the stereoscopic depth cues are such that a virtual image should appear in front of the screen, the edge of the screen appears to occlude the virtual object, as shown in Figure 8.13. Occlusion overrides the stereo depth information and the depth effect collapses. This is typically accompanied by a double image of the object that should appear in front.

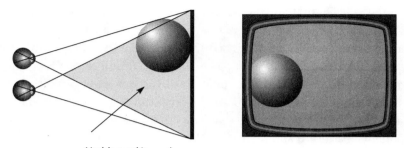

Usable working volume

Figure 8.13   Frame cancellation occurs when stereoscopic disparity cues
indicate that an object is in front of the monitor screen.
Because the edge of the screen clips the object, this acts as
an occlusion depth cue and the object appears to be behind
the window, canceling the stereo depth effect. Because of this,
the usable working volume of a stereoscopic display is
restricted as shown.

The Vergence-Focus Problem

When we change our fixation between objects placed at different distances,
two things happen: The convergence of the eyes changes (vergence) and the
focal lengths of the lenses in the eyes *accommodate* to bring the new object
into focus. The vergence and the focus mechanisms are coupled in the human
visual system. If one eye is covered, the vergence and the focus of the *covered*
eye change as the uncovered eye accommodates objects at different distances.
This illustrates vergence being driven by focus. The converse also occurs: A
change in vergence can drive a change in focus.

In a stereoscopic display, all objects lie in the same focal plane, regardless
of their apparent depth. However, accurate disparity and vergence information may fool the brain into perceiving them at different depths. Screen-based
stereo displays provide vergence and disparity information, but no focus
information. The failure to correctly present focus information coupled with
vergence may cause a form of eyestrain (Wann et al., 1995; Mon-Williams
and Wann, 1998). This problem is present in both stereoscopic head-
mounted systems and monitor-based stereo displays. Wann et al. concluded
that vergence and focus cross-coupling "prevents large depth intervals of
three-dimensional visual space being rendered with integrity through dual
two-dimensional displays." This may account for the common reports of eyestrain occurring with dynamic stereoscopic displays.

Distant Objects

The problems with stereoscopic viewing are not always related to disparities that are too large. Sometimes disparities may be too small. The stereoscopic depth cue is useful only for objects up to 30 meters from the viewer. Beyond this, disparities are too small to be resolved. For practical purposes, most useful stereoscopic depth is obtained within distances of less than 10 meters from the viewer and may be optimal for objects held roughly at arm's length.

Making Effective Stereoscopic Displays

There are ways of mitigating the diplopia, frame cancellation, and vergence-focus problems described above, although they will not be fully solved until true 3D displays become commercially viable. All the solutions involve reducing screen disparities by artificially bringing the computer graphics imagery into the fusional area. Valyus (1966) found experimentally that the diplopia problems were acceptable if no more than 1.6 degrees of disparity existed in the display. Based on this, he proposed that the screen disparity should be less than 0.03 times the distance to the screen. However, this provides only about ± 1.5 cm of useful depth at normal viewing distances. Using a more relaxed criterion, Williams and Parrish (1990) concluded that a practical viewing volume falls between –25% and +60% of the viewer-to-screen distance. This provides a more usable working space.

One obvious solution to the problem of creating useful stereoscopic displays is to simply create small virtual scenes that do not extend much in front of or behind the screen. However, in many situations this is not practical—for example, if we wish to make a stereoscopic view of extensive terrain. A more general solution is to compress the range of stereoscopic disparities so that they lie within a judiciously enlarged fusional area, such as that proposed by Williams and Parrish, and a method for doing this is described in the next two sections. But before going on, we must consider a potential problem. We should be concerned that tampering with stereoscopic depth may cause us to misjudge distance. There is conflicting evidence as to whether this is likely. Some studies have shown stereoscopic disparity to be relatively unimportant in making absolute depth judgments. For example, Wallach and Karsh (1963) found that when they rotated a wireframe cube viewed in stereo, only half the subjects they were trying to recruit were even aware of a doubling in their eye separation. Because increasing eye separation increases stereo disparities, this should have resulted in a grossly distorted cube. The fact that distortion was not perceived indicates that kinetic depth-effect information and rigidity assumptions are much stronger than stereo information. Ogle (1962) argued that stereopsis gives us information about the *relative* depths of objects that have small disparities, but when it comes to judging the overall layout of objects in space, other depth cues dominate. On the other hand, more recent evidence suggests that under the right circumstances, accurate depth judgments may be made on the basis of stereoscopic disparities (Durgin et al., 1995).

Overall, we can conclude that the brain is very flexible in weighing evidence from the different depth cues and that disparity information can be used as a flexible resource. Thus, it should be possible to artificially manipulate the overall pattern of stereo disparities and enhance local 3D space perception without distorting the overall sense of space if other strong cues to depth, such as linear perspective, are provided. Ware et al. (1998) found that they could dynamically change the disparity range by about 30% every three seconds, and so long as all the disparity ratios were preserved, subjects did not even notice the manipulation.

Cyclopean Scale

One simple method that we have developed to deal with diplopia problems is called a *cyclopean scale* (Ware et al., 1998). As illustrated in Figure 8.14, this manipulation involves scaling the virtual environment about the midpoint between the observer's estimated eye positions. The scaling variable is chosen so that the nearest part of the scene comes to a point just behind the monitor screen. To understand the effects of this operation, it is worthwhile to first consider that scaling a virtual world about a single viewpoint does not result in any change in computer graphics imagery (assuming depth of focus is not

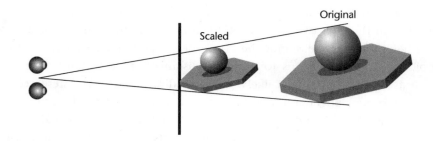

Figure 8.14   Cyclopean scale: A virtual environment is resized about a center point midway between the left and right viewpoints.

taken into account). Thus, the cyclopean scale does not change the overall sizes of objects as they are represented on a computer screen. The cyclopean scale has a number of benefits for stereo viewing:

- More distant objects, which would normally not benefit from stereo viewing because they are beyond the range where significant disparities exist, are brought into a position where usable disparities are present.

- The vergence-focus discrepancy is reduced; at least for the part of the virtual object that lies close to the screen, there is no vergence-focus conflict.

- Virtual objects that are closer to the observer than to the screen are also scaled so that they lie behind the screen. This removes the possibility of frame cancellation.

Virtual Eye Separation

The cyclopean scale, although useful, does not remove the possibility of disparities that result in diplopia. In order to do so, it is necessary to compress or expand the disparity range. To understand how this can be accomplished, it is useful to consider a device called a telestereoscope. This uses a system of mirrors to increase the effective separation of the eyes, as shown in Figure 8.15. A telestereoscope is generally used to increase disparities when distant objects are viewed. However, the same principle can also be used to decrease the range of disparities by optically moving the eyes closer together.

Figure 8.16 illustrates the concept of virtual eye separation and demonstrates how the apparent depth of an object decreases if the virtual viewpoint uses a wider eye separation than the actual viewpoint. We consider only a single point in the virtual space. If E_v is the virtual eye separation and E_a is the actual eye separation of some observer, the relationship between depth in the virtual image (z_v) and in the viewed stereo image (z_s) is a ratio:

$$\frac{E_v}{E_a} = \frac{z_s(z_v + z_e)}{z_v(z_s + z_e)} \tag{8.1}$$

where z_e represents the distance to the screen. By rearranging terms, we can get the stereo depth expressed as a function of the virtual depth and the virtual eye separation.

$$z_s = \frac{z_e z_v E_v}{E_a z_v + E_a z_e - E_v z_v} \tag{8.2}$$

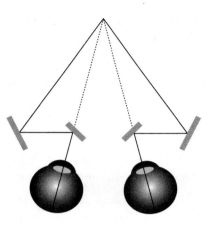

Figure 8.15   A telestereoscope is a device that increases the effective eye separation, thereby increasing stereoscopic depth information (disparities).

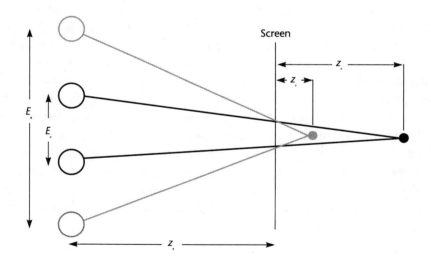

Figure 8.16   The geometry of virtual eye separation. In this example, the stereo depth is decreased by computing an image with a virtual eye separation that is smaller than the actual eye separation, but stereo depth can just as easily be increased.

If the virtual eye separation is smaller than the actual eye separation, stereo depth is decreased. If the virtual eye separation is larger than the actual eye separation, stereo depth is increased. $E_v = E_a$ for "correct" stereoscopic viewing of a virtual scene, although for the reasons stated, this may not be useful in practice. When $E_v = 0.0$, both eyes get the same image, as in single-viewpoint graphics. Note that stereo depth and perceived depth are not always equal. The brain is an imperfect processor of stereo information, and other depth cues may be much more important in determining the perceived depth.

Experimental evidence shows that subjects given control of their eye-separation parameters have no idea of what the "correct" setting should be (Ware et al., 1998). When asked to adjust the virtual eye-separation parameter, subjects tended to decrease the eye separation for scenes in which there was a lot of depth, but actually increased eye separation beyond the normal (enhancing the sensation of stereoscopic depth) when the scene was flat. This behavior can be mimicked by an algorithm designed to automatically test the depth in a virtual environment and adjust the eye-separation parameters appropriately (after cyclopean scale). We have found the following function to work well for a large variety of digital terrain models. It uses the ratio of the nearest point to the farthest point in the scene.

$$EyeSeparation = 2.5 + 5.0*(NearPoint/FarPoint)^2$$

This function increases the eye separation to 7.5 cm for shallow scenes (as compared to a normal value of 6.4 cm) and reduces it to 2.5 cm for very deep scenes.

Artificial Spatial Cues

There are effective ways of providing information about space that are not based directly on the way information is provided in the normal environment, although the best are probably effective because they make use of existing perceptual mechanisms. Here are two examples.

One common technique that is used to enhance 3D scatter plots is illustrated in Figure 8.17. A line is dropped from each data point to the ground plane. Without these lines, only a 2D judgment of spatial layout is possible. With the lines, it is possible to estimate 3D position. Kim et al. (1991) showed that this artificial spatial cue can be at least as effective as stereopsis in providing 3D position information.

It should be understood that although the vertical line segments in Figure 8.17 can be considered artificial additions to the plot, there is nothing artificial about the way they operate as depth cues. Gibson (1986) pointed out that one of the most effective ways of estimating the sizes of objects is with reference to the ground plane. This enables local texture size and linear perspective cues to be used. Adding the vertical lines creates a link to the ground plane, and this enables perspective cues to be used.

Computer graphics systems sometimes provide a facility for what is called *proximity luminance covariance* by vision researchers (Dosher et al., 1986) and is simply called (rather confusingly) *depth cueing* by computer graphics texts. Depth cueing in computer graphics is the ability to vary the color of an object depending on its distance from the viewpoint, as illustrated in Figure 8.18. Normally, this is done so that more distant objects are faded toward the background color, becoming darker if the background is dark and lighter if the background is light.

Proximity luminance covariance mirrors an environmental depth cue sometimes called *atmospheric depth*. This refers to the reduction in contrast for distant objects in the environment, especially under hazy viewing conditions. However the depth cueing is used in computer graphics, it is generally much more extreme than any atmospheric effects that occur in nature, and

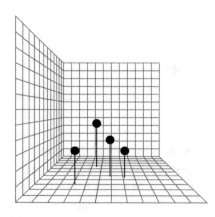

Figure 8.17   Dropping lines to a ground plane is an effective artificial spatial cue.

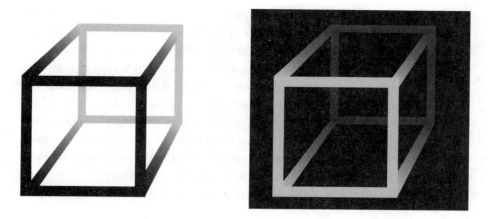

Figure 8.18   Proximity luminance covariance as a depth cue. Object color is altered with distance in the direction of the background color. This simulates extreme atmospheric effects.

for this reason it can be considered an "artificial" cue. Dosher et al. showed that proximity luminance covariance could function as an effective depth cue, but was weaker than stereo for static displays. With moving displays, however, proximity luminance covariance became a relatively stronger cue in making an ambiguous 3D scene unambiguous.

Depth Cues in Combination

In computer-graphics-based data displays, the designer has considerable freedom as to which depth cues to include in a data visualization and which to leave out. One approach would be to simply include all of them. However, this is not always the best solution. There can be considerable costs associated with creating a stereoscopic display, or with using real-time animation to take advantage of structure-from-motion cues. Other cues, such as depth-of-focus information, are difficult or impossible to compute in the general case, because without knowing what object the observer is looking at, it is impossible to determine what should be shown in focus and what should be shown out of focus. A general theory of space perception should make it possible to determine which depth cues are likely to be most valuable. Such a theory would provide information about the relative values of different depth cues when they are used in combination.

Unfortunately, there is no single widely accepted unifying theory of space perception, although the issue of how depth cues interact has been addressed by a number of studies. For example, the weighted-average model assumes that depth perception is a weighted linear sum of the depth cues available in a display (Bruno and Cutting, 1988). Alternatively, depth cues may combine in a geometric sum (Dosher et al., 1986). Young et al. (1993) proposed that depth cues are combined additively, but are weighted according to their apparent reliability in the context of other cues and relevant information. However, there is also evidence that some depth cues—in particular, occlusion—work in a logical binary fashion rather than contributing to an arithmetic or geometric sum. For example, if one object overlaps another in the visual image, it is perceived as closer to the observer.

Most of the work on the combination of spatial information implicitly contains the notions that spatial information is combined into a single cognitive model of space and that this model is used as a resource in performing all spatial tasks. This theoretical position is illustrated in Figure 8.19. Evidence is accumulating that this unified model of cognitive space is fundamentally flawed. Studies that have investigated more than one spatial task generally show different patterns of results depending on the task, suggesting

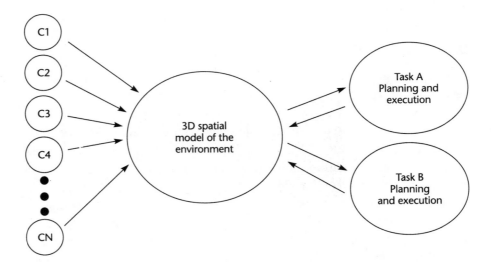

Figure 8.19   Most models of 3D space perception assume that spatial cues feed into a cognitive 3D model of the environment. This, in turn, is used as a resource for task planning and execution.

that cues are combined expeditiously depending on task requirements. For example, Wanger et al. (1992) showed that cast shadows and motion parallax cues both helped in the task of orienting a virtual object to match another. Correct linear perspective (as opposed to parallel orthographic perspective) actually increased errors; thus, it acted as a kind of negative depth cue for this particular task. However, when the task was one of translating an object, linear perspective was the most useful of the cues and motion parallax did not help at all.

The alternative to the unified model of the visual system is a flexible and adaptive system that applies different rules for depth cue combinations according to the task requirements. This is illustrated in Figure 8.20. Depending on whether the task is threading a needle or running through a forest, different spatial information is valuable and judgments are made depending on the best available evidence.

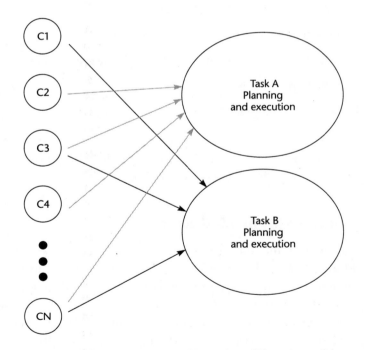

Figure 8.20   Experimental evidence shows that different spatial cues are weighted very differently for different tasks, suggesting that there is no unified cognitive spatial model.

Task-Based Space Perception

The obvious advantage of a theory of space perception that takes the task into account is that it can be directly applied to the design of interactive 3D information displays. The difficulty is that the number of tasks is potentially large and many tasks that appear at first sight to be simple and unified are found to be multifaceted upon more detailed examination. Nevertheless, taking the task into account is unavoidable; perception and action are intertwined. If we are to understand space perception, we must understand the purpose of perceiving. The best hope for progress lies in identifying a small number of elementary tasks that are as common as possible. Once this is done, informed design decisions can be made. The remainder of this chapter is devoted to analyzing the following tasks:

- Tracing data paths in 3D graphs

- Judging the morphology of surfaces and surface target detection

- Finding patterns of points in 3D space

- Judging the relative positions of objects in space

- Judging the relative movement of self within the environment

- Judging the "up" direction

- Feeling a sense of presence

This list of seven tasks is at best only a beginning; each of them has many variations. Two additional tasks, visually guided object positioning and navigation (or "wayfinding"), are discussed in Chapter 10.

Tracing Data Paths in 3D Graphs

Many kinds of information structures can be represented as networks of nodes and arcs, technically called *graphs*. Figure 8.21 shows an example of object-oriented computer software represented using a 3D graph. Nodes in the graph stand for various kinds of entities, such as modules, classes, variables, and methods. The 3D spars that connect the entities represent various kinds of relationships characteristic of object-oriented software, such as inheritance, function calls, and variable usage.

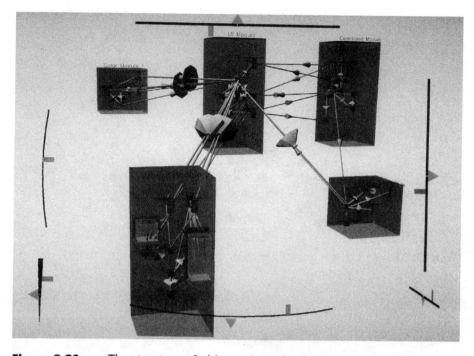

Figure 8.21   The structure of object-oriented software code is represented as a graph in 3D. See also color plates.

Information structures are becoming so complex that there has been considerable interest in the question of whether a 3D visualization will reveal more information than a 2D visualization.

One special kind of graph is a tree, illustrated in Figure 8.22. Trees are a standard technique for representing hierarchical information, such as organizational charts or the structure of information in a computer directory. The cone tree is a graphical technique for representing tree graph information in 3D (Robertson et al., 1993). It shows the tree branches arranged around a series of circles, as illustrated in Figure 8.23. The inventors of the cone tree claim that as many as 1000 nodes may be displayable without visual clutter using cone trees—clearly more than could be contained in a 2D layout. However, 3D cone trees require more complex user interactions to access some of the information than are necessary for 2D layouts.

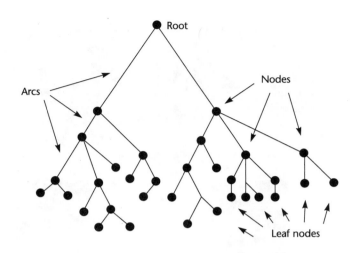

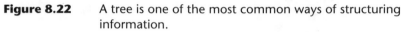

Figure 8.22   A tree is one of the most common ways of structuring information.

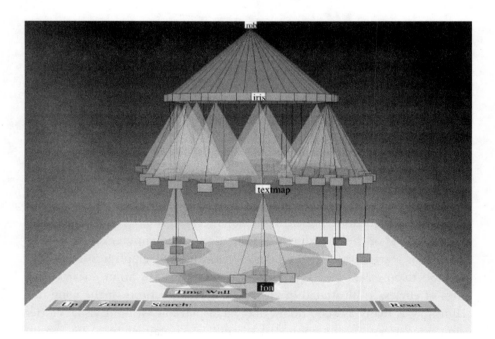

Figure 8.23   The cone tree invented by Robertson et al. (1993).

Empirical evidence also exists that shows that the number of errors in detecting paths in tree structures is substantially reduced if a 3D display method is used. Sollenberger and Milgram (1993) investigated a task involving two 3D trees with intermeshed branches. The task was to discover to which of two tree roots a highlighted leaf was attached. Subjects carried out the task both with and without stereo depth, and with and without rotation to provide kinetic depth. Their results showed that both stereo and kinetic depth viewing reduced errors, but that kinetic depth was the more potent cue.

A tree structure is not necessarily a good candidate for 3D visualization, for the reason that a tree can always be laid out on a 2D plane in such a way that none of the paths cross (path crossings are the main reason for errors in path-tracing tasks). The more general graph structures, such as that illustrated in Figure 8.21, usually cannot be laid on a plane without some paths crossing. Thus, the graph would seem to be a better candidate for applying 3D viewing techniques. To study the effects of stereo and kinetic depth cues on 3D visualization of graphs, we (Ware and Franck, 1996) systematically varied the size of a graph laid out in 3D and measured path-tracing ability with both stereoscopic and motion depth cues. Our results, illustrated in Figure 8.24, showed a factor-of-1.6 increase in the complexity that could be viewed when stereo was added to a static display, but a factor-of-2.2 improvement when kinetic depth cues were added. A factor-of-3.0 improvement occurred with both stereo and kinetic depth cues. These results held for a wide range of graph sizes. A subsequent experiment showed that the advantage of kinetic depth cues applied whether the motion was coupled to movements of the head or movements of the hand, or consisted of automatic oscillatory rotation of the graph.

Occlusion is one additional depth cue that should make it easier to differentiate arcs if they are colored differently, since occlusion makes it easier to see which arcs lie above and beneath. It seems unlikely that other depth cues will contribute much to a path-tracing task. There is no obvious reason why we should expect perspective viewing to aid the comprehension of connections between nodes in a 3D graph, and this was confirmed empirically by our study (Ware and Franck, 1996). There is also no reason to suppose that shading and cast shadows would provide any significant advantage in a task involving connectivity, although shading might help in revealing the orientation of the arcs.

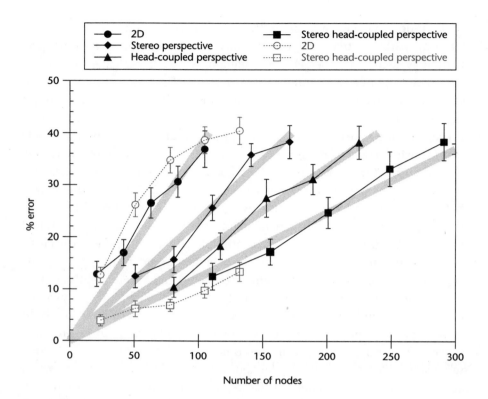

Figure 8.24   The plot shows how the errors increase as the number of nodes increases in a 3D graph representing stereo and motion depth cues.

Judging the Morphology of Surfaces and Surface Target Detection

Shape-from-shading and texture cues are extremely important in revealing surface shape, as discussed in Chapter 7. Here is some additional information on the value of stereoscopic and motion parallax information.

Experimental evidence suggests that the relative contribution of structure-from-motion and stereoscopic depth depends on very specific task-related factors. Surface shape detection cannot be considered as a simple problem. A study of the judged *heights* of cones showed that stereo depth was much more effective than structure-from-motion (Durgin et al., 1995). Conversely, Tittle et al. (1995) showed that structure-from-motion information was more important than stereo information in judging the *gradient* of a textured surface. Disparity curvature information may be considerably more important than absolute disparities in judging the shapes of surfaces, since this information is relatively invariant with viewing distance. Rogers and Cagenello (1989) showed that the kind of curvature matters. In a stereoscopic display, we are approximately twice as sensitive to the curvature of a horizontally oriented cylinder as we are to that of a vertically oriented cylinder.

There are also temporal factors to be taken into consideration. When we are viewing stereoscopic displays, it can take several seconds for the impression of depth to build up. However, stereoscopic depth and structure-from-motion information interact strongly. With moving stereoscopic displays, the time to fusion can be considerably shortened (Patterson and Martin, 1992). In determining shape from surfaces made from random dot patterns, using both stereoscopic and motion depth cues, Uomori and Nishida (1994) found that kinetic depth information dominated the initial perception of surface shape, but after an interval of four to six seconds, stereoscopic depth came to dominate.

Overall, it is clear that the way different depth cues combine in judgments of surface shape is highly complex. The relative values of stereo and structure-from-motion depend on the viewing distance, the texture of the surface, the kind of surface shape, and the viewing time. Because of this, when arbitrary surface shapes are being viewed, stereoscopic depth, kinetic depth, shape-from-shading, and surface textures can all add to our understanding of surface shape. The most important cues for any particular surface will vary, but including them all will ensure that good shape information is always presented.

Stereoscopic depth can also be used to enhance real-world imagery. Kalauger (1985) developed an intriguing technique that enabled a fusion of real-world imagery and photographic imagery. His method is simply to take a slide viewer out into the field, to the same place where a photographic slide image of the scene was previously taken. One eye is then used to view the photographic image while the other eye views the actual scene. Using this technique, it is possible to either enhance or reduce stereoscopic depth simply by moving laterally. Kalauger reported that with this viewing technique, otherwise invisible features, such as ledges on distant cliffs, could be seen. A variation of the technique can also be used to view changes in a landscape, such as landslides. When the eyes are alternately covered, these appear as anomalous depth or as movement effects.

Patterns of Points in 3D Space

The scatter plot is probably the most effective method for finding unknown patterns in 2D discrete data. In a 3D scatter plot, three data variables are used to position a point with respect to the *XYZ* axes. The resulting 3D scatter plot is usually rotated about a vertical axis, exploiting structure-from-motion to reveal its structure (Donoho et al., 1988). This technique can be added to the color- and shape-enhanced scatter plots discussed in Chapters 4 and 5.

There has been little or no empirical work on the role of depth cues in perceiving structures such as clusters and correlations in 3D. Nevertheless, a number of conclusions can be deduced from our understanding of the way depth cues function.

Perspective cues will not help us perceive depth in a 3D scatter plot, because a cloud of small, discrete points has no perspective information. If the points all have a constant and relatively large size, weak depth information will be produced by the size gradient. Similarly, with small points, occlusion will not provide useful depth information, but if the points are larger, some ordinal depth information will be perceivable. If there are a large number of points, cast shadows will not provide information, because it will be impossible to determine the association between a given point and its shadow. Shape-from-shading information will be missing, because a point has no orientation information. Each point will reflect light equally, no matter where it is placed and no matter where the light source is placed.

Hence, it is likely that the only important depth cues that can be exploited are stereoscopic depth and structure-from-motion. There seems to be little doubt that using both will be advantageous. As with the perception of surfaces, discussed above, the relative advantages of the different cues will depend on a number of factors. Stereo depth will be optimal for fine depth discriminations between points that lie near one another in depth. Structure-from-motion will be more important for points that lie farther apart in depth.

One of the problems with visualizing clouds of data points is that the overall shape of the cloud cannot easily be seen even when stereo and motion cues are provided. One way of adding extra shape information to a cloud of discrete points is to artificially add shape-from-shading information. It is possible to treat a cloud of data points as though each point were actually a small, flat oriented object. These flat particles can be artificially oriented, if they lie near the boundary of the point cloud, to reveal the shape of the cloud when shading is applied. In this way, perception of the shape of

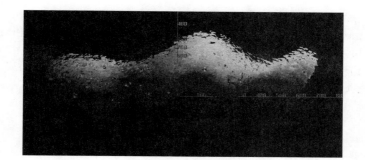

Figure 8.25 A cloud of discrete points is represented by oriented particles. The orientation is determined by using an inverse-square law of attraction between the particles. When the cloud is artificially shaded, its shape is revealed (Li, 1997). See also color plates.

the cloud can be considerably enhanced and shape information can be perceived without additional stereo and motion cues. At the same time, the positions of individual points can be perceived. Figure 8.25 illustrates this.

Judging Relative Positions of Objects in Space

Judging the relative positions of objects is a complex task, performed very differently depending on the overall scale and the context. When very fine depth judgments are made in the near vicinity, as in the task of threading a needle, stereopsis is the strongest single cue. Stereoscopic depth perception is a superacuity and is optimally useful for objects held at about arm's length. For these fine tasks, motion parallax is not very important, as evidenced by the fact that people hold their heads still when threading needles.

In larger environments, stereoscopic depth can play no role at all at distances beyond 30 m. Conversely, when we are judging the overall layout of objects in a larger environment, motion parallax, linear perspective, cast shadows, and texture gradients all contribute, depending on the exact spatial arrangement.

Gibson (1986) noted that much of size constancy can be explained by a referencing operation with respect to a textured ground plane. The sizes of objects that rest on a uniformly textured ground plane can be obtained by reference to the texture element size. Objects slightly above the ground plane can be related to the ground plane through the shadows they cast. In artificial environments, a very strong artificial reference can be provided by dropping a vertical line to the ground plane. A practical aid to visualizing spatial layout is a regular grid or checkerboard on the floor and walls, as illustrated in Figure 8.17. A grid provides a strong linear perspective cue, as well as providing a reference texture that may be optimal for many applications.

Judging the Relative Movement of Self within the Environment

When we are navigating through a virtual environment representing an information space, there are a number of frames of reference that may be adopted. For example, an observer may feel she is moving through the environment, or that she is stationary and the world is moving past. In virtual-environment systems that are either helmet-mounted or monitor-based, the user rarely actually physically moves any great distance, because real-world obstacles lie in the way. If self-movement is perceived, it is generally an illusion. Note that this applies only to linear motion, not to rotations; users with helmet-mounted displays can usually turn their heads quite freely.

A sensation of self-movement can be strongly induced even when the subject is not moving. This phenomenon, called *vection,* has been extensively studied. When observers are placed inside a large moving visual field—created either by a physical drum or by means of computer graphics within a virtual-reality helmet—they invariably feel that they are moving, even though they are not. A number of visual parameters influence the amount of vection that is perceived:

Field size. In general, the larger the area of the visual field that is moving, the stronger the experience of self-motion (Howard and Heckman, 1989).

Foreground/background. Much stronger vection is perceived if the moving part of the visual field is perceived as background more distant from the observer than foreground objects (Howard and Heckman, 1989). In fact, vection can be perceived even with quite a small moving field if that field is perceived to be relatively distant. The classic example occurs when someone is sitting in a train at a station and the movement of an adjacent vehicle (seen through a window) causes that person to feel he or she is moving even though this is not the case.

Frame. Vection effects are considerably increased if there is a static foreground frame between the observer and the moving background (Howard and Childerson, 1994).

Stereo. Stereoscopic depth can determine whether a moving pattern is perceived as background or foreground, and thereby increase or decrease vection (Lowther and Ware, 1996).

In aircraft simulators and other vehicle simulators, it is highly desirable that the user experience a sense of motion even though the simulator's actual physical motion is relatively small or nonexistent. One of the unfortunate side effects of this perceived motion is simulator sickness. The symptoms of simulator sickness can appear within minutes of acute exposure to extreme motion. Kennedy et al. (1989) report that between 10% and 60% of users of immersive displays report some symptoms of simulator sickness. This high incidence may ultimately be a major barrier to the adoption of fully immersive display systems.

Simulator sickness is thought to be caused by conflicting cues from the visual system and the vestibular system of the inner ear. When most of the visual field moves, the brain usually interprets this as a result of self-motion. But if the observer is in a simulator, no corresponding information comes from the vestibular system. According to this theory, the contradictory information results in nausea.

There are ways of ensuring that simulator sickness does occur, and ways of reducing its effects. Turning the head repeatedly while moving in a simulated virtual vehicle is almost certain to induce nausea (DiZio and Lackner, 1992). This means that a virtual ride should never be designed in which the participant is expected to look from side to side while wearing a helmet-mounted display. Simulator sickness in immersive virtual environments can be mitigated by initially restricting the participant's experience to short periods of exposure, lasting only a few minutes each day. This allows the user to build up a tolerance of the environment, and the periods of exposure can be gradually lengthened (McCauley and Sharkey, 1992).

Judging the "Up" Direction

In abstract 3D data spaces (for example, molecular models), there is often no sense of an "up" direction, and this can be confusing. The "up" direction is defined both by gravity, sensed by the vestibular system in the inner ear, and by the presence of the ground on which we walk. Much of the research that has been done on perceived "up" and "down" directions has been done as part of space research, to help us understand how people can best orient themselves in a gravity-free environment.

Nemire et al. (1994) showed that linear perspective provides a strong cue in defining objects perceived at the same horizontal level. They showed that a linear grid pattern on the virtual floor and walls of a display strongly influenced what the participants perceived as horizontal, and to some extent this overrode the perception of gravity. Other studies have shown that placing recognizable objects in the scene very strongly influences a person's sense of self-orientation. The presence of recognizable objects with a known normal orientation with respect to gravity, such as a chair or a standing person, can strongly influence which direction is perceived as up (Howard and Childerson, 1994). Both of these results can easily be adapted to virtual environments. Providing a clear reference ground plane and placing recognizable objects on it can to some extent define a vertical polarity for a data space.

The Esthetic Impression of 3D Space (Presence)

One of the most nebulous and ill-defined tasks related to 3D space perception is achieving a sense of *presence*. What is it that makes a virtual object or a whole environment seem vividly three-dimensional? What is it that makes us feel that we are actually present in an environment?

Much of presence has to do with a sense of engagement, and not necessarily with visual information. A reader of a powerfully descriptive novel may *visualize* (to use the word in its original cognitive sense) himself or herself in a world of the author's imagination—for example, watching Ahab on the back of the great white whale, Moby Dick.

Presence is somewhat anomalous in a task-based classification of spatial information, because presence as such does not have a clear task associated with it. It is simply the sense of being there. Nevertheless, a number of practical applications require a sense of presence. For an architect designing a virtual building to present to a client, the feeling of spaciousness and the esthetic quality of that space may be all-important. In virtual tourism, where the purpose is to give a potential traveler a sensation of what the Brazilian rain forest is really like, presence is also crucial.

A number of studies have used virtual-reality techniques for phobia desensitization. In one study by North et al. (1996), patients who had a fear of open spaces (agoraphobia) were exposed to progressively more challenging virtual open spaces. The technique of progressive desensitization involves taking people closer and closer to the situations that cause them fear. As they overcome their fears at one level of exposure, they can be taken to a slightly more stressful situation, and in this way they can overcome their phobias, one step at a time. The reason for phobia desensitization using VR simulations is to provide control over the degree of presence and to reduce the stress level by enabling the patient to exit the stressful environment instantaneously. After treatment in a number of virtual environments, the experimental subjects of North et al. scored lower on a standardized Subjective Units of Discomfort test.

In developing a virtual-reality theme park attraction for Disneyland, Pausch et al. (1996) observed that high frame rate and high level of detail were especially important in creating a sense of presence for users "flying on a magic carpet." Presenting a stereoscopic display did not enhance the experience. Empirical studies have also shown that high-quality structure-from-motion information contributes more to a sense of presence than does stereoscopic display (Arthur et al., 1993). However, the sense of presence may also be divided into subtasks. Hendrix and Barfield (1996) found stereoscopic viewing to be very important when subjects were asked to rate the extent to which they felt they could reach for and grasp virtual objects, but it did not contribute at all to the sense of the overall realism of the virtual condition. Hendrix and Barfield also found that having a large field of view was important to creating a sense of presence.

Conclusion

This chapter has been about the use of 3D spaces to display information. We asked whether a 3D display is better than a 2D display. The answer is that it depends on the task. Computer applications normally involve a substantial number of subtasks. Deciding whether or not to use a 3D display must involve deciding whether there are sufficient important subtasks for which 3D is clearly beneficial. The complexity and the consistency of the user interface for the whole application must be weighed into the decision. Even if 3D is better for one or two subtasks, the extra cost involved and the need for nonstandard interfaces for the 3D components may suggest that a 2D solution would be better overall. On the other hand, 3D may be better for the task, or it may be preferable simply because it is new and visually exciting.

The situation now with interactive 3D graphics can be likened to the one that existed 15 years ago with color displays. These displays were expensive and a number of studies showed that although color could be useful for labeling information, other techniques, such as shape coding or simply underlining, were equally effective. In addition, it was thought that the introduction of color would unnecessarily complicate the user interfaces to information display systems. However, in the intervening years, color displays have become cheap and designers have learned to use color effectively. It is now evident that many displays are made clearer and more informative through the use of color and other labeling techniques. Similarly, high-quality, interactive 3D displays are now becoming cheap, although even mediocre-quality VR systems are still expensive. But creating a 3D visualization environment is considerably more difficult than creating a 2D system with similar capabilities. We still lack design rules for 3D environments, and many interaction techniques are competing for adoption.

The strongest argument for the ultimate ascendancy of 3D visualization systems, and 3D user interfaces in general, must be that we live in a 3D world and our brains have evolved to recognize and interact with 3D. In the same way that color enriches the design environment, so also does 3D. The 3D design space is self-evidently richer than the 2D design space, because a 2D space is a part of 3D space. It is always possible to flatten out part of a 3D display and represent it in 2D.

Images and Words

This chapter addresses the relationship between visual information and verbal or textual information. Most visualizations are not purely graphical; they are composites, combining images with text or spoken language. But why do we need words? And when will images and words each be most effective? How should labels be used in diagrams? How should visual and verbal material be integrated in multimedia presentations? A particularly thorny but interesting problem is whether or not we should be using visual languages to program computers. Although computers are rapidly becoming common in every household, very few householders are programmers. It has been suggested that visual programming languages may help make it easier for "non-programmers" to program computers.

We begin by considering the differences between visual and verbal means of communication, then move on to the application areas.

Coding Words and Images

Bertin, in his seminal work, *The Semiology of Graphics,* distinguishes two distinct sign systems. One cluster of sign systems is associated with auditory information processing and includes mathematical symbols, natural language, and music. The second cluster is based on visual information processing and includes graphics together with abstract and figurative imagery. More recently, the dual coding of Paivio (1987) proposes that there are fundamentally different types of information stored in working memory; he calls them *imagens* and *logogens.* Roughly speaking, imagens denote the mental representation of visual information, while logogens denote the mental representation of language information. Visual imagens consist of objects, natural groupings of objects, and whole parts of objects (for example, an arm), together with spatial information about the way they are laid out in a particular environment, such as a room. Logogens store basic information pertaining to language, although not the sounds of the words. Logogens are processed by a set of functional subsystems that provide support for reading and writing, understanding and producing speech, and logical thought. Logogens need not necessarily be tied to speech. Even in the profoundly deaf, the same language subsystems exist and are used in the reading and production of Braille and sign language.

The architecture of dual coding theory is sketched in Figure 9.1. Visual-spatial information enters through the visual system and is fed into association structures in the nonverbal imagen system. Visual text is processed, but is then fed into the association structures of logogens. Accoustic verbal stimuli are processed primarily through the auditory system and then fed into the logogen system. Logogens and imagens, although based on separate subsystems, can be strongly interlinked. For example, the word *cat* and language-based concepts related to cats will be linked to visual information related to the appearance of cats and their environment.

Much of this theory is uncontroversial. It has been known for decades that there are different neural processing centers for verbal information (speech areas of the temporal cortex) and visual information (the visual cortex). But the idea that we can "think" visually is relatively recent. One line of evidence comes from mental imaging. When people are asked to compare the size of a light bulb with the size of a tennis ball, or the green of a pea with the green of a Christmas tree, most claim that they use mental images of

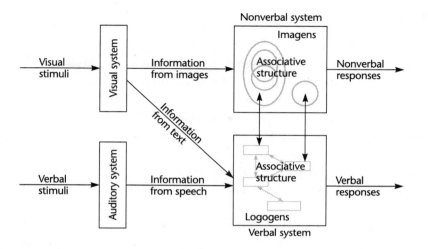

Figure 9.1   According to dual coding theory, the visual and verbal information is stored in different systems having different characteristics. Adapted from Paivio (1987).

these objects to carry out the task (Kosslyn, 1994). Other studies by Kosslyn and his coworkers show that people treat objects in mental images as if they have real sizes and locations in space. Recently, positron emission tomography (PET) has been used to reveal which parts of the brain are active during specific tasks. This shows that when people are asked to perform tasks involving mental imaging, the visual processing centers in the brain are activated. Also, when they mentally change the size and position of an imagined object, different visual areas of the brain are activated (Kosslyn et al., 1993). In addition, if visual processing centers in the brain are damaged, mental imaging ability is disrupted (Farah et al., 1992). Thus, it would seem that when we see a cow and when we mentally visualize a cow, the same neural pathways are excited, at least in part. Indeed, modern visual memory theory takes the position that visual object processing and visual object recognition are part of the same process. To some extent, the visual memory traces of objects and scenes are stored as part of the processing mechanism, and thus it is not necessary for an object to be fully processed for recognition to take place (Beardsley, 1997). This can account for the great superiority of recognition over recall. We can easily recognize that we have seen something before, but reproducing it in a drawing or with a verbal description is much harder.

The Nature of Language

Noam Chomsky revolutionized the study of natural language because he showed that there are aspects of the syntactic structure of language that generalize across cultures (Chomsky, 1965). A central theme of his work is the concept that there are "deep structures" of language, representing innate cognitive abilities, based on inherited neural structures. In many ways, this work forms the basis of modern linguistics. The fact that Chomsky's analysis of language is also one of the cornerstones of the theory of computer languages lends support to the idea that natural languages and computer languages have the same cognitive basis.

There is a critical period for normal language development that extends to about age ten. However, language is most easily acquired in the interval from birth to age three or four. If we do not obtain fluency in *some* language in our early years, we will never become fluent in any language.

Sign Language

Being *verbal* is not a defining characteristic of natural language. Sign languages are interesting because they are exemplars of true visual languages, but if we do not acquire these languages early in life, we will never become very adept at using them. Groups of deaf children spontaneously develop rich sign languages that have the same deep structures and grammatical patterns as spoken language. These languages are as syntactically rich and expressive as spoken language (Goldin-Meadow and Mylander, 1998). There are many sign languages; British sign language is a radically different language from American sign language, and the sign language of France is similarly different from the sign language of francophone Quebec (Armstrong et al., 1994). Sign languages grew out of the communities of deaf children and adults that were established in the nineteenth century, arising spontaneously from the interactions of deaf children with one another. In fact, until relatively recently, well-meaning social workers discouraged the use of sign languages in favor of lip reading.

Although in spoken languages words do not resemble the things they reference (with a few rare exceptions), signs are based partly on similarity. For example, see the signs for a tree illustrated in Figure 9.2. Sign languages have evolved rapidly. The pattern appears to be that a sign is originally created on the basis of a form of similarity in the shape and motion of the gesture, but

Figure 9.2 Three different sign-language representations of a tree. Note that they are all very different and all incorporate motion. From Bellugi and Klima (1976).

that over time the sign becomes more abstract, and similarity becomes less and less important (Deuchar, 1990). It is also the case that even signs apparently based on similarity are only recognized correctly about 10% of the time without instruction, and many signs are fully abstract.

Language Is Dynamic and Distributed over Time

We take in spoken, written, and sign language serially; it can take a few seconds to hear or read a short sentence. Armstrong et al. (1994) argue that in important ways, spoken language is essentially dynamic. Verbal expression does not consist of a set of fixed, discrete sounds; it is more accurately described as a set of vocal gestures producing dynamically changing sound patterns. The hand gestures of sign language are also dynamic, even when denoting static objects, as Figure 9.2 illustrates. There is a dynamic and inherently temporal phrasing at the syntactic level in the sequential structure of nouns and verbs. Even written language becomes a sequence of mentally re-created dynamic utterances when it is read.

In contrast with the dynamic, temporally ordered nature of language, relatively large sections of static pictures and diagrams can be understood in parallel. We can comprehend a complex visual structure in a fraction of a second, based on a single glance.

Visual and Spoken Language

The difficulty of writing and understanding computer programs has led to the development of a number of so-called visual languages in the hope that these can make the task easier. But we have to be very careful in discussing these as languages. Visual programming languages are mostly static diagramming systems, so unlike spoken languages that using the word *language* for both can be more misleading than helpful. Linguists and anthropologists commonly use the term *natural language* to refer to the spoken and written communications that make up our everyday human communication. Many of the cognitive operations required for computer programming have more in common with natural language than with visual processing.

Consider the following instructions that might be given to a mailroom clerk:

> Take a letter from the top of the In tray.
> Put a stamp on it.
> Put the letter in the Out tray.
> Continue until all the letters have stamps on them.

This is very like the following short program, which beginning programmers are often asked to write:

```
Repeat
    get a line of text from the input file
    change all the lowercase letters to uppercase
    write the line to the output file
Until (there is no more input)
```

This example program can also be expressed in the form of a graphical language called a flowchart (see Figure 9.3).

Flowcharts provide a salutary lesson to those who design visual programming languages. Flowcharts were once part of every introductory programming text, and it was often a contractual requirement that large bodies of software be documented with flowcharts describing the code structure. Having once been almost universally applied, flowcharts are now almost defunct.

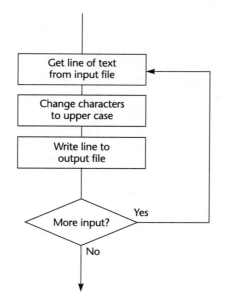

Figure 9.3   A flowchart is often a poor way of representing information that can be readily expressed in natural language–like pseudocode.

Why? It seems reasonable to attribute this to the similarity of pseudocode to natural language. We have already learned to make "while" statements and "if-then" structured expressions in everyday communications. Using natural language–like pseudocode transfers this skill. But a graphical flowchart representing the same program must be translated before it can be interpreted in the natural language processing centers.

Nevertheless, some information is much better described in the form of a diagram. A second example illustrates this. Suppose that we wish to express a set of propositions about the management hierarchy of a small company.

Jane is Jim's boss.

Jim is Joe's boss.

Anne works for Jane.

Mark works for Jim.

Anne is Mary's boss.

Anne is Mike's boss.

This pattern of relationships is far more clearly expressed in a diagram, as shown in Figure 9.4.

These two examples suggest that visual language, in the form of static diagrams, has certain expressive capabilities that are very different from, and perhaps complementary to, natural language. Diagrams should be used to

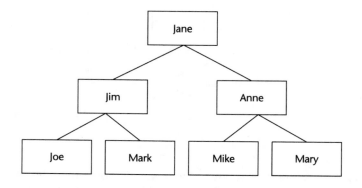

Figure 9.4   A structure diagram shows a hypothetical management
                     hierarchy.

express relationships among program elements, whereas words should be used to express detailed procedural logic.

However, the existence of the sign languages of the deaf suggests that there can be visual analogs to natural language and hence that effective visual programming languages are potentially possible, but if they are to be developed, they must be dynamically phrased, rely heavily on animation, and ideally be learned early in life. We will return to this concept later in this chapter.

Images versus Words

Often the visualization designer has the task of deciding whether to represent information visually or using words or both. Other, related choices involve the selection of static or moving images and spoken or written text. If both words and images are used, methods for linking them must be selected. Useful reviews of cognitive studies that bear on these issues have been summarized and applied to multimedia design by a number of authors, including Strothotte and Strothotte (1997), Najjar (1998), and Faraday (1998). What follows is a summary of some of the key findings, beginning with the issue of when to use images versus words. We start with static images, then consider animated images before moving to discuss the problem of combining images and words.

Static Images versus Words

As a general comment, images are better for spatial structures, location, and detail, whereas words are better for representing procedural information, logical conditions, and abstract verbal concepts. Here are some more detailed points:

- Images are best for showing structural relationships, such as links between entities and groups of entities. Bartram (1980) showed that planning trips on bus routes was better achieved with a graphical representation than with tables.

- Tasks involving localization information are better conveyed using images. Haring and Fry (1979) showed improved recall of compositional information for pictorial, as opposed to verbal, information.

- Visual information is generally remembered better than verbal information, but not for abstract images. A study by Bower et al. (1975) suggested that it is important that the visual information be meaningful and capable of incorporation into a cognitive framework for the visual advantage to be realized. This means that an image memory advantage cannot be relied on if the information is new and is represented abstractly and out of context.

- Images are best for providing detail and appearance. A study by Dwyer (1967) suggests that the amount of information that should be shown in a picture should be related to the amount of time available to study it. A number of studies support the idea that first we comprehend the shape and overall structure of an object, then we comprehend the details (Price and Humphreys, 1989; Venturino and Gagnon, 1992). Because of this, simple line drawings may be most effective for quick exposures.

- Text is better than graphics for conveying abstract concepts, such as freedom or efficiency (Najjar, 1998).

- Procedural information is best provided using text or spoken language, or sometimes text integrated with images (Chandler and Sweller, 1991). Static images by themselves are not effective in providing complex, nonspatial instructions.

- Qualifying information that specifies conditions under which something should or should not be done is better provided using text or spoken language (Faraday, 1998).

Animated Images versus Words

Computer animation opens up a whole range of new possibilities for conveying information. The work of researchers such as Michotte (1963), Heider and Semmel (1944), and Rimé et al. (1985), previously discussed in Chapter 6, shows that people can perceive events such as hitting, pushing, and aggression when geometric shapes are moved in simple ways. None of these things can be expressed with any directness using a static representation, although many of them can be well expressed using words. Thus, animation brings graphics closer to words in expressive capacity.

- Possibly the single greatest enhancement of a diagram that can be provided by animation is the ability to express causality (Michotte, 1963). With a static diagram, it is possible to use some device such

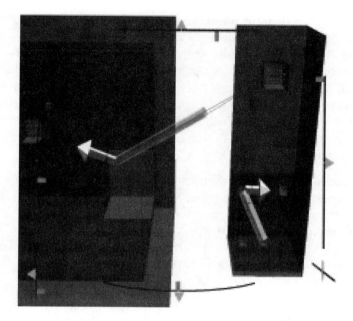

Figure 9.5   The "snakes" concept (Parker et al., 1998). Image courtesy of NVision Software Systems.

as an arrow to denote a causal relationship between two entities, but the arrowhead is a conventional device that perceptually shows that there is *some* relationship, not that it has to do with causality. The work of Michotte shows that with appropriate animation and timing of events, a causal relationship will be directly and unequivocally perceived.

- An act of communication can be expressed by means of a symbol representing a message moving from the message source object to the message destination object (Stasko, 1990). For example, Figure 9.5 shows a part of a message-passing sequence between parts of a distributed program using a graphical technique called "snakes" (Parker et al., 1998). Animation moves the head of the snake from one software component to the next as the locus of computation moves; the tail of the snake provides a sense of recent history. Although a verbal or text description of this is possible, it would be difficult to adequately describe the behavior of *multiple* process threads, each described by a snake.

- A structure can be transformed gradually using animation. In this way, processes of restructuring or rearrangement can be made explicit. However, only quite simple mechanisms can be readily interpreted. Based on studies that required the inference of hidden motion, Kaiser and Proffitt (1992) theorized that a kind of "naïve physics" is involved in perceiving action. This suggests that certain kinds of mechanical logic will be readily interpreted—for example, a simple hinge motion—but that complex interactions will not be correctly interpreted.

- A sequence of data movements can be captured with animation. The pioneering movie *Sorting Out Sorting* used animation to explain a number of different computer sorting algorithms by clearly showing the sequence in which elements were moved (Baecker, 1981). The smooth animated movement of elements enabled the direct comprehension of data movements in a way that could not be achieved using a static diagram.

- Some complex spatial actions can be conveyed using animation (Spangenberg, 1973). An animation illustrating the task of disassembling a machine gun was compared to a sequence of still shots. The animation was found to be superior for complex motions, but verbal instructions were just as effective for simple actions such as grasping some component part. Based on a study of mechanical troubleshooting, Boohrer (1975) concluded that an animated description is the best way of conveying perceptual-motor tasks, but that verbal instruction is useful to qualify the information. Teaching someone a golf swing would be better achieved with animation than with still images.

- The greatest advantage of words over graphical communication, either static or dynamic, is that natural language is ubiquitous. It is by far the most elaborate, complete, and widely shared system of symbols that we have available. For this reason alone, it is only when there is a clear advantage that visual techniques are preferred. In general, words should provide the general framework for the narrative of an extended communication, and they can also be used for the detailed structure.

Links between Images and Words

Images and words in combination are often more effective than either in isolation (Faraday and Sutcliffe, 1997; Wadill and McDaniel, 1992). Faraday and Sutcliffe (1999) showed that multimedia documents with frequent and explicit links between text and images can lead to better comprehension. Fach and Strothotte (1994) theorize that using graphical connecting devices between text and imagery can explicitly form cross-links between visual and verbal associative memory structures. But care should be taken in linking words and images. For obvious reasons, it is important that words be associated with the appropriate images. These links between the two kinds of information can be either static, as in the case of text and diagrams, or dynamic, as in the case of animations and spoken words.

Static Links

When text is integrated into a static diagram, the Gestalt principles discussed in Chapter 6 apply, as Figure 9.6 shows. Simple proximity is commonly used in labeling maps. A line drawn around the object and the text creates a common region, and this can also be used to associate groups of objects with a particular label. Arrows and speech balloons linking text and graphics also apply the principle of connectedness.

Beyond merely attaching text labels to parts of diagrams, there is the possibility of integrating more complex procedural information. Chandler

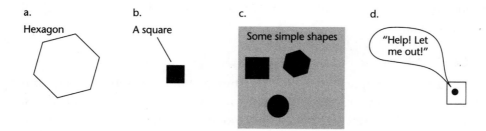

Figure 9.6   Various Gestalt principles are used to guide the linking of text and graphics: (a) Proximity. (b) Continuity/connectedness. (c) Common region. (d) Common region combined with connectedness.

and Sweller (1991) showed that a set of instructional procedures for testing an electrical system were understood better if blocks of text were integrated with the diagram, as shown in Figure 9.7. In this way, process steps could be read immediately adjacent to the relevant visual information. Sweller et al. (1990) use the concept of limited-capacity working memory to explain these and similar results. They argue that when the information is integrated, there is a reduced need to temporarily store information while switching back and forth between locations.

There can be a two-way synergy between text and images. Faraday and Sutcliffe (1997) found that propositions given with a combination of imagery and speech were recalled better than propositions given only through images. On the other hand, pictures can also enhance memory of text. Wadill and McDaniel (1992) provided images that were redundantly added to a text narrative, and even though no new information was presented, the images enhanced recall.

The nature of verbal labels can strongly influence the way visual information is encoded. Jorg and Horman (1978) showed that the choice of a general label (such as *fish*) or a specific label (such as *flounder*) to label an image influenced what would later be identified as previously seen. The broader-category label caused a greater variety of images to be identified (mostly erroneously). In some cases, it is desirable that people generalize specific instances into broader, more abstract categories, so this effect may sometimes be used to advantage.

Dynamic Links

Multimedia allows the integration of moving and static images, written and spoken text.

Deixis

In human communication theory, a gesture that links the subject of a spoken sentence with a visual reference is known as a *deictic gesture,* or simply *deixis.* When people engage in conversation, too, they sometimes point or indicate the subject of a sentence by pointing with a finger, or by glancing, or with a nod of the head. For example, a shopper might say "Give me that one," while pointing at a particular wedge of cheese at a delicatessen counter. The deictic gesture is considered to be the most elementary of linguistic acts. A

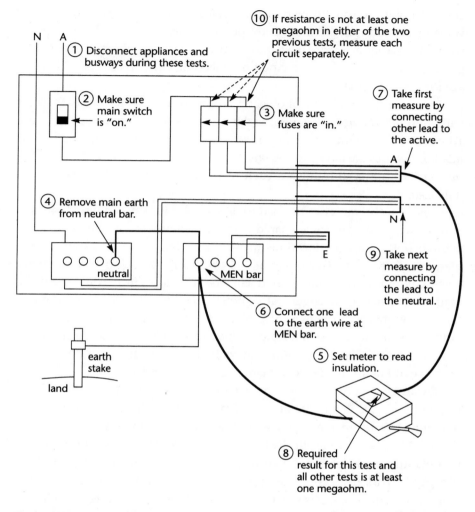

N A

① Disconnect appliances and busways during these tests.

⑩ If resistance is not at least one megaohm in either of the two previous tests, measure each circuit separately.

② Make sure main switch is "on."

③ Make sure fuses are "in."

⑦ Take first measure by connecting other lead to the active.

A

N

④ Remove main earth from neutral bar.

neutral

MEN bar

E

⑨ Take next measure by connecting the lead to the neutral.

⑥ Connect one lead to the earth wire at MEN bar.

⑤ Set meter to read insulation.

earth stake

land

⑧ Required result for this test and all other tests is at least one megaohm.

Figure 9.7   An illustration used in a study by Chandler and Sweller (1991). A sequence of short paragraphs is integrated with the diagram to show how to conduct an electrical testing procedure.

child can point to something desirable, usually long before she can ask for it verbally, and even adults frequently point to things they wish to be given without uttering a word. Deixis has its own rich vocabulary. An encircling gesture can indicate an entire group of objects or a region of space (Levelt et al., 1985; Oviatt et al., 1997).

To give a name to a visual object, we point and speak its name. Teachers will often *talk through* a diagram, making a series of linking deictic gestures. To explain a diagram of the respiratory system, a teacher might say, "*This tube* connecting the *larynx* to the *bronchial pathways* in the lungs is called the *trachea*," with a gesture toward each of the components whose names are italicized.

Deictic techniques can be used to bridge the gap between visual imagery and spoken language. Some shared computer environments are designed to allow people at remote locations to work together while developing documents and drawings. Gutwin et al. (1996) observed that in these systems, voice communication and shared cursors are the critical components in maintaining dialog. It is generally thought to be much less important to transmit an image of the person speaking. Another major advantage of combining gesture with visual media is that this *multimodal* communication results in fewer misunderstandings (Oviatt, 1999; Oviatt et al., 1997), especially when English is the second language of the speaker.

Oviatt et al. (1997) showed that when given the opportunity, people like to point and talk at the same time when discussing maps. They studied the ordering of events in a multimodal interface to a mapping system, in which a user could both point deictically and speak while instructing another person in a planning task using a shared map. The instructor might say something like "Add a park here," or "Erase this line," while pointing to regions of the map. One of their findings was that pointing generally preceded speech. The instructor would point to something and then talk about it.

Interestingly, the reverse order of events may be appropriate when we are integrating text (as opposed to spoken language) with a diagram. In a study of eye movements, Faraday and Sutcliffe (1999) found that people would read a sentence, then look for the reference in an accompanying diagram. Based on this finding, they created a method for making it easy for users to make the appropriate connections. A button at the end of each sentence caused the relevant part of the image to be highlighted or animated in some way, thus enabling readers to rapidly switch attention to the correct part of the diagram. They showed that this did indeed result in greater understanding.

This research suggests two rules of thumb:

- If spoken words are to be integrated with visual information, the relevant part of the visualization should be highlighted just before the start of the relevant speech segment.

- It written text is to be integrated with visual information, links should be made at the end of each relevant sentence or phrase.

Gestures can have an expressive dimension in addition to being deictic. Just as a line can be given a variety of qualities by being made thick, thin, jagged, or smooth, so a motion path can be made expressive (McNeil, 1992; Amaya et al., 1996). A particular kind of hand gesture, called a *beat,* sometimes accompanies speech, emphasizing critical elements in a narrative. Bull (1990) studied the way political orators use gestures to add emphasis. Vigorous gestures usually occurred at the same time as vocal stress. Also, the presence of both vigorous gestures and vocal stress often resulted in applause from the audience. In the domain of multimedia, animated pointers sometimes accompany a spoken narrative, but often quite mechanical movements are used to animate the pointer. The research on multimodal communication, together with the work on human motion perception by Johansson (1973), suggests that a variety of gestural styles could be used to enrich pointers without actually depicting a human hand.

Visual Momentum in Animated Sequences

Moving the viewpoint in a visualization can function as a form of narrative control. Often a virtual camera is moved from one part of a data space to another, drawing attention to different features. In some complex 3D visualizations, a sequence of *shots* is spliced together to explain a complex process. Hochberg and Brooks (1978) developed the concept of *visual momentum* in trying to understand how cinematographers link different camera shots together. As a starting point, they argued that in normal perception, people do not take more than a few glances at a simple static scene; following this, the scene "goes dead" visually. In cinematography, the device of the cut enables the director to create a kind of heightened visual awareness, because a new perspective can be provided every second or so. The problem faced by the director is that of maintaining perceptual continuity. If a car travels out of one side of the frame in one scene, it should arrive in the next scene traveling in the same direction (for example, from left to right); otherwise the audience may lose track of it and pay attention to something else. Wickens (1992) has extended the visual momentum concept to create a set of four principles for user interface design:

1. **Use consistent representations.** This is like the continuity problem in movies, which involves making sure that clothing, makeup, and props are consistent from one cut to another. In visualization, this means that the same visual mappings of data must be preserved. This includes presenting similar views of a 3D object.

2. **Use graceful transitions.** Smooth animations between one scale view and another allow context to be maintained. Also, the technique of smoothly morphing a large object into a small object when it is "iconified" helps to maintain the object's identity.

3. **Highlight anchors.** Certain visual objects may act as visual reference points, or anchors, tying one view of a data space to the next. An anchor is a constant invariant feature of a displayed world. Anchors become reference landmarks in subsequent views. When cuts are made from one view to another, ideally, several anchors should be visible from the previous frame. The concept of landmarks is discussed further in Chapter 10.

4. **Display continuous overview maps.** Common to many adventure video games and navigation systems used in aircraft or ground vehicles is the use of an overview map that places the user in a larger spatial context. This is usually supplemented by a more detailed local map. The same kind of technique can be used with large information spaces. The general problem of providing focus and context is also discussed further in Chapter 10.

Another technique used in cinematography is the use of an establishing shot. Hochberg (1986) showed that identification of image detail was better when an establishing shot preceded a detail shot than when the reverse ordering was used. This suggests that an overview map should be provided first when an extended spatial environment is being presented.

Animated Visual Languages

When people discuss computer programs, they frequently anthropomorphize, describing software objects as if they were people sending messages to each other and reacting to those messages by performing certain tasks. This is especially true for programs written using object-oriented programming techniques. Some computer languages explicitly incorporate anthropomorphism. ToonTalk™ is one such language (Kahn, 1996). ToonTalk uses animated cartoon characters in a cartoon city as the programming model. Houses stand for the subroutines and procedures used in conventional programming. Birds are used as message carriers, taking information from one house to another. Active methods are instantiated by robots, and comparison tests are symbolized by weight scales. The developers of ToonTalk derived their motivation from the observation that even quite young children can learn to control the behavior of virtual robots in games such as Nintendo's Mario Brothers®.

A ToonTalk example given by Kahn is programming the swapping of values stored in two locations. This is achieved by having an animated character take one object, put it to the side, take the second object and place it in the location of the first, and then take the first object and move it to the second location. Figure 9.8 illustrates this procedure.

KidSim is another interactive language, also intended to enable young children to acquire programming concepts using direct manipulation of graphical interfaces (Cypher and Canfield Smith, 1995). Here is the authors' own description:

> KidSim is an environment that allows children to create their own
> simulations. They create their own characters, and they create rules
> that specify how the characters are to behave and interact. KidSim
> is programmed by demonstration, so that users do not need to learn
> a conventional programming language.

In KidSim, as in ToonTalk, an important component is programming by example using direct manipulation techniques. In order to program a certain action, such as a movement of an object, the programmer moves the object using the mouse and the computer infers that this is a programming event that should occur when a certain set of conditions are met. For example, when an actor gets close to a rock, the actor should jump over the rock.

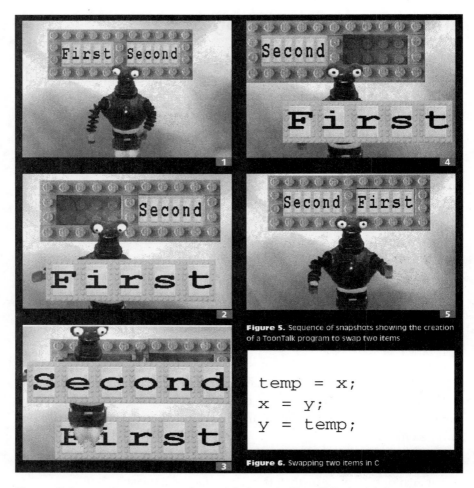

Figure 5. Sequence of snapshots showing the creation of a ToonTalk program to swap two items

```
temp = x;
x = y;
y = temp;
```

Figure 6. Swapping two items in C

Figure 9.8   A swap operation carried out in ToonTalk. In this language, animated characters can be instructed to move around and carry objects from place to place, just as they are in video games. (Kahn, 1996)

Programming by example always requires that the programmer make a number of assumptions about how the system should behave. In KidSim, programs are based on graphical rewrite rules—a picture is replaced by another picture specified by demonstration. Figure 9.9 illustrates how the rule "If there is an empty space to the right of me, move me into it" is created. The programmer must first specify the area to which the rule applies and then drag the object from its old position to the new position. There are implicit assumptions that the user must make: The rule will apply wherever the picture object occurs on the screen, and the rule is repeated in an animation cycle.

The use of animated characters as program components can often lead to false assumptions about programs that use them. Humans and animals get tired and bored, and can be expected to give up repetitive activities quite soon unless they are strongly motivated. Therefore, a child programming a computer with animated characters will expect them to stop and do something else after a while. But this is a poor metaphor for computers, which do not get tired or bored and can continue doing the same repetitive operation millions of times. Ultimately, both the strengths and the weaknesses of programming with animated characters will derive from the rich variety of visual metaphors that become available. Like all metaphors, these will be helpful if they are apt and harmful if they are not.

Rader et al. (1997) carried out an extensive independent evaluation of KidSim in two classrooms over the course of a year. The system was deliberately introduced without explicitly teaching the underlying programming

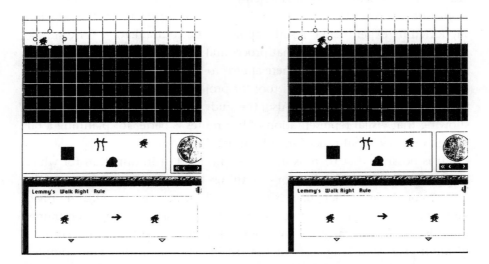

Figure 9.9   Creating a "Move Right" rule in KidSim. The user shapes a spotlight to outline the square to the right of the character, then drags the character into the adjacent square. At the bottom, the initial and final states for the rule are displayed. (Cypher and Smith, 1995)

concepts. They found that children rapidly learned the interactions needed to draw animated pictures, but failed to gain a deep understanding of the programs. They often tried to generalize the behavior they saw in ways that the machine did not understand. Students sometimes found it frustrating when they set up conditions they thought should cause some action, and then nothing happened.

A study by Palmeter et al. (1991) provided two different kinds of instruction for a procedural task. They reported that users were essentially mimicking the instructions. Thus using an animated demonstration to provide information about some procedural task may be optimal for the short term but may prove to be less effective in providing lasting gains.

Conclusion

Making general statements about the relative values of visual images and words is difficult, and much of what has been presented in this chapter is open to debate. Some of the advantages of visual representation, such as better comprehension of patterns and spatial relationships in general, seem clear and well documented. It is when we try to pin down the advantages of words that we run into difficulty. Indeed, some of the statements made, and supported by experimental results, appear to be contradictory. For example, some authors have suggested that procedural information is better described using words than images. But there appear to be counterexamples. The Gantt chart is a widely used graphical tool for project planning, and this is surely visual procedural information. Also, the study cited earlier by Bartram (1980), showing that visual representation of bus routes is better for planning a bus trip, is arguably about procedural planning.

It is possible that there is ultimately no kind of information for which words are demonstrably superior—all things being equal. But of course they are not equal. Natural language is the most elaborate, developed, and universal symbol system that we share. We are all experts at it, having been trained intensively from an early age. We are not similarly experts at visual communication. The sign languages of the deaf show that a rich and complete visual equivalent is possible, but these languages are inaccessible for most of us. Given the dominance of words as a medium of communication, visualizations will necessarily be hybrids, claiming ground only where a clear advantage can be obtained.

The evidence that we should use both images and words is stronger. Concepts presented using both kinds of coding are understood and remembered better. We evidently have cognitive subsystems dealing with each kind of information (as discussed in Chapter 10), and it is possible that using both kinds of information together may simply allow us to do more cognitive work. But to obtain a positive benefit from multimedia presentations, cross-references must be made so that the words and images can be conceptually integrated. Both time and space can be used to create these cross-links. The deictic gesture, wherein someone points at an object while speaking about it, is probably the most elementary of visual-verbal linking devices. It is deeply embedded in human discourse and probably provides the cognitive foundation for other linking devices.

The material presented in this chapter suggests a number of conclusions about how we should design easy-to-learn computer programming languages. They should be hybrids of visual and natural language codes. Structure should be presented visually, and perhaps also created visually using direct manipulation techniques. Modules can be represented as visual objects, easily connected by drawing lines between them, or by snapping them together. But the more detailed logical procedures should be programmed using words, not graphics. The use of speech recognition software may help with the difficulty of using a keyboard for beginning programmers. Pointing gestures should be used to bind spoken statements with visual objects.

Interacting with Visualizations

In some ways, a visualization can be considered an *internal* interface in a problem-solving system that has both human and computer components. A visualization can be the interface to a complex computer-based information system that supports data gathering and data analysis. On the human side, the visualization can act as an extension of cognitive processes, augmenting working memory by providing visual markers for concepts and by revealing structural relationships between problem components. A manager working with a spreadsheet and plotting projections is combining business knowledge with the computational power of the spreadsheet model. The plotted projections are visualizations that enable aspects of the model to be integrated efficiently into the cognitive decision-making process of the manager.

Interactive visualization is a process made up of a number of interlocking feedback loops that fall into three broad classes. At the lowest level is the data manipulation loop, through which objects are selected and moved using the basic skills of eye-hand coordination. Delays of even a fraction of a second in this interaction cycle can seriously disrupt the performance of higher-level tasks. At an intermediate level is an exploration and navigation loop, though which an analyst finds his or her way in a large visual data space. As people explore a new town, they build a cognitive spatial model using key landmarks and paths between them, and something similar occurs when they explore data spaces. But exploration can be generalized to more abstract searching operations. Kirsh and Maglio (1994) define a class of epistemic actions as activities whereby someone hopes to better understand or perceive a problem. At the highest level is a problem-solving loop through which the analyst forms hypotheses about the data and refines them through an augmented visualization process. The process may be repeated through multiple visualization cycles as new data is added, the problem is reformulated, possible solutions are identified, and the visualization is revised or replaced. Sometimes the visualization may act as a critical externalization of the problem, forming a crucial extension of the cognitive process.

This chapter is organized around these three loops: low-level interaction, exploration, and problem solving.

Visual-Manual Control Loop

There are a number of well-established "laws" that describe the simple, low-level control loops needed in tasks such as the visual control of hand position or the selection of an object on the screen.

Choice Reaction Time

Given an optimal state of readiness, with a finger poised over a button, a person can react to a simple visual signal in about 130 msec (Kohlberg, 1971). If the signals are very infrequent, the time can be considerably longer. Warrick et al. (1964) found reaction times as long as 700 milliseconds under conditions such that there could be as much as two days between signals. The participants were engaged in routine typing, so they were at least positioned appropriately to respond. If people are not positioned at workstations, their responses will naturally take longer.

Sometimes before someone can react to a signal, he or she must make a choice. A simple choice reaction-time task might involve pressing one button if a red light goes on and another if a green light goes on. This kind of task has been studied extensively, and it has been discovered that reaction times can be modeled by a simple rule called the Hick-Hyman law for choice reaction time (Hyman, 1953).

According to this law,

$$\text{Reaction time} = a + b \, \log_2 (C) \tag{10.1}$$

where C is the number of choices and a and b are empirically determined constants. The expression $\log_2 (C)$ represents the amount of information processed by the human operator, expressed in bits of information.

Many factors have been found to affect choice reaction time—the distinctness of the signal, the amount of visual noise, stimulus-response compatibility (see below), and so on—but under optimal conditions, the response time per bit of information processed is about 160 msec. Thus, if there are eight choices (3 bits of information), the response time will typically be on the order of the simple reaction time plus approximately 480 msec. Another important factor is the degree of accuracy required—people respond faster if they are allowed to make mistakes occasionally, and this effect is called a speed-accuracy trade-off. For a useful overview of factors involved in determining reaction time, see Card et al. (1983).

2D Positioning and Selection

In highly interactive visualization applications, it is useful to have graphical objects function not only as program output—a way of representing data— but also as program input, a way of finding out more about data.

Selection using a mouse or some similar input device (a joystick or a trackball) is one of the most common interactive operations in the modern graphical user interface, and it has been extensively studied. A simple mathematical model provides a useful estimation of the time taken to select a target that has a particular position and size.

$$\text{Selection time} = a + b \, \log_2 (D/W + 1.0) \tag{10.2}$$

where D is the distance to the center of the target, W is the width of the target, and a and b are constants determined empirically. These are different for different devices.

This formula is known as Fitts' law, after Fitts (1954). The term $\log_2(D/W + 1.0)$ is known as the *index of difficulty* (ID). The value $\frac{1}{b}$ is called the *index of performance* (IP), and is given in units of bits per second. There are a number of variations in the index-of-difficulty expression, but the one given here is the most robust (MacKenzie, 1992). Typical IP values for measured performance made with the fingertip, the wrist, and the forearm are all in the vicinity of 4 bits per second (Balakrishnan and MacKenzie, 1997). To put this into perspective, consider moving a cursor 16 cm across a screen to a small (0.5-cm) target. The index of difficulty will be about 5 bits. The selection will take more than a second longer than selecting a target that is already under the cursor.

Fitts' law can be thought of as describing an iterative process of eye-hand coordination, as illustrated in Figure 10.1. The human starts by judging the distance to the target and initiates the hand movement. On successive

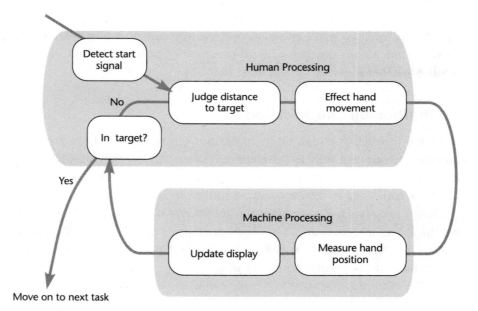

Figure 10.1   The visually guided reaching control loop. The human processor makes adjustments based on visual feedback provided by the computer.

iterations, a corrective adjustment is made to the hand movement based on visual feedback showing the cursor position. The number of iterations of the control loop increases both as the distance to the target gets larger and as the size of the target gets smaller. The logarithmic nature of the relationship derives from the fact that on each iteration the task difficulty is reduced in proportion to the remaining distance.

In many of the more complex data visualization systems, as well as in experimental data visualization systems using 3D virtual-reality technologies, there is a significant lag between a hand movement and the visual feedback provided on the display (Liang et al., 1991; Ware and Balakrishnan, 1994).

Fitts' law, modified to include lag, looks like this:

$$\text{Mean time} = a + b \ (\text{HumanTime} + \text{MachineLag}) \ \log_2 \ (D/W + 1.0) \qquad (10.3)$$

According to this equation, the effects of lag increase as the target gets smaller. Because of this, a fraction-of-a-second lag can result in a subject's taking several seconds longer to perform a simple selection task. This may not seem like much, but in a VR environment intended to make everything seem easy and natural, lag can make the simplest task difficult.

Skill Learning

Over time, people become more skilled at any task, barring fatigue, sickness, or injury. A simple expression known as the *power law of practice* describes the way task performance speeds up over time.

$$\log \ (T_n) = C - \alpha \log \ (n) \qquad (10.4)$$

where $C = T_1$ is the time to perform the task on the first trial and α is a constant that represents the steepness of the learning curve.

This law has generally been applied to simple human control tasks such as typing, but it also applies to complex perceptual tasks and to visual pattern recognition. For example, Kolers (1975) found that a power law applied to the reading of text in which the characters had been inverted. This is illustrated in Figure 10.2.

One of the ways in which skilled performance is obtained is through the *chunking* of small subtasks into programmed motor procedures. The beginning typist must make a conscious effort to hit the letters *t, h,* and *e* when

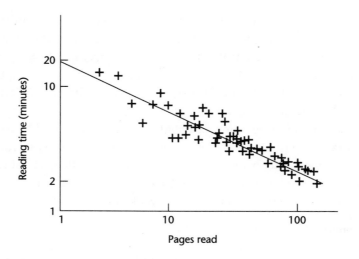

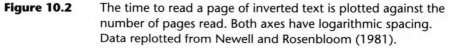

Figure 10.2   The time to read a page of inverted text is plotted against the number of pages read. Both axes have logarithmic spacing. Data replotted from Newell and Rosenbloom (1981).

typing the word *the,* but the brains of experienced typists can execute preprogrammed bursts of motor commands so that the entire word can be typed with a single mental command to the motor cortex. Skill learning is characterized by more and more of the task's becoming automated and encapsulated. To encourage skill automation, the computer system should provide rapid and clear feedback of the consequences of user actions (Hammond, 1987).

Control Compatibility

Some control movements are easier to learn than others, and this depends heavily on prior experience. If you move a computer mouse to the right and this causes an object on the screen to move to the right, this positioning method will be easy to learn. A skill is being applied that was gained very early in life and has been refined ever since. But if the system interface has been created such that a mouse movement to the right causes a graphical object to move to the left, this will be incompatible with everyday experience and positioning the object will be difficult. In the behaviorist tradition of psychology, this factor is generally called stimulus-response (S-R) compatibility.

In modern cognitive psychology, the effects of stimulus-response compatibility are readily understood in terms of skill learning and skill transfer.

In general, it will be easier to execute tasks in computer interfaces if the interfaces are designed in such a way that they take advantage of previously learned ways of doing things. Nevertheless, some inconsistencies are easily tolerated while others are not. For example, many user interfaces amplify the effect of a mouse movement so that a small hand movement results in a large cursor movement. Psychologists have conducted extensive experiments that involve changing the relationship between eye and hand. If a prism is used to laterally displace what is seen relative to what is felt, people can adapt in minutes or even seconds (Welch and Cohen, 1991). This is like using a mouse that is laterally displaced from the screen cursor being controlled. On the other hand, if people are asked to view the world inverted with a mirror, it can take weeks of adaptation for them to learn to operate in an upside-down world (Harris, 1965). Virtual-reality systems contain many distortions of the relationship between eye and hand, ranging from miscalibration errors to deliberate rescaling of hand movements so that users can move objects at a distance (Wang and MacKenzie, 1999). We can tolerate changes in the horizontal relationship between eye and hand, but misalignments due to rotations cause more disruption (Ware and Rose, 1999).

Consistency with real-world actions is only one factor in skill learning. There are also the simple physical affordances of the task itself. It is easier for us to make certain body movements than others. Very often we can make computer-mediated tasks easier to perform than their real-world counterparts. A single button click can be made to accomplish as much as a prolonged series of actions in the real world. For this reason, it would be naïve to conclude that computer interfaces should evolve toward virtual-reality simulations of real-world tasks. This discussion will be continued in the section on spatial-interaction metaphors.

Vigilance

A basic element of many interaction cycles is the detection of a target. Although several aspects of this have already been discussed in Chapter 5, a common and important problem remains to be covered: the detection of infrequently appearing targets.

The invention of radar during World War II created a need for radar operators to monitor radar screens for long hours, searching for visual signals representing incoming enemy aircraft. Out of this came a need to understand how people can maintain vigilance while performing monotonous tasks. This kind of task is common to airport baggage X-ray operators, industrial quality-control inspectors, and the operators of large power grids. Vigilance tasks commonly involve visual targets, although they can be auditory. There is an extensive literature concerning vigilance (see Davies and Parasuraman, 1980, for a detailed review). Here is an overview of some of the more general findings, adapted from Wickens (1992):

1. Vigilance performance falls substantially over the first hour.

2. Fatigue has a large negative influence on vigilance.

3. To perform a difficult vigilance task effectively requires a high level of sustained attention, using significant cognitive resources. This means that dual tasking is not an option for an important vigilance task. It is not possible for operators to perform some useful task in their "spare time" while simultaneously monitoring for some difficult-to-perceive signal.

4. Irrelevant signals reduce performance. The more irrelevant visual information is presented to an operative performing a vigilance task, the harder it becomes.

Overall, people perform poorly on vigilance tasks, but there are a number of techniques that can improve performance. One method is to provide reminders at frequent intervals about what the targets will look like. This is especially important if there are many different kinds of targets. Another is to use the sensitivity of the visual system to motion. A difficult target for a radar operator might be a slowly moving ship embedded in a great many irrelevant noise signals. Scanlan (1975) showed that if a number of radar images are stored up and rapidly replayed, the moving-ship image can easily be differentiated from the visual noise. As a more general comment, anything that can transfer the visual signal into the optimal spatial or temporal range of the visual system should help detection. If the signal can be made perceptually different or distinct from irrelevant information, this will also help. The various factors that make color, motion, and texture distinct can all be applied. These are discussed in Chapters 4 and 5.

View Refinement and Navigation Loop

View navigation is important in visualization when the data is mapped into an extended and detailed visual space. The problem is complex, encompassing, as it does, theories of pathfinding and map use, cognitive spatial metaphors, and issues related to direct manipulation and visual feedback.

Figure 10.3 sketches the basic navigation control loop. On the human side is a cognitive logical and spatial model whereby the user understands the data space and his or her progress through it. If the data space is maintained for an extended period, parts of its spatial model may become encoded in long-term memory. On the computer side, the visualization may be updated and refined from data mapped into the spatial model.

Here we start with the problem of 3D locomotion; we next consider the problem of pathfinding, and finally move on to the more abstract problem of maintaining focus and context in more abstract data spaces.

Locomotion and Viewpoint Control

Some data visualization environments show information in such a way that it looks like a 3D landscape, not just a flat map. This is naturally done with remote sensing data from other planets, or with maps of the ocean floor or other data related to the terrestrial environment. But the data landscape idea has also been applied to abstract data spaces such as the World Wide Web

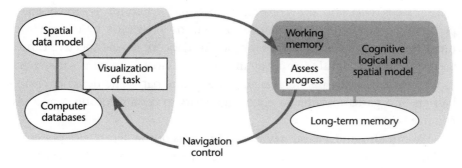

Figure 10.3 The navigation control loop.

Figure 10.4   Web sites arranged as a data landscape (Bray, 1996).

(see Figure 10.4 for an example). The idea is that we should find it easy to navigate through data presented in this way because we can harness our real-world spatial interpretation and navigation skills.

James Gibson (1986) offers an environmental perspective on the problem of perceiving for navigation:

> A path affords pedestrian locomotion from one place to another, between the terrain features that prevent locomotion. The preventers of locomotion consist of obstacles, barriers, water margins, and brinks (the edges of cliffs). A path must afford footing; it must be relatively free of rigid foot-sized obstacles. (Gibson, p. 36)

Gibson goes on to describe the characteristics of obstacles, margins, brinks, steps, and slopes. According to Gibson, locomotion is largely about perceiving and using the affordances offered for navigation by the environment (see Chapter 1 for a discussion of affordances). His perspective can be used in a quite straightforward way in designing virtual environments, much as we might design a public museum or a theme park. The designer creates barriers and paths in order to encourage visits to certain locations and discourage others.

We can also understand navigation in terms of the depth cues presented in Chapter 8. All the perspective cues are important in providing a sense of scale and distance, although the stereoscopic cue is important only for close-up navigation in situations such as walking through a crowd. When we are navigating at higher speed, in an automobile or a plane, stereoscopic depth is irrelevant since the important parts of the landscape are beyond the range of stereoscopic discrimination. Under these conditions, structure-from-motion cues and information based on perceived objects of known size are critical. It is usually assumed that smooth-motion flow of images across the retina is necessary for judgment of the direction of self-motion within the environment. But Vishton and Cutting (1995) investigated this problem using virtual-reality technology, with subjects moving through a forest-like virtual environment, and concluded that relative displacement over time of identifiable objects was the key, not smooth motion. Their subjects could do almost as well with a low frame rate, with images presented only 1.67 times per second, but performance declined markedly when updates were less than 1 per second. The lesson for the design of virtual navigation aids is that these environments should be sparsely populated with discrete but separately identifiable objects—there must be enough landmarks that several are always visible at any instant, and frame rates ideally should be at least 2 per second. However, it should also be recognized that although heading judgments are not impaired by low frame rates, other problems will result. Low frame rates cause lag in visual feedback and, as discussed previously, this can introduce serious performance problems.

Spatial Navigation Metaphors

Interaction metaphors are cognitive models for interaction that can profoundly change the design of interfaces to data spaces. Here are two sets of instructions for different viewpoint control interfaces:

1. "Imagine that the model environment shown on the screen is like a real model mounted on a special turntable that you can grasp, rotate with your hand, move sideways, or pull towards you."

2. "Imagine that you are flying a helicopter and its controls enable you to move up and down, forward and back, left and right."

With the first interface metaphor, if the user wishes to look at the right-hand side of some part of the scene, she must rotate the scene to the left to get the correct view. With the second interface metaphor, the user must fly her vehicle forward, around to the right, while turning in toward the target. Although the underlying geometry is the same, the user interface and the user's conception of the task are very different in the two cases.

Navigation metaphors have two fundamentally different kinds of constraints on their usefulness. The first of these constraints is essentially cognitive. The metaphor provides the user with a model that enables the prediction of system behavior given different kinds of input actions. A good metaphor is one that is apt, matches the system well, and is also easy to understand. The second constraint is more of a physical limitation. A particular metaphor will naturally make some actions easy to achieve, and others difficult to achieve, because of its implementation. For example, a walking metaphor limits the viewpoint to a few feet above ground level and the speed to a few meters per second. Both kinds of constraints are related to Gibson's concept of affordances—a particular interface affords certain kinds of movement and not others, but it must also be perceived to embody those affordances.

Note that, as discussed in Chapter 1, we are going beyond Gibson's view of affordances here. Gibsonian affordances are properties of the *physical* environment. In computer interfaces, the physical environment constitutes only a small part of the problem, since most interaction is mediated through the computer and Gibson's concept as he framed it does not strictly apply. We must extend the notion of affordances to apply to both the physical characteristics of the user interface and the representation of the data. A more useful definition of an interface with the right affordances is one that makes the possibility for action plain to the user and gives feedback that is easy to interpret.

Four main classes of metaphors have been employed in the problem of controlling the viewpoint in virtual 3D spaces. Figure 10.5 provides an illustration and summary. Each metaphor has a different set of affordances.

1. **World-in-hand.** In the world-in-hand metaphor, the user metaphorically grabs some part of the 3D environment and moves it (Houde, 1992; Ware and Osborne, 1990). Moving the viewpoint closer to some point in the environment actually involves pulling the environment closer to the user. Rotating the environment similarly involves twisting the world about some point as if it were held in the user's hand. A variation on this metaphor has the object mounted on a virtual turntable or gimbal. The world-in-hand model would seem to be optimal for viewing discrete, relatively compact data objects, such as virtual vases and telephones. It does not provide affordances for navigating for long distances over extended terrains.

2. **Eyeball-in-hand.** In the eyeball-in-hand metaphor, the user imagines that she is directly manipulating her viewpoint, much as she might control a camera by pointing it and positioning it with respect to an imaginary landscape. The resulting view is represented on the computer screen. This is one of the least effective methods for controlling the viewpoint. Badler et al. (1986) observed that "consciously calculated activity" was involved in setting a viewpoint.

Ware and Osborne (1990) found that while some viewpoints were easy to achieve, others led to considerable confusion. They also noted that with this technique, physical affordances are limited by the positions in which the user can physically place her hand. Certain views from far above or below cannot be achieved or are blocked by the physical objects in the room.

3. **Walking.** One way of allowing inhabitants of a virtual environment to navigate is simply to let them walk about. Unfortunately, even though a large extended virtual environment can be created, the user will soon run into the real walls of the room in which the equipment is housed. Most VR systems require a handler to prevent the inhabitant of the virtual world from tripping over the real furniture. A number of researchers have experimented with devices like exercise treadmills so that people can walk without actually moving. Typically, something like a pair of handlebars is used to steer. In an alternative approach, Slater et al. (1995) created a system that captures the characteristic up-and-down head motion that occurs when people walk in place. When this is detected, the system moves the virtual viewpoint forward in the direction of head orientation. This gets around the problem of bumping into walls, and may be useful for navigating in environments such as virtual museums. However, the affordances are still restrictive.

4. **Flying.** Modern digital terrain visualization packages commonly have "fly-through" interfaces that enable users to smoothly create an animated sequence of views of the environment. Some of these are more literal, having aircraft-like controls. Others use the flight metaphor only as a starting point. No attempt is made to model actual flight dynamics; rather, the goal is to make it easy for the user to get around in 3D space in a relatively unconstrained way. For example, Ware and Osborne (1990) developed a flying interface that used simple hand motions to control velocity. Unlike real aircraft, this interface makes it as easy to move up, down, or backward as it is to move forward. They reported that subjects with actual flying experience had the most difficulty; because of their expectations about flight dynamics, pilots did unnecessary things such as banking on turns and were uncomfortable with stopping or moving backward. Subjects without flying experience were able to pick up the interface more rapidly. Despite its lack of realism, this was rated as the most flexible and useful interface when compared to others based on the world-in-hand and eyeball-in-hand metaphors.

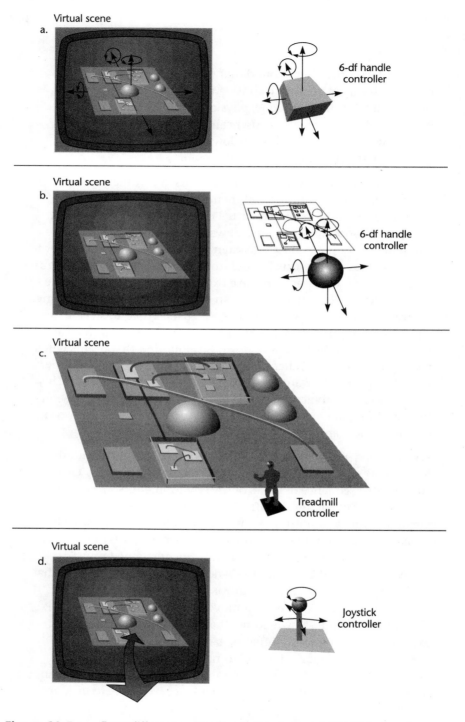

Figure 10.5   Four different navigation metaphors: (a) World-in-hand.
(b) Eyeball-in-hand. (c) Walking. (d) Flying.

The optimal navigation method depends on the exact nature of the task. A virtual walking interface may be the best way of giving a visitor a sense of presence in an architectural space; something loosely based on the flying metaphor may be a more useful way of navigating through spatially extended data landscapes. The affordances of the virtual data space, the real physical space, and the input device all interact with the mental model that the user has constructed of the task.

Wayfinding and Map Reading

In addition to the problem of moving through an environment in real time, there is the metalevel problem of how people build up an understanding of larger environments over time. This problem is usually called *wayfinding*. It encompasses both the way in which people build mental models of extended spatial environments and the way they use physical maps as aids to navigation.

Unfortunately, this area of research is plagued with a diversity of terminology. Through the following discussion, bear in mind that there are two clusters of concepts and the differences between these clusters relate to the dual coding theory discussed in Chapter 9.

One cluster includes the related concepts of *declarative knowledge, procedural knowledge, topological knowledge,* and *categorical representations*. These concepts are fundamentally logical and nonspatial.

The other cluster includes the related concepts of *spatial cognitive maps* and *coordinate representations*. These are fundamentally spatial.

Seigel and White (1975) proposed that there are three stages in the formation of wayfinding knowledge.

First, information about key landmarks is learned; initially there is no spatial understanding of the relationships between them. This is sometimes called *declarative knowledge*. We might learn to identify a post office, a church, and the hospital in a small town.

Second, *procedural knowledge* about routes from one location to another is developed. Landmarks function as decision points. Verbal instructions often consist of procedural statements related to landmarks, such as "Turn left at the church, go three blocks, and turn right by the gas station." This kind of information is also called *topological knowledge,* because it includes connecting links between locations but still no explicit representation of the spatial position of one landmark relative to another.

Third, a *cognitive spatial map* is formed. This is a representation of space that includes quantitative information about the distances between the different locations of interest. With a cognitive spatial map, it is possible to estimate the distance between any two points even though we have not traveled directly between them and to make statements such as "The university is about one kilometer northwest of the train station."

In Seigel and White's initial theory and in much of the subsequent work, there has been a presumption that spatial knowledge developed strictly in the order of these three stages: declarative knowledge, procedural knowledge, and cognitive spatial maps. Recent evidence from a study by Colle and Reid (1998) contradicts this. They conducted an experimental study using a virtual building consisting of a number of rooms connected by corridors. The rooms contained various objects. In a memory task following the exploration of the building, subjects were found to be very poor at indicating the relative positions of objects located in different rooms, but they were good at indicating the relative positions of objects within a given room. This suggests that cognitive spatial maps form easily and rapidly in environments where the viewer can see everything at once, whereas the paths from room to room were captured as procedural knowledge. A plausible conclusion is that cognitive spatial maps form naturally when it is possible to get an overview of the environment. The practical application of this is that overviews should be provided wherever possible in extended spatial information spaces.

The results of Colle and Reid's study fit well with a somewhat different theory of spatial knowledge proposed by Kosslyn (1987). He suggested that there are only two kinds of knowledge, not necessarily acquired in a particular order. He called them *categorical* and *coordinate* representations. For Kosslyn, categorical information is a combination of both declarative knowledge and topological knowledge, such as the identities of the landmarks and the paths between them. The coordinate representation is like the cognitive spatial map proposed by Seigel. A spatial coordinate representation would be expected to arise from the visual imagery obtained with an overview. Conversely, if knowledge were constructed from a sequence of turns along corridors when the subject was moving from room to room, the natural format would be categorical.

Landmarks provide the links between categorical and spatial coordinate representations. They are important both for cognitive spatial maps and for topological knowledge about routes. Vinson (1999) created a generalized classification of landmarks based on Lynch's classification (1960) of the "elements" of cognitive spatial maps. Figure 10.6 summarizes Vinson's design guidelines for the different classes of landmarks. This broad concept includes paths between locations, edges of geographical regions, districts, nodes such as public squares, and the conventional ideal of a point landmark such as a statue.

Vinson also created a set of design guidelines for landmarks in virtual environments. The following rules are derived from them:

- There should be enough landmarks that a small number are visible at all times.

- Each landmark should be visually distinct from the others.

- Landmarks should be visible and recognizable at all navigable scales.

- Landmarks should be placed on major paths and at intersections of paths.

Creating recognizable landmarks in 3D environments can be difficult because of multiple viewpoints. Darken et al. (1998) report that Navy pilots typically fail to recognize landmark terrain features on a return path, even if

Lynch's Types	Examples	Functions
Paths	Street, canal, transit line	Channel for navigator movement
Edges	Fence, riverbank	Indicates district limits
Districts	Neighborhood	Reference region
Nodes	Town square, public building	Focal point for travel
Landmarks	Statue	Reference point into which we cannot enter

Figure 10.6   The functions of different kinds of landmarks in a virtual environment. Adapted from Vinson (1999).

these were identified correctly on the outgoing leg of a low-flying exercise. This suggests that terrain features are not encoded in memory as fully three-dimensional structures, but rather are remembered in some viewpoint-dependent fashion. (See Chapter 7 for a discussion of viewpoint-dependent object memory.) An interesting way of assisting users in the encoding of landmarks for navigation in 3D environments was developed by Elvins et al. (1997). They presented subjects with small 3D subparts of a virtual cityscape that they called *worldlets,* as illustrated in Figure 10.7. The worldlets provided 3D views of key landmarks, presented in such a way that observers could rotate them to obtain a variety of views. Subsequently, when they were tested

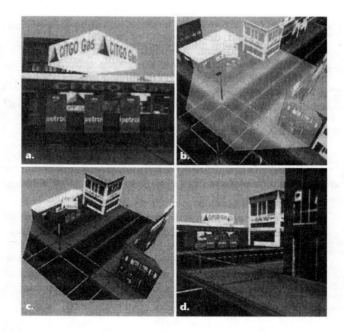

Figure 10.7   Elvins et al. (1998) conceived the idea of worldlets to be used as navigation aids. Each worldlet is a 3D representation of a landmark in a spatial landscape. (a) A straight-on view of the landmark. (b) The region extracted to create the worldlet. (c) The worldlet from above. (d) The worldlet from street level. Worldlets can be rotated to facilitate later recognition from an arbitrary viewpoint.

in a navigation task, subjects who had been shown the worldlets performed significantly better than subjects who had been given pictures of the landmarks, or subjects who had simply been given verbal instructions.

Cognitive maps can also be acquired directly from an actual map, much more rapidly than by traversing the terrain. To understand map-reading skills, Darken and Banker (1998) turned to orienteering, a sport that requires athletes to run from point to point over rugged and often difficult terrain with the aid of a map. Experienced orienteers are skilled map readers. One of the cognitive phenomena they observed was related to an initial scaling error rapidly remedied; they observed that "initial confusion caused by a scaling error is followed by a 'snapping' phenomenon where the world that is seen is instantaneously snapped into congruence with the mental representation" (Darken et al., 1998). This suggests that wherever possible, aids should be given to identify matching points on both an overview map and a focus map.

Map Orientation

How should a map be displayed? Two alternatives have been extensively studied: the track-up display and the north-up display. (See Figure 10.8 (a) and (b)). A track-up map is oriented so that the straight-ahead direction, from the point of view of the navigator, is the up direction on the map. The second alternative is to display the map so that north is always up, at the top of the map.

One way of considering the map orientation problem is in terms of control compatibility. Imagine yourself in a car, driving south from Berlin in Germany to Rome in Italy. With a north-up map, a right turn becomes a left direction on the map. Many people find this confusing and reorient the map, even though this means that the place names are upside down. Experimental studies of map use confirm this, showing that fewer errors are made when subjects use a track-up map (Eley, 1988). However, the north-up map does have advantages. Expert navigators often prefer this orientation because it provides a common frame of reference for communicating with someone else.

It is possible to enhance a north-up map and make it almost as effective as a track-up map, even for novices. Aretz (1991) provided a north-up map for helicopter navigators, but with the addition of a clear indicator of the forward field of view of the navigator. This significantly enhanced the ability of users to orient themselves. Figure 10.8(c) illustrates this kind of enhanced map.

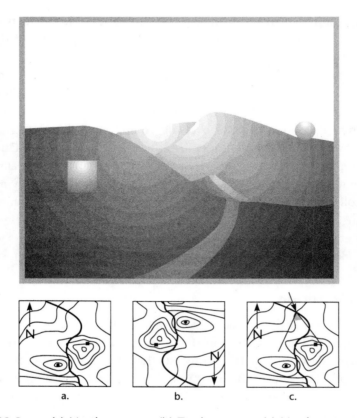

Figure 10.8   (a) North-up map. (b) Track-up map. (c) North-up map with user view explicitly displayed.

Supporting Visualizations with Maps

The research that has been reviewed suggests a number of ways that visualizations can be enhanced with maps:

- Overview maps should be provided when an information space is large. Given how hard it is to build up a mental map by exploring an environment, an overview can substantially reduce the cognitive load.

- User location and direction of view within the map should be indicated.

- Imagery of key landmarks should be provided. A landmark image on a map should be constructed from a viewpoint that will occur when the wayfinder encounters the actual landmark.

- Procedural instructions can be more useful than a map when the task itself requires navigating from landmark to landmark. In this case, the cognitive representation of the task is likely to be topological. If the problem is to guide a user from node to node through a virtual information space, providing a sequence of instructions may be more appropriate than providing a map. A verbal or written set of procedural instructions can also be enhanced with landmark imagery.

Focus, Context, and Scale

We have been dealing with the problem of how people navigate through 3D data spaces, under the assumption that the methods used should reflect the way we navigate in the "real" world. The various navigation metaphors are all based on this assumption. However, there are a number of successful spatial navigation techniques that do not use an explicit interaction metaphor, but do involve visual spatial maps. These techniques make it easy to move rapidly between views at different scales; because of this, they are said to solve the *focus-context* problem. If we think of the problem of wayfinding as one of discovering specific objects or locations in a larger landscape, the focus-context problem is simply a generalization of this, the problem of finding detail in a larger context. The focus-context problem is not always spatial; there are also structural and temporal variations. Here are examples of each:

Spatial Scale   Spatial-scale problems are common to all mapping applications. For example, a marine biologist might wish to understand the spatial behavior of codfish within a particular school of fish off the Grand Banks of Newfoundland. This information is understood in the context of the shape of the continental shelf and the boundary between cold arctic water and the warm waters of the Gulf Stream.

Structural Scale   Complex systems can have structural components at many levels. A prime example is computer software. This has structure within a single line of code, structure within a subroutine or procedure (perhaps 50 lines of code), structure at the object level for object-oriented code (perhaps 1000 lines of code), structure at the packet level, and structure at the system level. Supposing that we wish to visualize the structure of a large program such as a digital telephone switch (comprising as many as 20 million lines of code), we may wish to understand its structure through as many as six levels of detail.

Temporal Scale   Many data visualization problems involve understanding of the timing of events at very different scales. For example, in understanding data communications, it can be useful to know the overall traffic patterns in a network as they vary over the course of a day. It can also be useful to follow the path of an individual packet of information through a switch over the course of a few microseconds.

It is worth considering that the focus-context problem has already been solved by the human visual system. The brain continuously integrates detailed information from successive fixations of the fovea with the less detailed information that is available at the periphery. This must be combined with data coming from the prior sequence of fixations. For each new fixation, the brain must somehow match key objects in the previous view with those same objects moved to new locations. Differing levels of detail are supported in normal perception because objects are seen at much lower resolution at the periphery of vision than in the fovea. Since we have no difficulty in recognizing objects at different distances, this also means that scale-invariance operations are supported in normal perception. The best solutions to the problem of providing focus and context in a display are likely to take advantage of these perceptual capabilities.

Although the spatial scale of a map, the structural levels of detail of a computer program, and the temporal scale in communications monitoring are very different application domains, they can all be represented by means of spatial layouts of data and they belong to a class of related visualization problems. The same interactive techniques can usually be applied. In the following sections, we consider the perceptual properties of four different visualization techniques to solve the focus-context problem: distortion, rapid zooming, elision, and multiple windows.

Distortion Techniques

A number of techniques have been developed that spatially distort a data representation, giving more room to designated points of interest and decreasing the space given to regions away from those points. What is of specific interest is spatially expanded at the expense of what is not, thus providing both focus and context. Figure 10.9 illustrates one such method, called "intelligent zooming" (Bartram et al., 1994). Parts of the graph are dynamically repositioned and resized based on selected points of interest, and selected nodes are expanded to show their contents. Some techniques have been designed to work with a single focus, such as the hyperbolic tree browser (Lamping et al., 1995), shown in Figure 10.10. Others allow multiple foci to be simultaneously expanded; for example, the table lens (Rao and Card, 1994), illustrated in Figure 10.11. Many of these methods use simple algebraic functions to distort space based on the distance from each focus.

An obvious perceptual issue related to the use of distorting focus-context methods is whether the distortion makes it difficult to identify important parts of the structure. This problem can be especially acute when actual geographical maps are expanded. For example, Figure 10.12, from Sarkar and Brown (1994), shows a distorted view of a map of major cities in North

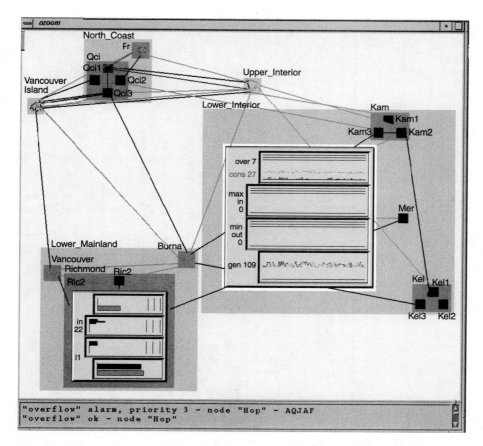

Figure 10.9   A view of the intelligent zoom system developed by Bartram et al. (Bartram et al., 1998)

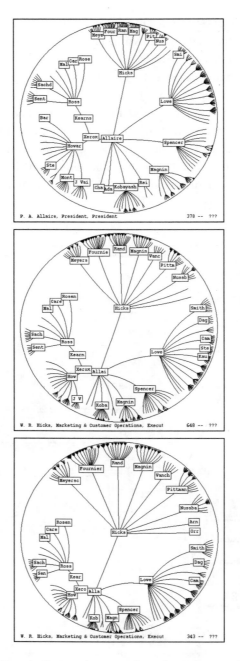

Figure 10.10   Hyperbolic tree browser from Lamping et al. (1995). The focus can be changed by dragging a node from the periphery into the center.

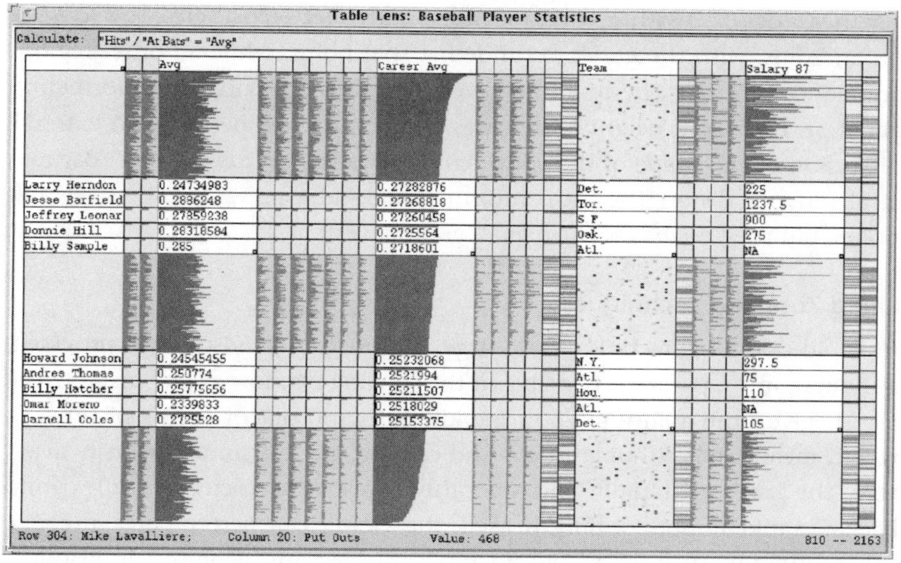

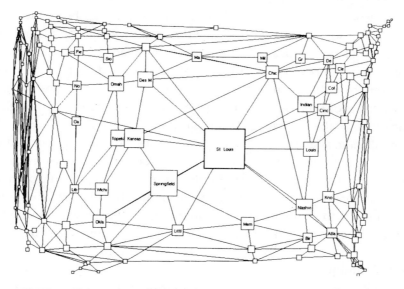

Figure 10.11   Table lens from Rao and Card (1994). Multiple row- and column-wise centers of focus can be created.

Figure 10.12   Fish-eye view of links between major American cities. The focus is on St. Louis. From Sarkar and Brown (1994).

America, together with communications paths between them. The focus is on St. Louis, with the graph expanded at that point, while all other regions are reduced in size. The result achieves the goal of making the information about St. Louis and neighboring cities clearer, at the expense of an extreme distortion of the shape of the continent. Compromises are possible; Bartram et al. do not distort the focal information locally presented in the graph nodes, but they do distort the overall graph layout.

Rapid Zooming Techniques

In rapid zooming techniques, a large information landscape is provided, although only a part of it is visible in the viewing window at any instant. The user is given the ability to zoom rapidly into and out of points of interest, which means that although focus and context are not simultaneously available, the user can rapidly and smoothly move from focus to context and back. If rapid smooth scaling is used, the viewer can perceptually integrate the information over time. The Pad and Pad++ systems (Bederson and Hollan, 1994) are based on this principle. They provide a large planar data landscape, with an interface using a simple point-and-click technique to rapidly move in and out. Care has been taken to make the animation smooth and continuous.

Mackinlay et al. (1990) invented a rapid-navigation technique for 3D scenes that they called *point of interest navigation*. This method moves the user's viewpoint rapidly in to a point of interest that has been selected on the surface of some object. At the same time, the view direction is smoothly adjusted to be perpendicular to the surface. A variant of this is to base the navigation on an object. Parker et al. (1998) developed a similar technique that is object- rather than surface-based; clicking an object scales the entire 3D "world" about the center of that object while simultaneously bringing it to the center of the workspace. This is illustrated in Figure 10.13.

In all these systems, the key perceptual issues are the rapidity and ease with which the view can be changed from a focal one to an overview and back. Less than a second of transition time is probably a good rule of thumb, but the animation must be smooth to maintain the identity of objects in their contexts. To maintain a sense of location, Landmark features should be designed to be recognized consistently, despite large changes in scale.

Elision Techniques

In visual elision, parts of a structure are hidden until they are needed. Typically, this is achieved by collapsing a large graphical structure into a single graphical object. This is an essential component of the Bartram et al. (1994)

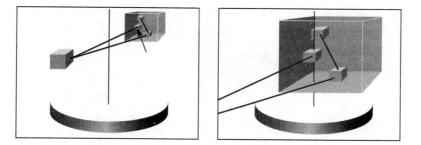

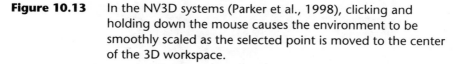

Figure 10.13   In the NV3D systems (Parker et al., 1998), clicking and holding down the mouse causes the environment to be smoothly scaled as the selected point is moved to the center of the 3D workspace.

system, illustrated in Figure 10.9, and of our NV3D system (Figure 8.21). In these systems, when a node is opened, it expands to reveal its contents.

The elision idea can be applied to text as well as graphics. In the "generalized fish-eye" technique, for viewing text data (Furnas, 1986), less and less detail is shown as the distance from the focus of interest increases. For example, in viewing code, the full text is shown at the focus, farther away only the subroutine headers are made visible, and the code internal to the subroutine is elided.

Elision in visualization is analogous to the cognitive process of chunking, discussed later in this chapter, whereby small concepts, facts, and procedures are cognitively grouped into larger "chunks." Replacing a cluster of objects, representing a cluster of related concepts with a single object, is very like chunking, and this similarity may be the reason that visual elision is so effective.

Multiple Windows

It is common, especially in mapping systems, to have one window that shows an overview and several others that show expanded details. The major perceptual problem with the multiple-window technique is that detailed information in one window is disconnected from the overview (context information) shown in another. A solution is to use lines to connect the boundaries of the zoom window to the source image in the larger view. Figure 10.14 illustrates a zooming window interface for an experimental calendar application. Multiple windows show day, month, and year views in separate windows (Card et al., 1994). The different windows are connected by lines that integrate the focus information in one table within the context

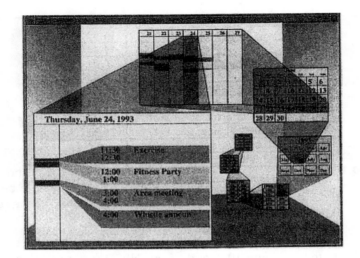

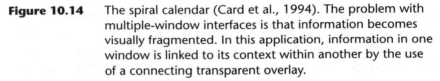

Figure 10.14   The spiral calendar (Card et al., 1994). The problem with multiple-window interfaces is that information becomes visually fragmented. In this application, information in one window is linked to its context within another by the use of a connecting transparent overlay.

provided by another. The great advantage of the multiple-window technique over the others listed above is that it is both nondistorting and able to show focus and context simultaneously.

Rapid Interaction with Data

In the data exploration interface, it is important that the mapping between the data and its visual representation be fluid and dynamic. Certain kinds of interactive techniques promote an experience of being in direct contact with the data. Rutkowski (1982) calls it the principle of transparency: When transparency is achieved, "the user is able to apply intellect directly to the task; the tool itself seems to disappear." There is nothing physically direct about using a mouse to drag a slider on the screen, but if the temporal feedback is rapid and compatible, the user can obtain the illusion of direct control. A key psychological variable in achieving this sense of control is the responsiveness of the computer system. If, for example, a mouse is used to select an object, or is used to rotate a cloud of data points in 3D space, as a rule of thumb visual feedback should be provided within $\frac{1}{10}$ second for people to feel that they are in direct control of the data (Shneiderman, 1987).

Interactive Data Display

Often data is transformed before being displayed. Interactive data mapping is
the process of adjusting the function that maps the data variables to the
display variables. A nonlinear mapping between the data and its visual representation can bring the data into a range where patterns are most easily made
visible. Figure 10.15 illustrates this concept. Often the interaction consists of
imposing some transforming function on the data. Logarithmic, square-root,
and other functions are commonly applied (Chambers et al., 1983). When the
display variable is color, techniques such as histogram equalization and interactive color mapping can be chosen (see Chapter 3). For large and complex
data sets, it is sometimes useful to limit the range of data values that are
visible and mapped to the display variable; this can be done through the use
of sliders. Ahlberg et al. (1992) called this kind of interface *dynamic queries* and
incorporated it into an interactive multivariate scatter plot application. By
adjusting data range sliders, subsets of the data can be isolated and visualized.

Another interactive technique is called *brushing* (Becker and Cleaveland,
1987). This enables subsets of the data elements to be interactively highlighted in a complex representation. Often data objects, or different attributes of them, simultaneously appear in more than one display window, or
different attributes can be distributed spatially within a single window. In

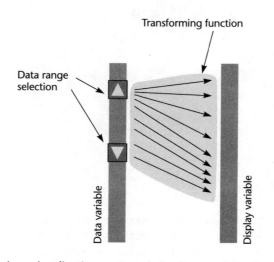

Figure 10.15   In a visualization system, is it often useful to interactively
change the function that maps data values to a display
variable.

brushing, a group of elements selected through one visual representation becomes highlighted in all the displays in which it appears. This enables visual linking of components of heterogeneous complex objects. For example, data elements represented in a scatter plot, a sorted list, and a 3D map can all be visually linked when simultaneously highlighted.

Brushing works particularly well with a graphical display technique called *parallel coordinates* (Inselberg and Dimsdale, 1990). Figure 10.16 shows an example in which a set of automobile statistics are displayed: miles per gallon, number of cylinders, horsepower, weight, and so on. A vertical line (parallel coordinate axis) is used for each of these variables. Each automobile is represented by a vertical height on each of the parallel coordinates, and the entire automobile is represented by a compound line running across the graph, connecting all its points. But because the pattern of lines is so dense, it

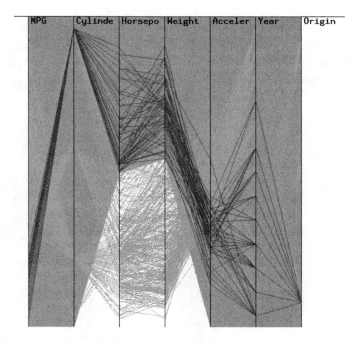

Figure 10.16   In a parallel-coordinates plot, each data dimension is represented by a vertical line. This example illustrates brushing. The user can interactively select a set of objects by dragging the cursor across them. (Courtesy of Matthew Ward) See also color plates.

is impossible to visually trace any individual line and thereby understand the characteristics of a particular automobile. With brushing, a user can select a single point on one of the variables, which has the result of highlighting the line connecting all the values for that automobile. This produces a kind of visual profile. Alternatively, it is possible to select a range on one of the variables, as illustrated in Figure 10.16, and all the lines associated with that range become highlighted. Once this is done, it is easy to understand the characteristics of a set of automobiles (those with low mileage, in this case) across all the variables.

As discussed in Chapter 5, it is possible to map different data attributes to a wide variety of visual variables: position, color, texture, motion, and so on. Each different mapping makes some relationships more distinct and others less distinct. Therefore, allowing a knowledgeable user to interactively change the mapping can be an advantage. (See Figure 10.17.) Of course, such mapping changes are in direct conflict with the important principle of consistency in user interface design, and in most cases, only the sophisticated visualization designer should change display mappings.

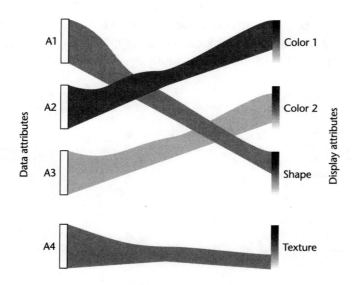

Figure 10.17 In some interactive visualization systems, it is possible to change the mapping between data attributes and the visual representation.

Problem-Solving Loop

People solve problems with diagrams differently from the way they do it without diagrams. What Zhang (1997) calls *external representations* extend and alter the cognitive process. Visualizations function in a straightforward way as memory extensions; more important, they enable cognitive operations that would otherwise be impossible.

Problem solving takes place in an interactive cycle. The user builds a conceptual model of the problem and develops a problem-solving strategy that contains a visualization as a key component. The visualization feeds into and enhances the hypothesis generation and testing operations of working memory. The loop is completed as the user makes control adjustments through the visual display, to seek more information or to alter the computer-based model. Figure 10.18 illustrates this basic loop. The remainder of this chapter is devoted to showing how visualization can be an integral part of some problem-solving processes, extending memory and cognition.

To understand computer-augmented problem solving, a unified model is needed, containing both human cognitive structures and a machine-based task environment. One such unified model is the executive process interactive control (EPIC), developed by Kieras and his coworkers (Kieras and Meyer, 1997). Its major structures are illustrated in Figure 10.19. Other models have been constructed by Card et al. (1983), Anderson et al. (1997), and Strothotte and Strothotte (1997). A fully developed model of cognition is

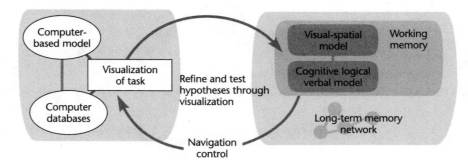

Figure 10.18   The visualization-centered problem-solving loop involves both computer-based modeling and a cognitive model integrated through a visualization.

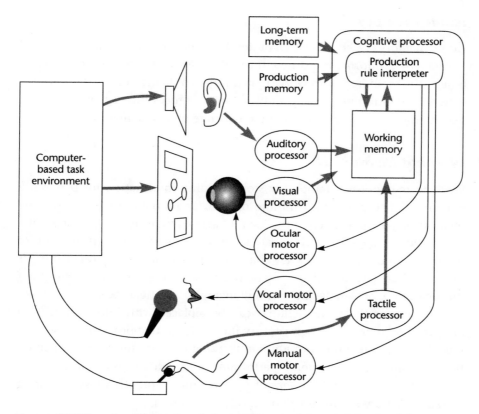

Figure 10.19   A unified extended cognitive model containing both human and machine processing systems. (Adapted from Kieras and Meyer, 1997.)

well beyond the scope of this book. The purpose of the following sections is to sketch, in broad outline, some of the key components and to show how visualization can function as an interface.

Memory structures provide the basic framework that underlies cognition and there are, as a first approximation, three different kinds of human memory—iconic, working, and long-term. In the following discussion, we begin with human memory structures, go on to describe computer augmentations, and finally use this integrated model to show how visualizations can be part of a problem-solving process.

Iconic Memory

Iconic memory is a kind of visual buffer that holds the information presented on the retina. Information stored in this way decays in a fraction of a second unless it is "read out" into working memory. Iconic memory is the interface between the computer display and the human processing system. The visual search processes described in Chapter 5 operate on iconic memory.

Working Memory

Working memory is a temporary store, holding information for between a fraction of a second and a minute or two. As its name suggests, working memory is the name given to the locus of active attention and problem solving. Although there is much debate about the exact nature and function of working memory, some of its key characteristics are clear. Working memory is limited in capacity; estimates vary between about three and seven chunks of information that can be held simultaneously. In the process of problem solving, any or all of these chunks can be replaced with information from long-term memory or by new sensory inputs. Cognitive-processing resources must be used to retain information in working memory for more than about three seconds. If someone is performing a cognitive task—for example, counting down from 100 in steps of 7—performance on other tasks requiring working memory resources will be drastically reduced.

Working memory is not a unitary system; rather, it has a number of inter-linked but separate components. There are, at least, separate systems for processing auditory and visual information, as well as subsystems for manual and verbal output. In addition to the sense-specific stores, there are also working memories for more abstract information. Kieras, for example, proposes an amodal control memory, containing the operations needed to accomplish current goals, and a general-purpose working memory containing other miscellaneous information.

Another feature of working memory is that it is usually filled with visual information about the outside world, but unlike information that is loaded internally from long-term memory, this externally referenced information requires no effort of maintenance—although it does require an effort of selective attention to take it in. A complex data visualization gives us access to far more complex spatial information than can be manipulated based on mentally stored images. The time required to load information from external visual sources into working memory is similar to that required for long-term memory—between 100 and 250 ms (Card et al., 1983; Kieras and Meyer, 1997). Because of this, and because of the high bandwidth of visual input, external visual aids should not be considered inferior to internal mental images used as supports for problem solving.

Long-Term Memory

Long-term memory contains the information that we build up over a lifetime. Subjectively, we tend to associate long-term memory with events we can consciously recall; this is called episodic memory (Tulving, 1983). However, long-term memory also includes motor skills, such as the finger movements involved in typing, and the perceptual skills, integral to our visual systems, that enable us to rapidly identify words and objects.

There is a common myth that we remember everything we experience (but we lose the indexing information), but in fact we remember only what gets encoded in the first 24 hours or so after an event occurs. The best estimates suggest that we do not actually store very much information in long-term memory. Using a reasonable set of assumptions, Landauer (1986) estimated that only about 10^9 bits of information are stored over a 35-year period. This is what we can currently expect to find in the solid state main memory of a personal computer. The power of human long-term memory is not its capacity, but its remarkable flexibility. The same information can be combined in many different ways and through many different kinds of cognitive operations.

Human long-term memory can be usefully characterized as a network of linked concepts (Collins and Loftus, 1975; Yufic and Sheridan, 1996). Our intuition supports this model. If we think of a particular concept—for example, data visualization—we can easily bring to mind a set of related concepts: computer graphics, perception, data analysis, potential applications. Each of these concepts is linked to many others. Figure 10.20 shows some of the concepts related to information visualization (at least in the author's mind).

The network model makes it clear why some ideas are harder to recall than others. Concepts and ideas that are distantly related naturally take longer to find, because it can be difficult to trace a path to them and easy to take wrong turns in traversing the concept net, since no map exists. For this reason, it can take minutes, hours, or days to retrieve some ideas. A study by Williams and Hollan (1981) investigated how people recalled names of

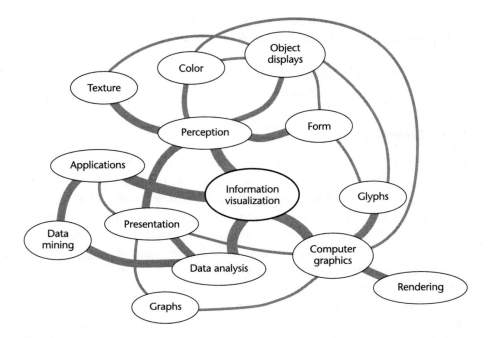

Figure 10.20   A concept map showing a set of linked concepts surrounding the idea of information visualization.

people from their high school graduating classes, seven years later. They continued to come up with new names for at least 10 hours, although the number of falsely remembered names also increased over time. The forgetting of information in long-term memory is thought to be more a loss of access than an erasure of the memory trace (Tulving and Madigan, 1970). Memory connections can easily become corrupted or misdirected, and as a result, people often misremember events with a strong feeling of subjective certainty (Loftus and Hoffman, 1989).

Chunks of information are continuously being prioritized, and to some extent reorganized, based on current cognitive requirements (Anderson and Milson, 1989). It is much easier to recall something that we have recently had in working memory. Seeing an image from the past will prime subsequent recognition.

Long-term memory and working memory appear to be overlapping, distributed, and specialized. Long-term visual memory involves parts of the visual cortex; long-term verbal memory involves parts of the temporal cortex specialized for speech. More abstract and linking concepts may be represented in areas such as the prefrontal cortex. Working memory is better thought of as existing within a context of long-term memory, rather than as a distinct processing module. As visual information is processed through the visual system, it activates the long-term memory of the visual objects that have previously been processed by the same system. This explains why visual recognition is much faster and more efficient than recall.

Chunks and Concepts

Human memory is much more than a simple repository like a telephone book; information is highly structured in overlapping and interconnected ways. The terms *chunk* and *concept* are both used in cognitive psychology to denote important units of stored information. The two terms are used interchangeably here. The process of grouping simple concepts into larger ones is called *chunking*. A chunk can be almost anything: a mental representation of an object, a plan, a group of objects, or a method for achieving some goal. The process of becoming an expert in a particular domain is largely one of creating effective high-level concepts (or chunks).

It is generally thought that concepts are formed by a kind of hypothesis-testing process (Levine, 1975). According to this view, multiple tentative hypotheses about the structure of the world are constantly being evaluated based on sensory evidence and evidence from internal long-term memory. In many cases, the initial hypotheses start with some existing concept, a mental model or metaphor. New concepts are distinguished from the prototype by means of transformations (Posner and Keele, 1968). For example, the concept of a zebra can be formed from the concept of a horse by adding a new node to a concept net containing a reference to a horse and distinguishing information, such as the addition of stripes.

Extending Memory and Cognition

Using this sketchy model of human processing, we are now in a position to say something about the way a data visualization system can extend the cognitive process. Let us start with the example of planning a route for a vacation trip across the country with the aid of a map. The map provides a visualization of the major and minor traffic arteries and the cities that can be visited. Although we may already have a good idea of the cities that we may wish to visit, the map reminds us of where they are and it may jog our memory about other nearby and interesting places. In many cases, the best route becomes obvious after a few seconds of looking at the map, but alternative routes can be rapidly identified. Once planning decisions have been made, parts of the route can be highlighted using a marker, and this reduces the cognitive load for the remaining planning. During the trip, the highlighted path is a useful augmentation of the original map. The highlighted path also makes it easy to track progress during the actual journey.

With a computer-based map, the possibilities for augmentation are even greater. In electronic charts used for ocean tankers, it is possible to show the position of the ship itself on the chart, as well as the ship's track and other ships in the vicinity. More computational enhancements are possible: While a ship's pilot might mentally calculate the turning radius of the ship in a particular situation, the computer can do this more accurately, based on a model of the ship, the wind loading, and the currents in the vicinity.

In these examples, there are three ways in which visualization extends human cognition. The first is as a fairly straightforward memory extension: The map preserves information about geography and about the route that has been planned. In this respect, a map is far superior to an internal mental image. The second is as a way of supporting spatial reasoning: The map enables much better route planning than would be possible with a set of poorly remembered facts about cities and their relative locations. The third is as a direct extension of the cognitive process: When the computer plots the ship's predicted course, it is taking over what was once a cognitive task for the pilot. The result gives the pilot the opportunity to pay attention to other task factors.

It is interesting to note that there is a rough correspondence between human memory and computer memory structures. The computer graphics frame buffer is a block of memory that holds currently displayed visual information. This is analogous to human iconic memory; it functions as a kind of visualization buffer, holding information created by a visualization for as long as it is required. Active applications running on a personal computer are analogous to human working memory. These are like the active thought processes involved in problem solving. Personal databases and the databases of the World Wide Web function like external long-term memory. There are even analogies with forgetting. Information is seldom deleted from personal, business, or Web databases. Instead, the "forgetting" process consists mostly of links being lost or rearranged to suit different purposes. These analogies, although intriguing, should not be taken too literally; there are also many differences. For instance, the level of detail that can be recalled from a visual image bank is far greater than what can be recalled from human visual memory.

At least one experimental user interface has been built to explicitly augment the different levels of human memory. The WebBook interface (Card et al., 1996) has distinct screen regions representing different memory types:

(1) a Focus Place (the large book or page) showing a page, a book, or an open book at full size for direct interaction between the user and content; (2) an Immediate Memory space (the air and the desk), where pages or books can be placed when they are in use, but not the immediate focus (like pages on a desk); (3) a Tertiary Place (the bookcase) where many pages and books can be stored.

A graphic object can function as a kind of extension for working memory, serving to hold information that can be used in cognitive operations. Links from graphical icons in hypermedia information systems serve to rapidly access new information. Click on the icon and additional information rapidly becomes available in a way that is somewhat analogous to following links in a concept net stored in long-term memory.

One way of describing the effectiveness of computer-based informational retrieval is to consider how long it takes to acquire useful information. Card et al. (1994) call this the *cost of knowledge characteristic function*. The cost of knowledge depends on the quality of the user interface—which may include a visualization—together with a particular user interface. If some measure of information quality is available, this can also be included. One thing that is immediately obvious from their work is that given a responsive, well-designed system, people can obtain information far more rapidly and accurately from external sources than from their own memories, even allowing that information from their own memories probably has the greatest utility and relevance.

When we consider the interfaces between human memory systems and computer-based memory, a great asymmetry is evident. As illustrated in Figure 10.21, by far the widest channel is the visual pathway from the computer into the human visual system. The flow of information across the visualization buffer and into the iconic memory of the observer is very large—up to tens of megabytes per second. This is visually analyzed through the powerful mechanisms of attention and pattern finding. Working in the other direction, people can output ideas to a computer by drawing diagrams or writing text, or by speaking, but these are all relatively low-bandwith pathways. The implication of this asymmetry is that a kind of steerable computing model

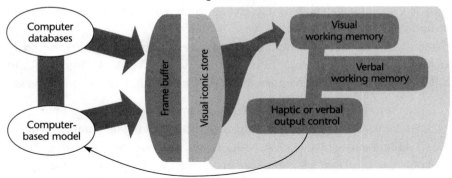
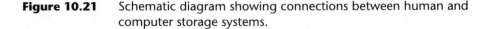

Figure 10.21   Schematic diagram showing connections between human and computer storage systems.

must be adopted for the efficient use of visualization. The user should be able to use low-bandwidth control actions to nudge a computer-based system so that it provides complete, well-structured, and timely information. Many systems are already designed with this in mind. In hypermedia, a single pointing action combined with a button click can generate a whole new screen, containing tens of thousands of bytes of new information. In scientific computation, huge computational simulations are often controlled by adjusting a few parameters, and the outcomes are visualized.

Visual Spatial Reasoning

In addition to providing a memory extension, visualizations can also support cognition and problem solving through a kind of spatial reasoning. Zhang (1997) argues that "external representations are not simply inputs and stimuli to the internal mind; rather they are so intrinsic to many cognitive tasks that they guide, constrain and even determine cognitive behavior." Applications such as project planners and computer-aided design (CAD) packages provide computational support for cognition with a visual interface, extending and distributing cognitive activity.

Zhang studied the way people played tic-tac-toe against a computer, using a number of different visual representations that are all logically equivalent. Three of them are illustrated in Figure 10.22 (with some modifications). One is the conventional game, in which players alternately insert Xs

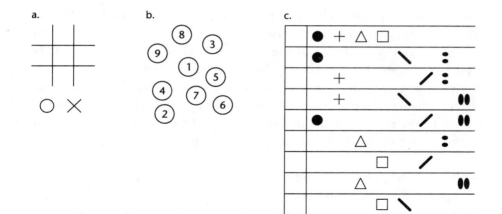

Figure 10.22   Three differerent representations of the tic-tac-toe game. This is a variation on the versions given in Zhang (1997).

and Os in a 3-×-3 grid until one person gets three in a straight line. A second is numeric: Players alternately choose numbers from a set of nine digits until one gets a set containing numbers that add up to 15. A third is visual, but players alternately select rows containing different sets of shapes, and winning involves getting a complete set of three shapes. Grid cells in Figure 10.22(a) are equivalent to numbers in (b) and rows in (c). For example, the center cell in (a), the number 5 in (b), and the top row in (c) are logically the same. Using standardized games played against computer opponents, Zhang found that people played better with both of the visual representations. He also showed that relatively subtle changes in the computer's playing strategy changed the relative advantages of different representations. Factors such as making an effective move visually salient were important. For example, it is usually a good strategy to choose the center square in tic-tac-toe, and this is visually salient because of its location and the many axes of symmetry that run through it. In (c), the top row is the equivalent of the center square. This is visually salient because it is at the top of the list and because it is the only one containing four objects. However, in (b), the equivalent number, 5, is not in any salient position, and although it is the median of the numbers 1 through 9, this fact requires calculation.

It should hardly surprise us that some representations lead to more effective problem solving. After all, if choices related to color, form, and layout were entirely arbitrary, one representation would be as good as another and design would be irrelevant. The more profound point that Zhang makes is that cognitive operations can become distributed into the visual representation. It is not necessary for the user to construct an internal model of the visualization because the visual representation allows problem solutions to be "directly perceived and used without being formulated explicitly." In the conventional tic-tac-toe game, we can see a partial line emerging, and hence can conclude that a particular move will result in a win. The kind of internal computation needed in the number version of the game is not required; instead, the problem has been partly externalized.

Concept Maps and Mind Maps

The technique of sketching out links between concepts, as shown in Figure 10.20, has received considerable attention from educational theorists. These *concept maps* (or *mind maps,* as they are sometimes called) are often recommended as study aids for students (Jonassen et al., 1993). Usually such maps are constructed informally by simply sketching them on paper, but computer-based tools also exist. Essentially, a concept map is a type of node-link diagram in which the nodes represent concepts and the links represent relationships between concepts. It can be used to make the structure of a cognitive concept network explicitly available. An individual can use a concept map as a tool for reorganizing his or her own personal concept structure, and it may reveal patterns of relationships between ideas that were not evident when the concepts were stored internally. A concept map can also be constructed in a group exercise, in which case it becomes a tool for building a common understanding.

Psychologists have developed a number of other tools for mapping the cognitive structures of concepts, besides simple sketching. One of these is multidimensional scaling (Shepard, 1962). The technique involves giving the participant pairs of examples of the ideas or objects to be mapped and asking him or her to rate the similarity. For example, if the goal is to find out how someone conceptualizes different kinds of animals, that person is given pairs such as cat-dog, mouse-cow, cat-elephant, and so on, and asked to give each pair a similarity rating. Once all pairwise ratings for the entire set have been obtained, the multidimensional scaling technique is used to compute a mathematical space in which similar animals are close together. This technique also reveals the most significant dimensions of this space. The multidimensional scaling technique does not show links between concepts; it shows only proximity. Concepts that are close together in the space are assumed to be related.

Multidimensional scaling can be used as a tool in visualizing concept spaces, but suffers from the problem that the space created can have a high dimensionality. However, the dimensionality can be reduced by simply showing the two or three most significant dimensions as a 2D or 3D scatter plot. More dimensions can be added by color coding or changing the shape of each data glyph, as discussed in Chapters 4 and 5.

The analysis of large text databases is an application area in which it is useful to get a view of a large number of points in a multidimensional conceptual space. The SPIRE system creates a classification of documents with respect to a keyword query and can be applied to databases (Wise et al., 1995) consisting of hundreds of thousands of documents. The result is a set of vectors in an *n*-dimensional space. To help people understand the resulting clusters of documents, Wise et al. created a visualization called a ThemeScape, which shows the two most important dimensions as a kind of data landscape. This is illustrated in Figure 10.23. Flags on the tops of hills label and identify the largest clusters of documents in this space. Essentially, a ThemeScape uses the two most significant dimensions of the space to create a smoothed two-dimensional histogram. This can be regarded as a different kind of concept map: one that does not show the links, but uses spatial proximity and salience to show the major concentrations of information and, to some extent, their relationships. This kind of display is useful when two dimensions really do capture most of the variability in the data. If more dimensions are involved, color coding as well as more interactive exploratory techniques may be necessary. In any case, the SPIRE system exemplifies the approach of using high-bandwidth visual output coupled with low-bandwidth control to help people understand very large amounts of information.

Trajectory mapping is a more recent psychological method for mapping out the structures of concept spaces (Richards and Koenderink, 1995). Unlike multidimensional scaling, trajectory mapping, explicitly finds links between concepts. In trajectory mapping, a participant is also given pairs of examples from the set of objects (or concepts) to be organized. However, in this case, the person is asked to look at the objects that make up the pair and extrapolate on the basis of some difference between them, and then select another sample concept that represents the result of that extrapolation. For example, someone who is given a mouse and a dog as exemplars might extrapolate to a cow based on the dimension of size, or might extrapolate to a monkey based on a concept of animal intelligence. Participants are also allowed to say that

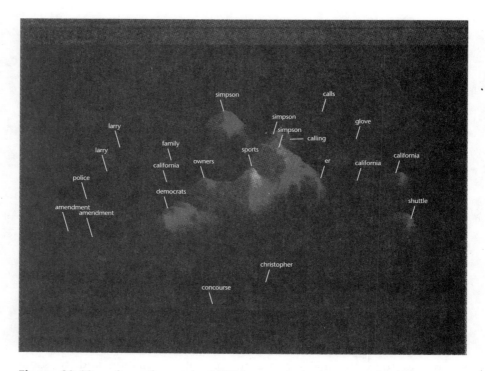

Figure 10.23   An entire week of CNN news stories is summarized in a
ThemeScape visualization (Wise et al., 1995).

there is no meaningful extrapolation, in which case one of the exemplars
becomes a terminator in the resulting concept graph. This exercise is designed
to produce a set of cognitive pathways linking concepts. Strong pathways can
be distinguished from weak ones. Lokuge et al. (1996) used a combination of
trajectory mapping and multidimensional scaling to create different visual
maps linking various tourist attractions in the Boston area, such as museums
and open-air markets. The results were based both on conceptual similarities
between the different items and on the pathways between them. One of the
results is shown in Figure 10.24. This technique could be used to automatically generate customized tours. All the tourist would have to do is enter a set
of interests, and the system would combine these with the database information to create a walking tour of relevant attractions.

It should be recognized that no matter how they are generated, concept
maps are somewhat crude instruments for making knowledge explicit. All of
them reveal only that there is *some* relationship between ideas, not the nature
of the relationship.

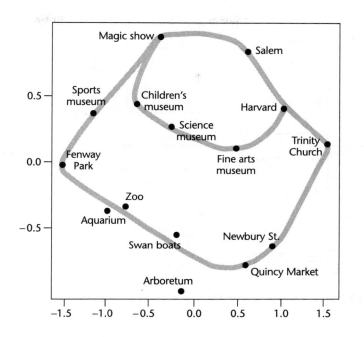

Figure 10.24 A trajectory map of tourist destinations in the Boston area, laid out according to the results of a multidimensional scaling experiment.

The Unified Modeling Language (UML) is a diagramming notation that has been specifically designed to represent very complex systems with multiple types of entities and relationships (Rumbaugh et al., 1999). Although UML was initially intended to model the components of computer software systems, it has been adapted for business modeling.

UML answers the need for visual representation of many kinds of complex entities and relationships. Figure 10.25 illustrates some of the many different kinds of relationships that can be modeled using UML.

Although UML is probably the best tool we possess for creating diagrams of complex systems visually, it has many shortcomings as a perceptual design. There are many kinds of entities and relationships in UML that are not differentiated in perceptually salient ways. Most of the variety is created by means of small cryptic symbols and written labels. There would seem to be an opportunity here for developing a visual knowledge modeling system using the flexibility and power of computer graphics systems. Color, texture, form, motion, and 3D structures could be used to more clearly differentiate multiple entities and relationships. Using perceptual principles, it should be

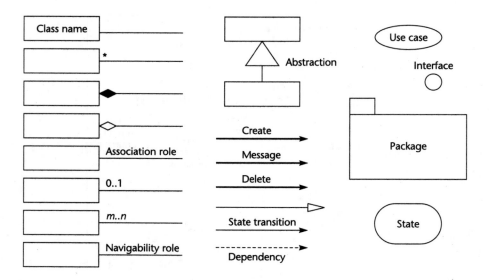

Figure 10.25   A subset of the Unified Modeling Language notation.

possible to design a notation in which both complex entities and multiple classes of relationships are made far more recognizable and visually distinct. This idea is also discussed with relation to the geon diagram in Chapter 7.

Creative Problem Solving

We commonly divide problem-solving activities into the routine and the creative. The essential difference is that in creative thinking the emphasis is on novelty. Theories of creative thinking generally break down the process into three states: preparation, production, and judgment (Matlin, 1994). Visualization can help with all three.

In the *preparation* stage, the problem solver acquires the background information needed to build a solution. Sometimes preparation involves a stage of exploratory data analysis; this is where visualization is most likely to be useful.

In the *production* stage, the problem solver generates a set of potential problem solutions. A problem solution often starts with a tentative suggestion, which is either rejected or later refined. Early theorists proposed that the quantity of ideas, rather than the quality, was the overriding consideration in the production of candidate solutions. However, experimental studies fail to support this idea (Gilhooly, 1988). Generating ideas irrespective of their value is probably not useful.

Possibly the most challenging problem posed in data visualization systems is to support the way sketchy diagrams are used by scientists and engineers in the production stage. Discoveries and inventions that began as table-napkin sketches are legendary. Here is a description of the role of a diagram by an architectural theorist (Alexander, 1964, p. 92):

> Each constructive diagram is a tentative assumption about the nature of the context. Like a hypothesis, it relates an unclear set of forces to one another conceptually; like a hypothesis, it is usually improved by clarity and economy of notation. Like a hypothesis, it cannot be obtained by deductive methods, but only by abstraction and invention. Like a hypothesis, it is rejected when a discrepancy turns up and shows that it fails to account for some new force in the context.

It is clear that if creativity is to be supported, the medium must afford tentative interactions. Imprecise, "loose" sketches gain from a lack of precision that affords multiple interpretations. The fact that a line can be interpreted in many different ways, as discussed in Chapter 9, can be a distinct benefit in enabling a diagram to support multiple tentative hypotheses. The sketches people construct as part of the creative process are rapid, not refined, and readily discarded. Giving a child high-quality watercolor paper and paints is likely to inhibit creativity if the child is made aware of the expense and is cautioned not to "waste" the materials. Schumann et al. (1996) carried out an empirical study of architectural perspective drawings executed in three different styles: a precise line drawing, a realistically shaded image, and a sketch. All the drawings contained the same features and had the same level of detail. The sketch version was rated substantially higher on measures of ability to stimulate creativity, changes in design, and discussions.

In the *judgment* stage, the problem solver analyzes the potential solutions. It is an exercise in quality control; as fast as hypotheses are created and patterns are discovered, most must be rejected. In the context of a visualization system used for something like data mining, the user may discover large numbers of patterns, but will also be willing to reject them almost as rapidly as they are discovered. Some will already be known, some will be irrelevant to the task at hand, only a few will be novel, and even fewer will lead to practical solutions. Many judgment aids are not visual; for example, statistical tools can be used to formally test hypotheses. But when visualization is part of the process, it should not be misleading, nor should it hide important information. This, of course, is the challenge of designing for perception that has occupied most of this book.

Conclusion

The best visualizations are not static images to be printed in books, but fluid, dynamic artifacts that respond to the need for a different view or for more detailed information. In some cases, the visualization can be an interface to a simulation of a complex system; the visualization, combined with the simulation, can create a powerful cognitive augmentation. An emerging view of human-computer interaction considers the human and the computer together as a problem-solving system (Zhang, 1997). In such a model, the data visualization becomes part of the interface between the human and machine system components. The visualization is a two-way interface, although highly asymmetric, with far higher bandwidth communication from the machine to the human than in the other direction. Because of this asymmetry in data rates, cognitive support systems must be constructed that are semiautomatic, with only occasional nudges from users steering them in a desired direction. The high-bandwidth visualization channel is then used to deliver the results of modeling exercises and database searches.

At the interface, the distinction between input and output becomes blurred. We are used to regarding a display screen as a passive output device and a mouse as an input device. This is not the way it is in the real world, where many things work both ways. A sheet of paper or a piece of clay can both record ideas (input) and display them (output). The coupling of input and output can also be achieved in interactive visualization. Each visual object in an interactive application can potentially provide output as a representation of data, and can also potentially receive input. Someone may click on it with a mouse, or may use it as an interface to change the parameters of a computer model. The ultimate challenge for this kind of highly interactive information visualization is to create an interface to support creative sketching of ideas, affording interactive sketching that is as fluid and inconsequential as the proverbial paper-napkin sketch.

The person who wishes to design a visualization must contend with two sets of conflicting forces. On the one hand, there is the requirement of the best possible visual representation, tailored exactly to the problem to be solved. On the other hand, there is the need for consistency in representation any time that two or more people work on a problem. This need is even greater when large international organizations have a common set of goals that demand industrywide visualization standards. At the stage of new discoveries, standardization is the enemy of innovation and innovation is the enemy of standardization. These are exciting times for information visualization, because we are still in the discovery phase, but it will not last for long. In the next few years, the wild inventions that are now being implemented will become standardized. Like clay sculptures that have been baked and hardened, the novel data visualization systems of today's laboratory will become cultural artifacts, everyday tools of the information professional.

Changing Primaries

This appendix describes the operation of transforming from one set of primaries to another. The mathematical name for this operation is a *change of basis.*

To convert a color from one set of primary lights to another, it is first necessary to define a conversion between the primaries themselves. We can think of this as matching each of the new primary lights using the old primary system. Suppose we designate our original set of primaries P_1, P_2, and P_3 and the new set of primaries Q_1, Q_2, and Q_3. We now use our original primaries to create matches with each of the new primaries in turn. Let us call the amount of each of the P primaries c_{ij}.

Thus,

$$Q_1 \equiv c_{11}P_1 + c_{12}P_2 + c_{13}P_3$$
$$Q_2 \equiv c_{21}P_1 + c_{22}P_2 + c_{23}P_3 \qquad \text{(A1.1)}$$
$$Q_3 \equiv c_{31}P_1 + c_{32}P_2 + c_{33}P_3$$

If we denote the matrix of c_{ij} values C, then

$$P = CQ \qquad\qquad\qquad (A1.2)$$

To reverse the transformation, invert the matrix:

$$P = C^{-1}Q \qquad\qquad\qquad (A1.3)$$

This same matrix can now be used to convert any set of values expressed in one set of primaries into the other set of primaries. Thus, the values p_1, p_2, and p_3 represent the amounts of the lights in primary system P needed to make a match.

$$\text{Sample} \equiv p_1 P_1 + p_2 P_2 + p_3 P_3 \qquad\qquad\qquad (A1.4)$$

Then we can calculate the values in primary system Q simply by solving.

$$q = Cp \qquad\qquad\qquad (A1.5)$$

CIE Color Measurement System

To determine a standard observer, a set of red, green, and blue lamps is used by a number of representative subjects to match all the pure colors of the spectrum. The result is called a set of color-matching functions. The set of color-matching functions for the Commission Internationale de L'Éclairage (CIE) standard observer are illustrated in Figure B1.1. They were obtained with red, green, and blue pure spectral hues at 700, 546, and 436 nanometers, respectively, using a number of trained observers. Notice that there are negative values in these functions. These exist for the reasons discussed in Chapter 4. It is not possible to directly match all spectral lights with these, or any other, primaries.

For a number of reasons, the CIE chose not to use the standard-observer color-matching functions directly as the color standard, although it would have been perfectly legitimate to do so. Instead, they chose a set of abstract primaries called the *XYZ* tristimulus values and transformed the original

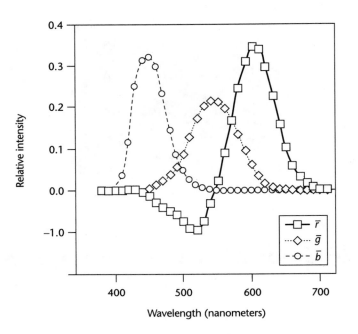

Figure B1.1   The color-matching functions that define the CIE 1931
standard observer. To obtain these, each pure spectral
wavelength was matched by a mixture of three primary lights.

color-matching functions into this new coordinate system. The process is the
transformation from one coordinate system to another, as described in
Appendix A. The transformed color-matching functions $\bar{x}, \bar{y}, \bar{z}$ are illustrated
in Figure B1.2.

The CIE *XYZ* tristimulus values have the following properties:

1. All tristimulus values are positive for all colors. To achieve this, it
   was necessary to create primaries that do not correspond to any
   real lights. The *XYZ* primary axes are purely abstract concepts.
   However, this model has the advantage that all perceivable colors
   fall within the CIE gamut. They are, in effect, a set of virtual
   primaries.

2. The *X* and *Z* tristimulus values have zero luminance. Only the *Y*
   tristimulus value contains luminance information, and the color-
   matching function ($\bar{y}$) is the same as the $V(\lambda)$ function, discussed
   in Chapter 3.

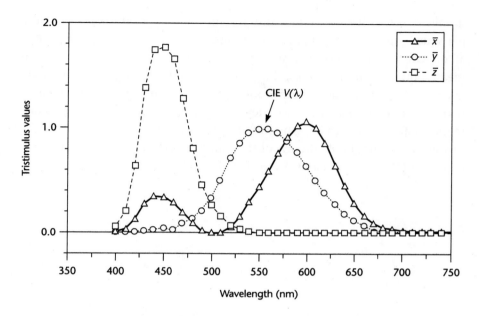

Figure B1.2   The CIE tristimulus functions used to define the color of a light in *XYZ* tristimulus coordinates.

To determine the *XYZ* tristimulus values for a given patch of light, we integrate the energy distribution with the three $\bar{x}, \bar{y}, \bar{z}$ color-matching functions that define the CIE standard. Note that this is a generalization of the process of obtaining luminance described in Chapter 3, only here we obtain three values to fully specify a color:

$$X = K_m \int_\lambda E(\lambda)\bar{x}_\lambda d\lambda$$

$$Y = K_m \int_\lambda E(\lambda)\bar{y}_\lambda d\lambda \qquad (B1.1)$$

$$Z = K_m \int_\lambda E(\lambda)\bar{z}_\lambda d\lambda$$

If $K_m = 680$ lumens/watt and $E(\lambda)$ is measured in watts per unit area solid angle (steradians), then *Y* gives luminance.

This appendix provides only a very brief introduction to the complex and technical subject of colorimetry. Many important issues have been neglected that must be taken into account in serious color measurement. One issue is whether the light to be measured is an extended source such as a monitor, in which case we measure in light emitted per unit area (candelas per square meter), or a lamp, in which case we measure total light output in all directions. The subject becomes still more complex when we consider the measurement of surface colors; the color of the illuminating source has to be taken into account, and we can no longer use a trichromatic system. Fortunately, computer monitors, since they emit light, do allow us to use a trichromatic system. The reader who intends to get involved in serious color measurement should obtain one of the standard textbooks, such as Wyszecki and Stiles (1982) or Judd and Wyszecki (1975).

Bibliography

Ahlberg, C., Williamson, C., and Schneiderman, B. (1992). Dynamic queries for information exploration. *Proceedings of CHI '92,* ACM, 619–626.

Alexander, C. (1964). *Notes on the Synthesis of Form,* Harvard University Press, Cambridge, MA.

Amaya, K., Bruderlin, A., and Calvert, T. (1996). Emotion from motion. *Proceedings of Graphics Interface '96,* 222–229.

Anderson, J.R. and Milson, R. (1989). Human memory: An adaptive perspective. *Psychological Review* 96(4): 703–719.

Anderson, J.R., Matessa, M., and Lebiere, C. (1997). ACT-R: A theory of higher-level cognition and its relation to visual attention. *Human-Computer Interaction* 12: 439–462.

Anstis, S.M. and Cavanaugh, P. (1983). A minimum motion technique for judging equiluminance in color vision. *Physiology and Psychophysics,* ed. J.D. Mollon and L.T. Sharpe. 156–166. Academic Press, London.

Arditi, A. (1987). Binocular vision. In *Handbook of Perception and Human Performance,* ed. K.R. Boff, L. Kaufman, and J.P. Thomas, 23–41. Wiley, New York.

Aretz, A.J. (1991). The design of electronic map displays. *Human Factors* 33(1): 85–101.

Armstrong, D.F., Stokoe, W.C., and Wilcox, S.E. (1994). Signs of the origin of syntax. *Current Anthropology* 35(4): 349–368.

Arthur, K.W., Booth, K.S., and Ware, C. (1993). Evaluating task performance for fish-tank virtual worlds. *ACM Tansactions on Information Systems* 11(3): 239–265.

Badler, N.I., Manoocherhri, K.H., and Baraff, D. (1986). Multi-dimensional interface techniques and articulated figure positioning by multiple constraints. *Proceedings Workshop on Interactive 3D Graphics,* ACM, October, 151–169.

Baecker, R., Small, I., and Mander, R. (1991). Bringing icons to life. *Proceedings CHI '91,* ACM, 1–12.

Baecker, R.M. (1981). *Sorting out Sorting.* Presented at ACM SIGGRAPH Conference, Dallas, Texas, 1981. Film and video versions available from Morgan Kaufmann, San Francisco.

Baecker, R.M. and Small, I. (1990). Animation at the Interface. In *The Art of Human-Computer Interface Design,* ed. B. Laurel, 251–267. Addison-Wesley, Reading, MA.

Balakrishnan, R. and MacKenzie, I.S. (1997). Performance differences in the fingers, wrist and forearm in computer input control. *CHI '97 Proceedings,* ACM, 303–310.

Ballesteros, S. (1989). Some determinants of perceived structure: Effects of stimulus and tasks. In *Object Perception: Structure and Process,* ed. B.E. Shepp and S. Ballesteros, 235–266. Lawrence Erlbaum Associates, Hillsdale, NJ.

Bar, M. and Biederman, I. (1998). Subliminal visual priming. *Psychological Science* 9: 464–469.

Barfield, W., Hendrix, C., Bjorneseth, O., Kaczmarek, K.A., and Lotens, W. (1995). Comparison of human sensory capabilities with technical specifications of virtual environment equipment. *Presence* 4(4): 329–356.

Barlow, H. (1972). Single units and sensation: A neuron doctrine for perceptual psychology? *Perception* 1: 371–394.

Bartram, D.J. (1980). Comprehending spatial information: The relative efficiencies of different methods for presenting information about bus routes. *Journal of Applied Psychology* 65: 103–110.

Bartram, L., Ovans, R., Dill, J., Dyck, M., Ho, A., and Harens, W.S. (1994). Contextual assistance in user interfaces to complex, time-critical systems: The intelligent zoom. *Graphics Interface '94,* 216–224.

Bartram, L., Ho, A., Dill, J., and Henigman, F. (1995). The continuous zoom: A constrained fisheye technique for viewing and navigating large information spaces. *Proceedings of UIST '95,* ACM, 207–215.

Bartram, L. (1998). Perceptual and interpretative properties of motion for information visualization. *Proceedings of the Workshop on New Paradigms in Information Visualization and Manipulation,* ACM, 3–7.

Bauer, B., Jolicoeur, P., and Cowan, W.B. (1996). Distractor heterogeneity versus linear separability in colour visual search. *Perception* 25: 1281–1294.

Beardsley, T. (1997). The machinery of thought. *Scientific American,* August, 78–83.

Beck, J. (1966). Effect of orientation and of shape similarity on perceptual grouping. *Perception and Psychophysics* 1: 300–302.

Beck, J. and Ivry, R. (1988). On the role of figural organization in perceptual transparency. *Perception and Psychophysics* 44: 585–594.

Becker, R.A. and Cleaveland, W.S. (1987). Brushing scatterplots. *Technometrics* 29(2): 127–142.

Bederson, B. and Hollan, J. (1994). Pad++: A zooming graphical interface for exploring alternate interface physics. *Proceedings of UIST' 94,* ACM, 17–36.

Bellugi, U. and Klima, E.S. (1976). Two faces of sign: Iconic and abstract. *Annals of the New York Academy of Sciences* 280: 514–538.

Benedikt, M. (1991). Cyberspace: Some proposals. In *Cyberspace: First Steps,* 119–224. MIT Press, Cambridge, MA.

Bennett, A. and Rabbetts, R.B. (1989). *Clinical Visual Optics,* 2d ed., 31. Butterworth Heinemann, Oxford.

Berlin, B. and Kay, P. (1969). *Basic Color Terms: Their Universality and Evolution.* University of California Press, Berkeley.

Berry, R.N. (1948). Quantitative relations among vernier, real depth and stereoscopic depth acuities. *Journal of Experimental Psychology* 38: 708–721.

Bertin, J. (1977). *Graphics and Graphic Information Processing.* de Gryter Press, Berlin.

Bertin, J. (1983). *Semiology of Graphics* (W.J. Berg, trans.). University of Wisconsin Press, Madison.

Bickerton, D. (1990). *Language and Species.* University of Chicago Press, Chicago.

Biederman, I. and Cooper, E. (1992). Size invariance in visual object priming. *Journal of Experimental Psychology, Human Perception and Performance* 18: 121–133.

Bieusheuvel, S. (1947). Psychological tests and their application to non-European peoples. In *Yearbook of Education,* ed. G.B. Jeffrey. University of London Press, London.

Blake, R. and Holopigan, K. (1985). Orientation selectivity in cats and humans assessed by masking. *Vision Research* 23(1): 1459–1467.

Booher, H.R. (1975). Comprehensibility of pictorial information and printed word in proceduralized instructions. *Human Factors* 17(3): 266–277.

Bower, G.H., Karlin, M.B., and Dueck, A. (1975). Comprehension and memory for pictures. *Memory and Cognition* 3(2): 216–220.

Bovik, A.C., Clark, M., and Geisler, W.S. (1990). Multichannel texture analysis using localized spatial filters. *IEEE Transactions on Pattern Analysis and Machine Intelligence* 12: 55–73.

Bray, T. (1996). Measuring the Web. *Computer Networks and ISDN Systems* 28: 993–1005.

Bridgeman, B. (1991). Separate visual representations for perception and visually guided behavior. In *Pictorial Communications in Virtual and Real Environments,* ed. S.R. Ellis, 316–327. Taylor and Francis, London.

Brooks, F.P. (1988). Grasping reality through illusion: Interactive graphics serving science. *Proceedings of CHI '88,* ACM, 1–11.

Bruce, V. and Morgan, M.J. (1975). Violations of symmetry and repetition in visual principles. *Perception* 4: 239–249.

Bruno, N. and Cutting, J.E. (1988). Minimodality and the perception of layout. *Journal of Experimental Psychology: General* 117: 161–170.

Bull, P. (1990). What does gesture add to the spoken word? In *Images and Understanding,* ed. H. Barlow, C. Blakemore, and M. Weston-Smith, 108–121. Cambridge University Press, Cambridge.

Caelli, T. and Bevan, P. (1983). Probing the spatial frequency spectrum for orientation sensitivity with stochastic textures. *Vision Research* 23(1): 39–45.

Caelli, T., Brettel, H., Rentschler, I., and Hilz, R. (1983). Discrimination thresholds in the two-dimensional spatial frequency domain. *Vision Research* 23(2): 129–133.

Caelli, T., Manning, M., and Finlay, D. (1993). A general correspondence approach to apparent motion. *Perception* 22: 185–192.

Caelli, T. and Moraglia G. (1985). On the detection of Gabor Signals and discrimination of Gabor Textures. *Vision Research* 25(5): 671–684.

Callaghan, T.C. (1989). Interference and dominance in texture segmentation: Hue, geometric form and line orientation. *Perception and Psychophysics* 46(4): 299–311.

Campbell, F.W. and Green, D.G. (1965). Monocular versus binocular visual acuity. *Nature* 208: 191–192.

Card, S.K., Moran, T.P., and Newell, A. (1983). *The Psychology of Human-Computer Interaction.* Lawrence Erlbaum Associates, Hillsdale, NJ.

Card, S.K., Pirolli, P., and Mackinlay, J.D. (1994). The cost-of-knowledge characteristic function: Display evaluation of direct-walk dynamic information visualizations. *CHI '94,* ACM, 238–244.

Card, S.K., Robertson, G.G., and York, W. (1996). The WebBook and the Web Forager: An information workspace for the World Wide Web. *SIGCHI '96 Proceedings,* ACM, 111–117.

Carroll, J.M. and Kellogg, W.A. (1989). Artifact as theory-nexus: Hermeneutics meets theory-based design. In *Proceedings of SIGCHI '89.* ACM Press, New York.

Casey, S. (1993). *Set Phasers on Stun and Other True Tales of Design, Technology and Human Error.* Aegean Publishing, Santa Barbara, CA.

Cataliotti, J. and Gilchrist, A.L. (1995). Local and global processes in lightness perception. *Perception and Psychophysics* 57(2): 125–135.

Chambers, J.M., Cleveland, W.S., Kleiner, B., and Tukey, P.A. (1983). *Graphical Methods for Data Analysis*. Wadsworth, Belmont, CA.

Chandler, P. and Sweller, J. (1991). Cognitive load theory and the format of instruction. *Cognition and Instruction* 8: 293–332.

Charbonnell, J.R., Ware, J.L., and Senders, J.W. (1968). A queuing model of visual sampling: Experimental validation. *IEEE Transactions on Man-Machine Systems*, MMS-9, 82–87.

Chau, A.W. and Yeh, Y.Y. (1995). Segregation by color and stereoscopic depth in three-dimensional visual space. *Perception and Psychophysics* 57(7): 1032–1044.

Chen, P.P.S. (1976). The entity-relationship model—toward a unified view of data. *ACM Transactions on Database Systems* 1: 1–22.

Chernoff, H. (1973). Using faces to represent points in k-dimensional space. *Journal of the American Statistical Association* 68: 361–368.

Chomsky, N. (1965). *Aspects of the Theory of Syntax*. MIT Press, Cambridge, MA.

CIE subcommittee E-1.3.1. (1971.) *Recommendations on Uniform Color Spaces.* Commission Internationale de L'Éclariage (CIE), Supplement #2 to CIE Publication #15, Paris.

Cleveland, W.S. and McGill, R.A. (1983). A color-caused optical illusion on a statistical graph. *American Statistician* 37(2): 101–105.

Cohen, M.F. and Greenberg, D.S. (1985). The hemi-cube: A radiosity solution for complex environments. *SIGGRAPH '85,* ACM, 31–40.

Cohen, M.F., Greenberg, D.P. (1985). Immel, D.S., and Brock, P.J. (1986). An efficient radiosity approach for realistic image synthesis. *IEEE Computer Graphics and Applications* 6(2): January, 26–35.

Colle, H.A. and Reid, G.B. (1998). The room effect: Metric spatial knowledge of local and separated regions. *Presence* 7(2): 116–128.

Collins, A.M. and Loftus, E.F. (1975). A spreading activation theory of semantic processing. *Psychological Review* 82: 407–428.

Coren, S., and Ward, L.M. (1989). *Sensation and Perception,* 3d ed. Harcourt Brace Jovanovich, New York.

Cornsweet, T.N. (1970). *Visual Perception,* Academic Press, New York.

Cowan, W.B. (1983). An inexpensive scheme for calibration of a colour monitor in terms of CIE standard coordinates. *SIGGRAPH '83 Proceedings,* ACM, 315–322.

Cross, A.R., Armstrong, R.L., Gobrecht, C., Paton, M., and Ware, C. (1997). Three-dimensional imaging of the Belousov-Zhabotinsky reaction using magnetic resonance. *Magnetic Resonance Imaging* 15(6): 719–728.

Cutting, J.E. (1986). *Perception with an Eye for Motion*. MIT Press, Cambridge, MA.

Cutting, J.E. (1991). On the efficacy of cinema, or what the visual systems did not evolve to do: Visual enhancements in pick-and-place tasks. In *Pictorial Communication in Virtual and Real Environments,* ed. S.R. Ellis, 486–495. Taylor and Francis, London.

Cutting, J.E., Springer, K., Braren, P.A., and Johnson, S.H. (1992). Wayfinding on foot from information in retinal, not optical flow. *Journal of Experimental Psychology: General* 121: 41–72.

Cypher, A. and Canfield Smith, D. (1995). KidSim: End user programming of simulations. *CHI '95 Proceedings,* ACM, 27–34.

D'Zmura, M., Lennie, P., and Tiana, C. (1997). Color search and visual field segregation. *Perception and Psychophysics* 59(3): 381–388.

Darken, R.P. and Banker, W.P. (1998). Navigating in natural environments: A virtual environment training transfer study. *Proceedings of VRAIS '98,* 12–19.

Darken, R.P. and Sibert, J.L. (1996). Wayfinding strategies and behaviors in large virtual worlds, *CHI '96, Proceedings,* 142–149.

Darken, R.P., Allard, T., and Achille, L.B. (1998). Spatial orientation and wayfinding in large-scale virtual spaces: An introduction. *Presence* 7(2): 101–107.

Daugman, J.G. (1984). Spatial visual channels in the Fourier plane. *Vision Research* 24: 891–910.

Daugman, J.G. (1985). Uncertainty relation for resolution in space, spatial frequency, and orientation optimized by two-dimensional visual cortical filters. *Journal of the Optical Society of America* A/2: 1160–1169.

Davies, D.R. and Parasuraman, R. (1980). *The Psychology of Vigilance*. Academic Press, London.

De Valois, R.L. and De Valois, K.K. (1975). Neural coding of color. In *Handbook of Perception,* ed. E.C. Carterette and M.P. Friedman, vol. 5, *Seeing,* ch. 5, 117–166. Academic Press, New York.

Deering, M. (1992). High-resolution virtual reality. In *Proceedings of SIGGRAPH '92. Computer Graphics* 26(2): 195–202.

Dehaene, S. (1997). *The Number Sense: How the Mind Creates Mathematics*. Oxford University Press, Oxford.

Deregowsky, J.B. (1968). Picture recognition in subjects from a relatively pictureless environment. *African Social Research* 5: 356–364.

Deuchar, M. (1990). Are the signs of language arbitrary? In *Images and Understanding,* ed. H. Barlow, C. Blakemore, and M. Weston Smith, 168–179. Cambridge University Press, Cambridge.

Distler, C., Boussaoud, D., Desmone, R., and Ungerleider, L.G. (1993). Cortical connections of inferior temporal area REO in Macaque monkeys. *Journal of Comparative Neurology* 334: 125–150.

DiZio, P. and Lackner, J.R. (1992). Spatial orientation, adaptation and motion sickness in real and virtual environments. *Presence* 1(3): 319–328.

Donoho, A.W., Donoho, D.L., and Gasko, M. (1988). MacSpin: Dynamic graphics on a desktop computer. *IEEE Computer Graphics and Applications,* July, 51–58.

Dosher, B.A., Sperling, G., and Wurst, S.A. (1986). Trade-offs between stereopsis and proximity luminance covariance as determinants of perceived 3D structure. *Vision Research* 26(6): 973–990.

Douglas, S. and Kirkpatrick, T. (1996). Do color models really make a difference? *ACM CHI '96 Proceedings,* 399–405.

Drasic, D. and Milgram, P. (1991). Positioning accuracy of a virtual stereoscopic pointer in a real stereoscopic video world. *SPIE Vol. 1457—Stereoscopic Displays and Applications II,* 58–69.

Driver, J., McLeod, P., and Dienes, Z. (1992). Motion coherence and conjunction search. *Perception and Psychophysics* 51(1): 79–85.

Drury, C.G. and Clement, N.R. (1978). The effect of area, density, and number of background characters on visual search. *Human Factors* 20: 597–603.

Duda, R. and Hart, P.E. (1973). *Pattern Classification and Scene Analysis*. Wiley, New York.

Durgin, F.H., Proffitt, D.R., Reinke, K.S., and Olson, T.J. (1995). Comparing depth from motion with depth from binocular disparity. *Journal of Experimental Psychology: Human Perception and Performance* 21(3): 679–699.

Dwyer, F.M. (1967). The effect of varying the amount of realistic detail in visual illustrations. *Journal of Experimental Education* 36: 34–42.

Edelman, S. (1995). Representation of similarity in 3D object discrimination. *Neural Computation* 7: 407–422.

Edelman, S. and Buelthoff, H.H. (1992). Orientation dependence in the recognition of familiar and novel views of 3D objects. *Vision Research* 32: 2385–2400.

Edwards, B. (1979). *Drawing on the Right Side of the Brain*. J.P. Tarcher, Los Angeles.

Eley, M.G. (1988). Determining the shapes of land surfaces from topographical maps. *Ergonomics* 31: 355–376.

Elvins, T.T., Nadeau, D.R., and Kirsh, D. (1997). Worldlets—3D thumbnails for wayfinding in virtual environments. *UIST '97 Proceedings,* 21–30.

Elvins, T.T., Nadeau, D.R., Schul, R., and Kirsh, D. (1998). Worldlets: 3D thumbnails for 3D browsing. *Proceedings of CHI '98,* ACM, 163–170.

Englehardt, Y., de Bruin, J., Janssen, T., and Scha, R. (1996). The visual grammar of information graphics. *Artificial Intelligence in Design (AID '96)* in the Workshop on Visual Representation, Reasoning and Interaction in Design, 24–27, June.

Fach, P.W. and Strothotte, T. (1994). Cognitive maps: A basis for designing user manuals for direct manipulation interfaces. In *Cognitive Aspects of Visual Languages and Visual Interfaces,* ed. M.J. Tauber, D.E. Mahling, and F. Arefi. Elsevier Science Inc., New York.

Faraday, P. (1998). Theory-based design and evaluation of multimedia presentation interfaces. Ph.D. thesis. School of Informatics, City University, London.

Faraday, P. and Sutcliffe, A. (1999). Authoring animated Web pages using "contact points." *Proceedings of CHI'99,* ACM, 458–465.

Faraday, P. and Sutcliffe, A. (1997). Designing effective multimedia presentations. *Proceedings of CHI '97,* ACM, 272–279.

Faraday, P. and Sutcliffe, A. (1998). Making contact points between text and images. ACM Multimedia, *http://www.kom.e-technik.tu-darmstadt.de/pr/workshops /acmmm98/electronic_proceedings/faraday*

Farah, M.J., Soso, M.J., and Dashieff, R.M. (1992). Visual angle of the mind's eye before and after unilateral occipital lobectomy. *Journal of Experimental Psychology: Human Perception and Performance* 18: 214–246.

Feiner, S., MacIntyre, B., Haupt, M., and Solomon, E. (1993). Windows on the world, 2D windows for 3D augmented reality. *Proceedings UIST '93,* ACM Atlanta, GA, Nov.: 145–155.

Feldman, J.A. (1985). Four frames suffice: A provisional model of vision and space. *Behavioural and Brain Sciences* 8: 265–289.

Field, D.J., Hayes, A., and Hess, R.F. (1993). Contour integration by the human visual system: Evidence for a local "association field." *Vision Research* 33(2): 173–193.

Fisher, S.K. and Cuiffreda, K.J. (1990). Adaptation to optically increased interocular separation under naturalistic viewing conditions. *Perception* 19: 171–180.

Fitts, P.M. (1954). The information capacity of the human motor system in controlling the amplitude of movements. *Journal of Experimental Psychology* 47: 381–391.

Fleet, D. (1998). *Visualization of Communications in 3D.* Unpublished master's thesis. Faculty of Computer Science, University of New Brunswick.

Foley, J.D., van Dam, A., Feiner, S.K., and Hughes, J.F. (1990). *Computer Graphics: Principles and Practice,* 2d ed. Addison-Wesley, Reading, MA.

Fowler, D. and Ware, C. (1989). Strokes for representing univariate vector field maps. *Graphics Interface '89 Proceedings,* 249–253.

Fowler, R.H. and Dearholt, D.W. (1990). Information retrieval using pathfinder networks. In *Pathfinder Associative Networks: Studies in Knowledge Organization,* ed. R.W. Schvaneveldt, 165–178. Ablex, Norwood, NJ.

Frisby, J.P. (1979). *Seeing, Illusion, Brain and Mind.* Oxford University Press, Oxford.

Frisby, J.P., Buckley, D., and Duke, P.A. (1996). Evidence for good recovery of lengths of real objects seen with natural stereo viewing. *Perception* 25: 129–154.

Furnas, G. New graphical reasoning models for understanding graphical interfaces. *Proceedings of CHI '91,* ACM, 71–78.

Furnas, G.W. (1986). Generalized fisheye views. *Proceedings of CHI '86,* ACM, 17–26.

Garner, W.R. (1974). *The Processing of Information and Structure.* Lawrence Erlbaum Associates, Hillsdale, NJ.

Geertz, C. (1973). *The Interpretation of Cultures.* Basic Books, New York.

Gibson, J.J. (1979). *The Ecological Approach to Visual Perception.* Houghton Mifflin, Boston. (Currently published by Lawrence Erlbaum, Hillsdale, NJ.)

Gibson, J.J. (1986). *The Ecological Approach to Visual Perception.* Lawrence Erlbaum Associates, Hillsdale, NJ.

Gilbert, S.A. (1997). Mapping mental spaces: How we organize perceptual and cognitive information. Ph.D. thesis. MIT.

Gilchrist, A.L. (1979). The perception of surface blacks and whites. *Scientific American,* March, 88–96.

Gilchrist, A.L. (1980). When does perceived lightness depend on perceived spatial arrangement? *Perception and Psychophysics* 28: 527–538.

Gilhooly, K.J. (1988). *Thinking: Directed, Undirected and Creative.* Academic Press, London.

Ginsburg, A.P., Evans, D.W., Sekuler, R., and Harp, S.A. (1982). Contrast sensitivity predicts pilots' performance in aircraft simulators. *American Journal of Optometry and Physiological Optics* 59: 105–108.

Goldin-Meadow, S. and Mylander, C. (1998). Spontaneous sign systems created by deaf children in two cultures. *Nature* 391: 279–281.

Goldstein, D.A. and Lamb, J.C. (1967). Visual coding using flashing lights. *Human Factors* 9: 405–408.

Gonzalez, R.C. and Wintz, P. (1987). *Digital Image Processing,* 2d ed. Addison-Wesley, Reading, MA.

Goodman, N. (1968). *Language of Art.* Bobbs Merrill, New York.

Gray, C.M., Konig, P., Engel, A.K., and Singer, W. (1989). Oscillatory responses in cat visual cortex exhibit intercolumnar synchronisation which reflects global stimulus properties. *Nature* 388: 334–337.

Gray, W.G.D., Mayer, L.A., and Hughes Clarke, J.E. (1997). Geomorphological applications of multibeam sonar and high-resolution DEM data from Passamaquoddy Bay. Geological Association of Canada, Ottawa, *'97 Proceedings Abstracts 57.*

Gregory, R.L. (1977). Vision with isoluminance color contrast: A projection technique and observations. *Perception* 6(1): 113–119.

Guitard, R. and Ware, C. (1990). A color sequence editor. *ACM Transactions on Graphics* 9(3): 338–341.

Gutwin, C., Greenberg, S., and Roseman, M. (1996). Workspace awareness support with radar views. *CHI '96 Conference Companion,* ACM, 210–211.

Hagen, M.A. (1974). Picture perception: Toward a theoretical model. *Psychology Bulletin* 81: 471–497.

Hagen, M.A. and Elliott, H.B. (1976). An investigation of the relationship between viewing conditions and preference for true and modified perspective with adults. *Journal of Experimental Psychology: Human Perception and Performance* 5: 479–490.

Hallett, P.E. (1986). Eye movements. In *Handbook of Perception and Human Performance,* ed. K.R. Boff, L. Kaufman, and J.P. Thomas. vol. 1, ch. 10. Wiley, New York.

Halverston, J. (1992). The first pictures: Perceptual foundations of paleolithic art. *Perception* 21: 389–404.

Hammond, N. (1987). Principles from the psychology of skill acquisition. In *Applying Cognitive Psychology to User Interface Design,* ed. M.M. Gardener and B. Christie, 163–188. Wiley, Chichester.

Haring, M.J. and Fry, M.A. (1979). Effect of pictures of children's comprehension of written text. *Educational Communication and Technology Journal* 27(3): 185–190.

Harris, C.S. (1965). Perceptual adaptation to inverted reversed and displaced vision. *Psychological Review* 72(6): 419–444.

Harrision, B. and Vincente, K.J. (1996). An experimental evaluation of transparent menu usage. *CHI Conference Proceedings,* ACM, 391–398.

Healey, C.G. (1996). Choosing effective colors for data visualization. *IEEE Visualization '96, Proceedings,* 263–270.

Healey, C.G., Booth, K.S., and Enns, J.T. (1998). High-speed visual estimation using pre-attentive processing. *ACM Transactions on Human-Computer Interaction* 3(2): 107–135.

Heider, F. and Simmel, M. (1944). An experimental study of apparent behaviour. *American Journal of Psychology* 57: 243–259.

Held, R., Efstanthiou, A., and Green, M. (1966). Adaptation to displaced and delayed visual feedback from the hand. *Journal of Experimental Psychology* 72: 887–891.

Hendrix, C. and Barfield, W. (1996). Presence within virtual environments as a function of visual display parameters. *Presence* 5(3): 272–289.

Hering, E. (1920). *Grundzuge der Lehr vom Lichtsinn.* Springer-Verlag, Berlin. (*Outlines of a Theory of Light Sense.* Translated by L.M. Hurvich and D. Jameson. Harvard University Press, Cambridge, MA, 1964.)

Herndon, K.P., Zelenik, R.C., Robbins, D.C., Conner, D.B., Snibbe, S.S., and van Dam, A. (1992). Interactive shadows. In *Proceedings of the ACM Symposium on User Interface Software and Technology, UIST '92,* ACM, 1–6.

Herskovits, R.J. (1948). *Man and His Works.* Knopf, New York.

Hill, B., Roger, T., and Vorhagen, F.W. (1997). Comparative analysis of the quantization of color spaces on the basis of the CIELAB color-difference formula. *ACM Transactions on Graphics,* 16(2): 109–154.

Hillstrom, A.P. and Yantis, S. (1994). Visual attention and motion capture. *Perception and Psychophysics* 55(4): 399–411.

Hochberg, J. (1986). Representation of motion and space in video and cinematic display. In *Handbook of Perception and Human Performance,* ed. K.R. Boff, L. Kaufman, and J.P.Thomas, 1–64. Wiley, New York.

Hochberg, J. and Brooks, V. (1978). Film cutting and visual momentum. In *Eye Movements and the Higher Psychological Functions,* ed. J.W. Senders, D.F. Fisher, and R.A. Mony. Lawrence Erlbaum Associates, Hillsdale, NJ.

Hochberg, J.E. and Brooks, V. (1962). Pictorial recognition as an unlearned ability. *American Journal of Psychology* 75: 624–628.

Houde, S. (1992). Iterative design of an interface for easy 3-D direct manipulation. *CHI '92, ACM, Monterey, May Proceedings.* 135–142.

Howard, I.P. (1991). Spatial vision within egocentric and exocentric frames of reference. In *Pictorial Communication in Virtual and Real Environments,* ed. S.R. Ellis, M.K. Kaiser, and A.J. Grunwald. 338–358. Taylor and Francis, London.

Howard, I.P. and Childerson, L. (1994). The contributions of motion, the visual frame, and visual polarity to sensations of body tilt. *Perception* 23: 753–762.

Howard, I.P. and Heckman, T. (1989). Circular vection as a function of the relative sizes, distances and positions of two competing visual displays. *Perception* 18(5): 657–667.

Howard, J.H. and Kerst, S.M. (1981). Memory and perception of cartographic information for familiar and unfamiliar environments. *Human Factors* 23(4): 495–504.

Hummel, J.E. and Biederman, I. (1992). Dynamic binding in a neural network for shape recognition. *Psychological Review* 99(3): 480–517.

Humphreys, G.W. and Bruce, V. (1989). *Visual Cognition: Computational, Experimental and Neurological Perspectives*. Lawrence Erlbaum Associates, Hillsdale, NJ.

Hurvich, L.M. (1981). *Color Vision*. Sinauer Associates: Sunderland, MA.

Hyman, R. (1953). Stimulus information as a determinant of reaction time. *Journal of Experimental Psychology* 45: 423–432.

Iavecchia, J.H., Iavecchia, H.P., and Roscoe, S.N. (1988). Eye accommodation to head-up virtual images. *Human Factors* 30(6): 689–702.

Inselberg, A. and Dimsdale, B. (1990). Parallel coordinates: A tool for visualizing multidimensional geometry. In *Proc. IEEE Conf. on Visualization, Los Angeles*, 361–378.

Interrrante, V., Fuchs, H., and Pizer, S.M. (1997). Conveying 3D shape of smoothly curving transparent surfaces via texture. *IEEE Transactions on Visualization and Computer Graphics* 3(2): 98–117.

Irani, P. and Ware, C. (1999). The geon diagram. *Grapics Interface '99 Poster Abstracts*, Kingston, Ontario, June.

Jackson, R., MacDonald, L., and Freeman, K. (1994). *Computer-Generated Color: A Practical Guide to Presentation and Display*. Wiley, New York.

Jackson, R., MacDonald, L., and Freeman, K. (1998). *Computer-Generated Color*. Wiley Professional Computing, Chichester.

Jacob, R.J.K. (1991). The use of eye movements in human-computer interaction techniques: What you look at is what you get. *ACM Transactions on Information Systems* 9(3): 152–169.

Jacob, R.J.K., Egeth, H.E., and Bevon, W. (1976). The face as a data display. *Human Factors* 18: 189–200.

Johansson, G. (1973). Visual perception of biological motion and a model for its analysis. *Perception and Psychophysics* 14(2): 201–211.

Johansson, G. (1975). Visual motion perception. *Scientific American* (232): June, 76–98.

Johnson, B. and Schneiderman, B. (1991). Tree-maps: A space-filling approach to the visualization of hierarchical information structures. *Proceedings IEEE Information Visualization '95*, 43–50.

Jonassen, D.H., Beissner, K., and Yacci, M.A. (1993). Structural knowledge: Techniques for conveying, assessing, and acquiring structural knowledge. Lawrence Erlbaum Associates, Hillsdale, NJ.

Jorg, S. and Hormann, H. (1978). The influence of general and specific labels on the recognition of labelled and unlabelled parts of pictures. *Journal of Verbal Learning and Verbal Behaviour* 17: 445–454.

Judd, D.B. and Wyszecki, G.W. (1975). *Color in Business, Science and Industry*, 3d. ed. Wiley, New York.

Kahn, K. (1996). Drawings on napkins, video-game animation and other ways to program computers. *Communications of the ACM* 39(8): 49–59.

Kahn, K. (1996). ToonTalk—an animated programming environment for children. *Journal of Visual Languages and Computing* 7(2): 197–217.

Kahneman, D. and Henik, A. (1981). Perceptual organization and attention. In *Perceptual Organization*, ed. M. Kubovy and J.R. Pomerantz, 181–209. Lawrence Erlbaum Associates, Hillsdale, NJ.

Kahneman, D., Triesman, A., and Gibbs, B.J. (1992). The reviewing of object files: Object-specific integration of information. *Cognitive Psychology* 24: 175–219.

Kaiser, M., Proffitt, D., Whelan, S., and Hecht, H. (1992). Influence of animation on dynamic judgments. *Journal of Experimental Psychology, Human Perception and Performance* 18(34): 669–690.

Kalaugher, P.G. (1985). Visual effects with a miniature Leonardo's window: Photographs and real scenes fused stereoscopically. *Perception* 14: 553–561.

Kanizsa, G. (1976). Subjective contours. *Scientific American* (234): April, 48–64.

Kawai, M., Uchikawa, K., and Ujike, H. (1995). Influence of color category on visual search. In *Annual Meeting of the Association for Research in Vision and Ophthalmology, Paper #2991,* Fort Lauderdale, FL.

Kelly, D.H. (1979). Motion and vision: II Stabilized spatio-temporal threshold surface. *Journal of the Optical Society of America* 69: 1340–1349.

Kennedy, J.M. (1974). *A Psychology of Picture Perception.* Jossey-Bass, San Francisco.

Kennedy, R.S., Lilienthal, M.G., Berbaum, K.S., Baltzley, D.R., and McCauley, M.E. (1989). Simulator sickness in U.S. Navy flight simulators. *Aviation, Space and Environmental Medicine* 15: 10–16.

Kersten, D., Mamassian, P., and Knill, D.C. (1997). Moving cast shadows induce apparent motion in depth. *Perception* 26: 171–192.

Kersten, D., Mamassian, P., Knill, D.C., and Bulthoff, I. (1996). Illusory motion from shadows, *Nature* 351: 228–230.

Kieras, D.E. and Meyer, D.E. (1997). An overview of the EPIC architecture for cognition and performance with application to human-computer interaction. *Human-Computer Interaction* 12: 391–438.

Kim, W.S., Tendick, F., and Stark, L. (1991). Visual enhancements in pick-and-place tasks. In *Pictorial Communication in Virtual and Real Environments,* ed. S.R. Ellis, 265–282. Taylor and Francis, London.

Kirsh, D. and Maglio, P. (1994). On distinguishing epistemic from pragmatic action. *Cognitive Science* 18: 513–549.

Koffka, K. (1935). *Principles of Gestalt Psychology.* Harcourt-Brace, New York.

Kohlberg, D.L. (1971). Simple reaction time as a function of stimulus intensity in decibels of light and sound. *Journal of Experimental Psychology* 54: 757–764.

Kolers, P.A. (1975). Memorial consequences of automatized encoding. *Journal of Experimental Psychology: Human Learning and Memory* 1: 689–701.

Kosslyn, S.M. (1987). Seeing and imagining in the cerebral hemispheres: A computational approach. *Psychological Review* 94: 148–175.

Kosslyn, S.M. (1994). *Image and Brain: The Resolution of the Imagery Debate.* MIT Press, Cambridge, MA.

Kosslyn, S.M., Alpert, N.M., Thompson, W.L., Maljkovic, S.B., Weise, C.F., Chabreis, S., Hamilton, E., Rauch, S.L., and Buonanno, F.S. (1993). Visual mental imagery activates topographically organized visual context: PET investigations. *Journal of Cognitive Neuroscience* 5: 263–287.

Kroll, J.F. and Potter, M.C. (1984). Recognizing words, pictures and concepts: A comparison of lexical, object and reality decisions. *Journal of Verbal Learning and Verbal Behaviour* 23: 39–66.

Kubovy, M. (1986). *The Psychology of Linear Perspective and Renaissance Art.* Cambridge University Press, Cambridge.

Lamping, J., Rao, R., and Pirolli, P. (1995). A focus+content technique based on hyperbolic geometry for viewing large hierarchies. *Proceedings CHI '95,* ACM, 401–408.

Landauer, T.K. (1986). How much do people remember? Some estimates of the quantity of learned information in long-term memory. *Cognitive Science* 10: 477–493.

Larkin, J.H. and Simon, H.A. (1987). Why a diagram is (sometimes) worth ten thousand words. *Cognitive Science* 11: 65–99.

Lawson, R., Humphreys, G.W., and Watson, D. (1994). Object recognition under sequential viewing conditions: Evidence for viewpoint-specific recognition procedures. *Perception* 23: 595–614.

Lennie, P. (1998). Single units and cortical organization. *Perception* 27: 889–935.

Leslie, A.M. and Keeble, S. (1987). Do six-month-old infants perceive causality? *Cognition* 25: 265–288.

Levelt, W., Richardson, G., and Heu, W. (1985). Pointing and voicing in deictic expressions. *Journal of Memory and Language* 24: 133–164.

Levine, M. (1975). *A Cognitive Theory of Learning.* Lawrence Erlbaum Associates, Hillsdale, NJ.

Levoy, M. and Whitaker, R. (1990). Gaze-directed volume rendering. *Proceedings of ACM Symposium on Interactive 3D Graphics, Computer Graphics* 24(2): 217–224.

Li, Y. (1997). Oriented particles for scientific visualization. M.S. thesis. Computer Science, University of New Brunswick.

Liang, J., Shaw, C., and Green, M. (1991). On temporal-spatial realism in the virtual reality environment. *Proceedings of UIST '91,* ACM, 19–25.

Limoges, S., Ware, C., and Knight, W. (1989). Displaying correlation using position, motion, point size, or point color. *Proceedings, Graphics Interface '89,* 262–265.

Linos, P.K., Aubet, P., Dumas, L., Helleboid, Y., Lejeune, D., and Tulula, P (1994). Visualizing program dependencies: An experimental study. *Software Practice and Experience* 24(4): 387–403.

Liu, F. and Picard, R.W. (1994). Periodicity, directionality, and randomness: World features for perceptual pattern recognition. *Proceedings of the 12th International Conference on Pattern Recognition,* Vol. II, 184–189, Jerusalem, October 9–13.

Livingston, M.S. and Hubel, D.H. (1988). Segregation of form, movement and depth: Anatomy, physiology and perception. *Science,* 240: 740–749.

Lloyd, R. (1997). Visual search processes used in map reading. *Cartographica* 34(1): 11–32.

Loftus, E.F. and Hoffman, H.G. (1989). Misinformation and memory: The creation of new memories. *Journal of Experimental Psychology: General* 118: 100–104.

Lokuge, I., Glibert, S.A., and Richards, W. (1996). Structuring information with mental models: A tour of Boston. *CHI '96 Proceedings,* ACM, 413–419.

Lowther, K. and Ware, C. (1996). Vection with large-screen 3D imagery. *CHI '96 Conference Companion,* ACM, 233–234.

Lu, C. and Fender, D.H. (1972). The interaction of color and luminance in stereoscopic vision. *Investigative Opthalmology* 11: 482–490.

Lynch, K. (1960). *The Image of the City.* MIT Press, Cambridge, MA.

MacKenzie, I.S. (1992). Fitts' law as a research and design tool in human-computer interaction. *Human-Computer Interaction* 7: 91–139.

Mackinlay, J.D., Card, S.K., and Robertson, G.G. (1990). Rapid controlled movement through a virtual 3D workspace. *Proceedings SIGGRAPH '90,* ACM, 24: 171–176.

Mackworth, N.H. (1976). Ways of recording line of sight. In *Eye Movements and Psychological Processing,* ed. R.A. Monty and J.W. Senders, 173–178. Erlbaum, Hillsdale, NJ.

Malik, J. and Perona, P. (1990). Preattentive texture discrimination with early vision mechanisms. *Journal of the Optical Society of America* A 7(5): 923–932.

Mark, D.M. and Franck, A.U. (1996). Experiential and formal models of geographical space. *Environment and Planning,* B. 23: 3–24.

Marr, D. (1982). *Vision.* W.H. Freeeman and Company, New York.

Marr, D. and Nishihara, H.K. (1978). Representation and recognition of the spatial organization of three-dimensional shapes. *Proceedings of the Royal Society of London,* B. 207: 269–294.

Masin, S.C. (1997). The luminance conditions of transparency. *Perception* 26: 39–50.

Matlin, M.W. (1994). *Cognition,* 3d ed. Harcourt Brace, Fort Worth.

Mayer, L.A., Dijkstra, S., Hughes Clarke, J., Paton, M., and Ware, C. (1997). High-frequency acoustics in shallow water. *SACLANT Conference Proceedings Series,* CP-45, ed. N.G. Pace, E. Pouliquen, O. Bergem, and J. Lyons.

McCauley, M.E. and Sharkey, T.J. (1992). Cybersickness: Perception of self-motion in virtual environments. *Presence* 1(3): 311–318.

McGreevy, M.W. (1992). The presence of field geologists in Mars-like terrain. *Presence* 1(4): 375–403.

McManus, I.C. (1977). Note: Half a million basic colour words: Berlin and Kay and the usage of color words in literature and science. *Perception* 26: 367–370.

McNeill, D. (1992). *Hand and Mind: What Gestures Reveal about Thought.* University of Chicago Press, Chicago.

Megaw, E.D. and Richardson, J. (1979). Target uncertainty and visual scanning strategies. *Human Factors* 21(3): 303–316.

Metelli, F. (1974). The perception of transparency. *Scientific American* (230): April, 91–98.

Meyer, G.W. and Greenberg, D.P. (1988). Color-defective vision and computer graphics displays. *IEEE Computer Graphics and Applications.* September: 28–40.

Michotte, A. (1963). *The Perception of Causality.* (Translated by T. Miles and E. Miles.) Methuen, London.

Milner, A.D. and Goodale, M.A. (1995). *The Visual Brain in Action.* Oxford Psychology Series 27. Oxford University Press, Oxford.

Mon-Williams, M. and Wann, J.P. (1998). Binocular virtual reality displays: When problems do and don't occur. *Human Factors* 40(1): 42–49.

Moray, N. (1981). Monitoring behavior and supervising control. In *Handbook of Perception and Human Performance,* ed. K.R. Boff, L. Kaufman, and J.P. Thomas. Wiley, New York.

Moray, N. and Rotenberg, I. (1989). Fault management in process control: Eye movements and action. *Ergonomics* 32(11): 1319–1342.

Mullen, K.Y. (1985). The contrast sensitivity of human color vision to red-green and blue-yellow chromatic gratings, *American Journal of Optometry and Physiological Optics* 359: 381–400.

Najjar, L.J. (1998). Principles of educational multimedia user interface design. *Human Factors* 40(2): 311–323.

Nakayama, K. and Silverman, G.H. (1986). Serial and parallel processing of visual feature conjunctions. *Nature* 320: 264–265.

Nakayama, K., Shimono, S., and Silverman, G.H. (1989). Stereoscopic depth: Its relation to image segmentation, grouping and the recognition of occluding objects. *Perception* 18: 55–68.

Nemire, K., Jacoby, R.H., and Ellis, S.R. (1994). Simulation fidelity of a virtual environment display. *Human Factors* 36(1): 79–93.

Neveau, C.F. and Stark, L.W. (1998). The virtual lens. *Presence* 7(4): 370–381.

Newell, A. (1990). *Unified Theories of Cognition.* Harvard University Press, Cambridge, MA.

Newell, A. and Rosenbloom, P. (1981). Mechanisms of skill acquisition and the law of practice. In *Cognitive Skills and Their Acquisition,* ed. J.R. Anderson. Lawrence Erlbaum Associates, Hillsdale, N.J.

Norman, D.A. (1988). *The Psychology of Everyday Things*. Basic Books, New York.

Norman, J.F., Todd, J.T., and Phillips, F. (1995). The perception of surface orientaiton from multiple sources of optical information. *Perception and Psychophysics* 57(5): 629–636.

Noro, K. (1993). Industrial application of virtual reality and possible health problems. *Japan. Journal Ergonomica* 29: 126–129.

North, M.N., North, S.M., and Coble, J.R. (1996). Effectiveness of virtual environment desensitization in the treatment of agoraphobia. *Presence* 5(3): 346–352.

Oakes, L.M. (1994). Development of infants' use of continuity cues in their perception of causality. *Developmental Psychology* 30: 869–879.

Ogle, K.N. (1962). The visual space sense. *Science* 135: 763–771.

Oviatt, S. (1999). Mutual disambiguation of recognition errors in a multimodal architecture. *Proceedings of CHI '99*, ACM, 576–583.

Oviatt, S., DeAngeli, A., and Kuhn, K. (1997). Integration and synchronization of input modes during multimodal human-computer interaction. *Proceedings of CHI '97*, ACM, 415–422.

Owlsley, C.J., Sekuler, R., and Siemensne, D. (1983). Contrast sensitivity through adulthood. *Vision Research* 23: 689–699.

Paivio, A. (1987). Mental representations: A dual coding approach. Oxford Psychology Series. Oxford University Press, Oxford.

Palmer, S.E. (1992). Common region: A new principle of perceptual grouping. *Cognitive Psychology* 24: 436–447.

Palmer, S.E. and Rock, I. (1994). Rethinking perceptual organization: The role of uniform connectedness. *Psychonomic Bulletin and Review* 1(1): 29–55.

Palmer, S.E., Rosh, E., and Chase, P. (1981). Canonical perspective and perception of objects. *Attention and Performance IX*, ed. J. Long and A. Baddeley, 135–151. Lawerence Erlbaum Associates, Hillsdale, N.J.

Palmiter, S., Elkerton, J., and Paggett, P. (1991). Animated demonstrations vs. written instructions for learning procedural tasks: A preliminary investigation. *International Journal of Man-Machine Studies* 34: 687–701.

Parker, G., Franck, G., and Ware, C. (1998). Visualizing of large nested graphs in 3D: Navigation and interaction. *Journal of Visual Languages* 9: 299–317.

Pashler, H. (1995). Attention and visual perception: Analyzing divided attention. In *An Invitation to Cognitive Science: Visual Cognition*, vol. 2, ed. S. Kosslyn and D. Osherson, 71–100. MIT Press, Cambridge, MA.

Patterson, R. and Martin, W.L. (1992). Human stereopsis. *Human Factors* 34(6): 669–692.

Pausch, R., Snoddy, J., Taylor, R., Watson, S., and Haseltine, E. (1996). Disney's Aladdin: First steps towards storytelling in virtual reality. *SIGGRAPH '96 Proceedings*, 193–203.

Pavio, A. and Csapo, K. (1969). Concrete image and verbal memory codes. *Journal of Experimental Psychology* 80: 279–285.

Pearson, D., Hanna, E., and Martinez, K. (1990). Computer-generated cartoons. In *Images and Understanding*, ed. H. Barlow, C. Blakemore, and M. Weston Smith. Cambridge University Press, Cambridge.

Perrett, D.I., Oram, M.W., Harries, M.H., Bevan, R., Hietanen, J.K., Benson, P.J., and Thomas, S. (1991). Viewer-centered and object-centered coding of heads in the Macaque temporal cortex. *Experimental Brain Research* 86: 159–173.

Peterson, H.E. and Dugas, D.J. (1972). The relative importance of contrast and motion in visual detection. *Human Factors* 14: 207–216.

Pickett, R.M. and Grinstein, G.G. (1988). Iconograhic displays for visualizing multidimensional data. *Proceedings of the 1988 IEEE Conference on Systems, Man and Cybernetics,* vol. I, 514–519.

Pickett, R.M., Grinstein, G.G., Levkowitz, H., and Smith, S. (1995). Harnessing pre-attentive perceptual processes in visualization. In *Perceptual Issues in Visualization,* ed. G.Grinstein and H. Levkowitz. 33–45. Springer, New York.

Posner, M.I. and Keele, S. (1968). On the generation of abstract ideas. *Journal of Experimental Psychology* 77: 353–363.

Post, D.L. and Greene, F.A. (1986). Color name boundaries for equally bright stimuli on a CRT: Phase I. *Society for Information Display, Digest of Technical Papers* 86: 70–73.

Postma, A. and De Haan, E.H.F. (1996). What was where? Memory for object locations. *Quarterly Journal of Experimental Psychology* 49A(1): 178–199.

Price, C.J. and Humphreys, G.W. (1989). The effects of surface detail on object categorization and naming. *Quarterly Journal of Experimental Psychology* 41A: 797–828.

Pylyshyn, Z.W. and Storm, R.W. (1988). Tracking of multiple independent targets: Evidence for a parallel tracking mechanism. *Spatial Vision* 3: 1–19.

Rader, C., Brand, C., and Lewis, C. (1997). Degrees of comprehension: Children's understanding of a visual programming environment. *Proceedings of CHI '97,* ACM, 351–358.

Ramachandran, V.S. (1988). Perception of shape from shading. *Nature* 331: 163–166.

Rao, R. and Card, S.K. (1994). The table lens: Merging graphical and symbolic representations in an interactive focus+context visualization for tabular information. *Proceedings of CHI '94,* ACM, 318–322.

Regan, D. (1989). Orientation discrimination for objects defined by relative motion and objects defined by luminance contrasts. *Vision Research* 18: 1389–1400.

Regan, D. and Hamstra, S. (1991). Shape discrimination for motion and contrast defined contours: Squareness is special. *Perception* 20: 315–336.

Rhodes, G. (1995). Face recognition and configurational coding. In *Cognitive and Computational Aspects of Face Recognition,* ed. T. Valentine. Routledge, New York.

Rhodes, P.A. and Luo, M.R. (1996). A system of WYSIWYG colour communication. Displays, Elsevier *Science* 16(4): 213–221.

Richards, W. (1967). Differences among color normals: Classes I and II. *Journal of the Optical Society of America* 57: 1047–1055.

Richards, W. and Koenderink, J.J. (1995). Trajectory mapping: A new non-metric scaling technique. *Perception* 24: 1315–1331.

Riggs, L.A., Merton, P.A., and Mortion, H.B. (1974). Suppression of visual phosphenes during saccadic eye movements. *Vision Research* 14: 997–1010.

Rimé, B., Boulanger, B., Laubin, P., Richants, M., and Stroobants, K. (1985). The perception of interpersonal emotions originated by patterns of movements. *Motivation and Emotion* 9: 241–260.

Robertson, G.G., Mackinlay, J.D., and Card, S.W. (1993). Invormation Visualization Using 3D Interactive Animation. *Communications of the ACM,* 36(4), 57–71.

Robertson, P.K. and O'Callaghan, J.F. (1986). The generation of color sequences for univariate and bivariate mapping. *IEEE Computer Graphics and Applications* 6(2): 24–32.

Robertson, P.K. and O'Callaghan, J.F. (1988). The application of perceptual colour spaces to the display of remotely sensed data. *IEEE Trans. on Geoscience and Remote Sensing* 26(1): 49–59.

Rogers, B. and Cagnello, R. (1989). Disparity curvature and the perception of three-dimensional surfaces. *Nature,* 339: May, 137–139.

Rogers, B. and Graham, M. (1979). Similarities between motion parallax and stereopsis in human depth perception. *Vision Research* 22: 261–270.

Rogers, E. (1995). A cognitive theory of visual interaction. In *Diagrammatic Reasoning: Cognitive and Computational Perspectives,* ed. J. Glasgos, N.H. Narayanan, and B. Chandraseekaran, 481–500. AAAI Press/MIT Press, Cambridge, MA.

Rogowitz, B.E. and Treinish, L.A. (1996). How not to lie with visualization. *Computers in Physics* 10(3): 268–273.

Rood, O.N. (1897). *Modern Chromatics*. Reprinted in facsimile, 1973, Van Nostrand Reinhold, New York.

Roscoe, S.R. (1991). The eyes prefer real images. *Pictoral Communication in Virtual and Real Environments,* ed. S.R. Ellis, M. Kaiser, and A.J. Grunwald, 577–585. Taylor and Francis, London.

Rosenthal, N.E. (1993). Diagnosis and treatment of seasonal affective disorder. *Journal of the American Medical Association* 270: 2717–2720.

Rumbaugh, J. Booch, G., and Jacobson, I. (1999). *Unified Modeling Language Reference Manual*. Addison-Wesley Object Technology Series, Reading, MA.

Russo, J.E. and Rosen, L.D. (1975). An eye fixation analysis of multi-alternative choice. *Memory and Cognition* 3: 267–276.

Rutkowski, C. (1982). An introduction to the Human Applications Standard Computer Interface, Part 1: Theory and principles. *BYTE* 7(11): 291–310.

Ryan, T.A. and Schwartz, C.B. (1956). Speed of perception as a function of mode of representation. *American Journal of Psychology* 69: 60–69.

Saito, T. and Takahashi, T. (1990). Comprehensible rendering of 3-D shapes. *Computer Graphics* 24(4): 197–206. *SIGGRAPH '90 Proceedings.*

Sarkar, M. and Brown, M.H. (1994). Graphical fisheye views. *Communications of the ACM* 37(12): 73–83.

Saussure, F. de (1959). *Course in General Linguistics*. Reprinted by Fontana/Collins, New York. (Published posthumously based on lectures originally given at the University of Geneva between 1906 and 1911.)

Scanlan, L.A. (1975). Visual time compression: Spatial and temporal cues. *Human Factors* 17: 337–345.

Schroeder, W., Martin, K., and Lorenson, B. (1997). *The Visualization Toolkit*. Prentice Hall, Upper Saddle River, NJ.

Schumann, J., Strotthotte, T., Raab, A., and Laser, S. (1996). Assessing the effect of non-photorealistic rendered images in CAD. *CHI '96 Proceedings,* ACM, 35–41.

Schwarz, M., Cowan, W., and Beatty, J. (1987). An experimental comparison of RGB, YIQ, LAB, HSV and opponent color models. *ACM Transactions on Graphics* 6(2): 123–158.

Seigel, A.W. and White, S.H. (1975). The development of spatial representations of large-scale environments. In *Advances in Child Development and Behaviour,* ed. H.W. Reese, 9–55. Academic Press, London.

Sekuler, R. and Blake, R. (1990). *Perception,* 2d ed. McGraw-Hill, New York.

Selker, T. and Koved, L. (1988). Elements of visual language. *IEEE Conference of Visual Languages, Proceedings,* 38–44.

Sellen, A., Buxton, B., and Arnott, J. (1992). Using spatial cues to improve videoconferencing. *CHI' 92 Proceedings,* ACM, 651–652. Plus CHI video proceedings, same year.

Serra, L., Hern, N., Choon, C.B., and Poston, T. (1997). Interactive vessel tracing in volume data. *1997 Symposium on Interactive 3D Graphics, Proceedings,* 131–137.

Shenker, M. (1987). Optical design criteria for binocular helmet-mounted display. In *Display System Optics, SPIE Proceedings* 778: 173–185.

Shepard, R.N. (1962). The analysis of proximities: Multidimensional scaling with unknown distance function, Part I. *Psychometrika* 27(2): 125–140.

Sheridan, T. (1972). On how often the supervisor should sample. *IEEE Transactions on Systems Man and Cybernetics* 6: 140–145.

Shneiderman, B. (1987). *Designing the User Interface*. Addison-Wesley, Reading, MA.

Singer, W. and Grey, C.M. (1995). Visual feature integration and the temporal correlation hypothesis. *Annual Review of Neuroscience* 18: 555–586.

Slater, M., Usoh, M., and Steed, A. (1995). Taking steps, the influence of walking technique on presence in virtual reality. *ACM Transactions on CHI* 2(3): 201–219.

Slocum, T.S. (1983). Predicting visual clusters on graduated circle maps. *American Cartographer* 10(1): 59–72.

Smith, A.R. (1978). Color gamut transform pairs. *Computer Graphics* 12: 12–19.

Smith, G. and Atchison, D.A. (1997). *The Eye and Visual Optical Instruments*. Cambridge University Press, Cambridge.

Sollenberger, R.L. and Milgram, P. (1993). The effects of stereoscopic and rotational displays in the three-dimensional path tracing task. *Human Factors* 35(3): 483–500.

Spangenberg, R.W. (1973). The motion variable in procedural learning. *AV Communications Review* 21(4): 419–436.

Sperling, G. (1960). The information available in brief visual presentations. *Psychological Monographs: General and Applied* 74(11).

Standing, L., Conezio, I., and Haber, R.N. (1970). Perception and memory for pictures: Single trial learning of 2560 visual stimuli. *Psychonomic Science* 19: 73–74.

Stasko, J.T. (1990). Tango: A framework and system for algorithm animation. *IEEE Computer* 23(9): 27–39.

State, A., Livingston, M.A., Garrett, W.F., Hirotal, G., Whitton, M.C., and Pisano, E.D. (1996). Technologies for augmented reality systems: Realizing ultrasound-guided needle biopsies. *SIGGRAPH' 96 Proceedings*, ACM, 439–446.

Stenning, K. and Oberlander, J. (1994). A cognitive theory of graphical and linguistic reasoning: Logic and implementation. *Cognitive Science* 19: 97–140.

Stevens, S.S. (1961). The psychophysics of sensory function. In *Sensory Communication*, ed. W.A. Rosenblith, 1–33. MIT Press, Cambridge, MA.

Stevens, S.S. (1946). On the theory of scales of measurement. *Science* 103: 677–680.

Stone, M.C., Cowan, W.B., and Beatty, J.C. (1988). Color gamut mapping and the printing of digital color images. *ACM Transactions on Graphics* 7(4): 249–292.

Stroop, J.R. (1935). Studies of interference in serial verbal reactions. *Journal of Experimental Psychology* 18: 643–662.

Strothotte, C. and Strothotte, T. (1997). *Seeing between the Pixels*. Springer-Verlag, Berlin.

Sun, F., Staerk, L., Nguyen, A., Wong, J., Lakshminarayanan, V., and Mueller, E. (1988). Changes in accommodation with age: Static and dynamic. *American Journal of Optometry and Physiological Optics* 65(6): 492–498.

Sweller, J., Chandler, P., Tierner, P., and Cooper, G. (1990). Cognitive load as a factor in the structuring of technical material. *Journal of Experimental Psychology* 119(2): 176–192.

Tittle, J.S., Todd, J.T., Perotti, V.J., and Norman, J.F. (1995). Systematic distortion of perceived three-dimensional structure from motion and binocular stereopsis. *Journal of Experimental Psychology: Human Perception and Performance* 21(3): 663–687.

Todd, J.T. and Mingolla, E. (1983). Perception of surface curvature and direction of illumination from patterns of shading. *Journal of Experimental Psychology: Human Perception and Performance* 9(4): 583–595.

Triesman, A. (1980). Preattentive processing in vision. *Computer Vision, Graphics and Image Processing* 31: 156–177.

Triesman, A. and Gormican, S. (1988). Feature analysis in early vision: Evidence from search asymmetries. *Psychological Review* 95(1): 15–48.

Trumbo, B.E. (1981). A theory for coloring bivariate statistical maps. *American Statistician* 35: 220–226.

Tufte, E.R. (1983). *The Visual Display of Quantitative Information.* Graphics Press, Cheshire, CT.

Tufte, E.R. (1990). *Envisioning Information.* Graphics Press, Cheshire, CT.

Tulving, E. (1983). *Elements of Episodic Memory.* Oxford University Press, New York.

Tulving, E. and Madigan, S.A. (1970). Memory and verbal learning. *Annual Review of Psychology* 21: 437–484.

Turk, G. and Banks, D. (1996). Image-guided streamline placement. *SIGGRAPH '96 Proceedings,* ACM, 453–460.

Tweedie, L. (1997). Characterizing interactive externalizations. *CHI '97, ACM, Atlanta Proceedings,* 375–382.

Tweedie, L., Spence, R., Dawkes, H., and Su, H. (1996). Externalizing abstract mathematical models. *CHI '96 Proceedings,* 406–412.

Uomori, K. and Nishida, S. (1994). The dynamics of the visual system in combining conflicting KDE and binocular stereopsis cues. *Perception and Psychophysics* 55(5): 526–536.

Valyus, N.A. (1966). *Stereoscopy.* (Translated from the original). Focal Press, London.

Venturino, M. and Gagnon, D. (1992). Information trade-offs in complex stimulus structures: Local and global levels in naturalistic scenes. *Perception and Psychophysics* 52(4): 425–436.

Veron, H., Southard, D.A., Leger, J.R., and Conway, J.L. (1990). Stereoscopic displays of terrain database visualization. *Proceedings of the 1992 ACM Symposium on Interactive 3D Graphics,* 39–42.

Vinson, N.G. (1999). Design guidelines for landmarks to support navigation in virtual environments. *Proceedings of CHI '99,* ACM, 278–285.

Vishton, P.M. and Cutting, J.E. (1995). Wayfinding, displacements, and mental maps: Velocity fields are not typically used to determine one's aimpoint. *Journal of Experimental Psychology: Human Perception and Performance* 21(5): 978–995.

Wade, N.J. and Swanston, M.T. (1966). A general model for the perception of space and motion. *Perception* 25: 187–194.

Wadill, P. and McDaniel, M. (1992). Pictorial enhancement of text memory: Limitations imposed by picture type and comprehension skill. *Memory and Cognition* 20(5): 472–482.

Wainer, H. and Francolini, C.M. (1980). An empirical enquiry concerning human understanding of two variable maps. *American Statistician* 34(2): 81–93.

Wallach, H. and O'Connell, D.N. (1953). The kinetic depth effect. *Journal of Experimental Psychology* 45: 205–217.

Wallach, H. (1959). The perception of motion. *Scientific American* 201: July, 56–60.

Wallach, H. and Karsh, E. (1963). The modification of stereoscopic depth perception based on oculomotor cues. *Perception and Psychophysics* 11: 110–116.

Wang, Y. and Frost, B.J. (1992). Time to collision is signaled by neurons in the nucleus rotundus of pigeons. *Nature* 356: 236–238.

Wang, Y., and MacKenzie, C.L. (1999). Object manipulation in virtual environments: Relative size matters. *Proceedings of CHI '99,* ACM, 48–55.

Wanger, L. (1992). The effect of shadow quality on the perception of spatial relationships in computer-generated images. *Proceedings of the 1992 ACM Symposium on Interactive 3D Graphics*, 39–42.

Wanger, L.R., Ferwander, J.A., and Greenberg, D.A. (1992). Perceiving spatial relationships in computer-generated images. *IEEE Computer Graphics and Applications*, May, 12(3): 44–58.

Wann, J.P., Rushton, S., and Mon-Williams, M. (1995). Natural problems for stereoscopic depth perception in virtual environments. *Vision Research* 35(19): 2731–2736.

Wann, J.P., Rushton, S.K., and Lee, D.N. (1995). Can you control where you are heading when you are looking at where you want to go? In *Studies in Perception and Action III*, ed. B.G. Bardy, R.J. Bootsmal, and Y. Guiard, 201–210. Lawrence Erlbaum Associates, Hillsdale, NJ.

Ware, C. (1988). Color sequences for univariate maps: Theory, experiments, and principles. *IEEE Computer Graphics and Applications*, Sept., 41–49.

Ware, C. (1989). Fast hill shading with specular reflection and cast shadows. *Computers and Geosciences* 15: 1327–1334.

Ware, C. and Balakrishnan, R. (1994). Object acquisition in VR displays: Lag and frame rate. *ACM Transactions on Computer Human Interaction* 1(4): 331–357.

Ware, C. and Beatty, J.C. (1988). Using color dimensions to display data dimensions. *Human Factors* 30(2): 127–142.

Ware, C. and Cowan, W.B. (1982). Changes in perceived color due to chromatic interactions. *Vision Research* 22: 1353–1362.

Ware, C. and Cowan, W.B. (1987). Chromatic mach bands: Behavioral evidence of lateral inhibition in color vision. *Perception and Psychophysics* 41: 173–178.

Ware, C. and Cowan, W.B. (1990). The RGYB color geometry. *ACM Transactions on Graphics* 9(2): 226–232.

Ware, C. and Franck, G. (1996). Evaluating stereo and motion cues for visualizing information nets in three dimensions. *ACM Transactions on Graphics* 15(2): 121–140.

Ware, C. and Knight, W. (1995). Using visual texture for information display. *ACM Transactions on Graphics* 14(1): 3–20.

Ware, C. and Mikaelian, H. (1987). An evaluation of an eye tracker as a device for computer input. *Proceedings of CHI '87*, ACM, 183–188.

Ware, C. and Osborne, S. (1990). Explorations and virtual camera control in virtual three-dimensional environments. *Computer Graphics* 24(2): 175–183.

Ware, C. and Rose, J. (1999). Rotating virtual objects with real handles. *ACM Transactions on Computer Human Interaction* 6(2): 1–19.

Ware, C., Arthur, K.W., and Booth, K.S. (1993). Fish-tank virtual reality. In *Proceedings of INTERCHI '93 Conference on Human Factors in Computing Systems*, ACM, New York, 37–42.

Ware, C., Bonner, J., Knight, W., and Cater, R. (1992). Moving icons as a human interrupt. *International Journal of Human-Computer Interaction* 4(4): 341–348.

Ware, C., Gobrecht, C., and Paton, M. (1998). Dynamic adjustment of stereo display parameters. *IEEE Transactions on Systems, Man and Cybernetics* 28(1): 56–65.

Warren, W.H. (1984). Perceiving affordances: Visual guidance of stair climbing. *Journal of Experimental Psychology: Human Perception and Performance* 10: 683–703.

Warrick, M.S., Kibler, A., Topmiller, D.H., and Bates, C. (1964). Response time to unexpected stimuli. *American Psychologist* 19: 528.

Watanabe, T. and Cavanaugh, P. (1996). Texture laciness: The texture equivalent of transparency. *Perception* 25: 293–303.

Welch, R.B. (1978). *Perceptual Modification: Adapting to Altered Sensory Environments.* Academic Press, New York.

Welch, R.B. and Cohen, M.M. (1991). Adaptation to variable prismatic displacement. In *Pictorial Communication in Virtual and Real Environments,* ed. S.R. Ellis, 295–304. Taylor and Francis, London.

Wickens, C.D. (1992). *Engineering Psychology and Human Performance,* 2d ed. Harper Collins, New York.

Wickens, C.D., Haskell I., and Harte, K. (1989). Ergonomic design for perspective flight path displays. *IEEE Control Systems Magazine* 9(4): 3–8.

Wilkins, A. (1995). *Visual Stress.* Oxford Psychology Series #24.

Williams, A.J. and Harris, R.L. (1985). Factors affecting dwell times on digital displays. *NASA Technical Memorandum 86406.* NASA Langley Research Center.

Williams, L.J. (1985). Tunnel vision induced by a foveal load manipulation. *Human Factors* 27(2): 221–227.

Williams, M.D. and Hollan, J.D. (1981). The process of retrieval from very long-term memory. *Cognitive Science* 5: 87–119.

Williams, S.P. and Parrish, R.V. (1990). New computational control techniques and increased understanding for stereo 3-D displays. *Proc. SPIE Stereoscopic Display Applications,* Santa Clara, CA, 73–82.

Wilson, H.R. and Bergen, J.R. (1979). A four mechanism model for threshold spatial vision. *Vision Research* 19: 19–32.

Wise, J.A., Thomas, J.J., Pennock, K., Lantrip, D., Pottier, M., Schur, A., and Crow, V. (1995). Visualizing the non-visual: Spatial analysis and interaction with information and text documents. *Proceedings of IEEE Information Visualization '95,* 51–58.

Witkin, A. and Kass, M. (1991). Reaction diffusion textures. *SIGGRAPH '91 Proceedings: Computer Graphics,* 25(4): 299–308.

Wyszecki, G. and Stiles, W.S. (1982). *Color Science Concepts and Methods, Quantitative Data and Formulae,* 2d ed. Wiley Interscience, New York.

Yaniv, I. and Mayer, D.E. Activation and metacognition of inaccessible stored information: Potential basis for incubation effects in problem solving. *Journal of Experimental Psychology: Learning, Memory and Cognition* 13: 187–205.

Yantis, S. (1992). Multielement visual tracking: Attention and perceptual organization. *Cognitive Psychology* 24: 295–340.

Yeh, Y. and Silverstein, L.D. (1990). Limits of fusion and depth judgment in stereoscopic color displays. *Human Factors* 32(1): 45–60.

Yoshimura, T., Nakamura, Y., and Sugiura, M. (1994). 3D direct manipulation interface: Development of the Zashiki-Warashi system. *Computers and Graphics* 18(2): 201–207.

Young, M.J., Landy, M.S., and Maloney, L.T. (1993). A perturbation analysis of depth perception from combinations of texture and motion cues. *Vision Research* 33: 2685–2696.

Yufic, Y.M. and Sheridan, T.B. (1996). Virtual networks: New framework for operator modeling and interface optimization in complex supervisory control systems. *Annual Review of Control* 20: 179–195.

Zeki, S. (1992). The visual image in mind and brain. *Scientific American,* Sept., 69–76.

Zhai, S., Buxton, W., and Milgram, P. (1994). The "silk cursor": Investigating transparency for 3D target acquisition. *CHI '94 Proceedings,* ACM, 459–464.

Zhang, J. (1997). The nature of external representations in problem solving. *Cognitive Science* 21(2): 179–217.

Index

About the Author

Colin Ware had an early interest in both art and science, which eventually led to a fascination with the effective display of information. He grew up in England, obtained a BSc in psychology at Durham University, and then moved to attend Dalhousie University in Canada. There he studied stereoscopic depth perception and completed a masters degree in psychology. At this point, he left the academic world for three years in an attempt to become an artist. But he continued to study on his own, pursuing the idea of applying the science of visual perception to the study of art.

After three years he returned to academia and began a Ph.D. at the University of Toronto to study picture perception under John Kennedy. This turned into a study of form perception, and he completed his doctorate in 1980. Next he moved to Ottawa to work with William Cowan and Gunter Wyszecki on problems of color perception, and with Cowan, he conducted series of applied color tutorials at SIGGRAPH. An emerging interest in computing and information display led him to the University of Waterloo to do an MMath in computer science—investigating the use of color for discrete information display. At the age of 35 he obtained his first "real" job at the University of New Brunswick where he concentrated his research on interactive display techniques for 14 years.

Ware has published over ninety articles in scientific and technical journals and at leading conferences. Many of these relate to the use of color, texture, motion, and interactive 3D displays for information visualization. His approach is always to combine theory with practice, and his publications range from rigorously scientific contributions in the *Journal of Physiology* and *Vision Research* to applications-oriented articles in *ACM Transactions on Graphics* and *IEEE Transactions on Systems, Man and Cybernetics*.

Ware also takes pride in building useful visualization systems. He is a founding member of the Ocean Mapping Group at the University of New Brunswick. He has been instrumental in the creation of two spin-off visualization companies based initially on his research. Interactive Visualization Systems Inc. makes visualization software for advanced ocean mapping applications. NVision Software Systems Inc. provides visualization tools to enhance the understanding of large highly interconnected datasets.

Recently Professor Ware transferred to the University of New Hampshire where he directs the Data Visualization Research Lab as part of the newly established Center for Coastal and Ocean Mapping.